S0-DHV-634

Global Markets
for Processed Foods

Global Markets for Processed Foods

Theoretical and Practical Issues

EDITED BY

Daniel H. Pick,
Dennis R. Henderson,
Jean D. Kinsey,
and Ian M. Sheldon

Published in 1998 in the United States of America by Westview Press, 5500 Central Avenue, Boulder, Colorado 80301-2877, and in the United Kingdom by Westview Press, 12 Hid's Copse Road, Cumnor Hill, Oxford OX2 9JJ

Library of Congress Cataloging-in-Publication Data
Global markets for processed foods : theoretical and practical issues
/ edited by Daniel H. Pick ... [et al.].
p. cm.
Based on the proceedings of a conference held in June 1996.
Includes bibliographical references (p.).
ISBN 0-8133-3279-6 (hardcover)
1. Food industry and trade—Congresses. 2. International business enterprises—Congresses. I. Pick, Daniel H.
HD9000.5.G586 1998
382'45664—dc21 97-29278
CIP

The paper used in this publication meets the requirements of the American National Standard for Permanence of Paper for Printed Library Materials Z39.48-1984.

10 9 8 7 6 5 4 3 2 1

Contents

Preface

This book is based on the proceedings of a conference held in June 1996 under co-sponsorship of the International Agricultural Trade Consortium and The Retail Food Industry Center.

The International Agricultural Trade Research Consortium (IATRC) is a group of 160 economists from 16 countries who are interested in fostering research relating to international trade of agricultural products and commodities and providing a forum for the exchange of ideas. Each summer the IATRC sponsors a symposium on a topic relating to trade and trade policy from which proceedings are published. A list of past symposia and related publications may be obtained from Laura Bipes, IATRC Executive Director, Department of Applied Economics, University of Minnesota, St. Paul, Minnesota 55108.

The Retail Food Industry Center at the University of Minnesota is a community of scholars that develops and disseminates knowledge and analysis about how food reaches consumers. The Center focuses on food retailers (grocers, restaurants, and take-out) and their interface with consumers and various suppliers, back to the food manufacturers and handlers wherever they may be. The community of scholars includes faculty, students, and industry leaders from across the nation and around the world. The Center introduces creative thinking and visionary solutions to tomorrow's challenges that arise out of new science, lifestyles, management relationships, and technology. The Center is funded by the Alfred P. Sloan Foundation as one of twelve industry study centers located in various universities in the United States. The Center focuses on educational programs that will produce more knowledgeable and flexible workers in the industry and disseminates information about how this industry operates and serves the well-being of people and the economy. Research projects focus on management practices and productivity, technology adoption, measurement of profits and consumer satisfaction, human resource practices, wage distribution, and career training. International comparisons are underway. Information is disseminated by seminars, working papers, short courses for industry leaders, conferences, professional and trade journals, a newsletter, and the World Wide Web (http://

rhetoric.agri.umn.edu/~trfic). The Center is housed in the Department of Applied Economics and includes research faculty and graduate students from that department, Food Science and Nutrition and four departments from the Carlson School of Management.

The financial support of the Economic Research Service, the Foreign Agricultural Service and Cooperative State Research Service of the U.S. Department of Agriculture, Agriculture and Agri-Food Canada and The Retail Food Industry Center, made this symposium and this book possible.

The editors acknowledge the help of Laura Bipes of the University of Minnesota for arranging the symposium. Nancy Ottum prepared the camera-ready copy of this book in a timely and precise manner.

Daniel H. Pick
Dennis R. Henderson
Jean D. Kinsey
Ian M. Sheldon

1

Introduction

Daniel H. Pick and Jean D. Kinsey

The collection of essays in this book are based on presentations at a conference titled "Global Markets for Processed Foods: Theoretical and Practical Issues." The conference was sponsored by the International Agricultural Trade Research Consortium and The Retail Food Industry Center. The purpose of the conference was twofold, first to focus attention of trade researchers on theoretical, methodological, and empirical issues arising from inconsistencies between neoclassical trade theory and actual international commerce in processed food and beverages; second to identify the implications of these issues for public policy.

The motivation behind organizing this conference was that the bulk of research and policy analysis up to this day has been directed at agricultural commodities such as wheat, corn, soybeans, rice, and others. However, the fact is that trade in processed foods exceeds that of agricultural commodities. Furthermore, international commerce in processed foods is characterized by traits not found in trade of agricultural commodities. These include intra-industry trade, economies of scale, foreign direct investment (FDI), multinational enterprises, vertical integration, foreign production, and others. Thus, existing trade models of agricultural commodities are not sufficient to explain trade in processed foods. Therefore, trade policy prescriptions are not symmetric between agricultural commodities and processed food products.

The chapters in this book shed light on the different characteristics of the international commerce in processed foods, both theoretically and empirically. The structure of this book can be divided into two parts. The first part contains chapters that are central to general issues underlying international commerce in processed foods. The second part contains six chapters that use research applied to specific regions or goods to investigate several aspects of the globalization of the processed food industry.

The second chapter, by Henderson, Sheldon and Pick provides the necessary background to the subsequent chapters. There, the authors define what is meant by the term "global food marketing system" and list the different players participating in the several stages of the marketing chain. The chapter highlights the growth of trade in processed foods and the importance of intra-industry trade observed.

Unlike trade in raw commodities where physical goods are shipped across borders, the globalization of processed food markets includes much more activity and production by firms in foreign countries. Henderson et al. provide a brief discussion and summary of these activities, which include foreign direct investment, contract production, international vertical ties, and trade in intellectual property. The authors then conclude by raising several issues directed at researchers and policy analysts that constitute the foundation of organizing this conference.

In the third chapter, Jones and Blandford aim to shed light on the relevant industrial policies affecting trade in processed food products. Given that the authors are both economists with the Organization for Economic Cooperation and Development (OECD), the discussion is motivated by OECD policy studies. Three policy areas are identified and discussed: agricultural policies, competition policies, and investment policies. The authors reach an important conclusion when they state that, "For analysts and policymakers concerned with the structure and performance of the agro-food sector, it is no longer sufficient to focus solely on agricultural policy. Trade, competition, and investment policy will increasingly influence the sector's development and growth."

Given that trade in processed food products is concentrated in very few countries and firms (chapter 2), the role of imperfect competition and strategic trade policy is outlined by Karp in the fourth chapter. While agriculture is often used as an example of a competitive market, the author points to the fact that government intervention and a high concentration ratio in the processed food industry implies the existence of oligopolistic markets. In such markets, the optimal trade policy will depend on the nature of market structure. Karp outlines different static and dynamic trade models to illustrate the possible strategic outcomes. Thus researchers are left with the challenge of incorporating elements of such models into empirical investigations of processed food markets.

In the fifth chapter, Carter and Yilmaz explore an important characteristic of trade in processed foods, intra-industry trade. The importance of exploring the determinants of intra-industry trade lies in the fact that conventional trade theory fails to explain trade between countries in similar products. The chapter reviews some of the empirical studies that have been applied to the food processing sector but concludes that "there exists a large gap between the theory of intra-industry trade and the empirical studies on food products." Thus, the future challenge to researchers is to incorporate characteristics such as import competition and differentiated products into their modeling effort.

With the continuing globalization of the sector, we see continuous emergence of multinational firms. Markusen, in the sixth chapter, attempts to reconcile the theory of international trade and the theory of multinational enterprises in the context of a general equilibrium framework. The reason such a framework is important is that policy analysis using the strategic trade policy models can be misleading in the presence of a sector that is dominated by large multinational firms. Though Markusen uses a simple general equilibrium model that incorporates the theory of multinationals, the results shed light on when and why one may observe multinational enterprises.

An important feature in the firms' decision process is FDI. As indicated in chapter 2, foreign affiliates' sales are more important than direct export sales of processed foods. In the seventh chapter, Rugman explores the reasons behind the decisions of multinational enterprises to invest abroad and internalize. His conclusion lends support to the finding that the theory of multinationals is consistent with multinational enterprises' behavior.

In chapter 8, Abbott and Solana-Rosillo provide an interesting empirical investigation into the internationalization model of firms in the industry. Using cost-benefit analysis for the case of wine export into the United States from Spain and Australia, the authors are able to isolate preferred entry modes to U.S. markets. More important, it is demonstrated how firm-level data can be used to identify firm decisions on how to penetrate certain markets. Their approach also raises the issue facing empirical researchers on the choice between using a computable general equilibrium model to analyze policy scenarios using aggregated data versus cost-benefit analysis at the disaggregated level.

Another important feature of the globalization of the processed food markets is vertical integration. In chapter 9, Jones lays out the theoretical foundation of vertical markets in international trade. The relevance of Jones's model to the sector is quite apparent. The model deals with a case in which both input and output are traded internationally, and where the market can be characterized as imperfectly competitive. Both of these characteristics can be applied to the food processing sector. Results of the model confirm the importance of knowing the market structure to draw policy conclusions.

In chapter 10, Antonovitz, Buhr, and Liu explore some international implications of vertical markets in the processed food sector. The authors pose the question, "What are the incentives for agricultural firms to vertically integrate across national boundaries?" To try and answer this question, the authors review the new trade and new industrial organization literature and draw conclusions applied to cases of international vertical integration in the processing sector.

Henderson and Sheldon, in chapter 11, attempt to synthesize the strands of theory discussed in the previous chapters, within the context of observed patterns of international commerce in processed foods. In doing so, they demonstrate how the works herein contribute to the emergence of an eclectic framework for understanding the impacts of strategic and policy actions on international trade in an imperfectly competitive sector.

The second part of the book contains six empirical studies, presented in the conference, on specific products or issues in the food processing sector. In chapter 12, Schamel, Gabbert, and von Witzke demonstrate how different characteristics of similar products affect the pricing of wine from the United States, France, Australia, and Chile. Since the production region is an important quality characteristic of wine, wine remains a traded good as opposed to a food process that can readily be sourced in the country where its consumers live. In chapter 13, Haley and Paarlberg investigate the case of subsidies under the Uruguay Round agreement as applied to the bulk commodity (wheat) versus the processed product (wheat flour). They found that returns to U.S. wheat and flour producers from meeting Uruguay Round commitments are not distributed evenly. However, in general, wheat producers lose while flour producers gain and the gains in the flour sector outweigh the losses in the wheat sector.

In chapter 14, Gopinath, Roe and Shane use a Gross Domestic Product (GDP) function approach to analyze the source of growth in the food processing sector. They found that large increases in total factor productivity in agriculture fed through to the food processing sector in the form of lower input prices, leading to lower food prices for consumers as well. The issue of economies of scale is brought forth in chapter 15 by Kalaitzandonakes, Hu and Bredahl. The authors develop a two-country, two-sector model to investigate the role of foreign direct investment and trade under the presence of economies of scale and then use the results to evaluate the U.S. pork-producing and pork-processing industry. They found that analysis of economies of scale provide insights about trade and multinational activity. In chapter 16, Burfisher, Robinson, and Thierfelder conduct a comparative analysis of increased processed food exports by the United States, Mexico, and Brazil. Using a multicountry, computable general equilibrium (CGE) model, they show how the backward links from food exports to farm output and employment are weakened by a shift toward imported inputs and more capital intensive food processing technologies. In the final case study, chapter 17, Hagen uses interviews conducted with executives in the processed meat industry and the preserved fruits and vegetables industry to analyze foreign production decisions by the firms. His results are consistent with the transaction cost theory of foreign production: food manufacturers tend to be located close to consumers rather than exporting finished goods.

PART ONE

Global Markets in Concept and Practice

2

International Commerce in Processed Foods: Patterns and Curiosities

Dennis R. Henderson, Ian M. Sheldon, and Daniel H. Pick

Introduction

Contrary to common perception, the value of global commerce in processed foods exceeds that of basic agricultural commodities by several magnitudes. Furthermore, global commerce in processed foods does not just entail international trade in goods. It also encompasses activities such as production abroad by foreign affiliates and a wide variety of cross-border contractual relationships between firms.

The purpose of this chapter is to characterize patterns of international market organization and behavior, as a means of providing an empirical framework for subsequent work that addresses specific research and policy issues relating to the global processed food market. This chapter is organized into four sections: In the first section, a definition is given for what is meant by the global market for processed foods; the structure of international trade in processed foods is depicted in the second, while the third describes other means by which international transactions are carried out. Some challenges for research and policy analysis are lifted up in the final section.

The Global Food Marketing System

The global market for processed food involves several distinct stages in a vertical chain, including the farm input industries, farmers, food manufacturers and distributors, and consumers. In the developed world, input suppliers and farmers account for a relatively small share of the processed food system. For example, in the United States, combined they contribute about 22 percent of total value added in the food chain. While these stages may not be participating directly in international commerce of processed foods, they are affected by activities elsewhere in the marketing chain. Through derived demand, both input suppliers and agricultural producers are affected by exports and imports of processed foods. Further, changes in the supply of farm commodities affect the cost of processed foods.

Downstream from farmers in the marketing chain are food manufacturing enterprises, which make up one of the largest stages of the chain. In the United States, food manufacturing accounts for about 25 percent of the system's total value added. Globalization of processed food markets affects food manufacturers in a number of ways: They gain business volume from exports and the development of foreign operations; they gain access to new or lower-cost imported processed food ingredients; and they experience increased competition from foreign producers and products.

The economic importance of the food manufacturing industries in developed countries can be observed in Table 2.1. In terms of gross value of processed food output, the United States has the largest food manufacturing sector ($384 billion), ahead of Japan ($281 billion). Germany, France, the United Kingdom, Canada, and Australia also have major food manufacturing sectors. In terms of relative importance, food manufacturing as a share of all manufacturing in these countries ranges from 9.8 percent in Japan to 20.8 percent in Australia. Employment in food manufacturing ranges from 188,000 in Australia to 1.6 million in the United States, and the value of output per employee ranges from $137 thousand in Australia to $237 thousand in the United States. In terms of labor productivity, the U.S.

TABLE 2.1 Output and Employment in Food Manufacturing, Selected Countries, 1990

	Gross Output ($billion)	*Share of Total Manufacturing (percent)*	*Total Employment (1,000)*	*Gross Output per Employee ($1000)*
United States	384	13.5	1,615	237.7
Japan	281	9.8	1,772	158.8
Germany	155	11.3	841	184.0
France	118	16.7	561	210.1
United Kingdom	93	16.3	559	165.6
Canada	39	14.8	223	177.1
Australia	26	20.8	188	137.3

Source: ERS (1996).

food manufacturing sector exceeds the average for other OECD (Organization for Economic Cooperation and Development) countries by 30 percent.

In order to define more precisely what constitutes the food manufacturing industries, the Standard Industrial Classification (SIC) system developed by the U.S. Department of Commerce is adopted. Under the SIC protocol, the sector is defined as *Food and Kindred Products* (SIC-20). At a three-digit SIC level, nine industry groups come under this definition. These are shown in Table 2.2, along with the corresponding levels of U.S. production and export shares. Because of national differences in reporting protocols, comparable industry-level data are not readily available for most other countries.

In order to give a sense of who the key players are in the food manufacturing sector, the world's fifty largest food manufacturing firms are identified (Table 2.3). It is evident that firms with headquarters in the United States, Japan, and Western Europe dominate the sector. Eight of the world's twelve largest food manufacturing firms, and twenty-one of the fifty largest, have their headquarters in the United States. The United Kingdom is second with eleven of the fifty largest firms, followed by Japan with ten. In 1993, Philip Morris/Kraft was second to Nestlé in terms of processed food sales ($36.3 billion) but had the highest total corporate sales at $50.6 billion. Combined, these fifty firms account for about 40 percent of the gross output of manufactured foods in the associated countries.

Downstream from food manufacturing, the next stage of the marketing

TABLE 2.2 Food Manufacturing Industries: SIC Three-Digit Definitions, and Value of U.S. Output and Exports, 1990

SIC	*Definition*	*Value of Gross Output ($million)*	*Percent Exported*
201	Meat products	90,776	5.3
202	Dairy products	50,962	0.8
203	Preserved fruit and vegetables	44,494	4.0
204	Grain and mill products	46,538	6.6
205	Bakery products	26,121	0.7
206	Sugar and confections	21,040	6.3
207	Fats and oils	19,499	11.7
208	Beverages	52,198	2.2
209	Miscellaneous foods	32,374	11.0
20	All food and kindred products	384,009	4.8

Source: U.S. Department of Commerce, Bureau of Economic Analysis: Annual Survey of Manufactures, Selected Issues.

TABLE 2.3 Country of Headquarters and Sales of the World's 50 Largest Food Processing Firms, 1993

Company	*Headquarters*	*Processed Food Sales ($billion)*	*Total Company Sales ($billion)*
1. Nestlé S.A.	Switzerland	36.3	39.1
2. Philip Morris/Kraft Foods	U.S.A.	33.8	50.6
3. Unilever	UK/Netherlands	21.6	41.9
4. ConAgra	U.S.A.	18.7	23.5
5. Cargill	U.S.A.	16.7	47.1
6. PepsiCo	U.S.A.	15.7	25.0
7. Coca Cola	U.S.A.	13.9	14.0
8. Danone S.A.	France	12.3	12.3
9. Kirin Brewery	Japan	12.1	12.1
10. IBP, Inc.	U.S.A.	11.2	11.7
11. Mars, Inc.	U.S.A.	11.1	12.0
12. Anheuser-Busch	U.S.A.	10.8	11.5
13. Montedison/Feruzzi/Eridania	Italy	9.9	12.3
14. Grand Metropolitan	UK	9.9	11.2
15. Archer Daniels Midland Co.	U.S.A.	8.9	11.4
16. Sara Lee	U.S.A.	7.6	15.5
17. Allied Domecq Plc	UK	7.2	7.2
18. RJR Nabisco	U.S.A.	7.0	15.1
19. Guinness Plc	UK	7.0	7.0
20. H.J. Heinz	U.S.A.	6.8	7.0
21. Asahi Breweries	Japan	6.8	6.8
22. CPC International	U.S.A.	6.7	6.7
23. Dalgety	UK	6.7	6.7
24. Campbell Soup	U.S.A.	6.6	6.6
25. Bass Plc	UK	6.6	6.6
26. Suntory Ltd.	Japan	6.6	6.6
27. Associated British Foods Plc	UK	6.5	6.5
28. Kellogg Company	U.S.A.	6.3	6.3
29. Hillsdown Plc	UK	5.8	6.0
30. Quaker Oats	U.S.A.	5.7	5.7
31. General Mills	U.S.A.	5.6	8.5
32. Tate & Lyle Plc	UK	5.6	5.6
33. Cadbury Schweppes	UK	5.6	5.6
34. Coca Cola Enterprises	U.S.A.	5.5	5.5
35. Seagram	Canada	5.2	5.2
36. Sapporo Breweries Ltd.	Japan	5.1	5.1
37. Borden, Inc.	U.S.A.	4.8	6.7

(continues)

TABLE 2.3 ***(continued)***

Company	Headquarters	Processed Food Sales ($billion)	Total Company Sales ($billion)
38. Nippon Meat Packers	Japan	4.8	4.8
39. Yamazaki Baking	Japan	4.8	4.8
40. Tyson Foods, Inc.	U.S.A.	4.6	4.7
41. Heineken	Netherlands	4.6	4.6
42. United Biscuits	UK	4.5	4.5
43. Fosters Brewing Group Ltd.	Australia	4.4	4.4
44. Ajinomoto Co., Inc.	Japan	4.3	5.2
45. Snow Brand Milk	Japan	4.3	4.8
46. LVMH Moet Hennessy	France	4.2	4.2
47. Besnier S.A.	France	4.1	4.1
48. Itoham Foods Inc.	Japan	3.9	3.9
49. Meiji Milk Products	Japan	3.9	3.9
50. Hershey Foods Corp.	U.S.A.	3.5	3.5

Source: Compiled by ERS from company reports and public records.

chain is food distribution. Firms at this stage are responsible for the wholesale and retail distribution of processed foods in both domestic and international markets. In the case of the United States, food wholesalers and retailers together account for about 32 percent of total value added in the system.

Through globalization, wholesalers generate increased volume, while retailers gain access to a wider variety of products and consumers. For example, U.S.-based wholesalers sold about $16 billion worth of goods abroad in 1993, an increase of 156 percent since 1982, while non-U.S. food wholesalers had 1993 sales of nearly $22 billion in the United States, up from $7 billion eleven years earlier (U.S. Department of Commerce, BEA). Among firms throughout the chain, food wholesalers appear to be more heavily involved in international joint ventures. For example, Wal-Mart has joined with the Hong Kong firm Ek Chor Distribution System Company to develop wholesale food operations in China, and with the Brazilian firm Lojas Americana to operate a wholesale distribution system in Argentina. Fleming, the leading U.S. food wholesaling firm, has formed a joint venture with Davids Holdings, the largest Australian wholesale firm, to establish distribution facilities throughout Asia.

Food retailing has experienced a great deal of foreign direct investment as firms have attempted to extend their store formats and merchandising systems to foreign markets. U.S. food retailers have been less aggressive in doing so than have non-U.S. firms. Foreign-owned firms accounted for more than $50 million in retail food sales in the United States in 1993, claiming nearly 15 percent of the market. At the same time, foreign operations of U.S. food retailers generated less than $12 billion in direct retail sales (ERS, 1996).

A smaller but growing link in the chain is the food service industry (eating places and related services), which in the United States accounts for about 21 percent of total value added. Globalization affects this stage primarily through foreign direct investment by food service chains and the use of international contractual arrangements such as franchising. McDonald's is the leading U.S. firm with foreign operations, generating foreign sales exceeding $11 billion in 1994, followed by $5.5 billion in sales by the PepsiCo subsidiaries KFC ($3.6 billion) and Pizza Hut ($1.9 billion). The U.K. firm, Grand Metropolitan, tallied sales exceeding $7 billion in the United States, followed by the Canadian firm, Imasco, with $3.5 billion in U.S. sales (ERS, 1996).

The food service industry has been affected by globalization in a relatively unique manner. Although firms in the industry export a range of intermediate goods for use in overseas outlets, the dominant characteristic of trade at this stage has been the export of things such as trademarks, logos, merchandising schemes, and quality control regimes, which are often licensed to overseas franchisees.

International Trade in Processed Foods

Trade in bulk agricultural commodities has generally been the dominant focus of research in the agricultural economics literature. This follows both from the fact that bulk commodity trade has been the target of a good deal of policy interventions, and because trade in commodities would seem to be a good candidate for the Heckscher-Ohlin-Samuelson (HOS) paradigm. The evidence suggests that this focus is now somewhat misplaced.

World trade in food and agricultural products has become increasingly dominated by the manufactured foods sector (Figure 2.1). Over the period 1972 to 1993, the value of trade in manufactured food products grew by 574 percent, while the value of bulk commodity trade grew by just 355 percent. Trade in manufactured food products now accounts for 67 percent of world trade, compared to 58 percent in 1972 (ERS, 1996).

Neoclassical trade theory predicts that the structure of trade will be *inter-industry* in nature, that is countries will specialize in the production and export of goods that use their abundant resources and will import goods using their scarce resources. There is evidence (e.g., McCorriston and Sheldon 1991), however, that the structure of trade in manufactured foods is, in part, of an *intra-industry* nature, that is, the simultaneous

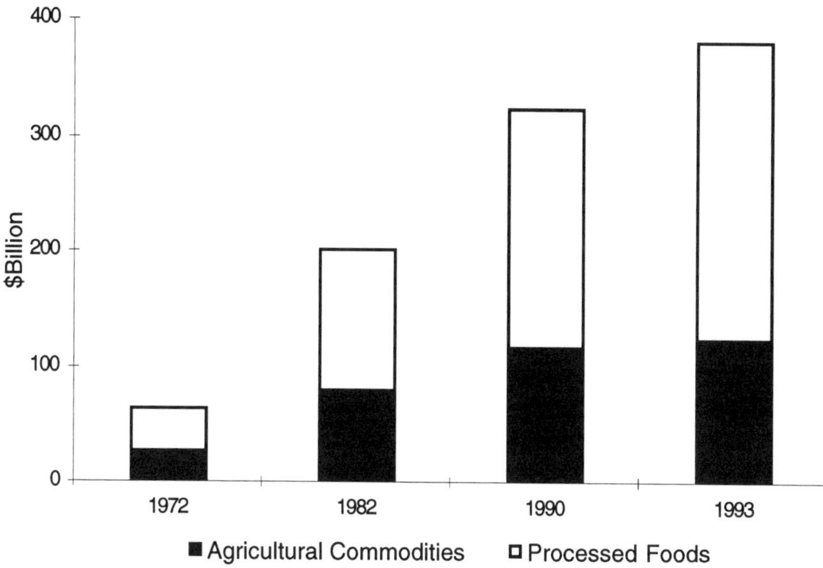

FIGURE 2.1 World Trade in Food and Agricultural Commodities. *Source:* ERS, 1996.

export and import of products that are very close substitutes for each other in terms of factor inputs and consumption (Tharakan 1985). This is a phenomenon that is difficult to explain with neoclassical trade theory. A closer examination of the structure of world trade in processed foods and an understanding of the expected determinants of intra-industry trade provides a clue as to why trade in this sector does not fit neatly into the neoclassical paradigm.

Structure of World Trade in Processed Foods

Global trade in processed or manufactured foods is concentrated among a few countries: twenty-four countries accounted for 80 percent of the shipments in 1990, compared to 68 percent in 1962 (United Nations 1990). In an analysis of 1990 United Nations trade data for processed food products, Handy and Henderson (1994) established that the countries comprising Western Europe, North America, Australasia, plus Japan, accounted for 63 percent of total exports and 84 percent of imports. Breaking this down further, the top five exporters accounted for 38 percent of manufactured food exports (Table 2.4), while the top five importers accounted for 53 percent of all imports (Table 2.5).

It is interesting to note that France, Germany, the United States and the United Kingdom are among both the top five importing and exporting

TABLE 2.4 Leading Exporters of Manufactured Foods, 1990

Country	*Share of World Total (percent)*
France	9.8
Netherlands	8.9
United States	8.5
Germany	6.7
United Kingdom	4.3
Belgium/Luxembourg	4.1
Denmark	3.9
Brazil	3.5
Italy	3.5
Canada	2.8

Source: Handy and Henderson 1994.

countries. Leading importing and exporting countries often trade with each other. For example, Canada is by far the dominant exporter to the United States with a total value of $3.5 billion (1990) and a 17 percent share of the U.S. import market. At the same time Canada is the second largest importer of U.S. processed food products, $2.7 billion in 1990, accounting for 14 percent of U.S. exports.

Intra-industry Trade

Empirical work on the evolution of the European Economic Community (Verdoorn 1960, Balassa 1965) and later work by Grubel and Lloyd (1975) indicates that much of the post-World War II growth in world trade

TABLE 2.5 Leading Importers of Manufactured Foods, 1990

Country	*Share of World Total (percent)*
Japan	12.0
Germany	11.8
United States	11.7
France	8.6
United Kingdom	8.6
Italy	8.1
Netherlands	5.2
Belgium/Luxembourg	4.0
Spain	3.5
Canada	2.6

Source: Handy and Henderson 1994.

has been between developed countries and has been of an intra-industry nature. Linder (1961), an early observer of this phenomenon, contended that, while export potential may exist on the basis of comparative advantage, such potential can only be realized where substantial domestic demand for the product exists and also where trade between two countries is limited to goods for which markets exist in both countries. Upon the assumption that income levels determine taste patterns, Linder predicted that trade in similar but differentiated products will take place between countries having similar per capita income levels.

That world trade in processed foods tends to be dominated by developed countries with relatively similar levels of gross domestic product (GDP) per capita should, therefore, come as no surprise. As incomes have risen in these countries, consumers have allocated expenditures toward more highly processed and differentiated food products as their basic subsistence needs have been satisfied. In addition, demographic characteristics of developed countries, such as increased participation of women in the workforce, have tended to reinforce trends toward purchase of highly processed foods.

A priori, it might also be expected that a portion of trade in the food and agricultural sector will be intra-industry in nature. Interestingly, most empirical work on intra-industry trade has focused almost entirely on other manufactured goods. Balassa and Bauwens (1987), for example, explicitly excluded food products from their sample. However, there is now a reasonable amount of empirical evidence indicating that trade in processed foods between developed countries is partly intra-industry (e.g., McCorriston and Sheldon 1991, Christodoulou 1992, Hartman et al. 1993, and Hirschberg et al. 1994).

The study by McCorriston and Sheldon, using export and import data at the three-digit SIC level, estimated the commonly used Grubel and Lloyd index of intra-industry trade for the United States, the EC-9, and the remainder of the OECD for a sample of processed foods in 1986. Their results suggest that the food manufacturing sector in the United States exhibited lower levels of intra-industry trade than in the European Community (EC), although the higher levels of intra-industry trade for the EC were influenced by intra-Community trade (Table 2.6). More recent estimates for the U.S. processed foods sector, based on 1994 four-digit SIC data, provide a detailed picture of intra-industry trade in the sector (Table 2.7), the average level of the Grubel and Lloyd index across the forty-eight industries being 0.57. Estimates of the Grubel and Lloyd index for U.S. trade with specific sets of trading partners are shown in Table 2.8. Not surprisingly, U.S. intra-industry trade tends to be higher with trade partners in the North American Free Trade Agreement (NAFTA) than for other trading blocs.

TABLE 2.6 Intra-Industry Trade in Processed Foods, 1986 Grubel and Lloyd Indices[a]

Product	*U.S.*	*EC-9*	*EC-9 External Trade*	*Rest of OECD*
Processed Meat	0.25	0.97	0.75	0.64
Cheese Products	0.21	0.97	0.70	0.92
Cereal Preparations	0.94	0.85	0.31	0.76
Processed Fruit	0.73	0.79	0.45	0.26
Processed Vegetables	0.53	0.95	0.74	0.79
Sugar Products	0.36	0.82	0.41	0.81
Chocolate Products	0.54	0.93	0.43	0.88
Non-Alcoholic Beverages	0.45	0.86	0.32	0.96
Alcoholic Beverages	0.17	0.73	0.14	0.54

[a]As value tends to 1, this indicates intra-industry trade.

Source: McCorriston and Sheldon 1991.

The latter point suggests that certain country characteristics are likely to affect the extent of intra-industry trade. Based on hypotheses advanced by Helpman and Krugman (1985), Hirschberg et al. (1994) analyzed the determinants of intra-industry trade in food manufacturing for a thirty-country sample over the period 1964–1985, using four-digit SIC data. Their results suggest that intra-industry trade in food manufacturing, as measured by the Grubel and Lloyd index, is a positive function of a country's GDP per capita and equality of per capita GDP between countries. In addition, they found that intra-industry trade is strongly influenced by distance between trading partners, membership in customs unions or free trade areas, and exchange rate volatility. Their results also show a general increase in intra-industry trade in processed foods over time.

As well as country characteristics, much of the literature on intra-industry trade in recent years appeals to industry-level characteristics to explain its occurrence. This has emphasized imperfect market structures, economies of scale, and product differentiation. Probably the best-known models are those that assume an industry structure of monopolistic competition, Helpman and Krugman having synthesized most of the earlier work of Krugman (1980), Lancaster (1981), and Helpman (1981). Assuming consumers have an aggregate demand for variety, where the number of varieties produced in a country is limited by economies of scale and two trading countries are similar in size, these models predict that the structure of trade will be intra-industry. In essence, each country produces, consumes, and exports part of a range of differentiated products and imports the rest.

TABLE 2.7 U.S. Intra-Industry Trade in Processed Foods, 1994

SIC Category	*Grubel and Lloyd Index*
Soft drinks and carbonated water	0.999
Chewing gum	0.992
Sausage and prepared meats	0.961
Frozen fruits and vegetables	0.958
Frozen bakery goods, exc. bread	0.944
Sauces and salad dressings	0.933
Other food preparations	0.893
Canned fruits and vegetables	0.829
Bread and other bakery goods	0.811
Condensed/evaporated milk	0.808
Roasted coffee	0.792
Cookies and crackers	0.768
Breakfast cereals	0.745
Chocolate and cocoa products	0.742
Meat packing	0.716
Candy and confectionery goods	0.713
Manufactured ice	0.690
Shortening and cooking oils	0.673
Canned specialties	0.664
Prepared fresh or frozen fish	0.639
Salted/roasted nuts and seeds	0.613
Malt	0.586
Processed fish products	0.584
Dried fruits and vegetables	0.583
Malt beverages	0.548
Prepared animal feed	0.546
Vegetable oil	0.476
Distilled and blended spirits	0.454
Refined cane sugar	0.394
Blended and prepared flours	0.381
Flour and grain mill products	0.374
Dog, cat and other pet food	0.357
Wet corn milling	0.319
Animal/marine fats and oils	0.315
Dry pasta	0.282
Wines, brandy, brandy spirits	0.274
Cheese	0.255
Rice milling	0.253
Flavorings, extracts, and syrups	0.201
Potato or corn chips and similar	0.182
Fluid milk	0.166
Cottonseed oil	0.146
Frozen specialties	0.124
Soybean oil	0.060
Creamery butter	0.038
Poultry	0.031
Ice cream/frozen desserts	0.030
Beet sugar	0.027

Source: ERS (1996).

TABLE 2.8 U.S. Intra-Industry Trade (Grubel and Lloyd Index) with Selected Regions, 1994

SIC	NAFTA[a]	European Union[b]	Asian Group[c]	South America[d]
2011 Meat packing	0.89	0.77	0	0.12
2013 Sausage	0.52	0.64	0.56	0.20
2015 Poultry meat	0.05	0.05	0.01	0
2021 Butter	0.04	0.33	0	0
2022 Cheese	0.38	0.01	0	0.56
2023 Dry/condensed dairy	0.32	0.13	0.03	0.01
2024 Ice cream	0	0.18	0.01	0
2026 Fluid milk	0.03	0.71	0.01	0
2032 Canned specialties	0.69	0.28	0.30	0.26
2033 Canned fruits and vegetables	0.56	0.71	0.43	0.16
2034 Dried fruits and vegetables	0.31	0.17	0.21	0.25
2035 Pickled fruits and vegetables	0.86	0.66	0.84	0.48
2037 Frozen fruits and vegetables	0.56	0.13	0.02	0.03
2038 Frozen specialties	0.04	0.67	0.78	0
2041 Grain mill products	0.93	0.06	0.09	0.05
2043 Breakfast cereals	0.89	0.75	0.15	0.15
2044 Rice milling	0.05	0.09	0	0.01
2045 Prepared flour mixes	0.60	0.17	0.02	0.01
2046 Wet corn milling	0.69	0.17	0.03	0.18
2047 Dog and cat food	0.50	0.02	0	0.06
2048 Prepared animal feeds	0.90	0.37	0.15	0.08
2051 Bread/bakery products	0.91	0.16	0.64	0.33
2052 Cookies and crackers	0.96	0.14	0.50	0.95
2053 Frozen bakery products	0.96	0.59	0.85	0.04
2062 Cane sugar	0.91	0.51	0.85	0.30
2063 Beet sugar	0.50	0	0	0
2064 Candy	0.95	0.28	0.86	0.21
2066 Chocolate products	0.99	0.13	1.00	0.16
2067 Chewing gum	0.65	0.94	0.33	0.74
2068 Nuts and seeds	0.39	0.05	0.24	0.04
2074 Cottonseed oil	0	0.38	0	0.92
2075 Soybean oil	0.14	0.19	0.06	0.06
2076 Peanut/olive/other oils	0.49	0.31	0.57	0.71
2077 Animal fats and oils	0.37	0.04	0.11	0.82
2079 Margarine	0.98	0.29	0.14	0.96
2082 Beer	0.25	0.19	0.20	0.14
2083 Malt	0.97	0.79	0.02	0
2084 Wines	0.36	0.11	0.34	0.12
2085 Distilled liquors	0.12	0.31	0.05	0.09
2086 Soft drinks	0.98	0.05	0.22	0.52
2087 Flavoring extracts/syrups	0.30	0.51	0.08	0.14
2091 Canned fish/seafoods	0.76	0.44	0.98	0.05
2092 Prepared fish/seafoods	0.38	0.60	0.35	0.01
2095 Roasted coffee	0.83	0.15	0.05	0.02
2096 Snack foods	0.61	0	0.07	0
2097 Manufactured ice	0.26	0.99	0	0
2098 Pasta	0.86	0.02	0.10	0.19
2099 Other	0.63	0.83	0.40	0.58

[a]Canada and Mexico; [b]EC-12; [c]Japan, Taiwan, Singapore, S. Korea, Malaysia; [d]Argentina, Brazil, Paraguay, Uruguay, Bolivia, Colombia, Ecuador, Peru, Venezuela, Chile.

Source: ERS (1996).

These types of model have resulted in a number of empirical studies that have attempted to establish the industry determinants of intra-industry trade using cross-sectional econometric methods (see Greenaway and Milner 1986 for a survey). While there are serious measurement problems with respect to crucial explanatory variables such as product differentiation, the bulk of the studies gives fairly robust and consistent support for market structure, product differentiation, and economies of scale as factors affecting cross-industry variation in intra-industry trade. Some validation of these explanatory variables for intra-industry trade in processed foods was found in a cross-sectional study using 1987 four-digit SIC data for the U.S. food manufacturing sector (Hartman et al. 1993).

Foreign Production

Even more so than in product trade, the international character of the processed foods sector is reflected in the direct foreign activities of food processing and distribution firms. These are dominated by firms' operation of foreign affiliates, that is, processing and distribution facilities located in other countries. Known as foreign direct investment (FDI), in essence this is how many firms "export" their home market strategies to markets abroad.

In 1994, sales from foreign affiliates of U.S. processed food firms exceeded $100 billion, more than four times the total value of U.S. exports of processed foods. Nearly all of these sales are in foreign markets; on average 79 percent of the sales by foreign affiliates of U.S. firms is in the host country and just 2 percent is shipped to the United States. At the same time, affiliates of foreign firms located in the United States sold more than $45 billion in processed foods, exceeding twice the level of U.S. imports. In addition to direct investment in foreign operations, firms engage in a variety of foreign contract operations, mostly licensing, franchising, and joint-venture arrangements.

Foreign Direct Investment

For purposes herein, foreign direct investment refers to investment in a foreign affiliate. The term *foreign affiliate* is used to identify a foreign entity in which a parent firm holds a substantial, but not necessarily majority, ownership. Parent firms are referred to as multinational firms (MNFs). Hereafter, investment by home-country firms in production facilities in other countries is referred to as outbound FDI, while investment by foreign firms in facilities located in a host country is called inbound FDI.

Sales by foreign affiliates is one indicator of FDI. This facilitates comparison of FDI and international trade in goods as alternative strategies for gaining access to foreign markets. The magnitudes of U.S. outbound and inbound FDI in the processed food sectors are shown in Tables 2.9 and 2.10. Sales from outbound FDI were slightly higher than sales from inbound FDI throughout the 1982–1993 period. Sales of all U.S. food marketing affiliates abroad totaled $132.5 billion in 1993, while sales of foreign-owned food marketing affiliates in the United States were $124.3 billion.

Foreign direct investment is distinctly different from foreign portfolio investment. Portfolio investment is characterized by a passive management role and does not seek control over decisionmaking. Foreign direct investment, by contrast, is defined as the ownership of assets in an affiliate by a foreign firm for the purpose of exercising control over the use of those assets. Until World War I, nearly all international investment was portfolio; the United Kingdom supplied about half of the world's total, followed by France and Germany. Younger, rapidly expanding economies, primarily the United States, Canada, Australia, and Latin America, were the main recipients.

Yet, even before World War I, outbound American investment was getting underway. From the outset, U.S. investment was different. To quote Södersten and Reed, "American investors seem to have been of a more dynamic type, not content to reap a fairly small interest-rate differential. Even before the First World War a dominant share of U.S. capital exports consisted of direct investments" (1994, p. 468). In short, from the beginning, Americans investing abroad have shown a propensity to transfer know-how (or intellectual capital), more so than financial capital.

Following World War II, the United States became the primary supplier of international finance, first in the form of official loans and gifts, and second in the form of FDI as American firms made major contributions to postwar industrial rebuilding. By 1960 the United States was supplying

TABLE 2.9 Sales by U.S.-Owned Food Marketing Affiliates Abroad, 1982–1993 (in $million)

Sector	*1982*	*1987*	*1992*	*1993*	*Share of Total (percent)*
Food manufacturing	39,023	50,067	89,159	95,782	72.3
Food wholesaling	6,172	9,206	14,388	15,783	11.9
Retail foodstores				11,930	9.0
}	8,691	9,674	21,169		
Eating & drinking places				9,007	6.8
Total	53,886	68,947	124,716	132,502	100

Source: ERS (1996).

TABLE 2.10 Sales by Foreign-Owned Food Marketing Affiliates in the United States, 1982–1993 (in $million)

Sector	*1982*	*1987*	*1992*	*1993*	*Share of Total (percent)*
Food manufacturing	14,847	22,862	46,799	45,765	36.8
Food wholesaling	7,039	13,953	18,984	21,734	17.5
Retail foodstores		24,312	48,159	51,537	41.5
}	18,758				
Eating & drinking places		498	4,904	5,236	4.2
Total	40,644	61,625	118,846	124,272	100

Source: ERS (1996).

about two-thirds of all international investment. By the 1980s, other countries—principally those of the European Union and Japan—observing U.S. industrial success throughout much of the free world, became more aggressive in exporting their management technology through FDI. Much of this landed in the United States. By the 1990s, FDI had become the main instrument for global industrialization. As the twentieth century ends, the nationality of multinational firms—the organizational result of FDI—has blurred in many cases to the point of being indistinguishable.

FDI in the processed food industries appears to be motivated by the potential to earn profits by exercising managerial control over international operations. Data from a worldwide sample of 118 multinational food processing firms were used to compare profitability based on extent of sales from foreign affiliates (Table 2.11). A profitability threshold was found at a level of foreign affiliate sales equal to 40 percent of total sales. Average net income as a percent of assets for firms above this threshold exceeded that for the firms below.

In aggregate, foreign affiliate sales appear to be significantly more important that processed food exports. However, firm-level data for the fifty U.S. food manufacturers with the largest foreign sales show that their

TABLE 2.11 Profitability of Food Firms with Foreign Sales (World Sample of 118 Firms, 1990)

	Net Income as a Percent of Total Assets
Foreign affiliate sales > 40 percent of total	8.1
Foreign affiliate sales < 40 percent of total	4.4

Source: Handy and Henderson 1994.

relative importance varies widely (Table 2.12). All of these firms export, and thirty-nine also supply processed food through their foreign affiliates. For these thirty-nine, the ratio of foreign affiliate sales to exports ranges from less than one (Dean Foods) to more than sixty (CPC International).

Contract Production

Multinational food manufacturers also supply foreign markets through contract arrangements. There are, however, few publicly available sources of information on contract operations. Perhaps the most is known about international brand licensing. In a survey of 120 of the world's largest publicly held food manufacturing firms, Henderson and Sheldon (1992) found that at least half mentioned involvement in some form of international product or brand-name licensing. Based on anecdotal evidence, they suggest that the total value of international sales of licensed food products exceeds that of direct product trade. U.S. and non-U.S. MNFs appear to be equally aggressive in brand-name licensing (Tables 2.13 and 2.14).

Licenses are often linked to product-specific technology, for example, the production of caramelized chocolate bars or cold-filtered draft beer. This is a way for the product developer (licensor) to maintain an equity position in the product once the licensee masters the technology. Further, licenses sometimes provide for the supply of critical ingredients by the licensor, such as cola syrup or chocolate paste, thus facilitating trade in intermediate products.

Some MNFs extend their operations internationally through joint ventures. The formation of Cereal Products Worldwide, a joint venture by General Mills and Nestlé to produce and market ready-to-eat breakfast cereals in Western Europe and other non-U.S. markets in direct competition with market leader Kellogg, has renewed interest in this phenomenon. Yet few examples of long-standing joint ventures in the food sector can be found. A study of joint ventures across all industries involving U.S. firms found that their average life is just 3.5 years (Harrigan 1988). A study of joint ventures in the Canadian food processing sector found that of 110 such entities in existence sometime between 1981 and 1988, 33 percent were created and 38 percent were dissolved during that period (Geringer 1990).

International Vertical Ties

Foreign direct investment and contract operations can be classified as horizontal or vertical. Horizontal refers to activities that are similar to those conducted by a firm in its home market (e.g. a U.S. food manufactur-

TABLE 2.12 Leading U.S. Food Manufacturers with Foreign Sales (1992–1993, Estimated)

Company	*Exports ($million)*	*Foreign Affiliate Sales ($million)*	*FDI Sales/Exports*
Ag Processing Inc.	98.0	170.6	1.7
American Brands	44.0	417.6	9.5
Anheuser Busch Cos. Inc.	608.4	968.9	1.6
Archer Daniels Midland Co.	937.5	2,232.1	2.4
Blue Diamond Growers	63.2	0	0
Borden Inc.	64.5	930.4	14.4
Bristol Myers Squibb	98.0	153.0	1.6
Brown-Forman Corp.	65.5	47.4	0.7
Campbell Soup	94.0	1,930.5	20.5
Chiquita Brands International Inc.	57.6	1,381.0	24.0
Clorox	3.1	80.7	26.1
Coca-Cola Co.	207.0	9,351.0	45.2
Colgate-Palmolive	64.0	0	0
ConAgra Inc.	1,328.9	1,310.9	1.0
Coors	114.5	0	0
CPC International Inc.	70.9	4,325.7	61.0
Curtis-Burns Inc.	15.2	46.6	3.1
Dean Foods Co.	144.7	5.0	0.1
Dole Foods Co.	66.2	1,657.0	25.0
General Mills Inc.	175.0	415.2	2.4
Gerber Products Co.	44.0	126.0	2.9
Grace (W.R.) & Co.	8.8	297.8	33.8
Heinz (H.J.) Co.	105.3	3,053.5	29.0
Hershey Foods Corp.	197.5	407.9	2.1
Hormel (Geo. A.) & Co.	106.2	0	0
IBP Inc.	1,388.9	0	0
International Flavors & Fragrance Inc.	6.4	293.6	46.2
Kellogg Co.	97.3	2,511.5	25.8
Land O'Lakes Inc.	106.0	0	0
McCormick & Co. Inc.	76.2	217.9	2.9
MM/Mars	120.0	4,000.0	33.3
Multifoods	28.4	556.1	19.6
Monsanto	70.5	0	0
Ocean Spray	98.0	0	0
PepsiCo Inc.	247.8	5,381.6	21.7
Pet Inc.	26.4	261.9	9.9
Philip Morris Cos. Inc.	1,340.0	11,945.0	8.9
Proctor & Gamble	101.0	329.0	3.3
Quaker Oats Co.	120.4	2,024.9	16.8
Ralston Purina	149.2	1,576.7	10.6
Riceland Foods Inc.	232.1	0	0
RJR Nabisco	243.0	1,540.0	6.3
Sara Lee Corp.	184.0	2,344.0	12.7
Seaboard Corp.	21.9	72.2	3.3
Smucker (J.M.) Co.	20.5	57.6	2.8
Sun-Diamond Growers of California	142.7	0	0
Tyson Foods Inc.	352.0	0	0
Universal Foods Corp.	45.0	139.2	3.1
Warner-Lambert Inc.	16.3	801.0	49.1
Wrigley (Wm. Jr.) Co.	34.5	634.7	18.4

Source: ERS (1996).

TABLE 2.13 U.S. Examples of International Food and Beverage Licenses

Licensor	*Brand Name*	*Licensee*
Anheuser-Busch (U.S.)	*Budweiser*	Labatt (Canada)
		United Breweries (Denmark)
		Guiness (Ireland)
		Suntory (Japan)
		Oriental Brewery (Korea)
		Grand Metropolitan (UK)
	Bud Light	Labatt (Canada)
Hershey Foods (U.S.)	*Hershey's*	Fujiya Confectionery (Japan)
CPC International (U.S.)	*Knorr*	Ajinomoto (Japan)
Geo. A. Hormel (U.S.)	*Spam*	Newforge Foods (UK)
		K.R. Darling Downs (Australia)
	Hormel	Lee Tan Farm Industries (Taiwan)
		Blue Ribbon Products (Panama)
	Bacon Bits	K.R. Darling Downs (Australia)
Adolph Coors (U.S.)	*Coors*	Molson (Canada)
Kraft General Foods (U.S.)	*Kraft*	Epic Oil Mills (S. Africa)
Miller Brewing (U.S.)	*High Life*	Molson (Canada)
	Miller Lite	Molson (Canada)
		Courage (UK)
Kellogg's (U.S.)	*Kellogg's*	Ajinomoto (Japan)
Ocean Spray (U.S.)	*Ocean Spray*	Pernod Ricard (France)
		Ranks Hovis McDougall (UK)
		Cadbury Schweppes (Canada)
		Pokka (Japan)
Sunkist Growers (U.S.)	*Sunkist*	Morinaga (Japan)
		Haitai Beverages (S. Korea)
		Rickertson (Germany)
		Cadbury Schweppes (UK)
Welch Foods (U.S.)	*Welch's*	Cadbury Schweppes (Canada)
RJR Nabisco (U.S.)	*Planters*	Britannia Brands (Singapore)
Cadbury Schweppes (UK)	*Cadbury*	Hershey Foods (U.S.)
	Peter Paul Mounds	Hershey Foods (U.S.)
	Almond Joy	Hershey Foods (U.S.)
Rowntree Mackintosh (UK)	*Rollos*	Hershey Foods (U.S.)
	Kit Kat	Hershey Foods (U.S.)
Haute Brasserie (France)	*Killian's Red*	Adolph Coors (U.S.)
Sodima (France)	*Yoplait*	Yoplait Foods (U.S.)
Löwenbrau (Germany)	*Löwenbrau Pils*	Miller Brewing (U.S.)

Source: Henderson, Sheldon, and Thomas 1994.

TABLE 2.14 Non-U.S. Examples of International Food and Beverage Licenses

Licensor	*Brand Name*	*Licensee*
Arla (Sweden)	*L – L*	Morinaga (Japan)
Bond (Australia)	*Castlemaine XXXX*	Allied Lyons (UK)
	Swan Premium	Allied Lyons (UK)
Brasserie Artois (Belgium)	*Stella Artois*	Whitbread (UK)
BSN (France)	*Kronenbourg*	Courage (UK)
Elders (Australia)	*Fosters*	Beamish & Crawford (Ireland)
		Pripps (Sweden)
Guinness (Ireland)	*Guinness Stout*	Elders (Australia)
Lutz (Germany)	*Lutz*	Nichieri (Japan)
Morinaga (Japan)	*Bifidus Yogurt*	St. Herbert (France)
		Südmilch (Germany)
	Morinaga	P.T. Enseval (Indonesia)
Unilever (Netherlands)	*Lipton*	Morinaga (Japan)
United Breweries (Denmark)	*Carlsberg*	Photos Photiades (Cyprus)
		Beamish & Crawford (Ireland)
		Suntory (Japan)
	Tuborg	Frydenlund Ringes (Norway)
		Unicer (Portugal)
Cerveceria Modelo (Mexico)	*Corona*	Molson (Canada)
Kirin (Japan)	*Kirin*	Molson (Canada)
		San Miguel (Hong Kong)
Labatt (Canada)	*Labatt*	Vaux Brewery (UK)
Löwenbrau (Germany)	*Löwenbrau Pils*	Allied Lyons (UK)
		Molson (Canada)
		Asahi (Japan)
		San Miguel (Hong Kong)
	Löwenbrau Strong	Allied Lyons (UK)
Jacob Suchard (Switzerland)	*Sugus*	Nestlé Produtos Alimentaros (Portugal)
		Beacon Sweets (S. Africa)
		Sanborn Hermanos (Mexico)
	Toblerone	Sanborn Hermanos (Mexico)
	Milka	Sanborn Hermanos (Mexico)
	Suchard	Sanborn Hermanos (Mexico)
		Tong Yang Confectionery (S. Korea)
		Nestlé Produtos Alimentaros (Portugal)
	Van Houten	Chocolate Products (Malaysia)
		General Food Industries (Indonesia)
		Sunshine Allied (Singapore)

Source: Henderson, Sheldon, and Thomas 1994.

ing firm engaging in food manufacturing abroad). Vertical organization refers to involvement in foreign operations in successive stages of production, upstream (away from final consumption) and/or downstream (toward final consumption) from the home-country operations (e.g. a U.S. food manufacturer with foreign commodity production or food wholesaling operations).

Unfortunately, few data are available to describe the extent to which foreign operations are horizontal or vertical. This is particularly so for contracts. General observation suggests that most international contracts are horizontal. In food service, for example, most foreign operations of U.S. firms are franchises. In food retailing, IGA is licensing its product procurement, branding, and merchandising procedures to foreign retailers. Circle K has joint venture and franchise agreements with convenience store operators in nineteen countries (ERS, 1996). Most of the licensing agreements of food manufacturers uncovered by Henderson and Sheldon (1992) were primarily horizontal market extensions of brand names.

However, there is some evidence of vertical contracts. For example, some product licenses require a foreign licensee to acquire selected ingredients from the licensor. Given considerable evidence of increasing use of vertical contracts in domestic food systems (e.g. O'Brien 1994), it may be conjectured that many international contracts have similar vertical functions. But we are unable to offer much documentation at this point.

The situation is somewhat clearer for FDI (Figure 2.2), where anecdotal information suggests that most is horizontal. The largest share of U.S. outbound FDI (72 percent) is in food processing, with just 12, 9, and 7 percent, respectively, involved in food wholesaling, retailing, and eating places (foodservice). Food manufacturers appear to originate at least a comparable share of all U.S. outbound FDI.

United States inbound FDI is more heavily oriented to food retailing (42 percent), followed by food manufacturing (37 percent), wholesaling (17 percent), and food service (4 percent). Food retailing firms appear to be the largest originators of U.S. inbound FDI. For example, with its recent acquisition of the Stop and Shop chain, Ahold (Netherlands) now holds the fourth largest share of the U.S. retail grocery market. Theo Albrecht (Germany) has the fifth largest market share through its Albertson's chain, followed by Tengelmann of Germany (A&P and others), and Delhaize of Belgium (Food Lion), with the eighth and ninth positions, respectively. Food manufacturers are also large originators of U.S. inbound FDI, led by Nestlé (Switzerland), Unilever (Netherlands/UK), and Grand Metropolitan (UK).

Thus, both outbound and inbound U.S. FDI appear to be primarily horizontal. An interesting question can be raised, however, regarding the markedly different composition of inbound and outbound operations.

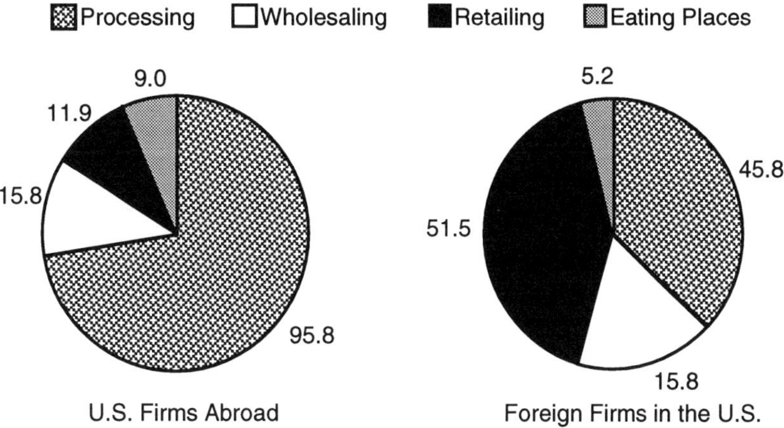

FIGURE 2.2 Food Operations of Foreign Affiliates, 1993 ($billion). *Source:* ERS, 1996.

Trade in Intellectual Property

Patterns of international commerce in processed foods are vested in part in the behavior of firms. Firm behavior is in part a product of environment, part a product of initiative by the people who make up the firms. This includes their intellectual productivity in terms of such things as devising new products, creating and promoting brand names, and developing sourcing, processing, merchandising, and distribution systems. Much of this intellectual effort creates unique, firm-specific assets, for example, technical production and merchandising knowledge, product formulations, brands, trademarks, copyrights, patents, and special relationships with suppliers and customers. These firm-specific assets can be thought of as a firm's intellectual property. In essence, intellectual property refers to those special skills and holdings that enable a firm to differentiate itself from its rivals.

Contemporary economic thought regarding multinational firms recognizes firm-specific intellectual property as a principal factor encouraging firms to develop foreign markets (e.g., Dunning 1981, and Markusen 1995). In essence, the rationale is that firms are motivated to expand the geographical boundary of their markets in order to spread their investment in firm-specific assets over a larger volume. Firm-specific assets, generally considered to be intangible assets, can be substantial, averaging nearly 20 percent of all assets for leading processed food MNFs (Table 2.15). Moving beyond their home market offers these firms the possibility of generating greater earnings from their investments in research, product development, brand names, and other intellectual property.

TABLE 2.15 Intellectual Property of Leading Multinational Food Manufacturing Firms (Means for a World Sample of Thirty Firms, circa 1990)

	Non-US Based	*US-Based*	*All*
Intangible Asset as a Percent of Total Assets	23.1	16.9	19.1
Number of Food Brands	38.2	29.8	32.7
Number of Brands per four-digit SIC Food Industry	7.5	4.5	5.5

Source: Handy and Henderson 1994.

A number of empirical studies of food manufacturers have demonstrated linkages between intellectual property and sales in foreign markets. For example, Connor (1983), using U.S. food manufacturing industry data, documented positive impacts of expenditures on advertising and research and development (R&D) on sales by foreign affiliates. Handy and MacDonald (1989), using similar data for 32 food manufacturing industries, and Henderson and Frank (1990), with data from forty-two food industries, both report positive relationships between R&D expenditures and home-country exports. Using pooled cross-section time series data for 628 food manufacturing firms with headquarters in sixteen countries, Henderson et al. (1996) found intangible assets and product differentiation positively associated with foreign affiliate sales.

The food service industry provides one of the clearest examples of U.S. firms advancing their firm-specific advantages in foreign markets. Much of what food service firms export is intangible: trademarks, logos, merchandising schemes, menu selections, quick service techniques, product formulation, quality control regimes, and the like. Indeed, from a U.S. perspective, food service stands as an example of commercial success in merchandising "Americana." Few other U.S. industries have accomplished so much in terms of selling American ideas and know-how abroad.

Perhaps the most distinct commercial transaction in intellectual property is the international licensing of brand names. Such a license is a contract by a firm who owns a brand name that is well established in one country with a firm in another country for the latter to manufacture and sell the branded product in its home market and/or in third countries. Here, it is mainly *image* that a firm is selling. In addition to the brand name, the seller often provides technical production assistance, a quality control regime, a product formula or recipe, and merchandising ideas. Firms originating international brand licensing have substantial investments in developing and promoting their brands. One measure is the book value of their licensed brand names. Henderson, Sheldon, and Thomas (1994) found the average value of licensed food brand names to exceed 12 percent of the originating firm's total assets. A study reported by Ourusoff

(1992) placed the average value of twelve leading internationally licensed food brands at just over $7 billion.

Not only are firms exploiting intellectual property by creating global markets for their products, they are developing global sourcing networks for product formulation and design, ingredients, engineering and plant construction, food processing equipment, and packaging systems. Specialized ingredient firms such as Pfizer, Genecor, Rhône Poulenc, Quest International, and Haarman and Reimer are forging long-term alliances with food processors to formulate new products and production and distribution techniques. Likewise, firms such as Calgene, Celltech, DeKalb Genetics, Genentech, and Monsanto are forging new relationships with agricultural producers to grow new varieties of crops and animals, often the products of biogenetic engineering, that provide basic feedstock for these innovative products and processes.

An example illustrates how quickly intellectual property can be transferred to a firm and country that have little or no production history. In this case, a producer of wine and soft drinks in Malta decided to enter the brewing business. The firm had extensive marketing and distribution know-how, but no experience as a brewer. The solution was to develop an alliance with Löwenbrau International. This resulted in a new state-of-the-art brewery incorporating the latest brewing and packaging technology gathered from around the world. The plant received *Food Engineering*'s International Plant-of the-Year award in 1991. This plant now supplies not only Malta but provides import competition to southern Europe.

Challenges for Research and Policy Analysis

In summary, the preceding discussion points up some key characteristics of international commerce in processed foods. Measured in terms of value of products sold in the marketplace, at least for the developed world, processed foods outweigh basic agricultural commodities by several magnitudes. This relative importance carries over into international commerce. Global trade in the food and agricultural sector is dominated by processed foods by a ratio of two to one, compared to basic commodities. What is more, measuring international commerce in food on the basis of international trade in goods misses what accounts for the biggest share of such commerce: foreign direct and contract production. A relatively small number of large, multinational firms are the main players.

Global commerce in processed foods is principally played out among the developed countries. These countries account for most of the trade in goods, as both buyers and sellers, and for most of the trade in direct investment capital and related corporate services, both as originators and as destinations. Of the international trade in goods, an important share is intra-industry. Of the international trade in direct investment capital, an important share is intellectual property. In short, there is little about global commerce in processed foods that resembles conditions that underlie neoclassical concepts of international trade, concepts that have been the springboard for truly extraordinary advances in liberalization of agricultural trade.

This situation presents a number of challenges to those conducting international trade research and policy analysis. Important questions to be worked out by researchers include the following.

- What are the relevant theories for explaining and predicting actual patterns of international commerce in processed foods?
- Is there a general theory that can rationalize foreign direct and contract production in the processed foods sector? Or, is international firm behavior in this sector so idiosyncratic as to limit meaningful analysis to case studies?
- How does the occurrence of foreign direct and contract production affect our understanding of patterns of international trade? Does it matter if foreign affiliation is horizontal or vertical?
- What data are needed for empirical studies, and what reporting protocols need to be established to obtain these data in an accurate and timely manner?

For policy analysts, relevant questions include the following.

- In the presence of intra-industry trade and foreign direct and contract production in the global processed food market, should trade policy prescriptions vary from those based on neoclassical trade theory?
- How can the impacts of trade policies be accurately predicted given the prevalence of intra- industry trade and foreign direct and contract production in processed food markets?
- How can the economic and social impacts of international trade in intellectual property be evaluated and assessed relative to those associated with trade in goods?
- How useful are trade policy prescriptions based on analysis of patterns of international commerce at upstream stages of the processed food chain in the absence of well-modeled linkages to downstream stages and a comprehensive understanding of downstream patterns of international commerce?

It is toward resolving these and related issues that we contribute to this volume.

References

Balassa, B. 1965. *Economic Development and Integration.* Mexico: Centro de Estudios Monetarios Latinoamericos.

Balassa, B. and L. Bauwens. 1987. Intra-Industry Specialization in a Multi-Country and Multi-Industry Framework. *Economic Journal,* 97:923–939.

Christodoulou, M. 1992. Intra-Industry Trade in Agrofood Sectors: The Case of the EEC Meat Market. *Applied Economics,* 24:875-884.

Connor, J. M. 1983. Foreign Investment in the U.S. Food Marketing System. *American Journal of Agricultural Economics,* 65:395-404.

Dunning, J. H. 1981. *International Production and the Multinational Enterprise.* London: Allen and Unwin.

ERS. 1996. *Globalization of the Processed Food Market.* D. Henderson, C. Handy, and S. Neff, eds. U.S. Department of Agriculture, Economic Research Service, Agricultural Economics Report, No. 742, Sept.

Geringer, J. M. 1990. Trends and Traits of Canadian Joint Ventures. *Investment Canada,* Working Paper Number 1990-IV, February.

Greenaway, D. and C. Milner. 1986. *The Economics of Intra-Industry Trade.* Oxford: Basil Blackwell.

Grubel, H. G. and P. J. Lloyd. 1975. *Intra-Industry Trade.* London: Macmillan.

Handy, C. R. and D. R. Henderson. 1994. Assessing the Role of Foreign Direct Investment in the Mood Manufacturing Industry. Ch. 11 in *Competitiveness in International Food Markets,* M. Bredahl, P. Abbott, and M. Reed, eds. Boulder, CO: Westview.

Handy, C. R. and J. M. MacDonald. 1989. Multinational Structures and Strategies of U.S. Food Firms. *American Journal of Agricultural Economics,* 71:1246–1254.

Harrigan, K. R. 1988. Strategic Alliances and Partner Asymmetries. *Cooperative Strategies in International Business,* F. Contractor and P. Lorange, eds. Toronto: Lexington Books, 205–226.

Hartman, D. A., D. R. Henderson, and I. M. Sheldon. 1993. A Cross-Section Analysis of Intra-Industry Trade in the U.S. Processed Food and Beverage Sectors. *Agricultural and Resource Economics Review,* 23: 189–198.

Helpman, E. 1981. International Trade in the Presence of Product Differentiation, Economies of Scale, and Monopolistic Competition. *Journal of International Economics,* 11:305–340.

Helpman, E. and P. R. Krugman. 1985. *Market Structure and Foreign Trade.* Cambridge, MA: MIT Press.

Henderson, D. R. and S.D. Frank. 1990. Industrial Organization and Export Competitiveness of U.S. Food Manufacturers. Ohio State University, North Central Regional Research Project NC-194, Report No. OP-4, March.

Henderson, D. R. and I. M. Sheldon. 1992. International Licensing of Branded Food Products. *Agribusiness: An International Journal,* Volume 8, Number 5, 399–412.

Henderson, D. R., I. M. Sheldon, and K. N. Thomas. 1994. International Licensing of Food and Beverages Makes Markets Truly Global. *Food Review,* Volume 13, Issue 3, 7–12.

Henderson, D. R., P. R. Vörös, and J. G. Hirschberg. 1996. Industrial Determinants of International Trade and Foreign Investment by Food and Beverage Manufacturing Firms. Ch. 12 in *Industrial Organization and Trade in the Food Industries*, I. Sheldon and P. Abbott, eds. Boulder, CO: Westview.

Hirschberg, J. G., I. M. Sheldon, and J. R. Dayton. 1994. An Analysis of Bilateral Intra-Industry Trade in the Food Processing Sector. *Applied Economics*, 26:159–167.

Krugman, P. R. 1980. Scale Economies, Product Differentiation and the Pattern of Trade. *American Economic Review*, 70:950–959.

Lancaster, K. 1980. Intra-Industry Trade under Perfect Monopolistic Competition. *Journal of International Economics*, 10:151–176.

Linder, B. 1961. *An Essay on Trade and Transportation.* New York: Wiley.

Markusen, J. R. 1995. The Boundaries of Multinational Enterprises and the Theory of International Trade. *Journal of Economic Perspectives*, 9:169–189.

McCorriston, S. and I. M. Sheldon. 1991. Intra-Industry Trade and Specialization in Processed Agricultural Products: The Case of the U.S. and the E.C. *Review of Agricultural Economics*, 13:173–184.

O'Brien, P. M. 1994. Implications for Public Policy. Ch. 23 in *Food and Agricultural Markets, The Quiet Revolution*, L. Schertz and L. Daft, eds. Washington, DC: National Planning Association.

Ourusoff, A. 1992. What's in a Name? What the World's Top Brands are Worth. *Financial World*, September 1.

Södersten, B. and G. Reed. 1994. *International Economics*, 3d Edition. New York: St. Martin's Press.

Tharakan, P.K.M. 1985. Empirical Analyses of the Commodity Composition of Trade, in *Current Issues in International Trade*, D. Greenaway, ed. London: Macmillan.

United Nations. 1990. Statistical Papers, Commodity Trade Statistics, According to Standard International Trade Classification, Series D. Statistical Office, Department of Economic and Social Affairs.

U.S. Department of Commerce, BEA. 1995. *Foreign Direct Investment Abroad* and *Foreign Direct Investment in the United States: Operations of U.S. Affiliates of Foreign Companies.* U.S. Department of Commerce, Economics and Statistics Administration, Bureau of Economic Analysis, Preliminary 1993 estimates.

Verdoorn, P. J. 1960. The Intra-Bloc Trade of Benelux, in *Economic Consequences of Nations*, Proceedings of a Conference Held by the International Economic Association, London.

3

Trade and Industrial Policies Affecting Processed Foods

Wayne Jones and David Blandford

The growing globalization of the world economy—based upon trade liberalization, foreign direct investment, integrated financial markets—and the resulting increase in competition has significant implications for the structure and performance of the food processing industry. Product mix, scale of operation, vertical coordination, industry concentration, geographic location, and ownership are just some of the characteristics being rapidly transformed by globalization.

At the same time, continued technological advance in the agrofood sector is contributing to its closer integration into the rest of the economy in most countries, as well as strengthened linkages between primary production and downstream industries. Changes in primary production can be significant for processors because they may induce changes in the price, quality, stability, and source of supply of agricultural raw materials.

One of the principal factors influencing the pace and direction of adjustment is the evolving policy environment within which the industry operates. Agricultural policies, involving market price supports, supply controls, border measures, export subsidies, and other policy instruments distort market signals and inhibit adjustment to varying degrees and affect industry structure and performance in terms of product prices, resource allocation, regional distribution, scale of activity, balance of market power, and industry adaptability. Trade policies also have important effects. For the first time, agriculture has been brought under international disciplines through the Uruguay Round Agreement on Agriculture (URAA) with well-defined constraints on import barriers, export subsidies, and domestic support. Most regional trade agreements include agriculture, albeit often in a less comprehensive way than other sectors, but nevertheless their effects are being felt on the structure and performance of agriculture and the agrofood industry.

Two other policy areas, competition and investment polices, are increasingly seen as fundamental to achieving economic efficiency gains and liberalization of trade and therefore as complements to industrial and trade policy reforms. While trade policy seeks to constrain the ability of governments to impose barriers to the international flow of goods, competition policy constrains the ability of the private sector to impose similar barriers. For many competition authorities, unobstructed international trade is seen as the best way of assuring rivalry in domestic markets. The establishment of common disciplines for competition policy is frequently identified as an issue likely to be on the agenda for the next round of multilateral trade negotiations.

Trade and investment were traditionally viewed as alternative ways of securing access to a market, but investment, or market presence, is increasingly considered to be an essential accompaniment to trade. Liberal trade alone may not ensure market contestability. Investment policy is now the subject of discussion or negotiation in numerous international fora such as the OECD and United Nations Conference on Trade and Development (UNCTAD) and regional entities such as North American Free Trade Agreement (NAFTA) and Asia-Pacific Economic Cooperation (APEC). At their May 1996 Ministerial meeting, OECD countries agreed to "begin an examination of trade and investment in the World Trade Organization (WTO) and to further the progress on negotiation of a Multilateral Agreement on Investment" (OECD 1996c).

This chapter examines the current direction of policy reforms in these four broad areas—agriculture, trade, competition, and investment policy and makes some observations about the implications for the food processing industry.

Agricultural Policy

"The cost of agricultural policies is considerable, for government budgets, for consumers and for the economy as a whole." (OECD Communiqué of Agricultural Ministers, 1987).

There is a growing recognition in OECD countries that traditional agricultural policies, which rely heavily on price support, are failing to achieve their stated objectives, such as the stabilisation of farm incomes and protection of the family farm (OECD 1995a). Structural adjustment has continued despite high support. Indeed, it can be argued that such support has accelerated the process of adjustment by stimulating output and raising costs. The technology-driven industrialization of the sector combined with the increased number of activities of farm households has resulted in greater diversity, thereby eroding the effectiveness of support policies designed for a more homogeneous sector. Only a small part of the money transferred to the agricultural sector through price support translates into increased farm household incomes. OECD estimates of the transfer efficiency ratio of price support are very low, with as little as one dollar of additional income resulting from every five dollars of consumer and taxpayer expenditures.

Without downplaying the importance of international developments, pressures for change in agricultural policies are largely domestic in nature. Growing competition for scarce public funds is placing intense pressure on governments to ensure that resources are used efficiently. In agriculture, policies designed to benefit farmers are increasingly seen as too costly to consumers and taxpayers. Negative side effects, most notably on downstream industries and on the environment, are becoming more apparent. Broader concerns about industry competitiveness, the amount of value added, and the future of rural economies have also led to pressures for the reform of agricultural policies in many countries.

A recent OECD study examined the impact of dairy policies in selected countries on industry structure and performance with particular reference to downstream processing (OECD 1996d). The study provides a number of examples of market distortions caused at least in part by existing policy regimes and institutional arrangements. Some of the observations include the following:

- A shift in relative milk prices across regions under U.S. support policies has led to regional shifts in production. Higher state-mandated processing margins in California put other manufacturers at a competitive disadvantage; this has created regional tensions.
- Under Canada's supply management system, the base price for industrial milk continued to increase through the 1980s while there was a steady decline in U.S. support prices. For some products like yogurt and ice cream, Canadian processors were paying up to 50 percent more for industrial milk.
- In the Netherlands, production quotas restrict the availability of supplies to processors and consequently plant size. The lack of tradability of quotas across EU (European Union) member states has frozen the pattern of milk production and processing to that of 1984, inhibiting adjustment to changes in costs, technology, or demand.
- The operations of the Milk Marketing Boards in the United Kingdom reduced incentives for efficient processing, enabled the survival of processors whose basic aim was to produce bulk products (for intervention buying), and shielded those manufacturers from price competition.

- As a monopoly exporter, the New Zealand Dairy Board exerts a strong influence on downstream processing. There is evidence that the existence of the Board has inhibited innovation and the exploitation of new market opportunities.

Greater awareness of these and other impacts have led to changes in attitudes and increased efforts to redress the negative effects of agricultural policies. The study goes on to document a number of dairy policy reforms aimed at improving market orientation and increasing the competitiveness of the sector as a whole. Among these are: reductions in price support levels and modifications to U.S. milk marketing orders to reflect the shift in demand toward low-fat milk products; establishment of a low-price milk class in Canada to improve the competitiveness of processors and exporters in international and domestic high value-added markets; in New Zealand, the liberalization of entitlements to export specialized products, providing private processing companies greater access to international markets; and deregulation of the U.K. Milk Marketing Boards, to permit processors to bid for milk in an open market for the first time in sixty years.

Similar examples of policy reinstrumentation or fundamental policy reform exist for other commodities. Each year the OECD monitors agricultural policy developments in member countries against their stated goal of increased market orientation and reduced distortionary impacts for the economy through progressive and concerted reductions in agricultural support. The 1996 report shows that further progress was made in reforming agricultural policies, although overall levels of support remained high (estimated total transfers in 1995 were U.S.$336 billion, see Table 3.1) (OECD 1996a). The main findings are as follows.

TABLE 3.1 Total Agricultural Transfers in Selected OECD Countries, 1995

	Total transfers (billion US$)	*Total transfers (percent of GDP)*	*Agricultural GDP (percent of total GDP)*
United States	74.6	1.0	1.5[a]
Canada	5.3	0.9	1.6[a]
European Union (15)	144.9	1.7	1.9[a]
Japan	91.6	1.8	1.7[b]
OECD	336.0	1.7	1.7[c]

[a]1994.
[b]1990–92.
[c]1994. (Excluding Iceland, Japan and Turkey)
Source: OECD (1996a).

- A general shift away from market price support and towards direct payments has resulted in further reductions in the insulation of domestic producers and consumers from world markets, albeit with continued wide variations in the levels, composition, and trends across countries and commodities (see Figure 3.1).
- Market price support, often in conjunction with supply controls, is still the main form of assistance in most OECD countries with direct payments still closely linked to production and focusing more on compensating for reduced price support than on facilitating adjustment.
- Domestic agricultural policy reforms related to implementation of the URAA reflect a move in the direction of greater trade liberalization by improving market access, and by reducing export subsidies and other trade distorting practices.

The direction of policy reform augers well for the processing sector, although the slow and uneven pace of change may frustrate many in the industry, particularly if competitors in other countries are seen to be benefiting from reform. A shift from market price support to direct payments should lead to lower raw material costs and, through lower food prices, to higher consumer food demand. With the accession of Austria to the European Union, for example, commodity prices declined by as much as 50 percent, with consumer food prices also declining but less dramatically.

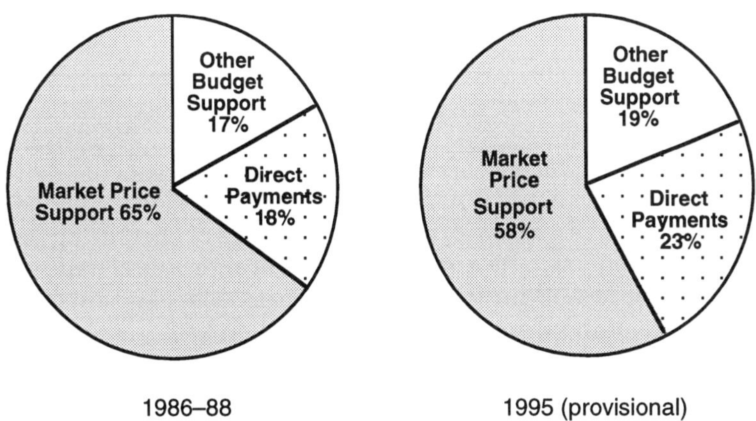

FIGURE 3.1 Composition of OECD[1] Agricultural Support (percent of total producer subsidy equivalent). *Source:* OECD (1996a).

[1] Excludes Czech Republic and Mexico.

This shift should also eventually lead to fewer of the supply controls commonly associated with market price support and the problems these create for the availability of supplies for processing. In 1995, Switzerland abolished limits on the size of individual milk quotas, Norway removed supply controls for pigmeat and eggs, Australia expanded land quotas on sugar cane production and the European Union and Iceland removed quotas for sheepmeat.

The movement toward less distortionary direct payments should reduce the tendency for support measures to mask market signals and inhibit adjustment, making producers more responsive to changing consumer demands and the needs of processors. Under the new U.S. farm legislation (the Federal Agricultural Improvement and Reform Act of 1996), for example, the link between income support payments and farm prices was removed by providing for fixed but declining "production flexibility contract payments." Thus, future production decisions should be based more on market conditions than on expected program payments.

Trade Policy

"The Agreement on Agriculture negotiated in the Uruguay Round is the most significant single package of changes to the international trading regime in agriculture ever agreed." (Stefan Tangermann, Institute of Agricultural Economics, University of Göttingen, 1996).

The three pillars of the Uruguay Round Agreement on Agriculture—market access, export subsidies, and domestic support—apply to all products, basic and processed alike. Market access is improved through the tariffication of nontariff barriers and the reduction of tariffs by 36 percent on average (simple average with a minimum reduction of 15 percent) as well as the introduction of tariff quotas. Outlays on export subsidies are to be cut by 36 percent from the base period level (21 percent reduction in eligible volume), and domestic support to agriculture, which distorts trade or affects production, is to be reduced by 20 percent.

An OECD study of the URAA came to the conclusion that, although the Agreement was a huge step forward in the process of liberalizing trade in agricultural products, only a modest increase in agricultural trade may be expected in the near future (OECD 1995c). That study, like most others on the outcomes of the Uruguay Round, focused on basic rather than processed agricultural commodities. Some observers have suggested that, by not examining the impacts of the Agreement on trade in processed agricultural products, its overall impact has been greatly underestimated.

In response to this, a study is underway by the OECD Secretariat, comparing the impacts of the URAA on trade in processed and basic agricultural products. Among other things, the study examines the allocation of tariff reductions, tariff escalation, and the effect of export subsidy commitments. The preliminary conclusion is that there is little evidence to support the assertion that the URAA will influence trade in processed products more than trade in basic commodities.

One relevant issue is the frequent use of tariffication not only for basic commodities, but also for processed products which contain "sensitive" basic commodities (dairy, sugar, vegetables, cereals). The level of tariffs resulting from the URAA is, in most cases, very high for both basic and processed products, and tariff reduction commitments for those products are below the average reduction of 36 percent (in many cases 15 percent, which is the minimum reduction allowed under the Agreement). Therefore, where tariffication has been used for processed products, trade is not expected to increase significantly in the short or medium term. Products containing dairy and sugar products as inputs stand out in this context (see Table 3.2).

The most important effects on trade in processed products are expected where tariffication was not used. In those cases, tariff reductions are to be applied to more "realistic" pre-existing levels, and, although tariffs are low in many cases, there will be some significant reductions. The products most affected are processed fruit and vegetables, prepared cereal products, alcoholic beverages, chocolate confectionery, and vegetable oils.

The percentage tariff reduction on processed products is no greater than for basic agricultural products, and, as these reductions have been allocated according to the simple average rule, countries have frequently reduced high tariffs less than low tariffs. This has led to a significant dilution of the potential impact of the agreement.

In general, the volume of imports of processed products was large enough in the base period to avoid the establishment of minimum access quotas. The main exceptions are dairy products, for which trade will be facilitated in some cases as a result of introduction of rather large minimum access quotas. The way in which tariff rate quotas (TRQs) are administered (e.g. first come–first serve, auctioning, historical, "prise-en-charge") is an important issue, but, as details of allocation mechanisms have only recently become available, no detailed analysis has been undertaken on their economic effects. The role of state trading enterprises in this context would warrant closer examination.

Before the implementation of the URAA, tariff escalation on agricultural products was difficult to analyze since nontariff barriers (NTBs) made the comparison meaningless in many cases. Now that most NTBs have been converted to tariffs, such analysis is possible. Escalation will be reduced in some cases as a result of the URAA but will continue to be a considerable impediment to trade in some processed products, especially those of importance to developing countries (coffee, cacao, fruit, and vegetables). For products such as meat and cereals, tariff escalation is either not considerable, or there is a de-escalating tariff structure. As indicated above, countries have frequently reduced high tariffs less than low tariffs and this has increased tariff escalation in some cases.

The use of export subsidies on processed products has now been explicitly embodied in the URAA, whereas under the General Agreement on Tariffs and Trade (GATT) such subsidies could arguably have been prohibited, as for other manufactured goods. There is, however, still some uncertainty about how the export subsidy commitments will be implemented.

In the URAA schedules a distinction is made between incorporated or

TABLE 3.2 Tariff Levels and Reduction Commitments

	Tariff Levels (percent)		*Percentage Reduction*	
Beef	**Basic**	**Processed**	**Basic**	**Processed**
Canada[a]	*37.9*	*11.2*	*30%*	*36%*
European Union	*195.0*	*36.0*	*36%*	*36%*
Japan	93.0	52.4	46%	44%
Norway	*404.9*	*404.9*	*15%*	*15%*
United States	*31.1*	6.6	*15%*	68%
Durum wheat	**Basic**	**Pasta**	**Basic**	**Pasta**
Canada[a]	*57.7*	*16.5*	*15%*	*15%*
European Union	*132.8*	59.9	*36%*	36%
Japan	*230.0*	45.0	*15%*	25%
Norway	*495.4*	*248.6*	*30%*	*15%*
United States	4.3	Duty free	16%	–
Dairy Products	**Milk: 1–6 % fat**	**SMP[b]**	**Milk**	**SMP[b]**
Australia	0%	2%	–	50%
Canada[a]	*283.8%*	*237.2%*	15%	15%
European Union	*340 ECU/t*	*1568 ECU/t*	*36%*	*20%*
Japan	*25% + 134 yen/kg*	*35% + 466 yen/kg*	*15%*	*15%*
Norway	*457%*	*461%*	*15%*	*15%*
United States	1.7 ¢/litre	*102 ¢/kg*	15%	*15%*
Oranges	**Fresh**	**Juice**	**Fresh**	**Juice**
Australia	2.0	41.8	50%	43%
Canada	0.0	1.5	–	36%
European Union	*27.6*	56.3	*20%*	20%
Japan	39.9	39.8	40%	36%
United States	2.6	48.7	15%	15%

[a]Over access commitments.

[b]Solid milk products.

Notes: i. Italics = tariffication applied.

ii. A simple average for tariffied and untariffied products is calculated for processed beef in Canada and the European Union.

iii. Specific tariff rates are converted to ad valorem rates except for dairy products.

Source: OECD Secretariat.

transformed products and other agricultural product categories. Primary and processed agricultural products are treated alike, except that no commitments on volume are included in the URAA schedules for incorporated products. Four OECD Member countries (Canada, the European Union, Norway, and Switzerland) have included export subsidy commitments on incorporated products in their schedules. These subsidies are mostly provided to compensate for the price difference between domestic and world markets.

Since there is no volume limit for export subsidies on incorporated products and the definition of processed products that received export support during the base period is quite wide, there is greater room for discretionary reallocation of subsidies among products and types of input than for export subsidies on basic products. However, since exports of incorporated products have generally been increasing during recent years, the export subsidy commitments affect trade in these products from the outset of the implementation period of the Agreement.

Export subsides for other processed agricultural products, such as dairy products, processed meat, and cereals are lumped together for a rather wide range of products in many cases. For example, export subsidy commitments for primary and processed meat products have been aggregated. In such cases, the allocation of export subsidies can be shifted between products at different levels of processing, depending on policy priorities at any given time. Thus the new Federal Agricultural Improvement and Reform (FAIR) Act in the United States involves an increased emphasis on market development for high value and value-added agricultural products, rather than simple export assistance for bulk commodities.

The reduction in export subsidies has already given rise to new arrangements to assist exporters whose international competitiveness has been affected. Examples of this are found in Norway and Switzerland, where duty-free imports of raw materials for food processing have recently been allowed, on condition that the final good is exported. In general, caps on export subsides are likely to lead to greater competition between exporters of basic and processed products for entitlement to export. Over time, these pressures could be reflected in demands from processors for more market-oriented reforms in policies affecting the basic commodities. At a minimum, processors are likely to demand further exemptions from import tariffs for basic agricultural inputs and price differentiation, with lower prices for products subjected to further processing.

The greatest impact of the export subsidy commitments of the URAA is likely to be on trade in cheese, as the European Union will be required to reduce substantially its export subsidies over the next few years. This will benefit traditional exporters of dairy products such as Australia and New Zealand.

Aspects other than tariff reductions and export subsidy commitments must be taken into account when examining the possible benefits of the UR agreement. Among these is an improved dispute settlement procedure. Trade disputes involving basic agricultural products have been frequent in recent years, and retaliatory trade measures have often involved processed food and beverages. Due to the multiplicity of processed agricultural products, they are easily grouped together to meet the value of trade and origin requirements for retaliation (Harris 1994). A reduction in the use of retaliation through an improved dispute settlement mechanism would therefore benefit trade in processed products.

The introduction of more stringent disciplines on the use of sanitary and phyto-sanitary (SPS) rules will likely have a positive impact on trade in processed agricultural commodities, but the size of the effects is difficult to forecast. SPS regulations apply to a lesser extent on processed than on basic products, due to the nature of the products—raw or fresh versus cooked or preserved. Other nontariff barriers such as variable levies have been used frequently as protective measures, alongside ordinary tariffs. The replacement of these and other nontariff barriers by ordinary tariffs has enhanced greatly the transparency of border measures. This is of great importance for future growth in trade in both basic and processed products.

Nonpolicy factors might have a greater impact on trade in high value and other processed agricultural products than the policy factors discussed above. Generally, it is clear that the international marketing of processed products is much more complex than that of homogeneous bulk commodities. Aspects such as brand awareness and product differentiation as well as concentration in the food industry are important. Strategic decisions by large multinational companies, which dominate the food industry, on international marketing versus foreign direct investment are based on many factors, not just tariffs. These factors are likely to counterbalance to some degree the impact of the tariff reduction commitments in the URAA (Malanoski 1994, Reed and Marchant 1991).

At the same time as the most important multilateral trade agreement for decades is being implemented, the importance of regional trading blocs and bilateral trade agreements is likely to be increasing. Since 1990, more than thirty regional agreements have been signalled to the GATT/WTO (Blandford, 1995). The proportion of world trade subject to such differential treatment is likely to expand. Some observers have raised the question whether regional agreements will compete with or complement the multilateral system.

As regional agreements provide preferential market access for the participating countries, they are inherently discriminatory for third parties. This can lead to increased intraregional trade and investment at the expense of extraregional trade and investment. The clearest example of a regional agreement contributing to increased protection in agriculture was the expansion of the Common Agricultural Policy to new members of the European Common Market during the 1970s and 1980s. However, in recent years there is evidence that, on balance, regional trading agreements have contributed to multilateral liberalization. They have done this by liberalizing faster and deeper than would be possible under multilateral agreements, and by providing laboratories for approaches and techniques that have subsequently found application in multilateral negotiations. Thus, for example, the creation of the single market in the European Union in 1993 provided the impetus for addressing more than two hundred nontariff barriers to trade in food and beverages between member countries. It is estimated that the elimination of these barriers will result in savings equivalent to 2–3 percent of the value added of the food processing sector in the Union (Commission of the European Communities 1990). The creation of the single market has also contributed to substantial merger activity in the food and beverage sector.

Whatever the net contribution of regional agreements to the liberalization of trade in processed agricultural products, it is of great importance that agriculture be fully incorporated from the outset in such arrangements. Otherwise the risk is that overall liberalization of trade in agricultural products, both basic and processed, will be at a slower pace than for other sectors.

Competition Policy

"The splendid provisions which prohibit price cartels, market sharing arrangements and abuses of market dominant positions lose nine-tenths of their force once they come within hailing distance of the farm gate." (Sir Leon Brittan, EU Competition Commissioner, 1990).

In general, competition policy is concerned with three issues: the diffusion of market power (e.g. threats from monopolies and cartels), the protection of market competition (e.g. from predatory pricing, boycotts, discrimination), and the enhancement of economic welfare (e.g. through allocative and productive efficiency) (Jacquemin 1990). Competition policy is a growing influence in the economic policy of OECD countries and is taking on greater prominence as a complement to, and instrument of, international trade policy. The lack of an effective competition policy in one country can seriously undermine the trade opportunities of other countries (e.g. through barriers to entry, discrimination in distribution chains), even if border controls and other measures used to protect domestic industries are relaxed. International aspects are expected to increase the pressure to broaden the scope of competition policy enforcement and to lead to a greater convergence of competition policies across OECD countries. Under such a scenario, it may become increasingly difficult for the agrofood sector to maintain its current exemptions and special rules regarding competition policy.

Competition policy is generally applied less comprehensively in the agrofood sector (or more specifically, primary production agriculture) than in other sectors. In many cases this relaxed treatment reflects the use of restrictive agreements associated with agricultural policy. Standards applied to the enforcement of anticompetitive disciplines and merger controls in the agrofood industries vary across OECD countries, reflecting the evolving state of competition policy and enforcement procedures.

A recent OECD report examined sectoral coverage, scope, and enforcement of competition policy, based on a country questionnaire and follow-up with twelve jurisdictions (Australia, Canada, European Union, France, Germany, Hungary, Japan, Mexico, Portugal, Sweden, United Kingdom, and United States). Of the twelve jurisdictions, Mexico was the only country to report no exclusions, partial exclusions, or special rules for agriculture. After employment relations, agriculture was the second most excluded, exempted, or favorably treated area under competition laws. Note that some exemptions are general in scope, while others apply only to specific products. However, none of the jurisdictions surveyed reported that agriculture was subject to relaxed merger control (OECD forthcoming).

As discussed in a recent OECD report on competition policy and the agrofood sector, there are several developments that are of significance to downstream industries (OECD 1996b). One is the deregulation of the production sector in the context of agricultural policy reform and the establishment of complementary measures to ensure competition. A second is the changing attitude of competition authorities toward mergers and acquisitions. A third is the growing influence of competition policy on market access and international trade.

Competition Policy and Agricultural Policy Reform

One of the main principles for agricultural policy reform agreed by OECD countries is improved market orientation. Deregulation and freer trade do not automatically result in greater competition. Agricultural policy reforms that reduce government intervention in the market may well require complementary measures to ensure effective competition. Recent experiences with agricultural policy reform in OECD member countries suggest that the existence of oligopolistic market structures and noncontestable markets may allow firms to benefit from deregulation and to capture the benefits of reform. Earlier studies of regulatory reform, privatization, and competition policy suggest that, where anticompetitive arrangements exist prior to reform, firms may be expected to seek "private" agreements that would continue such arrangements.

An example of this concern and the complementarity between agrofood policy reform and competition policy is the recent deregulation of the United Kingdom Milk Marketing Boards. The Boards were the sole buyers of milk from producers and the sole sellers of milk for processing. With the demise of the Boards in late 1994, producers were supposed to have a number of companies bidding for their milk for the first time in sixty years. Initially there were producer concerns about the loss of market power in dealing with processors but in fact market power has largely been maintained by producers through the establishment of voluntary producer-owned cooperatives—the largest, Milk Marque, accounts for over 50 percent of U.K. milk sales. Producer prices have increased significantly under the new arrangements as processors bid to increase their share of domestic milk supplies limited by quota, and through the reallocation of milk to more profitable uses. As a consequence, processors have expressed concerns about anticompetitive behavior, and both the U.K. government and the European Commission are monitoring the situation to ensure that there is no abuse of market power.

Swedish experience also highlights the importance of linking agricultural policy reform with measures to ensure effective competition. The Competition Commission found that most food markets in Sweden did not meet the conditions for contestable markets and argued for the introduction of specific competition legislation for agrofood in conjunction with internal deregulation of the industry. Producer cooperatives dominated primary processing and, via mergers and acquisitions, were obtaining greater control of markets further downstream. Markets outside the cooperative sphere were most often dominated by one or two major firms, and price collusion was frequent. As a result, there was a significant possibility that processors, wholesalers, and retailers would benefit from proposed internal deregulation by capturing the benefits of agricultural policy reform. Special legislation for the food sector was implemented, which restricted certain anticompetitive behavior, such as vertical price collusion, market segmentation, and unregulated marketing boards. However, producer cooperatives with less than 60 percent market share were exempted from the new legislation, effectively excluding many of the large cooperatives with dominant market position. A special internal commission is continuing to investigate the state of competition in the Swedish food industry.

Mergers and Acquisitions

In recent years, there has been considerable merger and acquisition activity in the food processing industry, while many other proposed arrangements have been prohibited. Mergers in the EU food industry account for a significant and growing share of total manufacturing mergers, increasing from 13 to 18 percent in recent years (see Table 3.3). Concerns over increased concentration and reduced competition are heightened by the fact that most of these mergers involve already very large firms. Almost half of recent mergers in the food industry were among domestic firms, with just over a third involving firms from different EU countries and 17 percent with firms outside the European Union (Figure 3.2).

Michael Porter and others suggest that intense interfirm rivalry can create and upgrade the competitive advantages of a nation's firms. Porter argues that a strong competition policy is essential to the economic performance of an industry, with particular emphasis on the monitoring of horizontal mergers, collusive behavior (e.g. price fixing, market sharing) and strategic alliances (Porter 1990).

Conversely, an increasing number of analysts contend that competition policy may interfere with efficient business practices, particularly with respect to mergers and acquisitions. Mergers and acquisitions are believed to enhance overall welfare if they yield offsetting cost reductions through economies of scale, synergies, or other means. It is also believed that the continual striving for efficiency gains is fundamental to international competitiveness. It is this line of thinking that has led to the adoption in a growing number of countries of a total welfare approach to competition policy enforcement. Most competition authorities now accept that, under certain circumstances, overall improvements of efficiency may permit mergers and acquisitions, which may have significant anticompetitive effects. Many merger

TABLE 3.3 Mergers in the EU Food Industry

	Mergers		*Large Mergers* [a]	
	Number of mergers	*Percent of manufacturing mergers*	*Number of mergers*	*Percent of manufacturing mergers*
1987–88	51	13.3	40	14.9
1989–90	102	16.9	86	16.8
1991–92	61	17.6	57	18.7

[a]Mergers with combined turnover of firms involved greater than 1,000 million ECUs.

Source: Oustapassidis, et al. (1995).

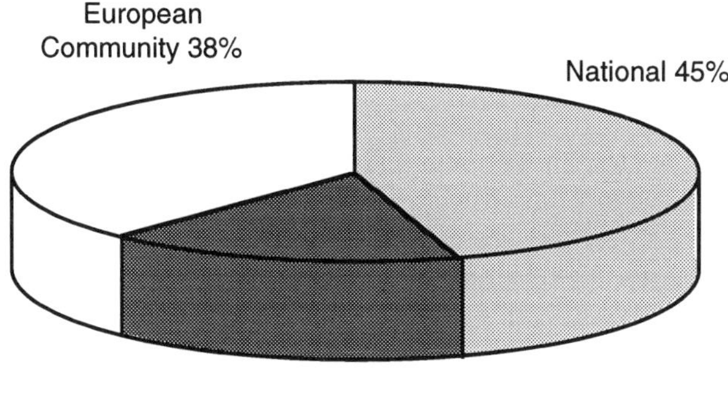

FIGURE 3.2 Mergers in the EU food industry, 1987–88 to 1991–92. *Source:* Oustapassidis, et al. (1995).

proposals in the agrofood sector use this efficiency defense when seeking approval from competition authorities.

A related consideration is the linkage between innovation and competition policy. Canadian competition authorities, for example, have maintained a particular interest in this relationship. Technological development and innovation are generally viewed as a key component in the economic growth of any industry. Active promotion of research, education, and technology transfer has long been a priority in the agrofood sector. Interfirm cooperation is often seen as a positive force in fostering innovation because of the externalities, indivisibilities, and economies of scale associated with research and intellectual property. As a result governments may, for the sake of more effective R&D, permit and even encourage horizontal business arrangements that might otherwise be suspect in terms of their effects on competition.

Market Access and Trade

Eliminating barriers to trade does not necessarily ensure access to markets. New dimensions are emerging in relation to market access as barriers to trade are relaxed. Restrictive business practices (and discriminatory investment laws) that limit foreign competition have become more visible and their impact on market access more significant as traditional constraints to trade are reduced. A number of contributors to a recent OECD Trade Committee roundtable suggested that business practices (which include the commercial activity of government enterprises) may now constitute a greater barrier to market access than border controls (OECD 1995b). While this is less likely to apply to agriculture currently because tariffs remain high, annual reports of competition policy case law cite examples in most OECD countries of business practices in the agrofood sector that were found to be in contravention of competition laws.

An OECD study argued that a weak competition policy that condones predatory or exclusionary behavior by domestic firms with respect to foreign goods, services, or investment may effectively serve as a substitute for "traditional" protection. It concluded that strengthening domestic competition laws to eliminate anticompetitive business practices that hinder market access would help alleviate the trade policy disputes arising from denials of market access (OECD forthcoming). The study suggested that, in contrast to all other areas with limited coverage (except employment relations), the limited coverage of competition laws in agriculture may depend less on judgments about "appropriate" economic considerations of natural monopoly and economies of scale and more on protectionist, political, cultural, or national security considerations. To the extent that these considerations deny a more market-oriented approach to policy, the potential for expanded coverage of the agrofood sector by competition law and its increased utility as an instrument to redress market access concerns were seen as limited. A key issue for agriculture is the scope of application of competition policy to governments, state enterprises, and government-encouraged private firm conduct because of the prevalence of government regulated or sanctioned activities (e.g. producer cooperatives, marketing boards) and the frequency of their exclusion from the provisions of competition law.

Export arrangements have so far proven to be the more contentious issue for both competition policy and trade policy. The American Bar Association (ABA) Special Committee on International Antitrust (1991) recommended that all countries repeal immunity for export cartels to the extent that such conduct would be unlawful in the country legislating such immunity. It also recommended that countries develop a multinational mechanism for the referral and prosecution of export cartels that unreasonably restrain trade in any particular country.

Both import and export arrangements have operated within the agrofood sector for many years, including State Trading Entities (STEs) with control over exports (e.g. Australian Wheat Board, Canadian Wheat Board, New Zealand Dairy Board); STEs with control over imports (e.g. Japan's Livestock Industry Promotion Corporation, Norwegian Grain Corporation); and voluntary restraints (e.g. U.S. voluntary export restraint agreements on beef with Australia and New Zealand). However, many of these arrangements have been ended or modified in response to commitments under the Uruguay Round Agreement. The extent to which continuing arrangements have the potential to affect market access and foreign competition depends on the existence of market power and prevalence of market distortions (e.g. limitations on market access, tariff rates, export subsidies). Where market power under the arrangement in question is relatively weak and/or markets are already highly distorted due to government intervention, the marginal impact of such arrangements on competition may not be large.

Investment Policy

"There are no foreign firms in the United Kingdom, only U.K. firms with foreign owners." (U.K. Department of Trade and Industry).

Investment policy is well beyond the expertise of the authors of this chapter but foreign direct investment in the food industry is one of the major structural trends of the last decade (consider the well known U.S. food firms Burger King, Dunkin' Donuts, and Pillsbury, which are actually U.K.-owned), while investment policy is an emerging international issue that warrants at least a brief comment. As documented in Chapter 2, sample data suggest foreign affiliate sales worldwide exceed processed food exports by a ratio of around five to one. Sales from foreign affiliates of U.S. processed food firms in 1994 (of over $100 million) were four times the value of U.S. exports of processed foods, and sales of foreign affiliates in the United States (more than $45 million) were twice the level of U.S. imports.

The relative importance of foreign direct investment (FDI) and direct investment abroad in the food manufacturing industry varies significantly across OECD countries. The United States and United Kingdom have been major hosts for foreign direct investment in the food industry in absolute terms with FDI in Canada also high given the relatively small size of its food industry. By comparison, inbound FDI in the Japanese food industry has been negligible, although the impact of protectionist policies on investment inflows is not clear (see Figure 3.3). The contribution of FDI to economic growth of the sector, however, depends on whether it reflects new investment or the acquisition of existing firms, which, for example, has characterised much of the foreign investment in the United States (OECD 1995d). Outbound FDI is also shown in Figure 3.3. Of the countries selected, the United States, Canada, and Germany have witnessed higher inbound than outbound FDI with the reverse situation for Japan, the United Kingdom, and France. To the extent that outbound FDI acts as a substitute for domestic production and exports, there are implications for the demand of domestic raw materials.

A 1993 survey of seventeen multinational firms (mainly U.S.-owned) suggested the main reason for expanding into international markets was the slow growth of domestic markets (Vaughn et al. 1994). Other reasons included risk reduction and the desire to capitalize on technological, product, and marketing expertise. The decision to produce in the host

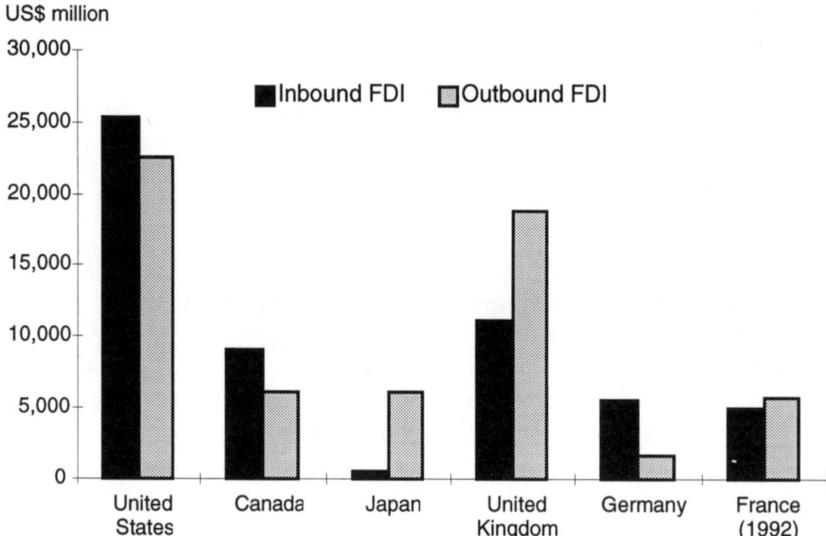

FIGURE 3.3 FDI and Direct Investment Abroad in the Food Industry (position at yearend 1993). *Source:* OECD (1995), International Direct Investment Statistics Yearbook.

country was primarily based on such factors as local market differentiation, service considerations, and transportation costs. The food processing firms interviewed indicated that public policies were generally not a key factor except for a few cases, such as Canada's supply management system for dairy and poultry and the U.S. sugar and peanut programs. Only a few firms mentioned investment regulations as a factor, although countries such as India and Mexico were identified as more attractive locations for FDI after deregulation.

However, as trade becomes more liberalized and competition increases, business decisions on where to locate become more sensitive to differences in domestic policies and practices. Paradoxically, as the barriers of protection are lowered and countries become more similar, their remaining differences become more significant in determining trade and investment flows (Lawrence 1996). There are differences in the treatment of foreign investment across OECD countries. With respect to R&D funding, for example, the trend in the European Union seems to be toward increased access for foreign direct investment. Proposed U.S. legislation that would limit participation by firms under foreign control in certain U.S. government-sponsored programs or link such participation to reciprocal treatment in other countries was proposed—but not passed into law—and was vigorously opposed by the European Union, Canada, and Japan, among others (Kleen 1995). There is also the recent example of the Helms-Burton Act, which seeks to impose sanctions on foreign companies doing business with or investing in Cuba, and the possible implementation of similar legislation to cover other countries, such as Iran and Libya.

Apart from these negative developments, the overall trend in investment policy during the last two decades has been towards the liberalization of restrictive measures. While there are always concerns expressed about foreign investors "buying up the country," there is general recognition of the benefits of foreign direct investment in terms of employment and capital generation, introduction of new technology, and increased competition. The progressive liberalization by OECD governments has since the early 1990s been promoted through a combination of formal commitments and constant peer pressure on member countries to remove remaining barriers. The OECD Code of Capital Movements and supplementary Code of Liberalization of Invisible Operations, together with the National Treatment Instrument, have to date provided the only multilateral framework of rules aimed at promoting nondiscrimination and investment liberalization among the world's developed economies. Countries in all regions of the world have reduced or eliminated restrictive elements in their FDI regimes and increased their protection and facilitation aspects in order to attract inbound investment.

A number of important developments at the international level have provided additional impetus in the 1990s. The conclusion of the Uruguay Round including the agreement on Trade Related Investment Measures (TRIMs), the agreement to establish NAFTA, and the increasing number of bilateral treaties for the promotion of FDI have been particularly instrumental. All these instruments share a common purpose of reducing restrictions on FDI flows and operations of multinationals and have led to significant convergence of policy approaches.

However, considerable differences remain in the nature, breadth, and depth of the measures regarding entry and establishment, ownership and control, investment incentives, standards of treatment, and market controls. Efforts are currently underway to consolidate and significantly strengthen existing OECD instruments through the development of a multilateral investment agreement. This will involve the elaboration of rules for liberalization, new or strengthened disciplines on privatization, monopolies and concessions, private practices and the movement of personnel, investment protection, and effective dispute settlement procedures. It will also identify possible ways of involving nonmember countries.

The two main areas of government intervention subject to review are investment incentives and performance requirements. The two policy areas are linked in that acceptance of certain performance requirements is sometimes the price to be paid for obtaining investment incentives. Most analysts agree that any international investment accord should ban or restrict both types of intervention, reasoning that these measures act in much the same way as trade restrictions, reducing allocative and dynamic efficiency and resulting in welfare losses. Although opinion is more strongly against incentives, recent bilateral, regional, and international attempts at rulemaking suggest there is a higher probability that performance requirements will be curtailed under a multilateral agreement on investment (Graham 1996).

Conclusions

Trade in processed foods has always been influenced by policy measures, such as tariffs and quotas, which are applied at the border. Policies for production agriculture also have important indirect effects on the food industry and food trade. However, globalization means that trade in processed foods is increasingly being affected by other policies, such as those relating to competition and investment. The international effects of these policies are a potential source of friction, and ways must be found to address this. The central challenge facing policymakers today is how best to promote and secure internationally contestable markets in which the ability of foreign and domestic firms to enter and compete is not unduly impaired or distorted by public or private anticompetitive conduct.

There is a growing recognition of the need for further policy reform in agriculture. The impetus for such reform will largely result from domestic pressures. These pressures need to be translated into further reductions in tariffs, export subsidies, and domestic support at the next round of international negotiations through the WTO scheduled to begin in 1999. While difficult to address, common disciplines for competition policies will be needed. Future negotiations also need to focus on the elimination of restrictions on international investment. As barriers to trade fall, the persistence of measures that limit market access by limiting competition will become increasingly untenable. To realize the full benefits of globalization, it will be necessary to ensure the free movement of both goods and capital, and this requires competitive markets.

For analysts and policymakers concerned with the structure and performance of the agrofood sector, it is no longer sufficient to focus solely on agricultural policy. Trade, competition, and investment policy will increasingly influence the sector's development and growth.

Notes

The authors would like to acknowledge the contribution of the work of many of their colleagues in the OECD Secretariat to this paper, in particular Eirikur Einarsson. Nevertheless, the views expressed are those of the authors and do not necessarily reflect those of the OECD or its Member countries.

References

American Bar Association (1991). "Special Committee on International Antitrust," B. E. Hawk, Chair.

Blandford, D. (1995), "Regionalism versus Multilateralism and the World Trading System." Paper presented at the *IATRC symposium on Economic Integration in the Western Hemisphere*, Costa Rica, June 7–9.

Commission of the European Communities (1990), "The Agro-Food Business in the Community." *CAP Working Notes*. Directorate General for Agriculture. Brussels.

Graham, E. M. (1996) "Investment and the New Multilateral Trade Context" in OECD (1996c), *Market Access After the Uruguay Round Investment, Competition and Technology Perspectives*, Paris, pp. 35–62.

Harris, S. A. (1994), "The Food Industry Perspective," *Agriculture in the Uruguay Round*, editors K. A. Ingersent, A. J. Rayner, and R. C. Hire, eds. MacMillan.

Jacquemin, A. (1990), "Competition and Competition Policy in Market Economies," in *Competition Policy in Europe and North America: Economic Issues and Institutions*, Harwood Academic Publishers, London, pp. 1–8.

Kleen, P. (1995), "The Case of Sweden" in OECD (1995), *New Dimensions of Market Access in a Globalising World Economy*, Paris, pp. 41–45.

Lawrence, R. Z. (1996), "Towards Globally Contestable Markets," in OECD (1996c), *Market Access After the Uruguay Round: Investment, Competition and Technology Perspectives*, Paris, pp. 25–33.

Malanoski, M. (1994), "U.S. Multinational Food Manufacturers Choose Production in Foreign Markets Over Exports," *Food Review*, USDA (1994) Washington, D.C.

OECD (1995a), *Adjustment in OECD Agriculture: Issues and Policy Responses*, Paris.

OECD (1995b), *New Dimensions of Market Access in a Globalising World Economy*, Paris.

OECD (1995c), *The Uruguay Round, A Preliminary Evaluation of the Impacts of the Agreement on Agriculture in the OECD countries*, Paris.

OECD (1995d), *OECD Reviews of Foreign Direct Investment*: United States, Paris.

OECD (1996a), *Agricultural Policies, Markets and Trade in OECD Countries: Monitoring and Evaluation 1996*, Paris.

OECD (1996b), *Competition Policy and the Agro-Food Sector*, Paris.

OECD (1996c), News Release 23 May, Meeting of the Council at Ministerial Level, Paris.

OECD (1996d), *Reforming Dairy Policy*, Paris.

OECD (forthcoming), *The Scope and Coverage of Competition Laws*, Paris.

Oustapassidis, K., A. Banterle, J. Briz, A. Collins, J. Gilpin, C. Noeme, S. Tonzauli, and H. Wendt (1995), *A Review of Some Preliminary Data Relating to Structural Changes within the European Food Industries and Factors Affecting It*, Discussion Paper No. 9, EU Concerted Action on Structural Change in the European Food Industries, Brussels.

Porter, M. (1990), *The Competitive Advantage of Nations*, New York: Free Press.

Reed, M. and M. Marchant (1991), *Globalisation of the U.S. Food Processing Sector*, Organisation and Performance of World Food System: NC-194. Department of Agricultural Economics, University of Kentucky.

Tangermann, S. (1996), "Implementation of the Uruguay Round Agreement on Agriculture: Issues and Prospects," paper presented to the Annual Meeting of the Agricultural Economics Association, Newcastle upon Tyne, March 27–29, 1996.

Vaughn, O., M. Malanoski, D. West, and C. Handy (1994), "Firm Strategies for Accessing Foreign Markets and The Role of Government Policy," a paper prepared for presentation to the NE-165/WRCC-72 Research Conference on Interactions Between Public Policies and Private Strategies in the Food Industries, Montreal, June 26–28.

4

Is Strategic Trade Policy Practical?

Larry S. Karp

Introduction

Governments require international rules to restrain their fondness for trade-related investment subsidies and export subsidies. Before the advent of the literature on strategic trade policy, there was no coherent *economic* rationale for why governments would want to use such policies. The optimal tariff model predicts that a country with market power should tax exports in order to induce domestic exporters to behave more like a cartel and, thus, to improve the terms of trade. The most coherent explanations for observed policy were based on *political economy* models. These models predict that the government is willing to transfer a dollar to domestic producers, even if the cost to domestic taxpayers is considerably greater than a dollar. A variety of factors having to do with lobbying or voter behavior rationalize the government's willingness to make this transfer. There have been many empirical attempts to measure governments' "revealed preference" for producer welfare.

The literature on strategic trade policies provides an economic rationale for many observed policies and is now central to trade theory. However, I do not think that the main contribution of the literature lies in either explaining government policies or in offering specific policy advice. Although (some) models offer specific policy prescriptions, no consensus emerges from the literature. If the strategic trade literature has limited positive and normative content, why has it become so important in trade theory?

The most important reason is that the literature addresses neomercantilist arguments. Politicians like to justify the policies they promote by appealing to principle rather than political expediency. When there is a principle behind interventionist trade policies, it is probably based on mercantilist beliefs. However thoroughly these beliefs are discredited by academic economists, they still seem correct to many people. Despite (neo)classical trade theory's limited success in convincing people of the benefits of free trade, it has at least been successful in changing the rhetoric of the debate. Contemporary mercantilists speak of the strategic benefits of tariffs and export promotion.

The theoretical literature on strategic trade policy confronts neomercantilist arguments. The response is somewhat indirect, since the academic and the popular uses of the term *strategic trade policy* are often different. This difference is probably inevitable, and not very serious, because the popular meaning is either vague or protean, and frequently both. The economic literature at least takes seriously the notion that there may be strategic reasons that justify the type of trade intervention that governments like to use. By forcing ourselves to be precise about what we mean by strategic trade policy, we can at least obtain a sense of how practical the policies are.

Although I intend to concentrate here on the lessons from theoretical models, it is important to recognize the parallel empirical literature that investigates the trade effects of imperfectly competitive agricultural markets. Agriculture is sometimes used as a textbook example of a perfectly competitive market, but government intervention and high concentration in processing make some agricultural markets oligopolistic. The empirical agricultural industrial organization literature examines these market imperfections; much of this literature is concerned with international markets. McCalla's (1966) study of the wheat market provides one of the earliest examples. More recent papers use econometric methods to estimate the degree of market power or use calibrated models to examine the effect of market power and government intervention. For example, Palm and Vogelvan (1986) and Karp and Perloff (1989; 1993) econometrically estimate oligopoly structure in commodity markets. McCorriston and Sheldon (1996) and Thursby and Thursby (1990) use calibrated models to study imperfectly competitive international banana and wheat markets, respectively. Elsewhere, McCorriston and Sheldon (1991; 1994) examine the effects of market structure on a government's ability to collect quota rents and on government incentives to intervene in the input markets. These papers illustrate how trade and industrial organization theory have guided empirical research in agricultural economics. They also illustrate the continued gap between theory and empirics, which exists in most fields of economic research.

This chapter is organized in three sections. The first section reviews three static models of strategic trade theory. Two of these models explain why trade policies may have strategic value and illustrate that the optimal policy may be either a tax or a subsidy. Strategic trade policy works by changing firm's incentives, and it requires that the government be able to make commitments. The third model shows how the effects of trade policy depend on the nature of the market. The next section explains why the introduction of dynamics may fundamentally change the policy prescriptions of static models. In these models the government does not have a commitment problem. The third section discusses dynamic models in which the government does have a commitment problem. Where the government's ability to commit to future policies is limited, strategic trade policies may be useless or harmful. The conclusion summarizes what I think we have learned from the literature on strategic trade policies.

Basic Static Models

A review of three static models of strategic trade policy illustrates the basic ideas in the literature. Brander (1995) provides a much more comprehensive review of the literature. The first two models show the commitment value of government policy and the sensitivity of the optimal policy to the type of game that firms play. The third model shows how strategic trade policy can alter the type of competition between domestic and foreign firms.

In each of two large exporting countries, to which I will refer as the United States and the European Community, there is a single firm. These firms export all production to a third market, where they are duopolists. This "third-market assumption" means that domestic consumers are absent from the model, so we can neglect the welfare effects of policies on consumers. The government of one country, say the United States, chooses an export tax or subsidy before firms make their decisions. The government of the second country is inactive. There are no transaction costs, and the government maximizes social welfare, in which a dollar of tax revenue has the same value as a dollar of firm profits. Later we discuss how the results change if any of these assumptions are dropped. When firms make their decisions, they take the trade policy as given. In the first model, due to Spencer and Brander (1983), the duopolists choose quantities. In the second model, studied by Eaton and Grossman (1986), firms choose prices. In both cases, the equilibrium in the game between firms is Nash.

Figure 4.1 shows the best-response function (BRF) for the U.S. firm in the quantity-setting (Cournot) game. The BRF is constructed using U.S. isoprofit loci, three of which are shown: π_i $(i = 1,2,3)$, $\pi_1 > \pi_2 > \pi_3$. All combinations of U.S. and E.C. exports on a given isoprofit locus lead to the same level of U.S. profits.

The subsequent argument turns on the shape and location of the U.S. isoprofit loci, so an explanation of these curves is worth a digression. Figure 4.2 graphs U.S. profits as a function of U.S. exports, for two levels of

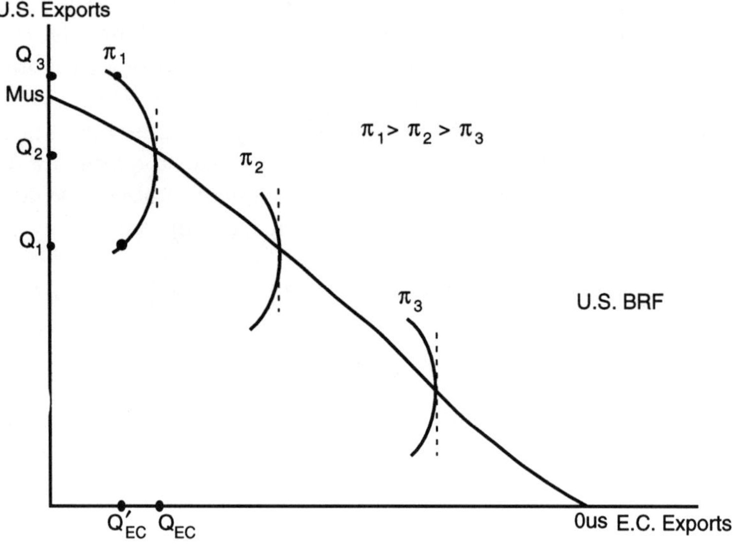

FIGURE 4.1 Reaction Function for The United States.

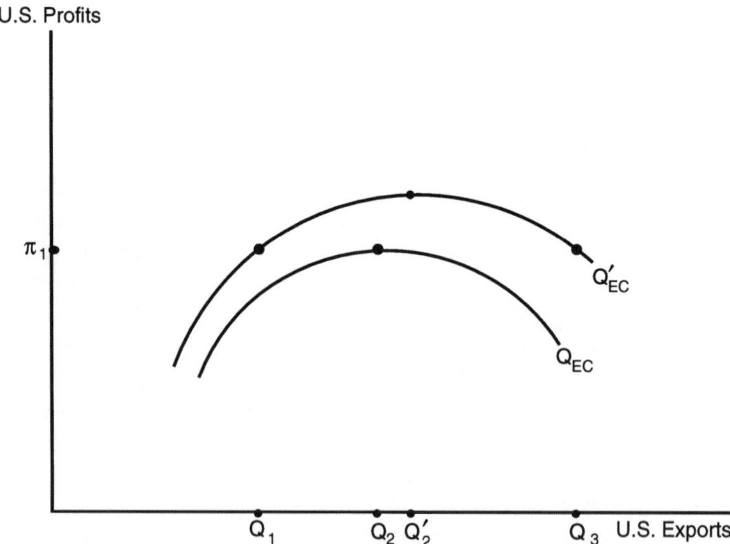

FIGURE 4.2 U.S. Profit Function.

E.C. exports ($Q_{EC} > Q'_{EC}$). These two curves illustrate three assumptions about the U.S. profit function: (i) It is concave in own exports; (ii) it is decreasing in E.C. exports; and (iii) the level of exports that maximizes U.S. profits is decreasing in E.C. exports. The third assumption is the crucial one. It means that U.S. and E.C. exports are "strategic substitutes" (see Bulow et al., 1985): A larger value of one country's exports makes the other country want to export less. Given E.C. exports of Q_{EC}, the United States receives the maximal level of profits, π_1, by exporting Q_2. If E.C. exports fall to Q'_{EC}, the United States can achieve π_1 by exporting either Q_1 or Q_3. (Of course, these levels of exports are no longer optimal given changed E.C. exports; the optimal level is now Q'_2.) Figures 4.1 and 4.2 both illustrate that, for a given level of E.C. exports, there is a unique level of U.S. exports that maximizes U.S. profits. For a lower level of E.C. exports, the United States can achieve the same level of profits by exporting either more or less than the optimal level. Hence, the U.S. isoprofit locus π_1 is convex, as shown in Figure 4.1.

For arbitrary levels of E.C. exports (the dotted vertical lines in Figure 4.1), U.S. profits are maximized by getting on the highest isoprofit curve. Profit maximization requires that the U.S. firm be on the curve tangent to the vertical line at the E.C. level of exports. The locus of points given by these tangencies is the U.S. BRF. Assumption (iii) about the U.S. profit function implies that the U.S. firm's BRF has a negative slope, as shown in Figure 4.1. The vertical intercept (M_{us}) of the U.S. BRF shows the monopoly level of U.S. exports (when $Q_{EC} = 0$), and the horizontal intercept (0_{us}) shows the level of E.C. exports that drives the United States out of the market.

Figure 4.3 shows the E.C.'s BRF, which is drawn using similar reasoning as above. The noncooperative Nash equilibrium occurs at point N, where each firm is on its own BRF. In Figure 4.3 the equilibrium is unique. A sufficient condition for uniqueness is that the E.C. BRF is everywhere steeper than the U.S. BRF. That condition on the slopes is guaranteed if each country's marginal profits are more sensitive to its own exports than to its rival's.

If the U.S. firm were a Stackelberg leader, it would choose its level of exports before the E.C. moves. As a Stackelberg leader, the U.S. firm maximizes profits, knowing how the E.C. firm will respond. That is, the United States chooses its preferred point on the E.C. BRF. This is shown as point S in Figure 4.3, where a U.S. isoprofit locus is tangent to the E.C. BRF. If the U.S. firm were able to commit to producing at point S, it would be rational for the E.C. firm to follow. However, there is no obvious commitment mechanism for the U.S. firm.

The fundamental insight of the strategic trade literature is that government policy can act as a substitute for a firm's commitment. For any level

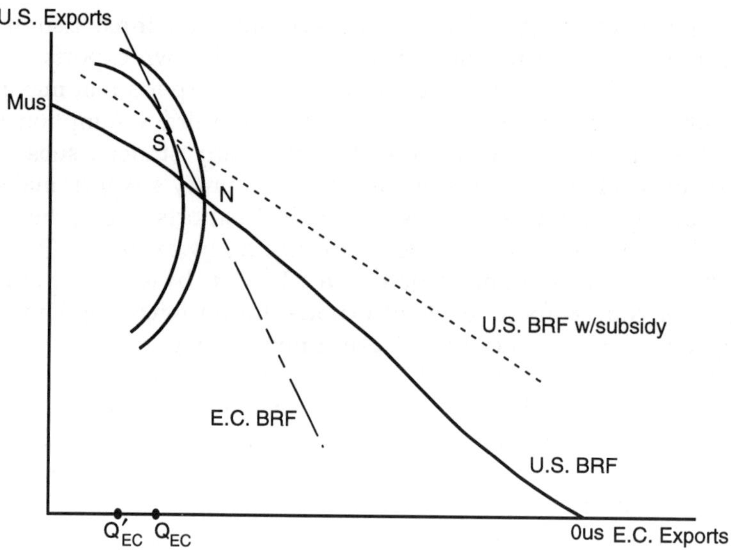

FIGURE 4.3 The Optimal Subsidy.

of E.C. exports, a U.S. export subsidy makes it optimal for the U.S. firm to export more. This policy-induced change in U.S. behavior is shown as shifting up the U.S. BRF (Figure 4.3), to the dotted curve. An appropriate level of the subsidy causes the U.S. BRF to shift up enough so that the Nash equilibrium occurs at point S. The conclusion is that if the government is able to commit to its trade policy before firms make their decisions, then government policy is a substitute for a firm's commitment.

By offering a sufficiently large export subsidy, the government can induce the U.S. firm to export any quantity, regardless of E.C. sales. When there are no transaction costs or domestic consumers, government welfare is identical to the domestic firm's profits net of the transfer. Therefore, the subsidy that induces production at point S is the optimal policy.

It is important to recognize that the government wants to increase domestic exports because it knows that this change will decrease foreign exports. The increase in domestic exports is not an end in itself but is valuable because it affects the rival's behavior. If the rival's exports did not depend on U.S. exports, that is, if the E.C. BRF were vertical, the optimal U.S. policy would be free trade. This is an obvious point and does not rely on whether the optimal policy is a tax or a subsidy; it will be important to recall this observation when we discuss dynamic games where commitment is problematic.

The U.S. firm is happy with the outcome S in Figure 4.3. It receives the Stackelberg leader's level of profits plus a subsidy. From construction of the BRFs, it is clear that E.C.'s profits decrease as we move northwest up its BRF. E.C. profits are lower at point S than at N, and the E.C. would not willingly choose to be a Stackelberg follower. The E.C. firm is worse off than at the Nash equilibrium. This model explains why an export subsidy, which benefits the domestic industry and harms the foreign rival, is rational for the U.S. government.

The policy recommendation changes if the firms compete in the third market by choosing prices rather than quantities. Figures 4.4 and 4.5 illustrate the price-setting (Bertrand) equilibrium. Figure 4.4 shows three U.S. isoprofit loci in price space. These loci can be constructed using the same type of argument illustrated in Figure 4.2, but now the assumptions on the U.S. profit function are: (i) It is concave in own price; (ii) it is increasing in E.C. price; and (iii) the U.S. price that maximizes U.S. profits is an increasing function of E.C. price. Again, the third assumption is the important one. It states that, if the E.C. firm unilaterally increases its price, it would be optimal for the U.S. firm to increase its price. In this game the firms' actions are strategic complements. For an arbitrary E.C. price, indicated by the dashed vertical lines in Figure 4.4, the optimal U.S. price is given by the tangency of the U.S. isoprofit locus and the vertical line. The locus of these points is the U.S. BRF.[1]

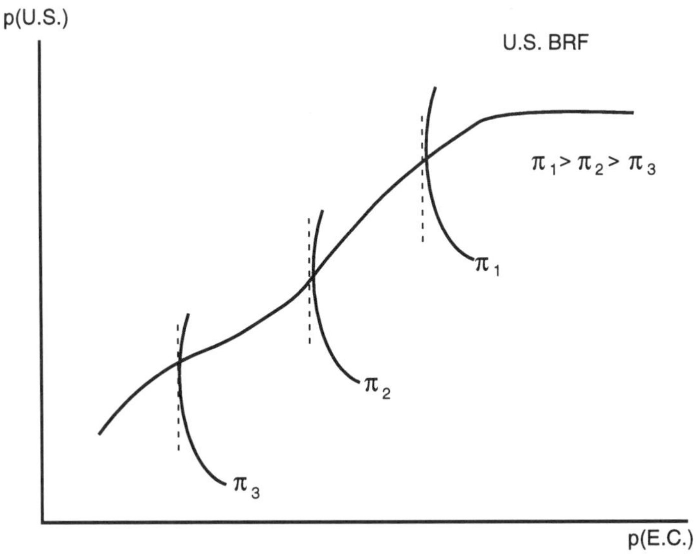

FIGURE 4.4 U.S. BRF in a Price-setting Game.

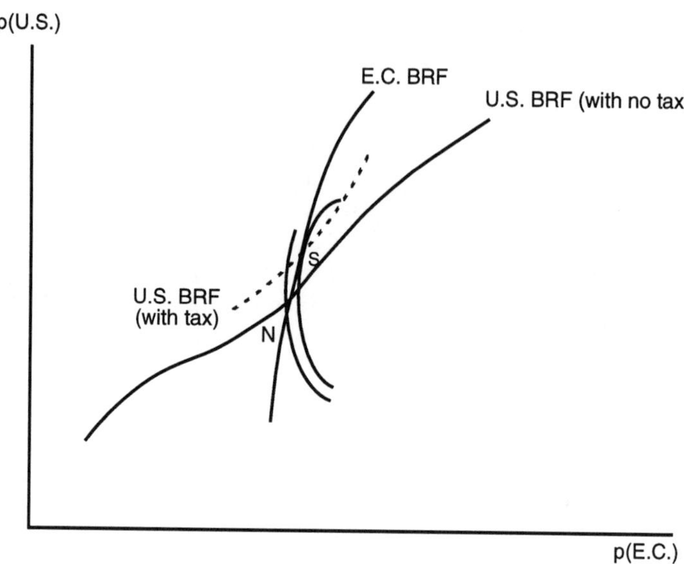

FIGURE 4.5 The Optimal Export Tax.

The E.C. BRF is graphed in Figure 4.5, where the Nash equilibrium occurs at N. The relative slopes of the two BRFs are as shown if the marginal (with respect to own-price) profits of a firm are more sensitive to own-price than to the rival's price. This assumption regarding marginal profits guarantees a unique equilibrium. The highest level of U.S. profits consistent with the E.C. being on its BRF occurs at S, the Stackelberg equilibrium, when the U.S. firm is the leader. Note that each country's profits increase as we move up its BRF. Therefore, E.C. profits are higher at S than at N; the United States obviously prefers S.

A U.S. export subsidy would encourage the U.S. firm to export more, which would require that it lower its price—the opposite of what is optimal. In order to induce the U.S. firm to raise its price, the U.S. government has to tax U.S. exports. An export tax shifts up the U.S. BRF, as shown by the dotted curve in Figure 4.5. By choosing an appropriate export tax, the U.S. government is able to induce point S as the Nash equilibrium: Point S is a feasible Nash equilibrium when the U.S. government can commit to an export tax. Once again, it is easy to see that point S is also optimal for the U.S. government in the absence of transaction costs and domestic consumers. When the tax/subsidy revenue is a pure transfer, the U.S. government welfare equals the U.S. firm's profits net of the transfer. Point S maximizes profits net of a transfer.

The policy implications are, thus, different when firms compete in prices rather than quantities. In the price-setting game it is optimal to tax exports. The foreign rival benefits from the policy, but the domestic firm may be worse off. The domestic firm gains by the move to its Stackelberg leader equilibrium, but it loses from having to pay taxes.

These two models illustrate several important aspects of strategic trade policy. First, government intervention is effective because, by assumption, the government is able to make a commitment about a policy that affects firm behavior. Government commitment is a substitute for the domestic firm's inability to commit, that is, to behave as a Stackelberg leader. Alternatively, we can think of government policy as correcting the domestic firm's "mistake" (or "distortion"[2]). The "mistake" is that the domestic firm takes its rival's action as given. In fact, the rival's equilibrium action is conditioned upon beliefs about what the domestic firm will do: if the domestic firm deviates from the Nash equilibrium, and if the rival anticipates this, then the rival would also deviate from the equilibrium.[3]

Second, the sign of the optimal policy (a tax or a subsidy) depends on the manner in which the rival firm would respond to a deviation from the original equilibrium by the home firm. In other words, the policy depends on the slope of the rival's BRF or, equivalently, whether the firms' actions are strategic substitutes or complements.

Third, the effect of government intervention on firms' profits is ambiguous. Government policy can be either "rent shifting" or "rent sharing." When firms' actions are strategic substitutes, government intervention heightens the competition between firms by decreasing the export cost of the domestic firm. This policy shifts oligopoly rents from the foreign to the domestic firm. However, when firms' actions are strategic complements, government policy softens the competition between firms by increasing the effective cost of the domestic firm. This policy moves the Nash equilibrium toward the cartel solution (decreased competition) and increases industry profits, benefiting the foreign firm.

Finally, in both cases government welfare is higher when it uses the optimal policy. The ability to intervene strategically never harms the government, which always has the option of using no policy. We will see that in slightly more complicated models this last conclusion no longer holds.

We briefly consider how the implications of the two previous models are changed when we relax some of the assumptions. For example, if there are $n > 1$ domestic firms in the quantity-setting game, competition is higher than when $n = 1$. As $n \rightarrow \infty$ the domestic industry behaves competitively. It ignores its collective market power. This is the standard large-country case, where we know that an export tax is optimal. For $1 < n < \infty$, the government balances the desire to restrain competition among domestic firms (which encourages the use of a tax) with the desire to shift profits from foreign firms (which encourages the use of a subsidy). Therefore, the optimal policy could be either a tax or a subsidy. In the price-setting game, the increase in the number of domestic firms increases the incentive to use an export tax.

If the rival government also intervenes, it has similar incentives to the home government's. When firms play a quantity-setting game, the rival government also subsidizes exports in order to shift profits. This beggar-thy-neighbor rivalry makes the final equilibrium more competitive, and, in a symmetric equilibrium, welfare in both countries is lower than in the nonintervention equilibrium. When firms play the price-setting game both countries choose export taxes. These policies move the final equilibrium closer to the cartel solution. Welfare in each country is higher as a result of the rival's intervention.

If some of the good is consumed domestically, consumer surplus becomes part of the government's objective. In that case, the government has to balance its desire to increase industry profits against the possible loss of consumer welfare. Including a social cost of transferring funds makes it optimal for the government to choose a lower level of its policy, whether this is a tax or subsidy.

The third and final model of this section describes a situation where the domestic and foreign duopolists sell in the home country, and the home government uses a trade policy. If the policy instrument is a tax, the government has the usual large-country incentive to tax imports to improve the terms of trade. A more interesting situation arises if the government policy is an import quota (Krishna, 1989). Consider, for example, the situation where the import quota is exactly at the free trade level of imports. The effect of the quota depends on whether the duopolists choose price or quantity. In the quantity-setting game (Figure 4.2), the quota causes the E.C. BRF to become vertical at point N. This change does not alter the equilibrium. The home firm would like to increase its own sales in order to induce the foreign firm to decrease exports. The quota imposed at the free-trade Nash equilibrium does not alter the foreign firm's incentive to change its decision, and therefore the quota has no effect. In the price-setting game (Figure 4.5), the quota fundamentally changes the game because it is no longer rational for the domestic firm to take the foreign price as given. For example, beginning at the free-trade price (point N in Figure 4.5, where by assumption the quota is exactly binding), the domestic firm knows that, if it were to raise its price, and the foreign firm did not respond, then the foreign firm would increase sales, violating the quota. Therefore, the domestic firm knows that the foreign firm would *have to* increase its price following a domestic price rise. Knowing this, the domestic firm wants to choose a higher price than the free trade level, as does the foreign firm (because policies are strategic substitutes). Here the imposition of an import quota at the free trade level increases each firm's equilibrium price.

This model captures some of the features of the voluntary export restraint (VER) imposed on Japanese car exports to the United States in the 1980s. Arguably, the VER assisted Japanese firms in colluding among themselves to restrict exports to the U.S. market. Japan was a large country vis-à-vis the United States in the car market and could have benefitted from using an export tax. The VER required participation of the Japanese government in the car market and essentially invited them to apply an export tax. The VER also made collusion among U.S. firms easier since it decreased the market discipline created by foreign competitors. Finally, the VER made collusion between the U.S. and Japanese auto industries easier since it provided Japanese firms with a credible commitment to restrict exports, and thus to increase price.

Strategic Trade Policy in a Dynamic Setting

In static models each agent makes only one decision; in a dynamic model at least one agent makes decisions at different times. There are two types of dynamics, and both can change the implications of strategic trade policy. First, the firms (and possibly the government) may play the same game repeatedly. Second, actions such as investment, which are taken in the current period, may change the game in subsequent periods. I briefly consider repeated games and then discuss the second type of dynamics. In the models discussed in this section the government moves only once, at the beginning of the game, so the government has no commitment problem.

In a one-shot game, "reasonable" assumptions ensure that the equilibrium is unique for a given level of government policy. In that case, the optimal government policy is typically unique, given the rules of the game. (Of course, when the game is changed, e.g., from price setting to quantity setting, we saw that the optimal trade policy changes.) However, when firms repeat the same game infinitely often, a wide range of equilibria can arise for a given government policy. This result is an application of the folk theorem. In order to use repeated game models to analyze strategic trade policy, we need a criterion for selecting the most plausible equilibrium. A popular choice is to assume that the most collusive subgame perfect equilibrium outcome—the outcome that gives highest joint profits—will emerge. Collusive outcomes can be supported by credible threats to compete fiercely if another firm cheats. Changes in the level of trade policies, or changes in the type of policies, for example, from tariffs to quotas, can alter the severity of threats. In this manner, trade policies can change the degree of collusion that can be supported. Davidson (1984) and Rotemberg and Saloner (1989) use repeated game models to demonstrate how trade policy can alter collusion.

The other source of dynamics occurs where actions in the current period affect behavior in subsequent periods. For example, firms may make research and development (R&D) investments, which reduce marginal costs, and then choose quantity (Spencer and Brander, 1983). In all other respects, the game is the same as the first model described in the previous section. In this situation, the optimal policy is to tax investment and subsidize exports.

The explanation for the export subsidy is the same as in the simpler game. The subsidy shifts rent from the foreign to the domestic firm; it corrects the distortion that arises from the domestic firm's failure to realize that the rival's decision would change if the domestic firm's decision were to change. The explanation for the investment tax is that the domestic firm has a strategic incentive to invest because, by lowering its costs, it discourages its rival's production. This strategic incentive causes the domestic firm to invest more than the cost-minimizing amount. However, the export subsidy induces the "correct" (from the standpoint of the government) level of exports, that is, the export subsidy targets the distortion at the export stage. The domestic firm's strategic investment incentive therefore constitutes a distortion, which is corrected using the investment tax.

This example illustrates the advantage of thinking of decision-making in an oligopolistic setting as giving rise to distortions. Economists are accustomed to the idea of using appropriate instruments to target distortions. When we apply the same reasoning to a strategic trade setting, we see how different tax policies are used to target different aspects of oligopoly rivalry. Also, we know that if the number of instruments is less than the number of distortions, it is typically not possible to achieve the first-best outcome, and the problem of matching distortions to instruments is more complicated.

For example, in the previous model, if the government has only an investment subsidy/tax, it uses this policy to correct the distortions at both the export and the investment stages. These distortions cut in different directions, so the sign of the optimal investment policy (absent the export policy) is not obvious. However, the optimal policy is an investment subsidy because R&D investments are strategic substitutes. The domestic firm, in taking as given the foreign R&D investment, commits the same type of mistake as it makes in the quantity-setting game. The investment subsidy corrects this mistake because it induces the domestic firm to invest more, which induces the foreign firm to invest less. That is, the investment subsidy shifts the equilibrium from the Nash to the

Stackelberg point in the investment game. Here the investment policy is an indirect lever on exports and a direct lever on investment. When the export subsidy was available, export levels could be targeted directly, making it unnecessary to use the investment subsidy for that purpose.

Dynamics can also lead to the breakdown of the equivalence of two policies. The specific manner in which this breakdown occurs can be surprising. In the original quantity-setting, third market model, we know that the optimal export policy is a subsidy. From the geometric argument that we used to show this result, it is fairly obvious that it does not matter whether a unit or an ad valorem subsidy is used. Both types of policies shift the domestic firm's BRF in the same manner (Figure 4.3), thus inducing the domestic firm to behave as a Stackelberg leader.

This conclusion changes when we introduce dynamics. Suppose that it is costly to alter exports, with average costs increasing with the size of the adjustment. For concreteness, let I_t^i be the change in firm i's output level in period t:I_t^i is greater or less than zero, as firm i increases or decreases its exports relative to the previous period. If q_{t-1}^i is firm i's output in the previous period, then current output is $q_t^i = q_{t-1}^i + I_t^i$. (We can also think of q as being capacity and I as being investment, in which case $I < 0$ means there is disinvestment.) Let the cost of adjustment be $c(I_t^i)$, a convex function, so that it is optimal to smooth adjustment. If firm i's government uses a unit adjustment subsidy of s, the domestic adjustment cost is $c(I_t^i) - sI_t^i$. If the government uses an ad valorem adjustment subsidy of σ, the domestic firm's adjustment cost is $(1-\sigma)c(I_t^i)$. Firm i maximizes the present discounted value of the stream of profits (a function of q_t^i and q_t^j) net of adjustment costs.

Karp and Perloff (1992) study the subgame perfect equilibrium in which firms condition their current adjustment decision on the parameters of the game (including s or σ) and lagged output. The government chooses a constant s or σ at the beginning of the game and wants to maximize the present discounted value of the stream of firm i's profits net of the government transfer. Since firms make many decisions, there are many "distortions," but (by assumption) the government has a single policy instrument, either s or σ. Each policy targets many distortions, so neither will achieve the first-best outcome. The two policies lead to different outcomes, since they have different effects on the domestic firm's marginal adjustment costs. A marginal increase in s decreases marginal adjustment costs by one unit, independent of the value of I_t^i. Therefore, a larger value of s makes growth for the home firm ($I > 0$) more attractive, regardless of the value of I. A marginal increase in σ decreases marginal adjustment costs by $c'(I_t^i)$, which is an increasing function of I_t^i. An increase in σ makes adjustment in either direction (growth or disinvestment) cheaper.

Using quadratic forms for the profit functions and for adjustment costs, Karp and Perloff construct examples in which the optimal value of s is positive (a subsidy) and the optimal value of σ is negative (a tax). The explanation for the optimality of a unit subsidy in the dynamic game is the same as in the one-shot game. In both cases, the subsidy encourages the domestic firm to export more, that is, to choose a larger value of I_t^i. In the dynamic game export growth occurs over time, whereas in the static game all of the growth occurs immediately, but in other respects the two games are the same.

With the ad valorem policy a tax increases adjustment costs. In this dynamic game, firms have a strategic incentive to grow (invest) today in order to induce the rival to disinvest, or grow more slowly, in the future. An ad valorem tax imposes a strategic cost on a firm that is initially small, that is, a firm that grows during the early stages of the game. However, the increased adjustment cost confers a strategic benefit on the domestic firm near the steady state. The tax provides the home firm with a credible commitment not to shrink. This commitment reduces the strategic incentive that the foreign firm has to grow large as a means of discouraging domestic growth. In an infinite horizon model, with a moderate discount rate (under 10 percent), the steady state strategic benefit of the adjustment tax is large relative to the transitional strategic cost. In some cases the optimal ad valorem policy is a tax, although the optimal unit policy is always a subsidy.

In our numerical examples, the optimal unit subsidy increases domestic welfare by 5 to 10 percent more than does the optimal ad valorem tax. However, using the subsidy, the transfer from the government to the domestic firm is large—over 50 percent of domestic welfare—whereas, with the tax, the transfer from the domestic firm to the government is under 10 percent of domestic welfare. Thus, at least for these examples, a large transfer is needed in order to obtain a moderate increase in social welfare. If there were a cost to making a transfer, the ad valorem tax might be the more efficient instrument.

Dynamics and Limited Commitment

The government had no commitment problem in the dynamic models discussed in the previous section. In those models the government chose a policy or policies at only one point in time, before firms made their decisions. The dynamics related only to the firms' actions. Here we consider the case where firms take some actions before the government chooses some policy. The government is not able to commit to a future policy before firms act in the present. The resulting commitment problem for the government may eliminate the benefits of strategic action, or it may make the use of strategic trade policy disadvantageous. Two models illustrate these two possibilities.

First, consider the dynamic adjustment game described above, in which firms incur convex costs for investing, that is, for changing their level of exports, or capacity. Now suppose that, instead of setting only one tax/subsidy level at the beginning of the entire game, the government is allowed to choose a different policy level at the beginning of each period, before firms choose their investment/adjustment. Again, we consider only Markov perfect equilibria: equilibria in which agents condition their actions and their beliefs about rivals' actions on the payoff-relevant variables, the lagged level of exports (or, in the other interpretation of the model, the lagged capacity). The restriction to Markov perfection means that the government cannot rely on its reputation as a means of committing to future subsidies. All agents know that in the future, as today, the government will choose the subsidy optimally, ignoring past events that do not affect current or future profits. The government uses a unit rather than an ad valorem tax/subsidy.

Although the government moves before both firms in each period, each firm in the current period moves before the government in the next period. Therefore, the game now involves alternating moves rather than a first mover as before. The length of a period is the amount of time between actions, and this is assumed to equal the amount of time for which the government can commit to a particular policy level.

Karp and Perloff (1995b) show that, as the length of time between decisions (and thus the period of commitment) becomes small, the government loses its incentive to subsidize the domestic firm. In the limit, as firms make their investment decisions continuously, rather than at discrete intervals, the government has no incentive to intervene, and the optimal subsidy is zero. The simplest explanation for this result is that the shorter the intervals between moves, the smaller is the government's first-mover advantage, and the closer the game is to a situation in which all agents move simultaneously. In the simultaneous move game, government policy has no commitment value, so the optimal policy is a zero subsidy.

Additional intuition for the result uses the observation that, in the static game, the government wants to use investment policy to alter the domestic firm's action *because by doing so it indirectly alters the action of the rival.* The government has this leverage in the static game, where the rival's optimal decision depends on the domestic firm's decision. (The rival's BRF is not vertical in Figures 4.3 and 4.5.) In the dynamic game, however, the rival's decision (the change in exports or capacity) depends on the payoff-relevant variables, which here are the export or capacity *levels.* The subsidy has a direct effect on the domestic firm's current decision, which in turn has a direct effect on its current export level but only an indirect effect on the rival's decision. More formally, the current subsidy has a first-order impact on the domestic firm's decision but only a second-order impact on the rival. As the decision period becomes small, a very large subsidy, and thus a very high adjustment cost, would be needed to induce a non-negligible change in the rival's decision. With small periods of commitment, investment policies are simply too expensive.

The result that the government's strategic incentive vanishes in the limit, as the period of commitment shrinks, depends on the fact that the firms' decisions affect a dynamic variable. The decisions taken today alter future profits. If the decision variable had no effect on future profits, the efficacy of government policy would not depend on the length of the period. Consider a variant of the game described above: in each period firms choose both investment, which affects their future cost function, and current output. If, at the beginning of each period, the government chose an output subsidy/tax rather than the investment subsidy/tax, then the strategic incentive would not depend on the period of commitment. Current output, unlike investment, is a "static decision." The value to the firm of current output depends on the current subsidy but not on future events. The value of investment, on the other hand, depends on future events. When policies are targeted at static decisions, the government's inability to commit to future policies does not weaken its strategic leverage in the current period.

The basic conclusion is that in environments where the government is unable to make credible commitments regarding future policies, investment policies may be of little strategic use. In these environments it is still tempting for the government to use output or export policies. This conclusion provides a rationale for the emphasis on restricting explicit trade policies, rather than investment policies, in GATT negotiations.[4]

We have seen that when a government's ability to commit to future policies is limited, it may lose all strategic leverage. Where that happens, the benefits of government intervention are zero. It is possible that government intervention reduces welfare when it has limited commitment ability. This result may seem paradoxical since it might appear that, if intervention reduces welfare, the government would simply choose not to intervene. However, the possibility arises when the government cannot credibly commit to refrain from intervening. By changing the timing of moves in the original Spencer and Brander model, we can construct an example where intervention is disadvantageous, but it nevertheless occurs in equilibrium (Karp and Perloff, 1995a).

In stage one the competing firms choose investment, which lowers their marginal costs. In stage two the government chooses an export tax/subsidy, and in stage three the firms choose quantities, which they sell in a third market. In the subgame perfect equilibrium, the government uses an export subsidy in the second period. Under reasonable assumptions, the export subsidy is an increasing function of the home firm's cost advantage. The anticipation of the subsidy gives both firms a strategic incentive to increase investment; the home firm wants to increase its cost advantage, and the foreign firm wants to decrease it. The benefit that the government receives from rent-shifting in the second stage may not be enough to compensate for the socially excessive level of investment at the first stage. Where that occurs, intervention is ex ante (before investment) disadvantageous, despite the fact that the ex post (after investment) optimal subsidy is positive. Unless the government can somehow commit not to use a subsidy, in circumstances where it would want to do so, firms will change their investment decisions in ways that may decrease social welfare.

Intervention can be disadvantageous because of the government's inability to commit to a level of the subsidy before investment occurs. The introduction of a stage zero, prior to the investment stage, when the government chooses an investment tax or subsidy, increases the government's leverage. This investment policy stage decreases but does not eliminate the possibility that intervention is disadvantageous. The investment tax can be used to achieve the efficient level of domestic investment, but the tax does not stop the foreign firm from investing strategically in order to reduce the stage-two export subsidy. The benefit that the government achieves by shifting rent in stage two, and influencing domestic investment in stage zero, may not be enough to compensate for having to face a lower cost foreign rival. The government has three targets, domestic and foreign investment and domestic exports, but only two instruments, the export subsidy and the investment tax.

The possibility that government intervention can be disadvantageous is merely another example of what is by now a well-known feature of industrial organization models: An increase in market power, or an increase in cooperation, can reduce welfare of the agents who we would expect to benefit from the change.

Conclusion

Five fundamental points emerge from this review of the literature on strategic trade policy. First, strategic trade policies work because they enable the government to change the incentives of domestic firms, creating a credible commitment for these firms to take a certain action and behave as if they were Stackelberg leaders. Government policy is a substitute for firm commitment.

Second, the literature shows that the optimal strategic policy and the welfare effects of the policy are sensitive to the type of competition among firms. The optimal policy might be a tax or subsidy. Both domestic and foreign firms might benefit from government intervention, or only one firm—either the domestic or the foreign firm—might benefit.

Third, policies that appear innocuous, such as imposing a quota at the existing level of imports, may have large effects on the nature of competition, and thus on the market outcome.

Fourth, dynamics may change the nature of strategic policy even when the government has no commitment problem. If firms solve dynamic problems in which current decisions affect future opportunities, and if the government has fewer policy variables than the number of firm decisions, then policies that would be equivalent in a static setting are no longer equivalent. For example, the optimal unit tax/subsidy may be a subsidy where the optimal ad valorem tax/subsidy is a tax. The two optimally chosen policies lead to different outcomes.

Fifth, when firms solve dynamic optimization problems and some of the government's decisions are made after firm decisions, government commitment becomes problematic. The inability to commit to future policies erodes the efficacy of strategic trade policy. It may become useless or even decrease national welfare. A government's inability to commit to future policies that are targeted at "static decisions" (those that do not alter future payoffs) does not erode the government's strategic leverage.

These five observations suggest that attempts to use strategic trade policy might lead to increased welfare, but they are also likely to backfire. Proposals to use strategic trade policy should be viewed with skepticism, and the presumption should be in favor of free trade. The burden of proof must be placed on those who advocate government intervention, and the proof has to rely on specific features of the situation rather than on an appeal to theories of strategic policy. Most strategic trade advocates want subsidies or "import protection" rather than optimal policies. They would be less likely to push for strategic trade policies if they knew that such policies might require taxes.

The presumption in favor of free trade is not a very radical conclusion. Even before the strategic trade literature, we knew of several types of market failure or distortions that could justify trade intervention (although rarely as a first-best policy). The new literature increases the number of such "distortions."

The strategic trade literature contributes to an important policy debate. However, there is another reason why the literature has become so prominent within the economics profession: Strategic trade models fit squarely into the paradigm of rational, utility, or welfare-maximizing agents. Many of these models help improve our intuition by uncovering "surprising" results, but the basic assumptions of the models are familiar. Strategic trade theory began by studying oligopolistic markets, and oligopoly remains the chief market failure in most recent models. We are likely to obtain future insights by broadening our scope to include other market failures, such as imperfect labor markets and environmental externalities.

Notes

1. Figure 4.4 shows the U.S. BRF as increasing in E.C. price. For a sufficiently high price, the E.C. prices itself out of the market and the United States charges the monopoly price. Further increases in E.C. prices have no effect on U.S. profits, so for this region of E.C. price the U.S. BRF is flat.

2. Bhagwati and Srinivasan (1983, Chapter 16) describe the failure of a large country to exercise market power as a distortion. We are using the word in this sense. In the large-country case, competitive domestic firms "mistakenly" take world price as given. In the duopoly case, the domestic firm "mistakenly" takes its rival's action as given.

3. In a conjectural variations model, each firm makes a conjecture about how the rival would respond if the firm were to deviate from the Nash equilibrium. The conjectures are said to be consistent if the conjecture equals the slope of the rival's BRF. With consistent conjectures, firms do not make "mistakes" in equilibrium. In this case, the optimal government policy is a zero tax (Eaton and Grossman, 1986).

4. Of course, investment policies have also been the subject of trade disputes. Other important reasons why trade negotiations have emphasized explicit trade policies are that they are easy to monitor and their objectives are relatively transparent.

References

Bhagwati, J. N. and T. N. Srinivasan (1983) *Lectures on International Trade,* MIT Press, Cambridge, MA.

Brander, J. A. (1995) "Strategic Trade Policy." In *Handbook of International Economics, vol III,* ed. Gene M. Grossman and Kenneth Rogoff, Amsterdam: Elsevier Press, 1395-1456.

Bulow, J. I., J. D. Geankoplos, and P. D. Klemperer (1985) "Multi Market Oligopoly: Strategic Substitutes and Complements." *Journal of Political Economy,* Vol. 93, 488–511.

Davidson, C. (1984) "Cartel Stability and Tariff Policy." *Journal of International Economics,* Vol. 17, 219-237.

Eaton, J., and G. M. Grossman (1986) "Optimal Trade and Industrial Policy under Oligopoly." *Quarterly Journal of Economics,* Vol. 101, 383–406.

Karp, L. S., and J. M. Perloff (1989) "Dynamic Oligopoly in the Rice Export Market." *Review of Economics and Statistics,* Vol. LXXI, 462–470.

———. (1992) "The Long Run Value of Inflexibility." In *Trade Flows and Trade Policy after 1992,* ed. L. Alan Winters. Cambridge: Cambridge University Press, 213–231.

———. (1993) "A Dynamic Model of Oligopoly in the Coffee Export Market." *American Journal of Agricultural Economics,* Vol. 75, 448–457.

———. (1995a) "The Failure of Strategic Industrial Policies Due to the Manipulation by Firms." *International Review of Economics and Finance,* Vol. 4, 1–16.

———. (1995b) "Why Industrial Policies Fail: Limited Commitment." *International Economic Review,* Vol. 36, 887–905.

Krishna, K. (1989) "Trade Restrictions as Facilitating Practices." *Journal of International Economics,* Vol. 26, 251–270.

McCalla, A. F. (1966) "A Duopoly Model of World Wheat Pricing." *Journal of Farm Economics,* Vol. 48, 711–727.

McCorriston, S. and I. M. Sheldon (1991) "Government Intervention in Imperfectly Competitive Agricultural Input Markets." *American Journal of Agricultural Economics,* Vol. 73, 621–632.

McCorriston, S. and I. M. Sheldon (1994) "Selling Import Quota Licenses: The U.S. Cheese Case." *American Journal of Agricultural Economics,* Vol. 76, 818–827.

———. (1996) "Incorporating Industrial Organization into Agricultural Trade Modelling." In *Agricultural Markets: Mechanisms, Failures, Regulations.* ed. D. Martimort, Amsterdam: North-Holland Publishing Company.

Palm, F. C. and E. Vogelvang (1986) "A Short-Run Econometric Analysis of the International Coffee Market." *European Review of Agricultural Economics,* Vol. 13, 451–476.

Rotemberg, J. and G. Saloner (1989) "Tariffs vs. Quotas with Implicit Collusion." *Canadian Journal of Economics,* Vol. 89, 237–244.

Spencer, B. J., and J. A. Brander (1983) "International R&D Rivalry and Industrial Strategy." *Review of Economic Studies,* Vol. 50, 707–722.

Thursby, M. C. and J. G. Thursby (1990) "Strategic Trade Theory and Agricultural Markets: An Application to Canadian and U.S. Wheat Exports to Japan." In *Imperfect Competition and Political Economy: The New Trade Theory in Agricultural Trade Research,* eds. C. Carter, A. McCalla, and J. Sharples, Boulder, CO: Westview Press.

5

Intra-industry Trade and Foreign Direct Investment in Processed Food as Alternatives to Trade Theory

Colin A. Carter and Alper Yilmaz

Introduction

There are surprisingly few empirical studies that have measured comparative advantage in agriculture and how this is changing over time, but it is generally accepted that the United States has a strong comparative advantage in raw agricultural commodities due to its relatively large endowment of cultivable land and favorable climate. Some have suggested that the United States also has a comparative advantage in processed food and have expressed concern that the U.S. market share in processed food appears to be falling (Bredahl, Abbott, and Reed, 1995).

Given the growth in processed food trade and in particular its intra-industry nature, it is indeed important to understand factors explaining this intra-industry trade. More than one-half of processed food trade is intra-industry trade, and the value of U.S. processed food exports exceeds bulk agricultural commodity exports (Dayton and Henderson, 1992; Henderson, Sheldon, and Pick, Ch. 2, this volume).

This is not an easy task, however, because empirical work on the topic of explaining trade flows has run into difficulties over the years. Conventional theories of comparative advantage have not adequately explained trade among industrial countries (Krugman, 1981). According to Krugman (pp. 959–60), three aspects of world trade that seem to contradict conventional theory are as follows:

> First, much of world trade is between countries with similar factor endowments. Second, a large part of trade is intra-industry in character—that is, it consists of two-way trade in similar products. Finally, much of the expansion of trade in the postwar period has taken place without sizable reallocation of resources or income-distribution effects.

Apart from international differences in factor endowments, economies of scale and imperfect competition could also drive countries to exchange goods produced with quite similar factor proportions (Helpman and Krugman, 1985), and this is called *intra-sectoral* or *intra-industry trade*. Helpman and Krugman (1989) define intra-industry trade as "the two-way exchange of goods in which neither country seems to have a comparative cost advantage" (p.133).

While the traditional theory of international trade is by no means passé, the new trade theory introduces a whole set of new possibilities and concerns (Krugman, 1990). The gap that cannot be explained by these two approaches is partially filled by the theory of foreign investment. Even if production costs are not very different in different countries, firms may prefer to produce near markets in order to save transportation costs (Brander and Krugman, 1983). In this respect, one-way or two-way foreign direct investment operates as an alternative to trade; that is, producing in a foreign country may be a better strategic alternative with respect to cost concerns and market penetration than producing in the home country and exporting.

There is a wide span of approaches in the empirical literature examining trade in processed foods. However, they lack the simultaneous explanatory power of the theories of comparative advantage, intra-industry trade, and foreign direct investment. These three approaches must be considered simultaneously for better understanding of trade in the processed food sector. In this chapter, we first outline the theory of intra-industry trade. Second, we discuss empirical studies, including applications of this theory aimed at explaining trade in processed food. Third, we review empirical studies of foreign direct investment in processed food industries as an alternative to product trade. Finally, the last section is devoted to concluding remarks.

Brief Review of the Theory of Intra-industry Trade

The classical Heckscher-Ohlin-Samuelson trade theory is not capable of explaining intra-industry exchange of commodities, even though it provides useful insights into inter-industry specialization and trade (Greenaway and Milner, 1986). This led to the development of a theory of trade in differentiated goods by Falvey (1981), which assumes the production of at least one differentiated good with a sector-specific factor of production, capital,[1] and a mobile factor, labor. The country with the higher capital-labor ratio then has a comparative advantage in the production of the higher-quality product and the other country has a comparative advantage in the lower-quality product. In this context, the seemingly same good with different qualities is traded between countries. This explanation of intra-industry trade is also consistent with constant returns to scale and perfect competition (Falvey, 1981).

Straying from the assumptions of constant returns to scale and perfect competition, Helpman and Krugman (1985, 1989) provide two alternative explanations of the phenomenon of intra-industry trade. According to the first explanation, intra-industry trade could result from an interaction between product differentiation and economies of scale. Differentiated products are regarded as imperfect substitutes by consumers, and countries can produce only a limited number of products because of scale economies. This results in each country specializing in the production of a slightly differentiated product and trading it with other countries' similar products, depending on consumer tastes.

The second explanation, first proposed by Brander (1981) and then elaborated on by Brander and Krugman (1983), argues that price discrimination could lead to two-way trade in identical products. In this approach, firms restrict deliveries to the domestic market in order to keep the price high while selling more aggressively abroad, and this results in market segmentation[2] (Helpman and Krugman, 1989).

Today, one of the most comprehensive theoretical pieces in this field is Helpman and Krugman's 1985 book. Their approach explains intra-industry trade based on Chamberlinian monopolistic competition. It stems from Krugman's earlier theoretical paper (Krugman, 1979) on monopolistic competition and international trade. A vast amount of empirical research in intra-industry trade today is based on this theory.

Helpman and Krugman's explanations of intra-industry trade employ the Spence-Dixit-Stiglitz (SDS) product differentiation model. With this framework, each country is assumed to have only one industry which produces a range of differentiated products and trade can occur between countries with identical costs.[3] Under free trade, a greater variety of products is produced, with fewer varieties produced in larger quantities in either country. Each country both imports and exports products in the same commodity classification (Vousden, 1990).

Helpman and Krugman's theory is derived from a two-sector, two-factor model in which one of the goods (namely food) is assumed to be a labor-intensive homogeneous product produced in the foreign country with constant returns to scale technology, and the capital-intensive second good (i.e. nonfood) is assumed to be differentiated and produced in both countries with increasing returns to scale technologies. Even in the case where both goods are produced with declining average costs, the results of the analysis do not differ. Together with the free-entry and -exit assumption, which leads to zero long-run profits, this model is consistent with Chamberlin's large group monopolistic competition case.

Helpman and Krugman's approach has key results that give way to the testing of refutable hypotheses. The first hypothesis is the negative relation between the share of intra-industry trade in total trade volume and the relative output of capital-intensive goods in the capital-abundant country. Therefore, the smaller the size of the capital-rich country measured in terms of GDP (gross domestic product), the larger is the share of intra-industry trade in that country's total trade.

The second hypothesis is the relationship between the intra-industry trade share and similarity in relative factor endowments, namely as relative factor endowments are more similar between countries, the intra-industry trade share will rise. In the generalized framework, which includes more than two countries, this hypothesis may be restated:

> This analysis suggests that we should expect relatively more intra- industry trade between a pair of countries with a similar factor composition than between a pair of countries with a dissimilar factor composition.
>
> —Helpman and Krugman, 1985, p. 172

Another important prediction of this model is the relationship between the income levels of the countries engaged in trade and the share of intra-industry trade in the bilateral trade volume. On average, the closer the per capita incomes of two countries, the larger the expected share of intra-industry trade. Moreover, countries with more capital per worker experience more intra-industry specialization than countries with less capital per worker.

Helpman and Krugman's model was not the first to suggest a relationship between the volume of trade and some measure of trading partners' incomes. Indeed, their approach just fits the general form of the *gravity equation* given by $VT_{ij} = f(Y_i, Y_j, Z)$ where VT_{ij} is the volume of trade between countries i and j, Y is a measure of income, and Z is a vector of variables measuring distance, trade barriers, effects of common language or culture, etc. (Hummels and Levinsohn, 1995). Nevertheless, their approach is the most comprehensive attempt to develop a theory examining the impact of scale economies and product differentiation on trade (Leamer and Levinsohn, 1995).

Empirical Work in Intra-industry Trade

Empirical Work in Nonfood Sectors

Theoretical developments actually came after many empirical studies in intra-industry trade, as opposed to the typical intellectual life cycle of a new trade theory (Leamer and Levinsohn, 1995). Grubel and Lloyd's (1975) work is among the important empirical pieces in this field. Using a measure of intra-industry trade, named the Grubel-Lloyd index,[4] they noted that a significant amount of international trade was within industry classifications.[5] However, their paper, along with others like that of Loertscher and Wolter (1980), did not include a formal theory.

Helpman's empirical paper (1987) was among the first studies that made use of the Helpman and Krugman theory. Using OECD data from 1956 to 1981, he examined the three hypotheses emerging from the theoretical models of monopolistic competition. The Grubel-Lloyd index was used as the measure of the importance of bilateral intra-industry trade in each industry. Using graphical rather than statistical tests, due to degrees of freedom problems, Helpman reported that both GDP size and GDP similarity between countries contributed positively to intra-industry trade. In order to test the third hypothesis, he proxied for differences in relative factor endowments by calculating the bilateral difference in per capita GDP and regressed the measure of intra-industry trade on this proxy. He found the coefficient on this regressor negative, which is consistent with the theory; that is, if two countries have identical relative endowments, all trade is intra-industry trade rather than inter-industry.

Even though the Helpman and Krugman theory was supported by the empirical works of Loertscher and Wolter (1980), Balassa and Bauwens (1987), and Helpman (1987), this class of studies does not discriminate between explanations due to consumer tastes versus monopolistic competition. Moreover, it does not answer the question of how much of the intra-industry trade is due to economies of scale and how much is due to factor supply differences (Leamer and Levinsohn, 1995, p. 39).

Hummels and Levinsohn (1995) followed up on Helpman's paper. They worked on two different models, which used country-pairs as the unit of observation. In this way, they created 2,002 observations (ninety-one country-pair observations for each of the twenty-two years for which they had OECD data, spanning 1962 to 1983). Their first model assumed all trade between countries to be intra-industry trade. The findings of this model are quite similar to those of Helpman; that is, country size dispersion dictated by the theory is highly significant in explaining trade volumes. However, when they worked with the same model on a different data set[6] for which an explanation of intra-industry trade based on monopolistic competition was known by them to be inappropriate, they ended up with similar results. This raises the question of whether or not there exists some other explanation for intra-industry trade besides monopolistic competition.

In their second model, in which they used the Grubel-Lloyd index as the measure of intra-industry trade, the underlying assumption that all trade was intra-industry was relaxed. Their results are similar to Helpman's findings as with their first model. In addition, they found that the share of intra-industry trade in total trade decreased as the difference in the land-to-labor ratio increased between country pairs. They explained this finding as follows:

> This may be because there is very little IIT [intra-industry trade] in agricultural products. Countries with much arable land tend to exchange agricultural products for manufactures and therefore engage in less IIT.
>
> —Hummels and Levinsohn, 1995, pp. 814–15

Hummels and Levinsohn's findings were stronger when they added certain factor measures, including land, to their model. Nevertheless, when they investigated the behavior of intra-industry trade over time, as opposed to their cross-sectional analysis, they found that country-pair–specific effects, such as geography, seasonal trade, cultural and language ties, and trade barriers, have more explanatory power than time-varying factor measures. They also speculated that variables such as distance and multinational corporations, which did not enter the theory, might be important variables in empirical studies of intra-industry trade.

Intra-industry Trade in Processed Food Industries

"The literature on intra-industry trade has generally focused on manufactured goods" wrote McCorriston and Sheldon in one of the early studies on intra-industry trade in food products (1991, p. 173). They examined trade in a sample of highly processed products (i.e., processed meat, cheese products, cereal preparations, processed fruit, processed vegetables, sugar products, chocolate products, nonalcoholic beverages, alcoholic beverages, and tobacco products) for the United States and the EC, using indices of intra-industry trade and intra-industry specialization. Using an adjusted version of the Grubel-Lloyd index,[7] they calculated the volume of intra-industry trade for the United States, the EC, the rest of OECD, and the EC excluding intra-EC trade for 1986. They noted that U.S. trade in processed agricultural products was characterized by endowment-based inter-industry specialization with the exception of exports to Canada.

Alternatively, the EC trade was characterized by intra-industry specialization, which was mostly due to intra-industry trade within the community. Among possible explanations for this difference in specialization, they emphasized the role of distance from foreign markets, particularly for the EC case, in which economic integration, proximity to community and other European markets due to geographical patterns, and economic ties with excolonial countries were the factors that influenced trade. Their explanation for the make-up of intra-industry trade between the United States and Canada is proximity to markets. They suggest that the increase in U.S. direct foreign investment in the processed food sector is likely the main explanation for the relatively lower importance of intra-industry trade for the United States. However, this gives rise to a paradox, given the considerable amount of foreign investment in the United States by European firms (McCorriston and Sheldon, 1991).

Christodoulou (1992) attempted to identify factors that explain cross-country variations in levels of intra-industry trade in the EEC meat and meat products industry in the late 1980s.[8] The independent variables used to explain intra-industry trade were country-specific factors on the demand side of the market, such as market size, taste overlap, and market proximity. The industry-specific factors on the supply side included product differentiation, scale economies, market structure, technological progressiveness, and stage of processing. The unadjusted version of the Grubel-Lloyd index[9] was used to measure intra-industry trade. GDP and GDP per capita expressed in purchasing power parity were proxies for market size and taste overlap, respectively. The Hufbauer index[10] was used in approximating the degree of product differentiation. In addition, the minimum efficient scale of operation compared to the size of the market, and the proportion of turnover accounted for by the largest firms, proxied for scale economies and market structure, respectively.

Taste overlap, on the demand side, and imperfect competition, on the supply side, seem to be the most important factors in explaining intra-industry trade in EEC meats. Another finding was that intra-industry trade was more significant for both raw and highly processed products, compared to lightly processed products. Christodoulou reasoned this was due to the fact that countries traded considerably in raw material for their processing industries and then re-traded the output (p. 883).

A more recent study is that by Hirschberg, Sheldon, and Dayton (1994), which analyzed intra-industry trade in food processing for a panel data set of thirty countries over the period 1964–85. Their model followed Helpman and Krugman, and they employed a weighted tobit model with fixed effects to account for the censored cross-section time-series nature of the data, a major difference from other existing studies. They calculated their measure of intra-industry trade by both adjusted and unadjusted versions of the Grubel-Lloyd index. The model they used is as follows:

$$IIT_{jkt} = \alpha_0 + \beta_1 INEQGDC_{jkt} + \beta_2 GDPSIZE_{jkt} + \beta_3 GDC_{jkt} + \beta_4 DEX_{jkt} + \beta_5 DIST_{jkt} + \beta_6 DIST2_{jkt} + \beta_7 DIST3_{jkt} + \beta_8 BORDER_{jkt} + \beta_9 EC_{jkt} + \beta_{10} EFTA_{jkt} + \sum_{j=1}^{29} \gamma_j DRC_j + \sum_{k=1}^{29} \lambda_k DPC_k + \sum_{t=1965}^{1985} \pi_i DYR_i + \varepsilon_{jkt}$$

where *IIT* is the intra-industry trade index; *INEQGDC* is an indicator of the bilateral inequality between GDP's per capita; *GDPSIZE* is an index of the size differential of the GDP's; *GDC* is the value of GDP per capita used as a proxy for the endowment of capital per worker; *DEX* is the absolute value of the annual proportional change in the exchange rate; *DIST, DIST2*, and *DIST3* are the variables of a cubic function that account for the distances between countries; *BORDER, EC,* and *EFTA* are dummy variables for common borders and mutual customs agreements between countries; *DRC* and *DPC* are dummy variables for the reporting country and reporting partner respectively; and *DYR* is a time trend.

The results of this study provide support for two predictions arising from the Helpman and Krugman model, indicating that intra-industry trade is a positive function of a country's GDP per capita and the equality of the GDP per capita between countries. They also noted that membership in a customs union or a free trade area would increase the rate of intra-industry trade among members. A stronger finding is the positive correlation between the level of trade and having a common border. In a similar context, distance is found to have a negative influence on intra-industry trade; that is, intra-industry trade between two countries increases the closer they are to one another. In a macro context, variation in long-run exchange rate is noted to reduce intra-industry trade.

A similar study was conducted by Hirschberg and Dayton (1996). In this study, they investigated the patterns of intra-industry trade in each processed food sector under SIC=20 concordance, as opposed to aggregating over all processed food industries and fitting one set of parameters, which is the method used by Hirschberg, Sheldon, and Dayton (1994). Accordingly, they estimated a total of forty-nine regression models, one for each of the sectors. Their regressions included, as explanatory variables, "...inter-country comparisons of capital-labor ratios, the comparative sizes of the economies, the distance between partners, long-term fluctuations in exchange rates, common borders, and membership in customs union/free trade zones" (Hirschberg and Dayton, 1996, p. 142). The form of the equation was exactly the same as Hirschberg, Sheldon and Dayton (1994).

Their findings support the Helpman and Krugman (1985) hypotheses for a majority of the individual sectors, although some coefficients are not significantly different from zero. For the purposes of their cluster results they aggregated commodity groups that resemble one another with respect to the estimated modified parameters of the model. The cluster results also support the Helpman and Krugman hypotheses, to a great extent, with several exceptions (Hirschberg and Dayton, 1996, pp. 156–57). These key results from the four studies discussed above are presented in detail in Table 5.1.

Foreign Direct Investment as a Substitute for Trade

The Definition of Foreign Direct Investment

Over the past few decades, the food processing industry has increasingly contributed to the globalization of industrial economies. Moreover, foreign affiliate sales appear to be significantly more important than processed food exports. For this reason, foreign direct investment (FDI) has become a topic of major interest. FDI may be a substitute for intra-industry trade (Greenaway and Milner, 1986). Further, they may both substitute for the theory of comparative advantage.

Because of the difficulties associated with defining the nationality of a firm and isolating all aspects of managerial and administrative control over production, a precise definition of FDI poses certain problems. Graham and Krugman (1989) define FDI as ownership of assets by foreign residents for purposes of controlling the use of those assets. In defining FDI, Cantwell (1994, p. 303) starts from the definition of international production. He defines it as "that production which is located in one country but controlled by a multinational corporation (MNC) based in another country. Such production is in large part financed by MNC's through foreign direct investment...."

There is a vast literature of the theory of FDI (Hymer, 1976; Dunning, 1981; Caves 1982; Markusen, 1995). Most of the existing empirical studies of FDI consider the role of the processed food sector, since food manufacturing has consistently ranked among the top industries that are characterized by FDI. In this chapter, the theory is not reviewed thoroughly, but rather empirical studies that focus on the processed food and beverage sectors are considered. Accordingly, the theoretical factors that affect FDI are noted and the relevant empirical results are discussed.

The Determinants of FDI and Empirical Work

"Contemporary theories of the determinants of FDI are eclectic blends of industrial organization, pure trade, and location theories with an occasional dash of theories of the firm, firm financing, and political economy" (Connor, 1983, pp. 397-98). In his survey of FDI determinants in the food

TABLE 5.1 Studies of Intra-industry Trade in Processed Food Industries

Author(s) and Commodities	*Key findings*
McCorriston and Sheldon (1991) highly processed products (meat, cheese, sugar, vegetables, chocolate, cereal, fruit, beverages, tobacco products)	• U.S. trade is characterized by endowment-based inter-industry specialization • EC trade is characterized by intra-industry specialization
Christodoulou (1992) meat	• taste overlap and imperfect competition are the most important factors explaining IIT in the EEC • IIT is more significant for raw and highly processed meat products compared to lightly processed products
Hirschberg, Sheldon, & Dayton (1994) all 4-digit SIC=20 industries (aggregated over all processed food industries)	• GDP/capita and the equality of this measure between two countries contributes positively to IIT • membership in a customs union/free trade area contributes positively to IIT • having common borders and shorter distances between countries contributes positively to IIT • long-run exchange rate variation tends to reduce the extent of IIT
Hirschberg & Dayton (1996) all 4-digit SIC=20 industries (for each processed food industry)	*Results of the Sectoral Regressions* • the equality of GDP/capita between two countries contributes positively to IIT (for 27 of the 49 sectors) • GDP size does not have a significant effect on IIT for a majority of sectors • GDP/capita affects IIT in 20 of 49 sectors, but there is sign indeterminacy • membership in a customs union/free trade area contributes positively to IIT • long run exchange rate variation tends to reduce IIT in 19 of 49 sectors *Cluster Results* • the equality of GDP/capita between two countries contributes positively to IIT (for 8 of the 10 clusters) • GDP size does not have a significant effect on IIT except for one cluster • GDP/capita affects IIT in 5 of 10 clusters, but there is sign indeterminacy • membership in a customs union/free trade area contributes positively to IIT • long run exchange rate variation tends to reduce IIT in 8 of 10 sectors

and tobacco manufacturing industries, he categorized the factors affecting the FDI decision into three groups:

- *firm-specific advantages* (patents, trademarks, consumer loyalty to brand, positive enterprise image, research and development resources yielding technological leadership, effective data gathering and information systems, special relationships with sources of financial capital, etc.)
- *industry-specific advantages* (stable or growing demand, open distribution systems, standard guarantees or warranties, industry quality grades recognized by purchasers, machinery or other inputs available from other industries, market information for purchase, special industry subsidies for exporting, etc.)
- *location-specific advantages* (worker education levels, climate, language facility, knowledge of business and general customs, military procurement programs, the power or prestige of the government, barriers to trade effectively protecting domestic commerce, etc.) (p. 398)

Based on previous cross-sectional studies of the determinants of FDI in manufacturing industries, Connor noted that expenditures on research and development and advertising are the most significant explanatory variables causing FDI.

In a study that examined FDI in U.S. food and tobacco manufacturing industries, Pagoulatos (1983) noted that even though there has been a significant increase in U.S. outflow of FDI in these industries, the gap between the outflow and inflow narrowed during the 1970s and a significant part of the inflow (about 95% of total food manufacturing) came from Canada and Europe. He also observed that most of the investors' primary concern has been the U.S. market rather than foreign trade, and they have preferred to enter the U.S. market via mergers and acquisitions of existing firms rather than establishing new firms, in order to gain quick access to U.S. technological and marketing skills.

Based on several previous studies, Pagoulatos (1983) noted that most foreign food affiliates have been established in highly concentrated industries. The competition in these industries is characterized by advertising and product proliferation, and FDI tends to move into those industries where international trade will not (pp. 407–408). Accordingly, advertising intensity (in terms of advertising per capita) and firm-specific factors like the size of firm sales, the degree of product diversification, and the firm's experience in food marketing are significant determinants of FDI in the United States. Another explanation for the inflow of FDI to the United States could be lower input costs in the United States. Pugel (1983) found this explanation insufficient by itself, since it does not account for input costs stemming from the lack of *local information*. In his discussion of the two papers by Connor (1983) and Pagoulatos (1983), Pugel pointed out their lack of clarity with regard to the relevant explanations of the determinants of FDI.

In a probit analysis of foreign investment flow into U.S. food retailing for the period 1971–80, Marion and Nash (1983) found a significant positive effect of product diversification on FDI.[11] The exchange rate also had a positive effect on FDI, whereas the combined effect of the exchange rate and the price-earnings ratio of U.S. grocery chains was negative. In addition, they viewed foreign investment in the U.S. food retailing system to be less alarming than the growth of acquisitions by large U.S. grocery chains, since the latter might increase the concentration ratio in the processed food industries.

In a more recent study, examining the surveys conducted by the U.S. Bureau of Economic Analysis, Handy and MacDonald (1989) observed that:

- major U.S. food manufacturers do relatively little exporting in comparison to manufacturers in other OECD countries,
- U.S. food manufacturers have extensive overseas interests through direct investment,
- the geographical pattern of food industry FDI has changed significantly in the last twenty years in favor of European countries,
- even though trade among the partners of a multinational firm accounts for an important share of nonfood manufacturing exports and imports, food manufacturers' affiliates in foreign countries focus on local sales, and
- breweries tend to license use of their brands to foreign producers rather than export or invest overseas. (1989, pp. 1247–49)

Based on the above observations and using an Economic Research Service (ERS) survey of sixty-two firms, Handy and MacDonald (1989) found a negative relationship between advertising expenditures and the level of exports. They found that firms with advertising-to-sales ratios of at least 1 percent have a tendency to practice FDI, which accounted for 96 percent of their total foreign sales, and firms with smaller advertising-to-sales ratios tend to export more. This study characterizes differentiated product industries by intensive advertising, large research and development investments, or both. Both of these factors were found to have a positive impact on FDI.[12]

A recent paper by Reed and Ning (1996) examined FDI by U.S. food manufacturers. They studied decisions based on the degree of FDI and related business strategies. In this study, FDI was specified as a function of research and development expenditures as a percentage of sales, marketing expenditures as a percentage of sales, sales per employee (a productivity measure), assets per employee (a measure of capital intensity), the number of four-digit SIC industries in which the firm was classified (a measure of diversity), total assets of the company, and the foreign sales as percentage of total sales divided by foreign assets as a percentage of total assets (the export competitiveness index). Among these explanatory variables, advertising and marketing were noted to be important in FDI success, but they were not related to the FDI entry decision by firms. FDI was found to be a diversification strategy, and, as opposed to a priori expectations, productivity and firm sizes were not found to be major factors in decisions to invest. Moreover, technology did not seem to play a large role in FDI decisions, even though capital-intensive firms were found more likely to invest in foreign markets. The study is consistent with previous ones in its finding that exports and FDI are substitute activities.

In another recent study, Henderson, Voros, and Hirschberg (1996) tried to explain export propensity versus FDI intensity. Their explanatory variables included a firm's dominance in its home market, product characteristics, and its investment in intangible assets. One of the findings of this study is that as a firm's size in terms of its domestic market share increases, it is more inclined to engage in FDI than to export (i.e., smaller firms have a tendency to export, whereas larger firms are inclined to practice FDI). The degree of specialization was found to have a positive impact on exports, and a neutral effect on FDI. As expected by the theory, product diversity or differentiation encourages FDI but discourages exports.

In his empirical model for examining FDI in the processed food industry, Reed (1996) established an explicit, dynamic optimization problem under the rational expectations hypothesis, in which firms maximize profits. Firms that have undertaken FDI were found to be less responsive to demand shifts. Moreover, scale economies were indicated to be more important in firms' responsiveness than internal adjustment costs or managerial skills, and they provided positive incentives to cereal-, soft drink-, and oil-manufacturing industries in considering FDI. Reed's empirical results also suggested that those firms undertaking FDI improved their information set on foreign markets and had a smoother supply response than firms that pursue export strategies.

Conclusions

This chapter has reviewed the existing literature on the determinants of intra-industry trade in processed food products, with a focus on the United States. Foreign direct investment (FDI) may be a substitute for intra-industry trade and for this reason, research on FDI in processed foods was also reviewed.

The theory of intra-industry trade predicts that intra-industry trade will be more important:

- for highly processed (differentiated) agricultural commodities than for raw (homogeneous) agricultural products;
- among developed countries and less important for developing countries;
- among countries located near one another; and
- among countries that are members of a trading bloc or customs union.

Intra-industry trade does account for a large share of agricultural trade among developed countries, and it is growing in importance. This is what trade theory would predict because during the process of economic development a country's comparative advantage in raw agricultural commodities declines, and the comparative advantage in processed food products increases (Anderson, 1987). This trend is due to the fact that factor requirements of agricultural products differ significantly according to their degree of processing (Lange, 1989), and highly processed foods are generally capital intensive.

Given the theory, intra-industry trade in processed foods should be growing rapidly for countries such as the United States. However, Bredahl, Abbott, and Reed (1995) find that, even though U.S. exports have grown, the U.S. market share in world trade of processed food products actually fell in the period 1970–90. Henderson, Handy, and Neff (1996) indicate that U.S. imports have grown more slowly than exports of processed foods.

The empirical work to date has not attempted to explain these trends in processed food trade noted by Bredahl, Abbott, and Reed (1995) and Henderson, Handy, and Neff (1996). Nor has it addressed the question of why the FDI to intra-industry trade ratio is larger for the United States as compared to the EU. A firm's decision to use FDI versus exporting should be incorporated in the same model along with the market structure parameters.

There exists a large gap between the theory of intra-industry trade and empirical studies on food products. Most of the empirical work claims to be consistent with the theory, but most of the theoretical assumptions (e.g. imperfect competition at the firm level) are not explicitly modeled empirically. In the utility function, the theory rests heavily on consumer tastes for differentiated products, but empirically these tastes never show up.

The studies to date have used SIC industry classifications, and this could be problematic due to aggregation issues. For instance, some SIC categories group goods with similar consumption uses but different factor inputs (Hummels and Levinsohn, 1995), and trade within this industry would be recorded as intra-industry trade when it might actually arise due to relative factor abundance. In addition, there is considerable aggregation across commodities under the SIC system, and trade in two unrelated food products would be counted as intra-industry trade. For example, the SIC aggregates tomato ketchup with canned avocados (SIC=2033, canned fruits, vegetables, preserves, jams, and jellies). So if the United States exports ketchup to Mexico and imports canned avocados, this is measured as intra-industry trade. The relative importance of this problem is unknown, but clearly some of the intra-industry trade in food products is a statistical artifact of SIC classification. This aggregation problem is not as prevalent in the Harmonized System (HS), which is another industry- and product-based system. Instead of the SIC industry classification, further empirical work should use the HS product code, which was adopted by the United States in 1989.

The empirical work to date does not attempt to explain what determines differences in intra-industry trade levels across products. For instance, we do not know why intra-industry trade is high for meat but low for dairy products and vegetable oil. It could have something to do with agricultural policy—but do we know anything about the impacts of policy on intra-industry trade?

In all these respects, testing the prevailing theories with different data sets as Hummels and Levinsohn (1995) did, will provide more evidence regarding the appropriateness of various models. This is the only way that we can determine whether a model is powerful enough to fully explain intra-industry trade. It is obvious that intra-industry trade increases as the level of aggregation increases. In order to understand the effectiveness of SIC and HS in product classifications, the empirical models must be estimated with data under each classification at the same level of aggregation.

Another attempt to increase our knowledge on the issue is to increase the number of studies at very detailed product levels as Christodoulou (1992) did for meat products in the EU. These studies can be made more comprehensive with our knowledge of the characteristics of the product and the resulting impacts on trade patterns. In future research, inter-industry trade, intra-industry trade and foreign direct investment should be handled within the same study under a multiequation approach.

Notes

1. This sector-specific capital is the key to the production of a continuum of qualities of a vertically differentiated product under constant returns to scale production technology and a perfectly elastic supply of labor at the prevailing wage rate. For a detailed explanation of this model, see Falvey (1981) or Vousden (1990).

2. The explicit segmentation of the domestic market from the international market has a long history in agricultural trade. Statutory marketing authorities were well positioned to practice price discrimination in agricultural commodity trade (Alston and Freebairn, 1988).

3. In this approach, because of the form of the consumer's utility function, as the number of varieties increases, the utility increases for a representative consumer with a given income. For a brief explanation of the utility function used in the SDS product differentiation model and its implications, as well as a comparison of the SDS model to that of Lancaster's, see Vousden (1990).

4.The Grubel-Lloyd index takes the following form:

$$IIT_{ijk} = \frac{2\,min(X_{ijk}, X_{ikj})}{X_{ijk} + X_{ikj}}$$

where i indexes the industry, and j and k index countries. So X_{ijk} represents the exports of commodities in the ith sector from country j to country k.

5. In its original form, the Grubel-Lloyd index poses some possible problems of interpretation, especially with regard to food products. There is some intra-industry trade that can be explained by seasonal factors, and this is not accounted for in the Grubel-Lloyd index. For example, during the northern hemisphere's summer months, California exports fresh tomatoes to Mexico, and the trade is reversed during winter months. See Cook (1992).

6. Instead of using data from the OECD countries, Hummels and Levinsohn (1995) created a data set comprised of Brazil, Cameroon, Colombia, Congo, Greece, Ivory Coast, South Korea, Nigeria, Norway, Pakistan, Paraguay, Peru, Philippines, and Thailand. They indicated that this data set was inappropriate for a model of monopolistic competition and international trade.

7. This version of the Grubel-Lloyd index is adjusted for any imbalance in aggregate trade, and it has the following form:

$$IIT_{jki} = 1 - \frac{\left| \frac{X_{jki}}{X_{jk}} - \frac{M_{jki}}{M_{jk}} \right|}{\frac{X_{jki}}{X_{jk}} + \frac{M_{jki}}{M_{jk}}}$$

where X_{jki} and M_{jki} stand for industry i's exports and imports between countries j and k, and X_{jk} and M_{jk} refer to total exports and imports between the two countries.

8. Meat is classified as a processed agricultural product. Dried, salted, or smoked meat is classified as highly processed, whereas fresh, chilled, or frozen meats are considered lightly processed agricultural products (Garner and Winton, 1992, p. 572).

9. The unadjusted version of the Grubel-Lloyd index is slightly different than the previous ones mentioned above. It has the following form:

$$IIT_{jki} = 1 - \frac{|X_{jki} - M_{jki}|}{X_{jki} + M_{jki}}$$

where X_{jki} stands for industry *i*'s value of imports reported by country *j* as originating from country *k*, and M_{jki} stands for the value of imports for industry *i* reported by country *k* as coming from country *j*. IIT_{jki} indicates, as in other versions of the index, intra-industry trade between country *j* and country *k* for industry *i*.

10. The Hufbauer index used in Christodoulou (1992) measures the ratio of the standard deviation of export unit values for the different product categories to their average, calculated for every country pair. It is formulated as:

$$H_{ij}^f = \frac{\sigma_{ij}}{\mu_{ij}^f}$$

where *f* is the product and *i*, *j* are the trading countries.

11. Marion and Nash (1983) defined FDI as a binary variable that equals one if a firm makes or increases an investment in a U.S. food retailing company during a particular year, and as zero if it does not (p. 416).

12. Handy and MacDonald's (1989) FDI measure is the share of foreign affiliate sales in the total consolidated (parent plus affiliate) sales.

References

Alston, Julian M. and Freebairn, John W. "Producer price equalization," *Review of Marketing and Agricultural Economics*, 1988, 56(3), pp. 306–39.

Anderson, Kym. "On Why Agriculture Declines with Economic Growth," *Agricultural Economics*, 1987, 1(3), pp. 195–207.

Balassa, Bela and Bauwens, Luc. "Intra-industry Specialisation in a Multi- country and Multi-industry Framework," *Economic Journal*, 1987, 97(388), pp. 923–39.

Brander, James. "Intra-industry Trade in Identical Commodities," *Journal of International Economics*, 1981, 11(1), pp. 1–14.

Brander, James and Krugman, Paul R. "A 'Reciprocal Dumping' Model of International Trade," *Journal of International Economics*, 1983, 15(3–4), pp. 313–21.

Bredahl, Maury E.; Abbott, Philip C. and Reed, Michael R. *Competitiveness of U.S. Agriculture and the Balance of Payments*. Council for Agricultural Science and Technology, Task Force Report No. 125, Ames: CAST, 1995.

Cantwell, John. "The Relationship Between International Trade and International Production," in *Surveys in International Trade*. Eds.: David Greenaway and L. Alan Winters. Oxford: Basil Blackwell, 1994, pp. 303–28.

Caves, Richard E. *Multinational Enterprise and Economics Analysis*. Cambridge: Cambridge University Press, 1982.

Christodoulou, Maria. "Intra-industry Trade in Agrofood Sectors: the Case of the EEC Meat Market," *Applied Economics*, 1992, 24(8), pp. 875–84.

Connor, John M. "Determinants of Foreign Direct Investment by Food and Tobacco Manufacturers," *American Journal of Agricultural Economics*, 1983, 65(2), pp. 395–404.

Cook, Roberta L. "From Competition to Coordination of Vegetable Trade: the Case of Mexico and California," in *Vegetable Markets in the Western Hemisphere*. Eds.: Rigoberto A. Lopez and Leo C. Polopolus. Ames: Iowa State University Press, 1992, pp. 129–47.

Dayton, James R. and Henderson, Dennis R. "Patterns of World Trade in Processed Foods," Organization and Performance of World Food Systems: NC-194, OP-32, Columbus, OH, 1992.

Dunning, John H. *International Production and the Multinational Enterprise*. London: George Allen & Unwin, 1981.

Falvey, Rodney E. "Commercial Policy and Intra-industry Trade," *Journal of International Economics*, 1981, 11(4), pp. 495-511.

Garner, Brett and Winton, Justin. "Impediments to Australian Processed Agricultural Exports to East Asia," *Agriculture and Resources Quarterly*, 1992, 4(4), pp. 570–83.

Graham, Edward M. and Krugman Paul R. *Foreign Direct Investment in the United States*. Washington, D.C.: Institute for International Economics, 1989.

Greenaway, David and Milner, Chris. *The economics of intra-industry trade*. Oxford: Basil Blackwell, 1986.

Grubel, Harry and Lloyd, Peter. *Intra-industry Trade: The Theory and Measurement of International Trade in Differentiated Products*. London: Macmillan, 1975.

Handy, Charles and MacDonald, James M. "Multinational Structures and Strategies of U.S. Food Firms," *American Journal of Agricultural Economics*, 1989, 71(4), pp. 1246–54.

Helpman, Elhanan. "Imperfect Competition and International Trade: Evidence from Fourteen Industrial Countries," *Journal of the Japanese and International Economics*, 1987, 1(1), pp. 62–81.

Helpman, Elhanan and Krugman, Paul R. *Market Structure and Foreign Trade: Increasing Returns, Imperfect Competition, and the International Economy*. Cambridge, MA: MIT Press, 1985.

———. *Trade Policy and Market Structure*. Cambridge, MA: MIT Press, 1989.

Henderson, Dennis R.; Handy, Charles and Neff, Steven A. (Eds.) *Globalization of the Processed Food Market*. U.S. Department of Agriculture, Economic Research Service, Agricultural Economic Report, Number 742, 1996.

Henderson, Dennis R., Voros, Peter R., and Hirschberg, Joseph G. "Industrial Determinants of International Trade and Foreign Investment by Food and Beverage Manufacturing Firms," in *Industrial Organization and Trade in the Food Industries*. Eds.: Ian M. Sheldon and Philip C. Abbott. Boulder, CO: Westview Press, 1996, pp. 197–215.

Hirschberg, Joseph G. and Dayton, James R. "Detailed Patterns of Intra-industry Trade in Processed Food," in *Industrial Organization and Trade in the Food Industries*. Eds.: Ian M. Sheldon and Philip C. Abbott. Boulder, CO: Westview Press, 1996, pp. 141–59.

Hirschberg, Joseph G., Sheldon, Ian M., and Dayton, James R. "An Analysis of Bilateral Intra-industry Trade in the Food Processing Sector," *Applied Economics*, 1994, 26(2), pp. 159–67.

Hummels, David and Levinsohn, James. "Monopolistic Competition and International Trade: Reconsidering the Evidence," *Quarterly Journal of Economics*, 1995, 110(3), pp. 799–836.

Hymer, Stephen H. *The International Operations of National Firms: a Study of Direct Foreign Investment*. Cambridge, MA: MIT Press, 1976.

Krugman, Paul R. "Increasing Returns, Monopolistic Competition, and International Trade," *Journal of International Economics*, 1979, 9(4), pp. 469–79.

———. "Intra-industry Specialization and the Gains from Trade," *Journal of Political Economy*, 1981, *89*(5), pp. 959-73.

———. "Rethinking International Trade: Introduction," in *Rethinking International Trade* by Paul R. Krugman. Cambridge, MA: MIT Press, 1990, pp. 1–8.

Lange, Dirk. "Economic Development and Agricultural Export Pattern: an Empirical Cross-Country Analysis," *European Review of Agricultural Economics*, 1989, 16(2), pp. 187–202.

Leamer, Edward E. and Levinsohn, James. "International Trade Theory: the Evidence," in *The Handbook of International Economics, Volume III*. Eds.: Gene M. Grossman and Kenneth Rogoff. Amsterdam: Elsevier, 1995, pp. 1339–94.

Loertscher, Rudolf. and Wolter, Frank. "Determinants of Intra-industry Trade: Among Countries and Across Industries," *Weltwirtschaftliches Archiv*, 1980, 116(2), pp. 280–93.

Marion, Bruce W. and Nash, Howard J. "Foreign Investment in U.S. Food-Retailing Industry," *American Journal of Agricultural Economics*, 1983, 65(2), pp. 413–20.

Markusen, James R. "The Boundaries of Multinational Enterprises and the Theory of International Trade," *Journal of Economic Perspectives*, 1995, 9(2), pp. 169–89.

McCorriston, Steve and Sheldon, Ian M. "Intra-industry Trade and Specialization in Processed Agricultural Products: the Case of the US and the EC," *Review of Agricultural Economics*, 1991, 13(2), pp. 173–84.

Pagoulatos, Emilio. "Foreign Direct Investment in US Food and Tobacco Manufacturing and Domestic Economic Performance," *American Journal of Agricultural Economics*, 1983, 65(2), pp. 405–12.

Pugel, Thomas A. "Foreign Investment in the U.S. Food-Marketing System: Discussion," *American Journal of Agricultural Economics*, 1983, 65(2), pp. 423–25.

Reed, Michael R. "An Empirical Model for Examining Foreign Direct Investment in the Processed Food Industry," in *Industrial Organization and Trade in the Food Industries*. Eds.: Ian M. Sheldon and Philip C. Abbott. Boulder, CO: Westview Press, 1996, pp. 218–36.

Reed, Michael R. and Ning, Yulin. "Foreign Investment Strategies of U.S. Multinational Food Firms," in *Industrial Organization and Trade in the Food Industries*. Eds.: Ian M. Sheldon and Philip C. Abbott. Boulder, CO: Westview Press, 1996, pp. 183–96.

Vousden, Neil. *The Economics of Trade Protection*. Cambridge: Cambridge University Press, 1990.

6

Multinational Enterprises and Trade Theory

James R. Markusen

Introduction

Literatures on international trade theory and the theory of the multinational enterprise have largely developed separately, with little overlap among either researchers or readers. Trade theory took a general equilibrium path, with models predominately based on the twin assumptions of constant returns to scale and perfect competition. In such a framework, there is essentially no role for multinational firms since there are no technological or other features to support their existence in equilibrium. Indeed, there is no role for firms at all, and authors speak only of "industries," not firms.

Trade theory was then revitalized in the 1980s, with models based on assumptions of increasing returns to scale, imperfect competition, and product differentiation. These features were incorporated into simple general equilibrium models with the intention of explaining certain stylized facts, in particular the large volume of trade between similar economies, which were viewed as anomalous from the perspective of traditional Heckscher-Ohlin theory.

Yet the new models are very limited in their treatment of firms. In these models, a firm is generally synonymous with a plant or production facility; that is, a firm is an independent organization that produces one good in one location. Multiplant and multiproduct production, whether horizontal or vertical, is generally excluded from the analysis. This is potentially troubling. After all, industries characterized by scale economies and imperfect competition are often dominated by multinationals.

As a result, the policy and normative analysis that comes out of the new trade theory may be significantly off base. For example, conclusions of the strategic trade policy literature are fundamentally bound up with the notion of clearly defined national firms competing via trade with the national champions of other countries. Substantial foreign ownership of domestic production facilities radically alters the policy implications (Dick, 1993).

On the other hand, the theory of the multinational enterprise has been predominantly a theory-of-the-firm literature focusing on the characteristics of individual firms that lead to multinationality. This permits a great richness in analyzing firms' multiple options for serving markets and their geographic arrangement of activities. But partial equilibrium analysis of industry structure is somewhat unusual, and general equilibrium considerations are rarely incorporated.

Each literature has strengths, but there is a need to integrate their contributions. Trade theory cannot afford to ignore multinationals given their tremendous empirical importance in international economic activity. The present state of the theory of the multinational enterprise leaves it ill equipped to answer questions such as why ownership of multinational firms is concentrated in a few countries, or why multinationals are much more important relative to trade among the high-income countries than between high-income and lower-income countries.

The purpose of this chapter is to survey recent contributions that attempt to integrate the theory of the multinational enterprise into the theory of international trade. The contributions reviewed are primarily by trade economists. The basic models of multinationals are extremely simple, so that they can be incorporated into a correspondingly simple general equilibrium model. There is no expectation on my part that I will teach readers anything new about multinational firms per se, and indeed I hope that I do not cause offense by presenting such a simple model.

The next section presents a number of "stylized facts" on characteristics of multinational firms and characteristics of countries that are sources of and/or hosts to multinational investment. The goal is to reconcile these two sets of facts, and sections three and four present a simple model that attempts to do so. Section five turns to the question of internalization and the problem of why a firm, having chosen to produce abroad, will chose direct investment over some alternative mode of serving the foreign market.

Some Stylized Facts

Many studies have documented the characteristics of multinational firms and the characteristics of industries dominated by multinationals, comparing the latter to industries in which multinationals play a minor role. Since many of these empirical regularities will be very familiar to readers of this book, I will simply list some of them with little comment.

Extensive empirical evidence offers us a picture of the characteristics of firms and industries that are dominated by multinationals.[1] Firm and industry characteristics include the following:

1. Multinationals are associated with high ratios of R&D relative to sales.
2. Multinationals employ large numbers of scientific, technical, and other white collar workers as a percentage of their work forces.
3. Multinationals tend to have a high value of intangible assets, roughly market value minus the value of tangible assets such as plant and equipment.
4. Multinationals are associated with new and/or technically complex products.
5. Evidence suggests that multinationality is negatively associated with plant-level scale economies.
6. Multinationals are associated with product-differentiation variables, such as advertising to sales ratios.
7. A minimum or "threshold" level of firm size seems to be important for a firm to be a multinational, but above that level firm size is of minimal importance.
8. Multinationals tend to be older, more established firms.

These data suggest that multinationals are important in industries in which intangible, firm-specific assets are important. These assets can generally be characterized as "knowledge capital," ranging from proprietary product or process know-how to reputations and trademarks. Plant-level scale economies are not associated with direct investment.

Other data give us an understanding of the country characteristics that are associated with source and host countries. Country characteristics include:

1. The high-income developed countries are not only the major source of direct investment; they are also the major recipients. Most direct investment seems to be horizontal, in the sense that the bulk of the affiliates output is sold in the host country.
2. High volumes of direct investment are associated with similarities among countries in terms of relative factor endowments and per capita incomes, not differences. But that portion of output that is shipped back to the home country is associated with endowment and income differences.

3. A high volume of outward direct investment is positively related to a country's endowment of skilled labor and insignificantly or negatively related to its physical capital endowment.[2]
4. There is little evidence that direct investment is primarily motivated by trade-barrier avoidance; the relative coefficients often have the wrong sign. Trade barriers seem to discourage both trade and investment, but have a substitution effect toward investment.[3]
5. Direct investment stocks, at least among the high-income countries, have grown significantly faster than trade flows over the last two decades, even though trade barriers have fallen dramatically.
6. There is mixed evidence that tax avoidance and/or risk diversification are important motives for direct investment. Some evidence does suggest that political risk discourages inward investment.[4]
7. Infrastructure, skill levels, and a minimum threshold level of per capita income seem to be very important determinants of direct investment.
8. There is evidence that agglomeration effects are important in direct investment. But it is admittedly difficult to distinguish agglomeration effects from firms being drawn to the same (unobserved) site-specific resources [5]

In summary, direct investment is concentrated among the high-income countries, and skilled labor in particular is an important determinant of outward direct investment. Taxes and trade barriers do not seem to be of first-order importance, but good infrastructure and agglomeration economies do seem to be significant.

An Organizing Framework

As noted in the previous section, the purpose of this chapter is to connect these firm characteristics with the country characteristics. To do so we first need a very simple model of a multinational firm. Because of the quantitative importance of horizontal direct investment, I will concentrate on that case, but many of the ideas apply equally well to a model of a vertically integrated multinational.

Many authors begin by noting that there are inherent difficulties and costs to doing business abroad, such that multinationals are assumed to be disadvantaged relative to local firms. Because of these inherent disadvantages and higher costs of foreign production, it is necessary to identify offsetting advantages and conditions under which direct investment will occur. One organizing framework was proposed by Dunning (1977, 1981), who suggested that three conditions are necessary for a firm to undertake direct investment (that is, all three factors need to be present for a firm to have a strong motive for direct investment). This has become well known as the OLI framework: ownership, location, and internalization.

A firm's *ownership advantage* could be a product or a production process to which other firms do not have access, such as a patent, blueprint, or trade secret. It could also be something intangible, like a trademark or reputation for quality. Whatever its form, the ownership advantage confers some valuable market power or cost advantage on the firm sufficient to outweigh the disadvantages of doing business abroad.

In addition, the foreign market must offer a *location advantage* that makes it profitable to produce the product in the foreign country rather than simply produce it at home and export it to the foreign market. Although tariffs, quotas, transport costs, and cheap factor prices are the most obvious sources of location advantages, factors such as access to customers can also be important. Indeed, many multinationals are in service industries (for example, hotels) in which on-site provision of the services is an inherent part of the companies' business.[6]

Finally, the multinational enterprise must have an *internalization advantage*. This condition is the most abstract of the three. If a company has a proprietary product or production process, and if, due to tariffs and transport costs, it is advantageous to produce the product abroad rather than export it, it is still not obvious that the company should set up a foreign subsidiary. One of several alternatives is to license a foreign firm to produce the product or use the production process. Why not just sell the blueprints to a foreign firm rather than go through the costly and difficult process of setting up a foreign production facility? Reasons for wishing to do so are referred to as internalization advantages; that is, the product or process is exploited internally within the firm rather than at arm's length through markets.[7]

Ownership advantages come in many possible forms, and a good approach to identifying them is to seek guidance from the firm-level characteristics about direct foreign investment. Remember, the evidence finds that an industry tends to have a greater proportion of multinational enterprises when the output of that industry is characterized by R&D, marketing expenditures, scientific and technical workers, product newness and complexity, and product differentiation. At a broader level, multinational enterprises are identified with a high ratio of intangible assets of the firm to its total market value. These explanatory variables give rise to the concept of knowledge-based, firm-specific assets. These proprietary assets of the firm are embodied in such things as the human capital of the employees, patents or other exclusive technical knowledge, copyrights or trademarks, or even more intangible assets such as management "know-how" or the reputation of the firm.

There are two good reasons why these knowledge-based assets are more likely to give rise to direct foreign investment than physical capital assets. First, knowledge-based assets can be transferred easily back and forth across space at low cost. An engineer or manager can visit many separate production facilities at relatively low cost. Second, knowledge often has a joint-input characteristic, like a public good, in that it can be supplied to additional production facilities at very low cost. Blueprints, chemical formulae and pharmaceuticals, and trademarks and other marketing devices all have this characteristic—but assets based on physical capital such as machinery usually do not. That is, physical capital usually cannot yield a flow of services in one location without reducing its productivity in others.

In turn, the joint-input characteristic of knowledge-based assets has implications for the efficiency of the firm and for market structure. These implications are encapsulated in the notion of economies of multiplant production. Such economies arise because a single two-plant firm has a cost efficiency over two independent single-plant firms. The multiplant firm (that is, the multinational enterprise) need only make a single investment in R&D, for example, while two independent firms must each make the investment. Cost efficiency then dictates that multinational enterprises arise as the equilibrium market structure in industries where firm-specific assets are important, which is consistent with the empirical evidence.[8]

The converse proposition also deserves emphasis. Scale economies based on physical capital intensity do not by themselves lead to foreign direct investment, an argument supported by some evidence (Brainard, 1993c; Beaudreau, 1986; Ekholm, 1995). This type of scale economy implies the cost efficiency of centralized production rather than geographically dispersed production. Of course, some industries with high physical capital intensity may also be industries in which firm-specific assets are important (like automobiles).

What then is being traded when we observe multinational production? Basically, multinational enterprises in this framework are exporters of the services of firm-specific assets. These include management, engineering, marketing, and financial services, many of which are based on human capital. They also include the "services" of patents and trademarks, which are other knowledge-based assets. Subsidiaries import these services in exchange for repatriated profits, royalties, fees, or output.

A Simple General-Equilibrium Model

A small number of authors working from the international trade perspective have constructed models in which multinationals arise endogenously in equilibrium. These authors have combined elements of ownership and location advantages, generally leaving aside the question of internalization. Early papers by Helpman (1984) and Markusen (1984) allowed for a headquarters or firm-level activity such as R&D that could be separated from production. Helpman's model was constructed such that firms have a single production facility, that could be in a different country than the headquarters. The absence of tariffs or transport costs mean that the firm will never open more than one production facility, so the model is really one of a vertically integrated firm. In Markusen's model, the multinational enterprise would choose production facilities in both countries, becoming a horizontally integrated multinational enterprise. The headquarter's activity is modeled as a joint input (a nonrival input) such that adding additional plants does not reduce the value of the input to existing plants. The respective approaches are extended in Helpman (1985), Helpman and Krugman (1985), and Horstmann and Markusen (1987a).

More recently, Brainard (1993a) and Horstmann and Markusen (1992) have produced models in which horizontal multinationals arise endogenously and in which two-way investment, a characteristic of the North Atlantic economy, can arise in equilibrium. The three key elements of both papers are firm-level activities (like R&D) that are joint inputs across plants, plant-level scale economies, and tariffs or transport costs between countries. Although Brainard models firms as producing differentiated products, whereas goods are homogeneous in the Horstmann and Markusen model, the results are strikingly similar. Multinationals are supported in equilibrium when firm-level fixed costs and tariff/transport costs are large relative to plant-level scale economies. Multinationals are more likely to exist in equilibrium when the countries are large (both papers) and when the countries have similar relative factor endowments (Brainard). These results fit well with the empirical evidence noted above.

It may be useful to offer an outline of these newer models. The model sketched here is drawn from Markusen and Venables (1995a). It assumes homogenous goods, but it is clear from Brainard (1993a) that a differentiated-good model generates similar conclusions.

A. Two countries (h and f) produce two goods (X and Y), using the factors *land* and *labor* (R and L). Factors are immobile between countries.
B. Y is a homogeneous good produced with constant returns to scale by a competitive industry. Y production uses all of the land (R) and some of the labor (L).[9]
C. X is a homogeneous good produced with increasing returns to scale by Cournot firms. Markets are segmented (arbitrage conditions need not hold). X uses labor as its single factor of production.

D. The costs for producers of X can be measured in units of labor. The costs are to be divided into four types:
   1. firm-specific fixed cost (F)
   2. plant-specific fixed cost (one G per plant)
   3. constant marginal cost (c)
   4. unit shipping cost (t) between markets, assumed symmetric in both directions.

The model employs three firm types, with free entry and exit into and out of firm types. Type m firms are multinationals that maintain plants in both countries.[10] Type h firms are national firms that maintain a single plant in country h. Type h firms may or may not export to country f. Finally, type f firms are national firms that maintain a single plant in country f. Type f firms may or may not export to country h. The term *regime* denotes the set of firm types active in equilibrium.

In the context of this model, consider first two countries absolutely identical in technologies, preferences, and endowments. If transport costs were zero, then there would exist only national firms exporting to each other's markets, since no firm would incur the fixed costs of a second plant. If transport costs were very high, there would exist only multinational (two-plant) firms: in this case, a multinational has lower fixed costs per market and therefore outcompetes national firms that face prohibitive export costs. At intermediate levels of transport costs, multinational firms exist if firm-specific fixed costs and transport costs are large relative to plant-specific fixed costs (plant-level scale economies).[11] Thus, this model predicts that we should find multinationals concentrated in industries that fit at least one of three conditions: firm-level activities or intangible assets are important and plant scale economies are not particularly important; the overall market is large; and tariffs and transport costs are high but barriers to direct investment are relatively low.

Figures 6.1 and 6.2 present the results of some simulations for this model when the two countries are identical. The shading in the cells gives qualitative information on the equilibrium regime. On the horizontal axis is transport costs, measured as a proportion of marginal production costs. The vertical axis of Figure 6.1 measures the absolute factor endowment (economic size) of each of the identical economies (100 is the value used in subsequent simulations). We see the result that national firms dominate when transport costs are low and/or the markets are of modest size: in region a (light shade), there is intra-industry competition in exports between type h and type f national firms, reminiscent of the new trade theory mentioned in the introduction. Multinationals dominate under the opposite circumstances (region b, dark shade).

The vertical axis of Figure 6.2 gives the ratio of fixed costs for a two-

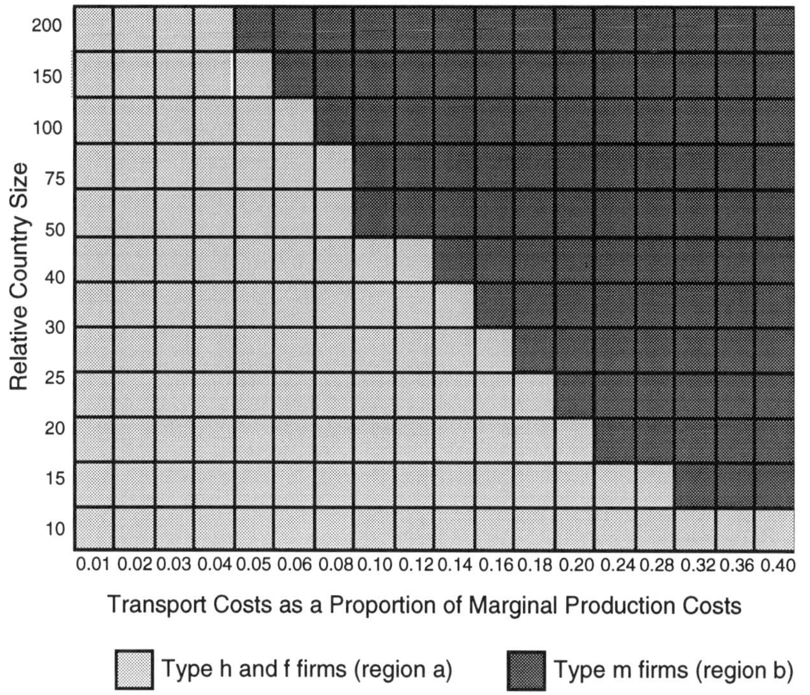

FIGURE 6.1 Absolute Country Size (Countries Identical). (100 is the value used in other simulations).

plant multinational to the fixed costs for a one-plant national firm (1.60 is the value used in the other simulations). This value is reduced below two by the joint-input nature of knowledge capital discussed above. It is raised above one by the physical capital costs of plant construction and by various transactions costs, including foreign investment barriers (assuming the latter fall on fixed costs). National firms dominate in equilibrium when trade costs are low and/or multiplant economies of scale are weak (or investment barriers are high). Multinationals dominate under the opposite circumstances.

The empirical evidence is consistent with these results, but it also indicates that multinationals are of greater importance between countries that are relatively similar in size, per capita income, and relative factor endowments, like Western Europe and the United States. It is interesting that the simple model does a good job of capturing the association of direct foreign investment and multinational enterprises with the *similarity* of countries.

Figures 6.3 and 6.4 consider country asymmetries. The horizonal axis of

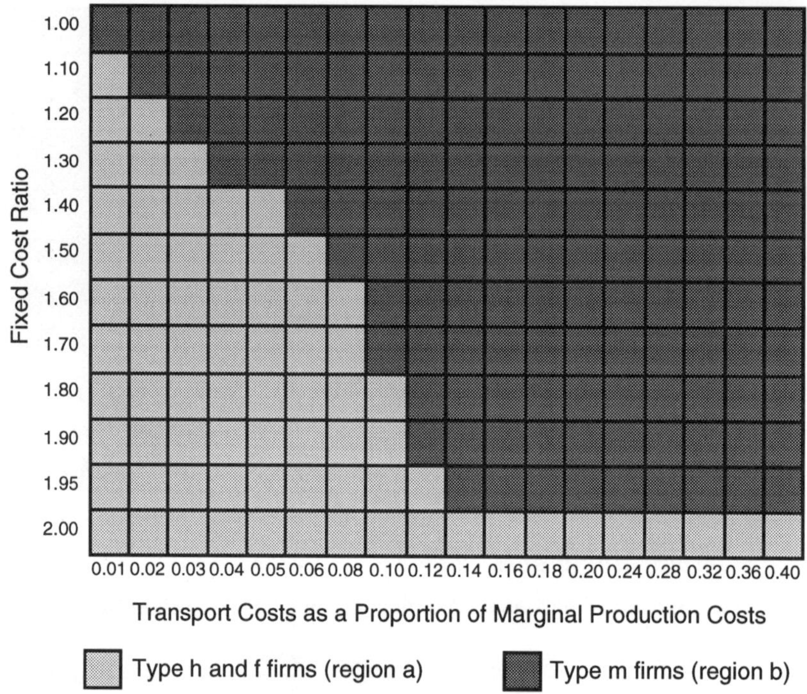

FIGURE 6.2 Ratio of Two-Plant to One-Plant Fixed Costs (Countries Identical). (1.60 is the value used in other simulations).

each of these figures is the same as for Figures 6.1 and 6.2. Figure 6.3 considers differences in country size, holding the total world endowment of factors constant. Countries are identical in the top row. Moving down a column, factors are transferred from country f to country h. The numbers on the vertical axis measure country f's factor endowment as a proportion of its initial endowment, with country h's endowment correspondingly larger.

Figure 6.3 shows that national firms dominate at low levels of trade costs (for a given level of the investment cost ratio): there is intra-industry competition in exports by nation firms (region a, light shade). At higher levels of transport costs, the pattern is more complex. If the countries are of similar size, only multinational firms exist (region b, dark shade). At a moderate degree of difference, multinationals firms compete with national firms located in country h, the large country (region d, no shade). When the size difference is very large, only national firms headquartered in country h exist in equilibrium (region c, hatched area).

In order to grasp the intuition behind these results, consider moving

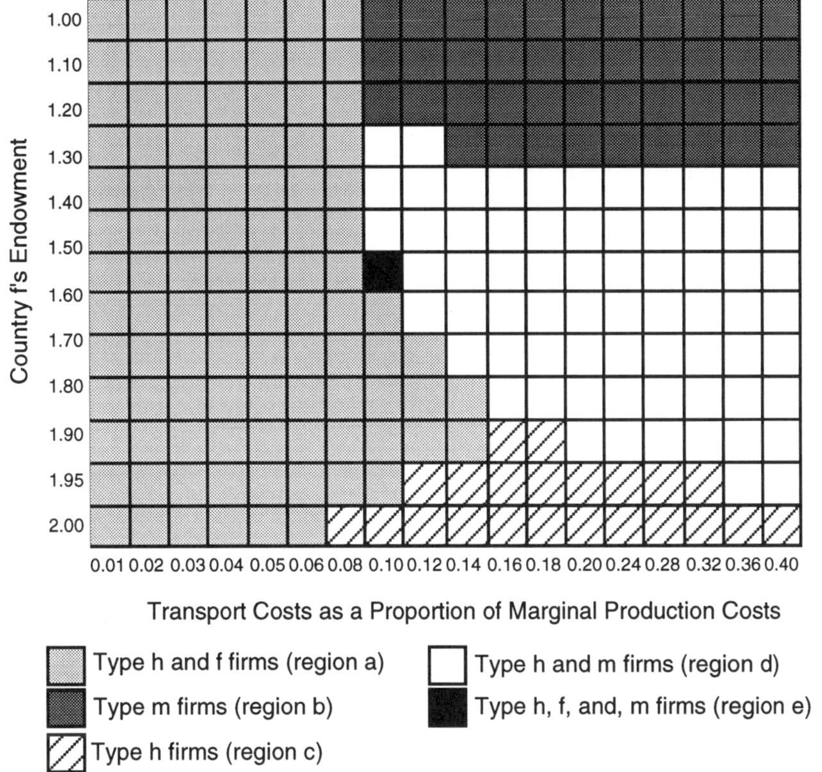

FIGURE 6.3 Countries Differ in Size.

down a column of Figure 6.3, such as t = .20. When the countries are very similar, only multinational firms exist in equilibrium. As the countries diverge in size, potential national firms headquartered in country h become more (potentially) profitable. Type h firms have lower fixed costs than the multinational firms, and most of their sales are concentrated in the large and low-cost (no transport cost) market. Multinationals must make an additional fixed-cost investment to serve an ever-shrinking market. Eventually, type h firms can dominate. Conversely, type f firms cannot enter, because their low-cost domestic market is small, and shipping costs would have to be incurred in order to serve market h.

As the difference in market sizes becomes extreme, multinational firms cannot exist at all, and only type h firms exist in equilibrium (region c of Figure 6.3). As country f's market becomes very small, no firm can afford a fixed-cost investment in that market (type m and type f firms), and all supply is from imports from type h national firms. Note the contrast

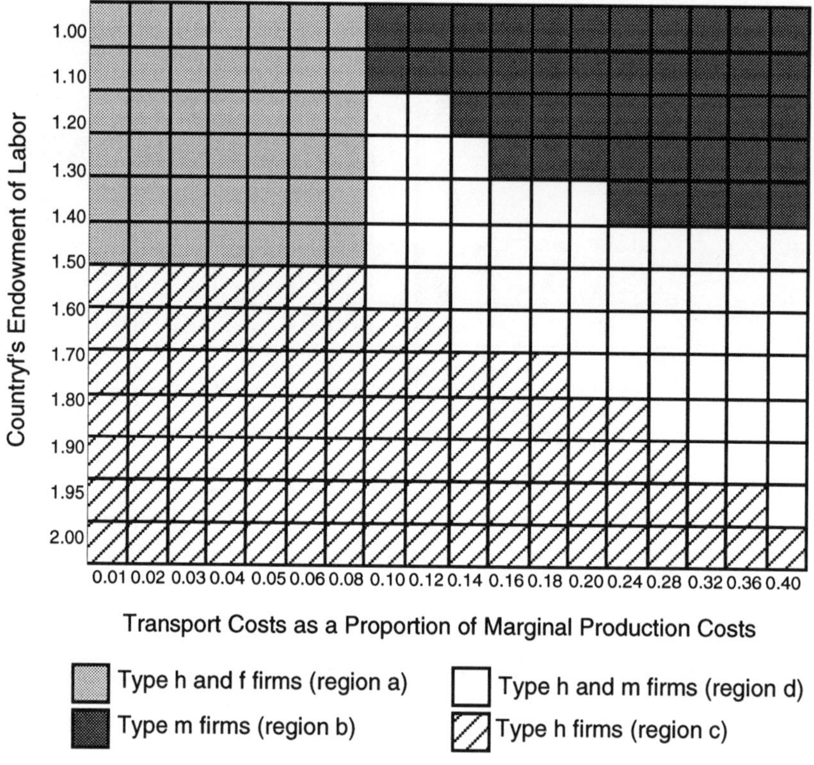

FIGURE 6.4 Countries Differ in Relative Endowments.

between this result and a traditional constant-returns Heckscher-Ohlin model, where difference in country size is not a source of comparative advantage (i.e., at no point in Figure 6.3 would there be any trade or investment).

Figure 6.4 considers differences in relative endowments across the countries, again holding the total world endowment of factors constant as in Figure 6.3. The countries are identical in the top row of Figure 6.4. Moving down a column of Figure 6.4, we transfer units of labor from country f to country h, and units of the Y-sector-specific factor from country h to country f. Moving down a column, we are then creating a Heckscher-Ohlin basis of comparative advantage, in X for country h and in Y for country f. Total incomes of the two countries remain approximately equal as we move down each column. At low levels of trade costs, there is intra-industry competition in exports (region a, light shade) when the endowment differences are modest, but only inter-industry trade when the endowment differences are large (only type h firms produce X in region c, hatched area). Region c could be termed a Heckscher-Ohlin region whereas region a could be dubbed the new trade theory region as noted earlier.

At higher levels of trade costs in Figure 6.4, we see a pattern qualitatively similar to that shown in Figure 6.3, where the differences are in relative country sizes. Moving down a column of Figure 6.4 such as t = .20, multinationals alone exist when the countries are relatively similar in relative endowments. But as the difference becomes more pronounced, factor price become unequal across countries, with the price of labor lower in country h, the labor-abundant country. Even though the market sizes are approximately the same, there is now a cost-side advantage for type h firms that incur all of their fixed costs in country h. Type m firms must incur fixed costs in both markets, including costs in the high-labor-cost market f. Type h firms can eventually enter in competition with multinational firms, whereas type-f firms cannot. Eventually, these costs factors are sufficiently strong such that only type h firms exist in equilibrium. Not surprisingly, the endowment difference at which the switch from type m to types (m,h) and the switch from types (m,h) to type h occur is increasing in the level of trade costs.

To summarize this section, we see that our very simple model generates outcomes that are at least superficially consistent with many of the stylized facts listed earlier. In particular the model predicts that direct investment will be important relative to trade when (a) countries are large (high income), (b) countries are similar in size, (c) countries are similar in relative factor endowments (crudely proxied by per capita income), and (d) trade costs are modest or high relative to foreign investment costs. Looking at a cross-section of industries between two countries with given characteristics, the model predicts that industries with large levels of multiplant economies of scale (a low ratio of two-plant to one-plant fixed costs in Figure 6.2) will be more multinationalized. This is also consistent with the stylized facts under the strong suspicion that multiplant economies are more important for knowledge-intensive industries than for physical-capital intensive industries.

Internalization

Even if foreign production makes economic sense in the terms of the models laid out in the previous section, there is a further question to tackle. A firm might be able to realize many of the advantages of multinational production while shielding itself from the costs, by signing a licensing agreement with a firm in the foreign country. Thus, a complementary part of the argument must explain why firms choose direct investment rather than some other mode of foreign entry. Licensing is only one of many such options; other include joint ventures, subcontracting, management contracts, and so forth. Following Dunning's terminology, the question of the mode of foreign entry can be referred to as the internalization problem.

Much has been written on whether a firm transfers a firm-specific asset (or the services thereof) within that particular firm or through an alternative arm's length arrangement with an independent foreign firm. As one might expect, the optimal scope of a firm is determined by factors like the form of corporate governance, the cost of internal transactions versus those in arm's length markets, the specific characteristics of the knowledge and information to be transferred, along with resulting market failures involving concepts like bounded rationality, agent opportunism, and asset specificity (Williamson, 1975, 1981).

Since many of the readers of this volume may be familiar with the writings of international business economists on internalization problems, I will limit my discussion here to some fairly specific, formal models produced by international trade economists using the broader notions developed by Williamson (1975, 1981), Casson (1987), Rugman (1986), Teece (1977, 1986), and others. I will also limit myself to a comparison among only three options of serving a foreign market: exports, direct investment, and licensing. These three illustrate some of the key tradeoffs firms face.

As in earlier sections, I am interested in a synthesis between the theory of the multinational and trade theory. Therefore, I will focus on a set of ideas that are quite compatible and complementary with the model developed above, in addition to fitting well with most of the firm-level stylized facts laid out earlier and some of the country-level stylized facts. With respect to the latter, most of the models discussed below generate the empirically relevant prediction that (horizontal) direct investment is more likely to arise between large countries with similar levels of investment.

Many or most of the reasons to transfer assets internally arise from the basic property that knowledge capital can be a joint input to a number of plants; this same property, the reader will recall, was used in the model of the previous section and is consistent with the association of multinational enterprises with R&D, advertising, and product newness and complexity. A number of papers show quite convincingly that transfers tend to be internal, rather than arms' length, when the products are new, complex, have no prior commercial application, and are produced by R&D-intensive firms (Davidson and McFetridge, 1984; Mansfield and Romeo, 1980; Teece, 1977; Wilson, 1977). Thus, the same features that create multiplant economies of scale may be responsible for creating advantages of internalization.

But although models of internalization do share an underlying commonality with the ownership-location models discussed in the previous section, internalization models tend to be somewhat different. Because they focus on characteristics of knowledge capital like nonexcludability, asymmetric information, moral hazard, adverse selection, and incomplete contracting, the models are often partial equilibrium in nature and bring to bear quite different tools of analysis. Nevertheless, despite their partial-equilibrium nature, many of the models generate empirically plausible predictions as noted above. In what follows, I will outline some of the ideas that have been advanced in formal models of internalization and present a simple analytical example at the end, much the same as I did in the section on ownership and location.

All of the models to be discussed share a common point of departure: firms would like to license due to the costs of doing business abroad, but licensing carries costs as well. These models can be categorized according to how they draw the link from information issues to difficulties in licensing, and hence why direct foreign investment occurs.

A first problem is that because of the nonexcludability property of new knowledge, a firm may not want to reveal (or truthfully reveal) its process or product technology to a potential licensee. After all, the licensee could reject a deal and go and copy the technology at little cost. Conversely, the licensee is not going to deal without knowing exactly what it is getting, which requires revelation on the part of the seller. A complete contract may be costly or infeasible under these circumstances, so the technology is transferred instead to an owned subsidiary (Ethier, 1986). More general discussions of buyer uncertainty of this type can be found in Teece (1986) and Rugman (1986).

This asymmetric information problem arises because the firm wants to maintain proprietary control over the results of its research due to the public goods nature of knowledge capital. But this asymmetric information problem then creates a moral hazard problem as well, in the Ethier model. The licensing contract is written before the results of the research are known or even before the research is undertaken (perhaps there could be string of products). But if the firm is going to maintain secrecy about the results of the research, how can the licensee know that the firm has put forth the contracted amount of research effort? The firm may claim that the results are poor when in fact it is due to a lack of effort (expense) on the firm's part. Of course, there exist the standard mechanism-design arguments to motivate full revelation, but the necessary contingent contracts might be difficult to write, particularly when there are multiple dimensions to the uncertainty. Internalization may be preferred to costly (rent dissipating) and/or incomplete contracts (Ethier, 1986). More general discussions of contracting costs and agent opportunism may be found in the writings of Buckley, Casson, Rugman, Teece, and Williamson.

A nice feature of the Ethier model is that it generates some predictions that are consistent with some of the stylized facts discussed earlier. For some rather complicated general equilibrium reasons that will not be explored here, the Ethier model predicts that direct investment is more likely to arise between similar countries, and for new and/or technically complex products (where the uncertainly of research outcomes is high).

A third informational asymmetry associated with newness focuses on the case where the potential licensee has superior information, usually about how the product will sell in its local market. This is more or less the opposite of Ethier's informational asymmetry. The multinational enterprise is reluctant to build a foreign plant without information about whether sales will be high or low, information that could be provided by the foreign agent. But the agent knows that if it reveals demand to be high, the firm may decide to produce directly, or a large share of the rents will be extracted from the foreign agent in subsequent periods. Thus, the agent's incentives can cause sales to be low even when demand is high. The multinational enterprise can avoid having to share informational rents with the licensee by direct investment (Horstmann and Markusen, 1996). This model has nice empirical implications in that direct investment is predicted as more likely when the host country is large, and the degree of uncertainty is small (e.g. highly developed host countries). Empirically, many firms do set up foreign wholesaling and servicing subsidiaries, possibly to deal with this sort of problem (Nicholas 1982, 1983; Nicholas et. al 1994; Thompson 1994; Zeile 1993).

A fourth problem is that the same property that makes knowledge easy to transfer internationally may mean that it is easily learned by new employees. If a firm licenses a technology to a foreign producer, the managers and workers may learn the technology quickly and be able to "defect," starting a new domestic firm in competition with the multinational enterprise. While this problem would exist to some extent within a firm as well, it is argued that a firm may more credibly commit than can a licensee to sharing the rents from a string of (uncertain) future products with the employees (Ethier and Markusen, 1996). Although many writers have discussed this problem in general terms, Rugman (1985, 1986) in particular views this as a cornerstone of internalization theory.

A fifth problem focusses on the costs of transferring technology. Certain aspects of a knowledge-intensive technology are bound up in the human capital of a firm's employees and even in the "company culture" (Teece, 1977, 1986). Such technology is costly to transfer arm's length, which does not contradict the possibility mentioned in the previous paragraph that the technology's value could be easily dissipated once the transfer does take place.

A sixth potential problem for licensing arises when the firm's intangible asset is a reputation for product quality. Product quality may only be observed after the product is purchased and used by the buyer. In this situation, the multinational enterprise cannot extract all rents from a licensee because, if it attempts to do so, the licensee can skimp on quality by producing an inferior substitute product for one period and earn positive single-period rents. To avoid this problem, it may be profitable to produce and sell through an owned subsidiary despite the added direct costs (Horstmann and Markusen, 1987b). This problem arises especially in franchising, where the firm wants a uniform level of quality across outlets. Each outlet manager (licensee) has an incentive to free ride on the reputation of the whole (Caves and Murphy, 1976). Among other empirically appealing results, the Horstmann-Markusen (1987b) model predicts that direct investment is more likely in larger markets, where the rent-sharing with the licensee that is necessary to sustain the firm's reputation is larger.

Finally, when a firm employs licensees, it must be concerned about a number of possible forms of moral hazard. For example, licensees may divert selling effort to competing products of other firms or simply shirk (Nicholas, 1983; Mathewson and Winter, 1985). Of course, these problems can occur within firms as well. Carlos (1994) and Carlos and Nicholas (1990) document how private trading on the part of agents caused difficulties for the Hudson's Bay and Royal African Companies, and how the Hudson's Bay Company was able to create an internal structure and company culture to mitigate the moral hazard and attendant losses. On the other hand, the Royal African Company went bankrupt. Intensive monitoring is one way to deal with licensees, but if a firm is going to monitor licensees with great care, it may be easier simply to own the foreign operation outright.

To add some concreteness to the idea of asset dissipation, we can outline a highly simplified version of Ethier and Markusen (1996). Consider a simple two-period model in which the multinational wishes to exploit a technology in a foreign market by licensing a foreign firm or by setting up a subsidiary (we will ignore exporting in this simple example). Because of the costs of doing business abroad, a licensing arrangement generates the most potential rents. The licensee masters the technology in the first period and can defect to start a rival firm in the second period. Similarly, the multinational can defect by issuing a license to a second firm in the second period. In other words, we make the strong assumption that no binding contracts can be written to prevent either firm from undertaking such a defection.

We will assume here, with no justification, that defection will not occur from within a subsidiary: that is, a part of a subsidiary will not split off to form another competitor. (This assumption is relaxed in Ethier and Markusen, 1996.) A subsidiary is thus (by definition) costly but "secure."

An example might be a multinational firm stationing home-country nationals in its foreign owned plant. While it is costly to keep home-country nationals oversees as opposed to hiring foreign nationals with roughly equivalent qualifications, it is reasonable to conjecture that the home-country nationals are less likely to defect and start a rival firm in the host country (due to language, cultural, visa barriers).

At the beginning of the second period, the multinational and the licensee make simultaneous moves, choosing whether to continue their original relationship. If both the multinational and the licensee defect, then the original licensee and the new licensee will compete as duopolists in the second period. For a two-period licensing contract to be self-enforcing, neither the multinational enterprise nor the licensee must wish to defect in the second period.

For the sake of illustration, and with some loss of generality, let us make some assumptions about the rents available in these different scenarios. If the license continues for both periods, let us refer to the total rents as 2R – F, where R are the rents available in each period and F as the physical capital cost that the licensee (or multinational) must incur to start production. (For simplicity, this example assumes no discounting.) If the multinational sets up a subsidiary, then the rents will be M, where M represents the rents (net of all costs) received when the subsidiary operates on its own. We will assume that $2R - F > M$, which means that the rents are larger if the licensing agreement continues. This assumption captures the idea discussed earlier that there are costs to establishing a business abroad.

The third situation is where the one-period license is followed by duopoly. In this case, the rents will be $R + D - 2F$, where D represents the total rents for both members of the duopoly in one period, and the capital costs F must be multiplied by 2 because with two separate producers the start-up costs must be incurred twice. For the purposes of this example, we posit that the rents from the duopoly option are lowest of these three scenarios; that is, $(2R - F) > M > (R + D - 2F)$.

As one final piece of notation, consider the licensing fee, which we will refer to as L_1 in period 1, and L_2 in period 2.

In this setting, what conditions must hold so that the licensing arrangement continues through both periods? For the license to continue, it must be better than the alternative, from the point of view of both the multinational and the subsidiary. Let us posit that, if one partner defects, that partner must incur the additional costs of F, and the nondefecting partner retains the original F.

For the licensee not to defect and start up production on its own, its second-period earnings ($R - L_2$, with no additional start-up costs) must be at least equal to $R - F$, its payoff from defecting. For the multinational enterprise, its licensing fee L_2 must be at least equal to $R - F$, its payoff from defecting.

$$R - L_2 \geq R - F \qquad \text{(incentive compatibility for the agent)}$$

$$L_2 \geq R - F \qquad \text{(incentive compatibility for the firms)}$$

Combining these two inequalities, licensing will be continued in the second period if $R < 2F$ that is, if the rent is no greater than twice the fixed costs.

Furthermore, if the $R < 2F$ condition holds, then the multinational can extract all rents from its licensee. In the second period, the fee $L_2 = F$ is the largest fee that the multinational can charge without causing the licensee to defect, and such a fee will also lead the firm to honor the agreement. The fee $L_2 = F$ leaves the licensee with rents $R - L_2 = R - F$ in the second period. The multinational can extract these with a fee $L_1 = 2R - F$ in the first period. In other words, the fee schedule $L_1 = 2R - F$ and $L_2 = F$ satisfies the (incentive compatibility) condition that neither partner will wish to defect in the second period and the (participation or individual rationality) condition that the licensee earns nonnegative profits (exactly zero in this case). Notice that $L_1 + L_2 = 2R$, which is to say that all the rents are collected by the multinational through the license fees. To sum up, if the condition $R < 2F$ holds, then the multinational will license, and it will earn all of the rents.

If the $R < 2F$ condition fails to hold—that is, if the rents are greater than twice the fixed costs—then both the firm and the licensee will defect in the second period. In this case, a duopoly game will result in the second period between the original and a second licensee. Assume that ownership of the original fixed cost F remains with the multinational. Then, the original licensee, now on its own, generates a net second–period income of $D/2 - F$, while the second licensee generates $D/2$ (using the original capital stock F). Knowing that defection is coming in the second period, the multinational is limited in what it can charge in the first period. All it can do is charge the first licensee a first–period fee of $L_1 = R + D/2 - F$, which just means that the most the multinational can demand is the second–period profits of the prospective defector. For the same reason, the multinational can charge the second licensee a second–period fee of $L_2 = D/2$. In this case, the total two– period profit for the multinational is $L_1 + L_2 - F = R + D - 2F$. Both licensees earn zero profits under this fee schedule, but while the multinational captures all rents, additional fixed costs are incurred, and some rents are dissipated by the duopoly competition. Thus, if the licensing condition fails to hold, the multinational will seek to avoid this duopoly outcome and will instead set up a subsidiary.

Remember, our earlier assumption was that the rents of a subsidiary arrangement are M, which exceed the rents of duopoly $R + D - 2F$.

Finally, consider the situation where $F = 0$. This can be interpreted as the case of a "pure" knowledge–capital technology; that is, when $F = 0$, the licensee can costlessly enter production in the second period after one period of learning–by–doing. Under the assumption that $F = 0$, it is clear that $R < 2F$ will fail to hold, and licensing will not sustain itself. As a result, the multinational chooses a costly subsidiary over a rent–dissipating licensing contract. We thus have a result that is consistent with both the theoretical ideas developed here and with some of the micro facts listed earlier. Direct investment in a subsidiary is more likely in cases where the technology has the joint–input characteristic of knowledge capital. The Ethier–Markusen model also predicts that multinationals (long–term relationships covering generations of products) are more likely to occur the more similar the home and host countries are in size and in relative factor endowments. While the latter involves subtle general equilibrium factor–market effects that I will not discuss here, the former (country size) result is easily seen in terms of the much simplified model presented here. A large host–country market is interpreted as a larger R relative to F, generating a larger incentive to defect from a licensing contract. Thus a subsidiary is chosen in a large market.

Conclusion

In some sense, this entire chapter is a summary of a great deal of literature, and to provide a summary of the summary seems a bit tedious. Thus, let me focus on a few points only.

The purpose of the chapter is to take a small step toward integrating the theory of the multinational enterprise with the theory of international trade and associated empirical evidence. A successful attempt should use a micromodel of the firm as suggested by the former literature and should predict that multinationals arise in situations consistent with actual evidence from the trade literature.

I use a micromodel of the firm based on the notion of knowledge capital, which has a joint-input characteristic across geographically separated production facilities, creating multiplant economies of scale. Such a model is consistent with extensive firm- and industry-level data on multinationals as noted earlier. Multinationals are then high fixed–cost firms competing with high marginal–cost domestic firms. In a general equilibrium setting, the model predicts that multinationals will dominate in equilibrium between countries that (a) have a high total income, (b) are similar in economic size, and (c) are similar in relative factor endowments. While much formal empirical work needs to be done, these predictions are at least superficially consistent with data that show two things: (1) direct investment has grown much faster than trade over the last two decades among the similar, high–income countries, and (2) direct investment from developed countries to other developed countries accounts for a larger share of all direct investment than the corresponding statistic for exports.

The knowledge-capital model (for lack of a better term) also fits well with the literature on internationalization motives for direct investment. The same public-goods property of knowledge capital that allows firms to exploit it in geographically separate production facilities also implies that the assets of the firm can be easily dissipated. Thus the risk of asset dissipation due to various informational difficulties suggests that firms may have a tendency to transfer knowledge-based assets internally rather that through arm's-length arrangements such as licensing

Notes

This is a revision and update of my paper, "The Boundaries of Multinational Firms and the Theory of International Trade," *Journal of Economic Perspectives* 9 (1995), 169–189. I would like to thank the American Economic Association for permission to reprint substantial portions of the *JEP* paper.

1. Much discussion, data, and many references are found in Caves (1996). For recent evidence on the points to follow, see Morck and Yeung (1991, 1992), Brainard (1993b,c), Blomstrom and Lipsey (1991), Grubaugh (1987), Dunning (1993), Ekholm (1995) and Beaudreau (1986). For events in which firms do transfer technology abroad, articles by Davidson and McFetridge (1984), Mansfield and Romeo (1980), Teece (1986), and Wilson (1977) show technology is more likely to be transferred internally within the firm by R&D–intensive firms producing new and technically complex products. Blomstrom and Zejan (1991) get similar results with respect to joint ventures: firms are less likely to seek a foreign partner when intangible assets are important.

2. For points 1, 2, and 3 see Brainard (1993a,b) and Ekholm (1995) in particular.

3. Regression coefficients on tariffs and transport costs or distance have often been insignificant and/or had the wrong sign in equations with some measure of multinationality as the dependent variable; for example, Beaudreau (1986) using extensive firm–specific data. Brainard (1993c) has mixed results for equations explaining the level of affiliate sales abroad. Part of the explanation seems to be that many firms have substantial imported content in their foreign production and export modest amounts (on average as noted above) back to their parent. In these respects tariffs and transport costs discourage affiliate production just like they discourage exports. However, using share equations, the share of affiliate sales in the total of affiliate sales and exports is increasing and significant in both freight charges and tariffs.

4. Insignificant effects of host–country taxes on inward direct investment have been found by Brainard (1993a,b), Morck and Yeung (1991), Hackett and Srinivasan (1997), and Wheeler and Mody (1992). Negative effects have been found by Grubert and Mutti (1991) and in a number of articles in Feldstein, Hines, and

Hubbard (1995). Schneider and Frey (1985) examine the role of political as well as economic variables.

5. See Hackett and Srinivasan (1997) and Wheeler and Mody (1992) for evidence on infrastructure. See Head, Ries, and Swenson (1995) and Wheeler and Mody (1992) for evidence on agglomeration.

6. Of course, it is possible to think of such services as simply being characterized by very high transport costs.

7. Attachment to the OLI framework is not universal, although it has been very appealing to trade economists. Rugman (1985, 1986, 1981) in particular argues that internalization is really the only thing that matters to understanding the multinational. OLI is also limited in that it only considers the conditions necessary for direct investment. It has little to offer about the choice among alternatives, such as licensing versus joint venture and versus exporting.

8. R&D, advertising, and technical/scientific workers are often used as proxies for firm–specific assets, and hence multinationality is highly correlated with firm–specific assets using these proxies (for citations, see the studies listed in footnote 2). Alternatively, firm–specific assets (intangible assets) are proxied as the market value of the firm minus the value of tangible assets (Morck and Yeung, 1991). In this case, firm–specific assets are defined as a residual, and this residual is highly correlated with multinationality. Care needs to be taken lest the argument become tautological: multinational enterprises tend to be firms with big residual values (unobserved intangible assets), and these residuals are firm–specific assets by definition.

9. The existence of the specific factor R in Y produces a general–equilibrium effect: the wage rate in terms of Y rises as the X sector expands, drawing more labor from Y. This effect "convexifies" the model and tends to limit the concentration of the X sector into one country.

10. Assume that multinational firms, when they exist in equilibrium, draw their labor for firm–specific fixed costs evenly between countries, so that we make no attempt in this minimal model to associate multinationals with particular countries.

11. This last statement is what Brainard (1993c) refers to as the "proximity–concentration hypothesis."

References

Beaudreau, Bernard C., *Managers, Learning and the Multinational Firm: Theory and Evidence*, PhD Dissertation, University of Western Ontario (unpublished). 1986.

Blomstrom, Magnus and Robert Lipsey, "Firm Size and Foreign Operations of Multinationals". *The Scandinavian Journal of Economics*, 1991, 93:1, 101–107.

Blomstrom, Magnus and Mario Zejan, "Why Do Multinational Firms Seek Out Joint Ventures?" *Journal of International Development*, 1991, 3:1, 53–63.

Blomstrom, Magnus, Robert Lipsey, and Ksenia Kulchycky, "U.S. and Swedish Direct Investment and Exports," in Robert E. Baldwin (ed.), *Trade Policy Issues and Empirical Analysis*. Chicago: University of Chicago Press. 1988, 259–297.

Brainard, S. Lael, "A Simple Theory of Multinational Corporations and Trade with a Trade–off between Proximity and Concentration," NBER Working Paper No. 4269, February 1993a.

———, "An Empirical Assessment of the Factor Proportions Explanation of Multinationals Sales," NBER Working Paper No. 4580, December 1993b.

———, "An Empirical Assessment of the Proximity–Concentration Tradeoff between Multinational Sales and Trade," NBER Working Paper No. 4583, December 1993c.

Buckley, Peter J. and Mark Casson, *The Economic Theory of the Multinational Enterprise*. London: Macmillan. 1985.

———, *The Future of the Multinational Enterprise*. London: Macmillan. 1989 (second edition).

Carlos, Ann, "Bonding and the Agency Problem: Evidence from the Royal African Company 1672–1691," *Explorations in Economic History*, July 1994, 31:313–335.

Carlos, Ann and Stephen Nicholas, "Agency Problems in Early Chartered Companies: The Case of the Hudson's Bay Company," *Journal of Economic History*, December 1990, 50:4, 853–875.

Casson, Mark, *The Firm and the Market: Studies in Multinational Enterprise and the Scope of the Firm*. Oxford: Blackwell and Cambridge: MIT Press. 1987.

Caves, Richard E., *Multinational Enterprise and Economic Analysis*. London: Cambridge University Press. 1996, second edition.

Caves, Richard E. and William F. Murphy II, "Franchising: Firms, Markets, and Intangible Assets, *Southern Economic Journal*, April 1976, 572–586.

Davidson William H. and Donald G. McFetridge, "International Technology Transactions and the Theory of the Firm," *Journal of Industrial Economics*. 1984, 32, 253–264.

Denekamp, Johannes and Michael J. Ferrantino, "Substitution and Complementarity of U.S. Exports and Foreign Based Affiliate Sales in a Demand Based Gravity System." Working paper, 1992.

Dick, Andrew R, "Strategic Trade Policy and Welfare: The Empirical Consequences of Cross–Ownership," *Journal of International Economics*. 1993, 35, 227–249.

Dunning, John H., *International Production and the Multinational Enterprise*. London: George Allen and Unwin. 1981.

———, "Trade, Location of Economic Activity and MNE: A Search for an Eclectic Approach," in B. Ohlin, P. O. Hesselborn, and P.M. Wijkman (eds.), *The International Allocation of Economic Activity*. London: Macmillan. 1977.

———, *The Globalization of Business*. London: Routledge, 1993.

Ekholm, Karolina, *Multinational Production and Trade in Technological Knowledge*, Lund Economic Studies, no. 58, 1995.

Ethier, Wilfred J., "The Multinational Firm", *Quarterly Journal of Economics*, 1986, 101, 805–833.

Ethier, Wilfred J., "Multinational Firms in the Theory of International Trade," in E. Bacha (ed.), *Economics in a Changing World, Vol. 4: Development, Trade, and the Environment*. London: Macmillan. 1994.

Ethier, Wilfred J. and James R. Markusen, "Multinational Firms, Technology Diffusion and Trade," *Journal of International Economics*, 1996, 41, 1–28.

Feldstein, Martin, James R. Hines Jr., and R. Glenn Hubbard, (eds.), The *Effects of Taxation on Multinational Corporations*, Chicago: University of Chicago Press. 1995.

Froot, Kenneth A., *Foreign Direct Investment*, Chicago: University of Chicago Press. 1993.

Graham, Edward M. and Paul R. Krugman, "The Surge in Foreign Direct Investment in the 1980s," in Kenneth A. Froot, (ed.), *Foreign Direct Investment*, Chicago: University of Chicago Press. 1993. 13–36.

Grubaugh, S., "Determinants of Direct Foreign Investment", *Review of Economics and Statistics*, February 1987, 69, 149–151.

Grubert, Harry and John Mutti (1991), "Taxes, Tariffs, and Transfer Pricing in Multinational Corporate Decision Making," *Review of Economics and Statistics*, 285–293.

Hackett, Steven C. and Krisna Srinivasan, "Do supplier Switching Costs Differ Across Japanese and U.S. Multinational Firms?" *Japan and the World Economy*, 1997, forthcoming.

Haddad, M. and Ann Harrison (1993), "Are There Positive Spillovers from Direct Foreign Investment?" *Journal of Development Economics* 42, 51–74.

Head, Keith, John Ries, and Deborah Swenson (1995), "Agglomeration Benefits and Location Choice: Evidence from Japanese Manufacturing Investments in the United States," *Journal of International Economics* 38, 223–247.

Helpman, Elhanan, "A Simple Theory of Trade with Multinational Corporations," *Journal of Political Economy*, 1984, 92, 451–471.

———, "Multinational Corporations and Trade Structure," *Review of Economic Studies*, 1985, 52, 443–458.

Helpman, Elhanan and Paul R. Krugman, *Market Structure and Foreign Trade*, Cambridge: MIT Press. 1985.

Horstmann, Ignatius J. and James R. Markusen, "Strategic Investments and the Development of Multinationals," *International Economic Review*, 1987a, 28, 109–121.

———, "Licensing Versus Direct Investment: A Model of Internalization by the Multinational Enterprise," *Canadian Journal of Economics*, 1987b, 20, 464–481.

———, "Endogenous Market Structures in International Trade," *Journal of International Economics*, 1992, 32, 109–129.

———, "Exploring New Markets: Direct Investment, Contractual Relations, and the Multinational Enterprise," *International Economic Review*, 1996, 37, 1–19.

Hummels, David L. and Robert M. Stern, "Evolving Patterns of North American Merchandise Trade and Foreign Direct Investment, 1960–1990," *The World Economy*, January 1994, 17:1, 5– 29.

Hymer, Stephen H., The International Operations of National Firms: A Study of Direct Foreign Investment. Cambridge: MIT Press. 1976.

Julius, DeAnne, *Global Companies and Public Policy*, London: Royal Institute of International Affairs. 1990.

Kindleberger, Charles P., *American Business Abroad*, New Haven: Yale University Press. 1969.

———, *Multinational Excursions*, Cambridge: MIT Press. 1978.

Levinsohn, James A., "Strategic Trade Policy When Firms Can Invest Abroad: When Are Tariffs and Quotas Equivalent?" *Journal of International Economics*, August 1989, 27:1/2, 129–146.

Lipsey, Robert E., "Foreign Direct Investment in the United States: Changes over Three Decades," in Kenneth A. Froot (ed.), *Foreign Direct Investment*, Chicago: University of Chicago Press. 1993. 113–172.

———, "Outward Direct Investment and the U.S. Economy," NBER Working Paper No. 4691, March 1994.

Mansfield, Edwin and Anthony Romeo, "Technology Transfer to Overseas Subsidiaries by U.S. Firms," *Quarterly Journal of Economics* 1980, 94, 737–750.

Markusen, James R., "Multinationals, Multi–Plant Economies, and the Gains from Trade," *Journal of International Economics* 1984, 16, 205–226.

Markusen, James R., Thomas F. Rutherford, and Linda Hunter, "Trade Liberalization in a Multinational–Dominated Industry", *Journal of International Economics*, 1995, 38, 95–118.

Markusen, James R. and Anthony J. Venables, "The Increased Importance of Multinationals in North American Economic Relationships: A Convergence Hypothesis," in Matthew W. Canzoneri, Wilfred J. Ethier, and Vitoria Grilli (eds), *The New Transatlantic Economy*, London: Cambridge University Press, 1996.

———, "Multinational Firms and the New Trade Theory," NBER and University of Colorado Working Paper, 1996.

Mathewson, G. Frank and Ralph A. Winter, "The Economics of Franchise Contracts," *Journal of Law and Economics*, 1985, 28, 503–526.

Morck, Randall and Bernard Yeung, "Why Investors Value Multinationality," *Journal of Business*, 1991, 64:2, 165–187.

———, "Internalization: An Event Study Test," *Journal of International Economics*, August 1992, 33:1/2, 41–56.

Motta, Massimo, "Multinational Firms and the Tariff–Jumping Argument," *European Economic Review*, 1992, 36, 1557–1571.

Nicholas, Stephen, "British Multinational Investment Before 1939," *Journal of European Economic History* 1982, 11, 605–630.

———, "Agency Contracts, Institutional Modes, and the Transition to Foreign Direct Investment by British Manufacturing Multinationals Before 1939," *Journal of Economic History*, 1983, 43, 675–686.

Nicholas, Stephen, William Purcell, David Merritt, and A. Whitwell, *Foreign Direct Investment in Australia in the 1990s.* University of Melbourne unpublished manuscript, 1994.

Rugman, Alan M., *Inside the Multinationals: The Economics of Internal Markets*, London: Croom Helm and New York: Columbia University Press. 1981.

———, "Internalization is Still a General Theory of Foreign Direct Investment," *Weltwirtschaftliches Archiv*, 1985.

———, "New Theories of the Multinational Enterprise: An Assessment of Internalization Theory," *Bulletin of Economic Research*, 1986. 38:2, 101–118.

Schneider, Friedrich and Bruno S. Frey, "Economic and Political Determinatnts of Foreign Direct Investment," *World Development*, 1985, 13, 161–175.

Smith, Alasdair, "Strategic Investment, Multinational Corporations, and Trade Policy," *European Economic Review*, 1987, 31, 89–96.

Teece, David, *The Multinational Corporation and the Resource Cost of International Technology Transfer*, Cambridge: Ballinger. 1986.

———, "Technology Transfer By Multinational Firms: The Resource Cost of Transferring Technological Know–How", *Economic Journal*, 1977, 87, 242–261.

Thompson, A. G., "Relational Problems in Australian Business Ventures in Southeast Asia," mimeo, University of Melbourne, 1994.

UNCTAD, *World Investment Report 1993: Transnational Corporations and Integrated International Production*, New York: United Nations. 1993.

Wheeler, David and Ashoka Mody, "International Investment Location Decisions," *Journal of International Economics*, 1992, 33, 57–76.

Williamson, Oliver E., *Markets and Hierarchies: Analysis and Antitrust Implications: A Study in the Economics of Internal Organizations*, New York: Free Press. 1975.

———, "The Modern Corporation: Origins, Evolution, Attributes," *Journal of Economic Literature*, 1981, 19:4, 1537–1568.

Wilson, Robert W., "The Effect of Technological Environment and Product Rivalry on R&D Effort and Licensing of Inventions," *Review of Economics and Statistics*, 1977, 59, 171–78.

Zeile, William J., "Merchandise Trade of U.S. Affiliates of Foreign Companies," *Survey of Current Business*, October 1993, 52–65.

7

Foreign Direct Investment and Internalization in Processed Foods

Alan M. Rugman

Introduction

For over a decade it has been well known that international trade and investment is dominated by a small set of multinational enterprises (MNEs). These MNEs, in turn, have their home bases and headquarters in the large triad markets of the United States, Japan, and the European Community. An MNE is defined as a company with production in at least one foreign market besides its domestic market, that is, an MNE is engaged in international production.

Today, there are over thirty thousand MNEs, as identified by the *World Investment Report* of the United Nations (1996). However, the largest five hundred of these MNEs account for well over 80 percent of the world's stock of foreign direct investment (FDI). Of these five hundred large MNEs, over 80 percent of them are from the triad (Rugman, 1981, 1996). In addition, these super MNEs account for over half of the world's merchandise trade (Rugman, 1993).

An example may help. The largest trading partner of the United States is Canada. Nearly one-third of Canada's imports from the United States are made by three MNEs: Ford Canada, GM Canada, and Chrysler Canada. These three (foreign-owned) MNEs also account for one-third of Canada's exports. In other words, there is a large amount of intra-industry, indeed intra-firm, trade conducted by a very small number of large MNEs. As few as fifty MNEs, Canadian-owned as well as U.S.-owned, account for well over 70 percent of Canada's two-way trade with the United States. These fifty MNEs also account for well over 80 percent of the two-way stocks of FDI (Rugman, 1990). The Canadian pattern is representative of other advanced countries. In the triad, there is an asymmetric influence of a few hundred very large MNEs accounting for the majority of international trade and FDI. The food processing MNEs are part of this group.

In Table 7.1, data are reported on the home base and headquarters of the world's fifty largest food processing firms as identified by Henderson, Sheldon and Pick (see Ch. 2, this volume), who state that "these 50 firms account for 40 percent of the gross output of manufactured foods in the associated countries." As can be seen, all but three of these fifty MNEs are in the triad, with twenty-one of them being U.S.-owned and based.

The objective of this chapter is to review literature on the theory of the MNE that is relevant to producing models of the activities of these fifty large food processing MNEs. The principal focus will be upon internalization theory and its key variants, including the resource-based view of the firm.

Internalization by Food Processing MNEs

The advantages of internalization are that the integrated MNE can monitor, meter, and regulate internally the nature and extent of its firm-specific advantage (FSA). For food processing MNEs internalization thereby reduces such transaction costs as buyer uncertainty, information asymmetries, and opportunism.

The internalization of the vertical supply chain by the MNE ensures that high-quality products can reach final consumers more efficiently than under any alternative system. The MNEs can realize a premium on their food products because they guarantee high quality and regular supply, thereby reducing the risks to final consumers of inferior alternative sources of supply.

Vertical integration in the food industry allows MNEs to better control the sources of supply, reducing the risks of interruptions in supply and variation in quality of the product. Control of the transportation and

TABLE 7.1 The Triad Basis of the World's Fifty Largest Food Processing Firms, 1993

Headquarters Country/Bloc	*Number of Firms*
United States	21
European Community	16
Japan	10
Other	3

Source: Adapted from Table 2.3 in Henderson, Sheldon, and Pick (Ch. 2, this volume).

distribution of the product reduces the risks of spoilage and waste and helps to ensure high, uniform quality in the final delivered product. Through internalization the MNE can meter and monitor the use of its product, since it is then able to use centralized information control systems to extract, produce, and distribute a high-quality, uniform final product to consumers at a premium price. The MNE can better time the coordination of the stages in the value chain than can independent contractors, and the MNE develops internal managerial skills in the techniques of coordination and internalization. These managerial skills, in time, become synonymous with the image of the MNE and turn the MNE itself into a brand-name, differentiated product.

Another transaction cost arising from perishability is opportunism, that is, the ability to act out of self interest and in a manner prejudicial to others. Again, internalization will help the MNE to minimize opportunistic behavior. When there is a perishable product, there is an incentive for rival firms (especially in a different political regime) to deny market access or entry for a specific time period, thereby destroying the product. To prevent such opportunistic behavior, the MNE can internalize and start to process the food product. The greater the degree of processing (in general) the harder it is for rivals to succeed in opportunistic behavior since the degree of perishability of the produce has fallen.

Internalization should not be confused with nonequity forms of foreign activity such as licensing and joint ventures. There will be a tendency to use internalization as opposed to other modes when there is a high risk of dissipation of the FSA (Rugman, 1981). This occurs when property rights have been developed by the MNE to protect its FSAs, such as new knowledge, process technology and management, marketing, and distribution skills. To some extent, internal know-how can be codified and made into routines. However, many of the FSAs of an MNE involve intangible management skills and related know-how that cannot be separated from the process of internal management. The MNE is an institution that embodies the joint product of intangible know-how and an organizational structure to prevent the dissipation of its FSAs.

Licensing, franchising, and joint ventures are some of the alternative modes of international activity to FDI. In general, the MNE will use such modes when the risk of dissipation of the FSA is low, for example when a mature product is being produced, when strong legal contracts can be developed, or when interpersonal managerial relationships can be cultivated. Franchising is an alternative to internalization by horizontal integration when routines can be established and the knowledge or brand name codified such that the risk of dissipation is lowered. Licensing is a viable alternative when there are government regulations that prevent entry of an MNE (as in the beer industry) and when the product is mature or when intangible FSAs can be codified. Joint ventures occur under similar circumstances but are perhaps likely to be less common in food processing than in more research and development and capital intensive sectors such as autos and aerospace.

Given the diversity of products produced by the world's fifty largest food processing companies, it is to be expected that a mix of such modes will exist. Even within the same MNE, it is possible that some product lines will be internalized (where there are high risks of dissipation), whereas more mature product lines, or ones with routines and codification, can be conducted through licensing, franchising and/or joint venture agreements. The choice of foreign entry mode and switches between entry modes for an MNE has been explored by Rugman (1981). There is no reason to think that these principles would not apply to food processing MNEs.

Related Literature on Internalization Theory

Casson (1982) has examined the transaction cost of buyer uncertainty as applied to multinational food processors. In the food industry he has found that the lack of information by consumers about quality leads to the creation of MNEs with brand names to reduce buyer uncertainty. These food processing MNEs engage in backward integration to reduce the variation in supply, which would occur through the risks of independent contracting. Casson finds that internalization theory explains the development of the banana industry.

An application of internalization theory to the fish processing industry has been made by Rutenberg (1982) and Acheson (1985). Fish are perishable and have erratic availability and great variation in quality. A fish MNE sells a "portfolio" of fish products to the final consumer, diversifying risks through the advantages of economies of scale not available to smaller, independent fish producers.

The fishing industry retains a large number of independent contractors, with a history and culture of self-sufficiency. The MNE buys from these independent suppliers but is subject to the variable supply and quality of the seasonal fish market. Consequently, there is pressure on the MNE to integrate backwards by the use of factory ships and related capital-intensive measures to bypass the risks of the fish extraction market. The fish MNE can freeze and store the fish better than smaller producers and it can better access the distribution system through internalization. For historical reasons, Canadian and U.S. fishermen have been able to retain an independent position for the "in-shore" fishery. Thus North American-based MNEs have not succeeded in full backward integration. In contrast, the Japanese-based factory ships are more efficient in this dimension.

However, all triad-based MNEs are in a similar state of competitiveness in terms of distribution and marketing, since they all control sales of a wide variety of species and can provide both economies of scale and economies of scope.

The fish MNEs offer a portfolio of fish products and are able to practice brand management through internalization of most of the value chain in fish production. In Canada, the East coast-based National Sea Products has survived as an MNE in the last five years, despite the virtual destruction of its staple, the cod fishery. It has been able to lay off processing workers and close some smaller fish processing plants while keeping others open by importing fish from other sources. If it were not for the integrated nature of its operations and the advantage of internalization, I doubt that National Sea could have survived these last five years. In 1995, it recorded a net profit on its activities.

The Resource-Based View

Another stream of literature of relevance in the modelling of food-based MNEs is the resource-based view (RBV) of the firm developed by organization theorists and economists. The RBV identifies managerial (Penrose, 1959) or related resources as the sources of competitive advantage and core competencies in a firm (Wernerfelt, 1984; Conner, 1991). More generally, managerial resources confer enduring competitive advantages when they are rare, hard to imitate, have no direct substitutes, and provide entry barriers (Barney, 1991). In this manner, firm-specific resources generate rents to the firm. Resources need to have firm-specific value, which means that they must be difficult to create, buy, substitute, or imitate (Peteraf, 1993).

Advocates of the RBV state that internalization is not due to market imperfections but to performance gains from the access to internal routines (Conner, 1991), such as the codification of know-how within organizations (Kogut and Zander, 1992, 1993). The latter authors state that a market imperfection (such as the externality in the pricing of knowledge as a public good) is not required to deduce that an MNE will internalize. All that is necessary is that the internal transfer of knowledge is done more efficiently than by rival firms. This gives the MNE its FSA and competitive advantage.

I believe that the resource-based view is a subcase of internalization theory, as developed by Rugman (1981), building upon the transaction cost economics approach (TCE) of Coase (1937) and Williamson (1975). For example, in the aforementioned public goods argument for knowledge, the key aspect of internalization is the securing of property rights (ownership) to overcome the externality of market failure. The MNE is an internalizer with ownership of its FSA, and, if any rents eventually occur, then these are part of the benefits of internalization. Thus, the RBV is not a stand-alone explanation of organizational learning and management skills but is a subcase of internalization theory. To this extent, the TCE approach is fully consistent with internalization theory.

A confusing point is that the RBV argues that the TCE view of markets and hierarchies is too extreme and that there are middle (in between) cases of business networks. These networks are built upon relational exchanges of organizations embedded in their social and institutional context. Since embeddedness (in networks) inhibits opportunistic behavior, Granovetter (1985) has shown that business networks are efficient modes of organization. However, he has not argued that the RBV is an alternative to ownership-based internalization. Again, this would be a wrong-headed approach, since networks are fully consistent with internalization theory—all that happens is that there is deinternalization to the network when the costs of internalization outweigh the benefits. This has been demonstrated by Rugman, Verbeke, and D'Cruz (1995).

While the TCE approach is associated with market failure leading to internalization, some writers have overstated their criticisms of TCE. One example is when Ghoshal and Moran state that "opportunism is a central concept in Williamson's TCE logic" and is the "ultimate cause for the failure of markets and for the existence of organization" (Ghoshal and Moran, 1996). But there are many aspects of TCE apart from opportunism that are relevant for the internalization decisions of food MNEs, such as buyer uncertainty and information asymmetries. In any case, as discussed earlier, there are examples of opportunism in the value chain of the food processing sector that provide incentives for internalization by MNEs.

The key attribute of internalization theory is that it provides a broad framework with a focus upon the key actor on the stage of global business, the MNE. The MNE will have an FSA (now called a "core competence" by writers in strategic management). The risk of dissipation of the FSA can be minimized through its strategic use within the internal market of the MNE. The FSA can be knowledge- or know-how-based, and it can depend upon the skills of its management team for successful exploitation. This part of the internalization approach has been taken on board by international economists, as reviewed by Markusen (1995). However, the extent of internalization is an empirical issue that is difficult to test since know-how-type FSAs are intangible and need to be measured by proxies such as the profitability and performance of the MNE against counterfactual modes of exporting, licensing, joint venture or network activities. This is a messy business that has led to considerable confusion in the empirical literature and a reluctance by economists to fully accept internalization theory.

Classification of the World's Fifty Largest Food Processing MNEs

An additional source of confusion in the potential application of internalization theory to food processing MNEs is that TCE makes a strong distinction between markets and hierarchies (Williamson, 1975, 1985). The original insight that the firm is an alternative to the market is in Coase (1937); it won him the Nobel Prize in Economics for 1991. Many forms of transaction are a mix of markets and hierarchies (Hennart, 1993). Firms and markets have institutional frameworks that enable a mix of organizing principles to exist. Hennart (1993) argues that there are two basic methods of organization:

1. the hierarchy (MNE) control of behavior, which involves the MNE in minimizing opportunism by imposing shirking costs and through behavioral organization; and
2. the market's control of output through a price system, which also involves the minimization of cheating costs and requires that output be measured.

The first method of MNE hierarchical control of behavior involves an indirect control of output. The second method of markets uses the prices system to control output with indirect control of behavior. However, as it is apparent that control of output and behavior are the critical organizing principles, then in practice what we observe is a mix of organizing principles in institutions like MNEs and markets. The allocation between the choice of behavior and price constraints will depend upon the marginal cost of using each organizing principle.

Hennart (1993) demonstrates that the total costs of using each organizing principle (method of organization) is the cost of constraining behavior (or measuring output) plus the residual cost of failing to do it fully. Since the marginal cost of using each organizing principle is usually increasing, institutions rarely specialize in the exclusive use of a single organizing principle. Therefore, the end result is usually a mix of markets (prices) and hierarchy (MNEs).

To illustrate this, consider Table 7.2. Here five types of firm-specific advantages are listed. Each of these can be internalized by the MNE, by either backward or forward vertical integration, or by other methods of FDI. Alternatively, there is a contractual solution, as listed in the final column, that is, a form of deintegration. As discussed by Hennart (1993) and Rugman (1996), the choice of internalization versus deinternalization will depend upon the relative costs and benefits of each mode, taking into account the overall organizational context of the MNE as an institution.

Food processing firms will be explained by different combinations of modes in Table 7.2. For example, McDonald's has been very successful

TABLE 7.2 Firm-Specific Advantages and Modes of Internalization and Contracting

Type of FSA	*Type of Internalization*	*Type of Contractual Solution*
Knowledge	Horizontal FDI	License
Reputation	Horizontal FDI	Franchise
Control over Raw Materials	Vertical FDI (backward)	Supply Contracts
Distribution Services	Vertical FDI (forward)	Distribution Contracts
Financial Capital	FDI	Loans

Source: J.-F. Hennart, 1993.

through the mode of franchising and it has developed a competitive advantage through its skills in building a global reputation on its brand name. The franchising mode has allowed McDonald's to monitor and meter the use of its FSA and it has not been necessary for McDonald's to be an internalized MNE. Other food MNEs with franchising strengths include Pepsi and Coca Cola.

In contrast, most of the food MNEs in Table 7.1 are engaged in internalization. For example, in an earlier piece of research (Rugman and McIlveen, 1995), Seagram was found to have strong FSAs in its internationally recognized brand-name products, in its marketing, and in its distribution network of affiliated dealers. The success of Seagram was fully explained by internalization theory. In order to reach this conclusion it was necessary to conduct extensive research using company annual reports, company histories, industry analyses, but of greatest importance, detailed interviews with senior company executives.

To properly classify the fifty largest food processing firms in Table 7.1 by internalization or contracting mode would require a similar research effort. However, it is possible to use some judgment in preparing a preliminary classification.

From our analysis of these food processing MNEs, it is apparent that the majority of them are internalizing and have FSAs in brand names. This would include most of the beer and beverage firms (Kirin, Anheuser-Busch, Guinness, Asahi, Bass, Suntory, Seagram, Sapporo, Heineken, and Fosters). The beer firms have to deal with government regulations, which often discriminate in favor of domestic brewers and deny market entry to foreign MNEs unless they license. Some firms like Heineken rely on exports from a home base to gain entry, while most others attempt to buy up breweries in protected markets or agree to license.

Another set of food MNEs with strong brand-name FSAs realized as internalization advantages would include firms like Nestlé, Philip Morris/Kraft, Mars, Sara Lee, RJR Nabisco, Heinz, Campbell Soup, Kellogg, Quaker Oats, Tate & Lyle, United Biscuits, and so on. These are MNEs with a variety of high-quality food products well known to consumers through advertising and efficient distribution networks. The requirement of providing consistently high and uniform quality to final consumers requires internalization and access to regular shelf space in retail stores and supermarkets. There does not have to be ownership of the retailers provided the food MNEs can make long-term arrangements to place their branded products with the retailers. The salespeople and agents of the MNE maintain and monitor this relationship in order to reduce opportunism, and their compensation can be determined by a combination of salary and commission depending upon the strength of the interfirm linkages between MNE and retailer.

To reiterate, it is necessary to conduct original research in order to properly classify the top fifty food processing firms in Table 7.1. The preliminary classification here is into three types: franchising MNEs (such as Coca Cola), brand-name brewers and distillers (such as Guinness and Seagram), and brand-name packaged food MNEs (such as Nestlé and Kellogg). However, what is apparent even from this preliminary look at the fifty largest food processing MNEs is how useful the internalization theory concept is as a starting point for analysis and classification.

Business Network Relationships

The Japanese food MNEs in Table 7.1 are affiliated with other companies in the *keiretsu* form of business networks. For example, Kirin Brewery is part of the Mitsubishi *keiretsu*, Suntory is part of Sanwa, and Sapporo is part of Fuji. In Japan, the distribution of beer is closely regulated by each of the *keiretsu*. For example, Gerlach (1992) shows that Kirin Brewery was a previous member of the Mitsubishi group. Today, Kirin beer only is stocked at supermarkets in the Mitsubishi *keiretsu*. Similarly, since the 1960s, Sapporo beer only is available in retail outlets affiliated with the Fuji group. Asahi Breweries has been an exclusive supplier to all other parts of the Sumitono *keiretsu* since the early 1970s. The fourth brewery in Japan is Suntory, and since the 1980s it has developed closer ties with the Sanwa *keiretsu*.

As exclusive suppliers, these four beer firms do not need to develop vertical integration and internalization, since their key supplier position with the *keiretsu* achieves all of the benefits of internalization without equity control being required. To a large extent this is a location-bound FSA that is determined by a lack of opportunism exhibited in Japanese cultural and business dealings.

In a North American and European context, it is unlikely that the *keiretsu* form of organization could operate, due to a more competitive and individualistic set of cultural and business norms. Indeed, the Japanese form of business network has been difficult to transplant to North America in the auto sector and will be even more difficult when access to distribution networks and marketing outlets is required. An attempt to develop a related "five partners/flagship" model of business networks within the cultural context of North America has been made by D'Cruz and Rugman (1992, 1993) and it would be useful to apply it to the food processing sector.

In general, such an exercise would reveal that most of the North American and European food processing MNEs would still prefer internalization when there is the need to maintain such nonlocation-bound FSAs as brand-name products and global distribution networks. There will be some movement toward the growing use of business networks once "flagship" relationships can be developed. These are intangible managerial relationships between key suppliers, key customers, MNEs, and key partners in the nonbusiness infrastructure. I am not aware of such developments in the non-Japanese MNEs listed in Table 7.1, but research could be conducted into these network relationships.

Foreign companies that are successful in Japan are those with strong brand names plus an ability to adapt to the different culture and network system in Japan. Examples of successful foreign-affiliated companies are Coca Cola, McDonald's, and Nestlé, which are the leaders in soft drink, fast foods, and instant coffee, respectively. Others that are successful are Del Monte for tomato juice and Remy Martin for liquor (Czinkota and Woronoff, 1991). In terms of sales in Japan, Nestlé ranks second in the foodstuffs sector after Kirin Brewery (Morgan and Morgan, 1991).

A key implication of the business network approach for the food processing sector can serve as a warning against simplistic applications of trade and investment models. The traditional measure of an industry's international exposure is its ratio of exports to total sales. As reported by Henderson, Sheldon, and Pick (Ch. 2, this volume), the U.S. "all food and kindred products" category of food manufacturing industries has only 4.8 percent of its gross output exported. Even if processed seafood and liquors were to be added to this category (as they should be), it would not increase this ratio substantially. In terms of international trade theory, this is a "nontraded" sector. Yet, as interpreted correctly by these authors, international business activity is better measured by the ratio of all foreign sales to total sales, where foreign sales include overseas production (by MNE subsidiaries) as well as exports from the home base. Since sales by foreign affiliates of U.S. processed food firms are over four times the value of U.S. exports of processed foods, the total foreign sales ratio is over 20 percent of total sales. For MNEs from nations smaller than the United States, the proportion of foreign to total sales will be much greater. For example, Rugman and McIlveen (1985) reported foreign to total sales for Seagram of 92 percent.

Another implication is that the economic impact of the food processing sector is probably even greater than is explained by measurement of the activities of MNEs. Using the D'Cruz and Rugman (1992, 1993) business network model, it can be noted that some firms with zero exports are actually engaged in international business, for example as key suppliers or key customers to a food processing MNE. The extent and nature of international competition is pervasive across most sectors of manufacturing, and the food processing sector is no exception.

Role of Government in Internalization

Several implications follow from the recognition of the key role of MNEs as international producers, whereby both exports and foreign affiliate sales are important. Due to the concentration of the fifty largest food processing MNEs in the triad, the behavior of individual MNEs needs to be modelled in a strategic dimension. Success in food processing will not just depend upon the efficient use of home based natural resources and the development of natural FSAs, but it will also be dependent upon securing market access to other triad markets. There is a large scope for lobbying of governments in order to erect protectionist entry barriers. The result can be a "shelter-type" strategy, which will have differential effects across the triad (Rugman and Verbeke, 1990).

It can be useful to think of government-imposed barriers to trade (such as tariffs) and other regulations (such as nontariff barriers to trade such as the discriminatory use of health codes and environmental regulations) as "unnatural" market imperfections. Such a distinction is made in Rugman, Lecraw, and Booth (1985). In general, the existence of unnatural market imperfections can provide a stream of reasons for internalization, which are parallel to the TCE reasons.

In turn, it is possible for MNEs to operate strategically in their use of unnatural market imperfections, as demonstrated by Rugman and Verbeke (1990). For example, in terms of the use of countervailing duty and antidumping actions, it is possible for Canadian agricultural producers, being denied access to the larger U.S. market, to use the dispute settlement mechanism of the North American Free Trade Agreement to help remove the role of unnatural market imperfections that would otherwise lead to internalization (Rugman and Anderson, 1990).

Conclusion

The central point of this paper is that the modern theory of the MNE, namely the theory of internalization (Rugman, 1981), can be applied to food processing. The fifty largest food processing MNEs are engaged in vertical integration to overcome market imperfections affecting the quality, perishability, and timely delivery of food products to final consumers who suffer from buyer uncertainty. A prevalent characteristic of food processing is the existence of brand-name products and well-known MNEs that internalize to reduce buyer uncertainty and overcome other transaction costs such as opportunism and information asymmetries.

Despite much of the food processing sector being a mature commodity business, the incentive to internalize remains when its benefits outweigh its costs. The existence of franchising, licensing, and joint ventures in food processing does not invalidate internalization theory as a general theory of FDI. For example, there will be franchises when horizontal investment no longer needs to be internalized. This could occur where there is a low risk of dissipation of an FSA due to the codification of know-how and the use of routines to manage the governance of organizational relationships. The behavior of food processing MNEs is not idiosyncratic but is fully compatible with the modern theory of the MNE. Indeed, even a business networks/cluster approach builds upon the central role of internalization theory as an explanation of MNEs.

Notes

I am grateful to my colleagues Ed Safarian and Brian Silverman at the University of Toronto for very helpful comments on an earlier draft. Also useful were questions asked by the participants at the Minneapolis conference of June 1996, in particular the discussant, Michèle Veeman of the University of Alberta.

References

Acheson, James M. (1985) "The Maine Lobster Market: Between Market and Hierarchy," *Journal of Law, Economics and Organizations* 1:2 (Fall), pp. 385–398.

Barney, Jay (1991) "Firm Resources and Sustained Competitive Advantage," *Journal of Management* 17, pp.99–120.

Casson, Mark (1982) "Transaction Costs and the Theory of the Multinational Enterprise," pp. 24–42 in Alan M. Rugman (ed.) *New Theories of the Multinational Enterprise* (New York: St. Martin's Press).

Coase, Ronald H. (1937) "The Nature of the Firm," *Economica* IV:386–403.

Conner, Kathleen R. (1991) "A Historical Comparison of Resource-Based Theory and Five Schools of Thought within Industrial Economics," *Journal of Management* 17, pp.121–54.

Czinkota, Michael R. and Jon Woronoff (1991) *Unlocking Japan's Markets: Seizing Marketing and Distribution Opportunities in Today's Japan* (Chicago: Probus).

D'Cruz, Joseph R. and Alan M. Rugman (1992) "Business Networks for International Competitiveness," *Business Quarterly* 56:4 (Spring): 101–7.

———. (1993) "Developing International Competitiveness: The Five Partners Model," *Business Quarterly* 58:2 (Winter): 60–72.

Gerlach, Michael L. (1992) *Alliance Capitalism: The Social Organization of Japanese Business* (Berkeley, CA: University of California Press).

Ghoshal, Sumantra and Peter Moran (1996) "Bad for Practice: A Critique of the Transaction Cost Theory," *Academy of Management Review* 21:1 (January), pp.13–47.

Granovetter, Mark (1985) "Economic Action and Social Structure: The Problem of Embeddedness," *American Journal of Sociology* 91:3, pp.481–510.

Hennart, Jean-François (1993) "Explaining the Swollen Middle: Why Most Transactions are a Mix of Price and Hierarchy," *Organization Science* 4:4, pp. 529–47.

Kogut, Bruce and Udo Zander (1992) "Knowledge of the Firm, Combinative Capabilities and the Replication of Technology," *Organization Science* 3:3, pp.383–97.

——— (1993) "Knowledge of the Firm and the Evolutionary Theory of the Multinational Corporation," *Journal of International Business Studies* 244 (December), pp.625–45.

Markusen, James R. (1995) "The Boundaries of Multinational Firms and the Theory of International Trade," *Journal of Economic Perspectives* 9: 169–189.

Morgan, James C. and J. Jeffrey Morgan (1991) *Cracking the Japanese Market: Strategies for Success in the New Global Economy* (New York: The Free Press-Macmillan).

Penrose, Edith (1959) *The Theory of the Growth of the Firm* (London: Basil Blackwell).

Peteraf, Margaret A. (1993) "The Cornerstones of Competitive Advantage: A Resource-Based View," *Strategic Management Journal* 14, pp. 179–92.

Rugman, Alan M. (1981) *Inside the Multinationals: The Economics of Internal Markets* (New York: Columbia University Press).

——— (1990) *Multinationals and Canada-United States Free Trade* (Columbia, S.C.: University of South Carolina Press).

——— (1993) "A Canadian Perspective on NAFTA," *The International Executive* 36: 1 (January–February), pp. 33–54.

——— (1996) *The Theory of Multinational Enterprises: Volume One of the Selected Scientific Papers of Alan M. Rugman* (Cheltenham, U.K.: Edward Elgar).

Rugman, Alan M. and Andrew D. M. Anderson (1990) "The Canada-U.S. Free Trade Agreement and Canada's Agri-Food Industries," *Northeastern Journal of Agricultural and Resource Economics* 19:2 (October): 70–79.

Rugman, Alan M. and John McIlveen (1995) *Megafirms: Strategies for Canada's Multinationals* (Toronto: Methuen).

Rugman, Alan M. and Alain Verbeke (1990) *Global Corporate Strategy and Trade Policy* (London and New York: Routledge).

Rugman, Alan M., Donald J. Lecraw, and Laurence Booth (1985) *International Business: Firm and Environment* (New York: McGraw-Hill).

Rugman, Alan M., Alain Verbeke, and Joseph R. D'Cruz (1995) "Internalization and De-internalization: Will Business Networks Replace Multinationals?" in Gavin Boyd (ed.) *Competitive and Cooperative Macromanagement: The Challenges of Structural Interdependence* (Aldershot, UK: Edward Elgar), pp.107–28.

Rutenberg, David (1982) "Multinational Food and Fish Corporations," pp. 217–237 in Alan M. Rugman (ed.) *New Theories of the Multinational Enterprise* (New York: St. Martin's Press).

United Nations (1996) *World Investment Report: 1995* (New York and Geneva: United Nations Conference on Trade and Development, Division on Transnational Corporations and Investment).

Wernerfelt, Birger (1984) "A Resource-based View of the Firm," *Strategic Management Journal* 5, pp. 171–80.

Williamson, Oliver (1975) *Markets and Hierarchies: Analysis and Antitrust Implications* (New York: Free Press).

——— (1985) *The Economic Institutions of Capitalism* (New York: Free Press).

8

International Firms in the Manufacture and Distribution of Processed Foods

Philip C. Abbott and Juan B. Solana-Rosillo

Introduction

Several economists have noted that traditional trade theory as embodied in the Heckscher-Ohlin-Samuelson (HOS) model has very little to say about processing, distribution, marketing strategies, or the role of multinational firms in trade (Ethier, 1994). This model has also failed to explain observed trade patterns, and confrontations with the reality of trade have led to both theoretical and empirical innovations. The first example of this is the famous Leontief paradox in the 1950s. Leontief demonstrated that, contrary to the predictions of the HOS model, the United States imported capital intensive goods—presumably its more abundant factor—and exported labor intensive goods. Several explanations for this observation emerged, based on demand differences, technical change, resource heterogeneity, and other factors that essentially became caveats to the standard trade model. Among these were Vernon's product cycle hypothesis, the first attempt to integrate firm strategy into a trade model.

The "new trade theory" emerged out of a second round of perceived failure of trade models to explain observed trade practices—intra-industry trade, intra-firm trade (IFT), East-West rather than North-South trade and foreign direct investment (FDI), and the prevalence of export subsidies (e.g. Ethier, 1994; Krugman, 1989). This new trade theory has drawn from approaches in industrial organization literature, emphasizing imperfect competition, product differentiation, and economies of scale. Trade economists have also drawn from the business strategy literature, introducing the concepts of transactions costs (Williamson, Coase), sunk costs (Sutton), firm level competitiveness (Porter), and Dunning's OLI (ownership-location-internalization) paradigm into trade models (Ethier, 1986, 1994; Hortsman and Markusen, 1996). Similar empirical crises in the industrial organization and business strategy literatures have forced those fields to consider international issues and the lessons from trade theory. Several ideas that can lead to modifications of the HOS model in order to explain the role of firms and market institutions in trade have emerged.

The various bodies of theoretical literature examining trade and alternative means of penetrating international markets have focused on binary decisions. For example, some studies examine why firms choose trade or foreign direct investment to go overseas (e.g. Connor and Wang, Reed and Ning for the food industries). Others consider the choice between investment and contractual arrangements, such as licensing or franchising (e.g. Henderson and Sheldon, see Ch. 2, this volume). In practice, a firm faces a matrix of choices, not the binary decisions depicted in the literature, and may employ several of the alternative modes of internationalization (to be defined shortly) in different market segments, in different geographical markets, and at different points in time.

One objective of this chapter is to examine the relevance of that theoretical literature to empirical work on trade and foreign direct investment for food, taking into consideration the importance of a firm's strategy, especially toward the distribution and marketing system.

Key firm decisions are identified here as the location of production (hence whether or not to use trade) and how to penetrate the marketing and distribution system of the importing country. The notions identified in the theoretical literatures on new trade theory, business strategy, and industrial organization are useful and important in examining how such decisions are made. We reject, however, the emphasis in the trade literature on force-fitting firm-level phenomenon into aggregate general equilibrium frameworks for empirical investigations. Rather, we follow the lead of the economic development literature and will recommend a methodology based on the cost-benefit approach, noting that trade economists have shown the link between that approach and general equilibrium trade models (Srinivasan and Bhagwati).

An empirical investigation of food, beverage, and wine trade by the United States in comparison with the relevance of alternative internationalization modes illustrates the issues we find to be critical to empirical analysis. Firm-level data show that aggregation, both by product and by country, can give rise to misleading conclusions. The cases examined here also emphasize product characteristics, market institutions, and especially the strategies pursued by firms to market their products overseas as being critical determinants of competitiveness. The focus of these cases in the remainder of the chapter is to consider the importance of and methods for analyzing internationalization mode choice in the context of empirical trade analysis.

Internationalization Mode

Multinational firms may penetrate overseas market via trade, foreign direct investment, or by contracting with foreign firms. Firm-level decisions on how to go overseas involve two key dimensions: where to produce (at home or abroad) and what degree of control to exercise over marketing and distribution of its product. Root defines this ensemble of decisions as the firms' internationalization mode. More formally, "An international market entry mode is an institutional arrangement that makes possible the entry of a company's products, technology, human skills, management or other resources into a foreign country" (Root, p.5). The various alternative means of doing this may be categorized according to these two dimensions as shown in Table 8.1, which presents the matrix of decision possibilities among which firms choose.

The decision to produce at home or abroad distinguishes modes involving trade from those involving production abroad. The relationships with middlemen determine whether trade is indirect, direct, or intra-firm. The distinction between IFT and FDI is shown to involve a decision on production location by a firm that has chosen to maintain control over marketing and distribution. The choice between contracting (or licensing) and FDI involves a decision on control over marketing, given that production is to be conducted abroad.

These distinctions are often blurred in practice as firms utilize several modes to enter different markets, or even different modes in the same market. For example, our case study of Spanish firms entering the U.S. market showed firms with a U.S. marketing subsidiary importing some product (IFT), while the bulk of sales are from the parent firm in Spain to U.S. distributors (direct exports), and a small quantity sold to Spanish or international middlemen who subsequently export to the United States (indirect exports). In the case of licensing versus FDI, it was interesting to

TABLE 8.1 International Entry Modes

Marketing and Distribution Control	*Manufacturing Location*	
	Home	Abroad
Independent Middlemen		
Home	Indirect Export	—
Abroad	Direct Export	Contractual
Manufacturer control/ownership	IFT	FDI

note also that the majority of license payments (90 percent for U.S. food processors) are payments by an affiliate, not an unrelated foreign entity. This mixture of FDI and contracting occurs in a world where FDI often involves only partial ownership of a subsidiary by the parent firm and may be a vehicle for repatriating earnings of the foreign subsidiary. These distinctions between modes according to production and marketing decisions are nevertheless useful in putting into perspective the literatures addressing these institutions.

Three key issues are identified here in determining where a firm (in theory) might choose to locate its facilities in this internationalization mode matrix. First, FDI is an investment decision, and trade outcomes are ultimately driven by the production capacity that is the consequence of such decisions. Any trade model addressing internationalization mode choice must incorporate investment dynamics. The literature also argues that firm specific assets and advantages matter, so capital endowments in a trade model would need to reflect that. This leads to consideration of two alternative methodologies for evaluating the relationship between trade and investment: growth models and cost-benefit analysis. Growth models would take a macroeconomic perspective and require modeling of investment fund allocation and growth in sector specific capital stocks. Cost-benefit analysis emphasizes a microeconomic perspective, is likely more feasible from a data requirement perspective, and is adaptable to firm-level decisions.

Second, distribution system relationships are crucial to internationalization mode choice. As the Spanish wine example will show, markups along the distribution chain, and so presumably distribution and transactions costs, are substantial. This is likely to be especially important for food products where perishability and safety concerns increase transportation and handling costs, and products require timely marketing or safe storage methods. In the wine case, these markups are much larger than are tariffs, and so distribution relationships seem much more important than traditional trade policy concerns. Therefore, the case study emphasizes penetrations of foreign distribution systems, and the cost-benefit framework proposed here is designed to incorporate costs and returns along the distribution chain.

Third, internationalization mode decisions depend on specific industry or firm characteristics. It is not uncommon for a single firm to choose multiple modes, nor is it uncommon for leading firms in an industry to choose different modes, as the empirical investigation will illustrate. Initial conditions and product characteristics matter, at a highly disaggregated level, as does market structure. This lesson from the new trade theory—outcomes depend on market specific institutions—must be explicitly addressed in examining these firm level decisions.

Internationalization Mode Trends in U.S. Processed Food Markets

To put the issues raised above in perspective and set the stage for our evaluation of alternative methodologies, data on the magnitudes of each internationalization mode choice for the U.S. manufacturing sector, food and kindred products, and beverages is presented in Table 8.2 for U.S. firms going abroad and in Table 8.3 for foreign firms entering the U.S. market (Bureau of Economic Analysis, 1995a, b). Trade trends are illustrated in Figure 8.1 for U.S. agricultural and food trade (United Nations, 1993).

Figure 8.1 (and growth rates calculated from the underlying data [United Nations, 1993]) demonstrates the familiar result that exports of processed foods have been growing more rapidly than agricultural commodities (until the exceptional recent circumstances in commodity markets) and were less prone to downturns in demand in the early 1980s. USDA's trade outlook expects this trend to resume, with processed food exports leading the gains in upcoming years. While processed food imports have grown less rapidly, they started at a higher level. Figure 8.1 also illustrates the likely consequences of the U.S. exchange rate adjustment after 1986, when the value of the dollar was at a high point and subsequently has declined. Beverage trade has been growing steadily but less rapidly than other agricultural exports.

Table 8.2 shows the importance of FDI relative to trade, updating statistics reported by Handy and Henderson (1994). Sales by affiliates of U.S. parents were more than six times exports of processed foods in 1989 and were about 4.9 times exports in 1993, reflecting the rapid increase in processed food exports since 1986. This table shows that FDI is substantially more often utilized as an entry mode by the processed food sector than by the overall manufacturing sector, where affiliate sales were twice exports; again, export importance has grown in the last decade. For beverages, where product characteristics make transport costs high, the importance of FDI is much greater, with affiliate sales now twenty-five times exports. Table 8.3 shows that FDI has been less important relative to exports for foreign firms entering the United States, but again FDI is more important for food products, and its relative importance has increased since 1987. It is important to keep in perspective, however, that sales by affiliates seldom arise from firms deciding to construct new plant and equipment overseas—90 percent of FDI by foreigners in the U.S. food industries is for acquisition of existing entities (Bolling).

TABLE 8.2 Internationalization Modes for U.S. Firm Entry into Foreign Markets

MANUFACTURING	*in Million U.S. Dollars*			*Average Annual Growth (percent)*	
Entry Mode	1982	1989	1993	1982-89	1989-93
Exports	212,277	363,634	464,757	10	7
Direct Exports	172,455	288,956	366,028	10	7
Intra-firm Trade					
IFT (Export) by U.S. Parent Firms	37,180	70,187	86,883	13	6
IFT (Exports) to Foreign Parents	2,642	4,491	11,846	10	41
Licensing Net Revenue	4,616	11,212	na	20	
From Affiliates	3,356	9,376	na	26	
From Unaffiliated Foreigners	1,260	1,836	na	7	
Foreign Direct Investment					
Sales by U.S. Affiliates	359,269	789,562	760,037	17	-1
Sales by Majority-Owned Affiliates	271,099	509,308	622,707	13	6
Net Income	8,914	40,492	29,265	4	-7
FOOD AND KINDRED PRODUCTS					
Exports	8,627	12,877	19,628	7	13
Direct Exports	6,215	10,507	16,203	10	14
Intra-firm Trade					
IFT (Export) by U.S. Parent Firms	2,287	2,170	2,582	-1	5
IFT (Exports) to Foreign Parents	125	200	843	9	80
Licensing Net Revenue	170	567	na	33	
From Affiliates	147	511	na	35	
From Unaffiliated Foreigners	23	55	na	20	
Foreign Direct Investment					
Sales by U.S. Affiliates	39,023	79,614	95,782	15	5
Sales by Majority-Owned Affiliates	32,585	50,791	79,874	8	14
Net Income	1,354	3,864	6,399	26	16
Exports	191	680	1,013	37	12
Direct Exports	na	na	na		
Intra-firm Trade					
IFT (Export) by U.S. Parent Firms	84	9	*d*	-13	
IFT (Exports) to Foreign Parents	*d*	*d*	111		
Licensing Net Revenue	31	*d*	na		
From Affiliates	*d*	*d*	na		
From Unaffiliated Foreigners	*d*	29	na		
Foreign Direct Investment					
Sales by U.S. Affiliates	6,297	20,082	25,333	31	7
Sales by Majority-Owned Affiliates	5,518	9,598	16,402	11	18
Net Income	333	1,722	2,924	60	17

Note: *d* means data not disclosed due to too few firms; *na* means not available.
Source: Bureau of Economic Analysis, *U.S. Direct Investment Abroad*, various years.

TABLE 8.3 Internationalization Modes for Entry into the United States

MANUFACTURING	*in Million U.S. Dollars*			*Average Annual Growth (percent)*	
Entry Mode	1980	1987	1993	1989-87	1987-93
Imports	252,997	493,056	603,154	13.56	5.58
Direct Imports	212,911	415,882	461,701	13.62	2.75
Intra-firm Trade					
IFT (Import) by U.S. Parent Firms	*32,278*	59,604	101,851	12.09	17.72
IFT (Imports) to Foreign Parents	7,808	17,570	39,602	17.86	25.08
Licensing Net Revenue	122	672	na	64.40	
Foreign Direct Investment					
Sales by Foreign Affiliates	100,382	218,540	442,147	16.82	25.58
Sales by Majority-Owned Affiliates	na	na	375,011		
Net Income	1,053	4,985	5,900	53.34	4.59
FOOD AND KINDRED PRODUCTS					
Imports	16,636	20,628	23,033	3.43	2.91
Direct Imports	15,378	18,257	18,550	2.67	0.40
Intra-firm Trade					
IFT (Import) by U.S. Parent Firms	*792*	1,464	2,618	12.12	19.71
IFT (Imports) to Foreign Parents	466	907	1,865	13.52	21.12
Licensing Net Revenue	*d*	158	na		
Foreign Direct Investment					
Sales by Foreign Affiliates	13,604	26,459	50,150	13.50	22.38
Sales by Majority-Owned Affiliates	na	na	44,395		
Net Income	216	353	361	9.06	0.57
Imports	2,468	3,891	4,234	8.24	2.20
Direct Imports	na	3,263	3,227		-0.28
Intra-firm Trade					
IFT (Import) by U.S. Parent Firms	*d*	210	490		33.33
IFT (Imports) to Foreign Parents	324	418	517	4.14	4.74
Licensing Net Revenue	d	d	na		
Foreign Direct Investment					
Sales by Foreign Affiliates	na	4,593	8,679		22.24
Sales by Majority-Owned Affiliates			6,553		
Net Income	177	276	136	7.99	-10.14

Note: *d* means data not disclosed due to too few firms and *na* means not available.
Numbers in *italics* correspond to 1982 data instead of 1980.
Source: Bureau of Economic Analysis, *Foreign Direct Investment in the United States*, various years.

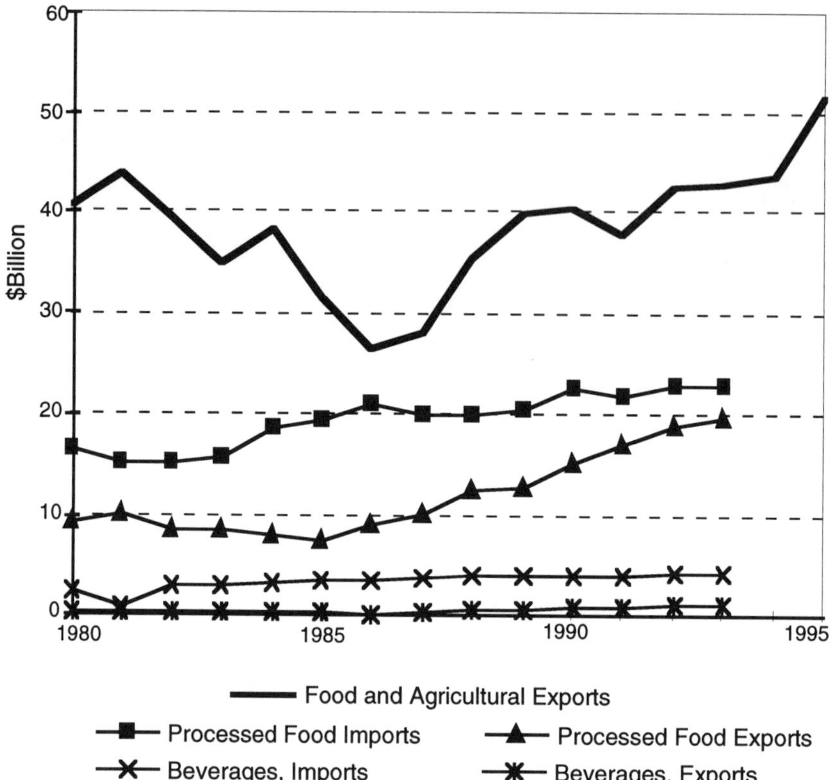

FIGURE 8.1 U.S. Agricultural and Food Trade. *Source:* United Nations, 1993.

Tables 8.2 and 8.3 also demonstrate that contractual entry modes are used less extensively than FDI. For food and kindred product going abroad (from the United States), net revenues from licensing are only 15 percent of net income from FDI sales. Furthermore, 90 percent of licensing net revenues come from affiliates or subsidiaries, not from unrelated firms. These data also highlight the difficulty in comparing magnitudes of any alternative modes, since the added value generated in the home country is likely to differ for each mode, affecting who benefits from the internationalization mode pursued by a firm.

Both indirect exports and intra-firm trade are also seen to be less important than direct exports, which account for about 80 percent of exports for both manufactures and food products. The relative importance of direct exports is comparable for entry modes into and out of the United States. It appears that an important step in exporting processed goods is to establish links with middlemen and the marketing system in the target country.

These data embody two apparent trends. First, a general appreciation in the value of the U.S. dollar until 1986 appears to coincide with slower rates of growth in exports than in FDI. A general depreciation in the value of the dollar since 1986 appears to correspond with a reversal in these relative rates of growth. Secondly, behavior of foreign firms entering the United States is becoming a bit more like that of U.S. firms going abroad, with growth in FDI being much more rapid than trade, especially since 1987. High growth rates in IFT to foreign parents also reflect this trend.

We have also observed that entry mode, especially for food products, depends strongly on product characteristics. Subsequent case studies will also highlight this concern, which makes aggregate analysis of the food industry problematic.

Addressing Alternative Internationalization Modes in Global Trade Models

As noted earlier, literature on the role of firms in trade has generally sought to modify general equilibrium models to incorporate market institutions and firm specific characteristics. The new trade theory explicitly incorporates product differentiation, economies of scale and market power, whereas studies on trade and FDI by multinationals also looks at internalization advantages, transactions costs, and the role of information. Addressing these in empirical trade investigations would then logically involve adding these features to computable general equilibrium (CGE) models as were used to investigate trade liberalization impacts from GATT, NAFTA, and agricultural policy reform. Having attempted to examine these issues using one such model (Hertel; Reca and Abbott), we will examine some of the lessons from that exercise relevant to the issues under examination here.

Some features of CGE models are suited to investigation of FDI and trade as alternative internationalization modes. The underlying theory of such models corresponds to a Ricardo-Viner trade model, with sector specific capital stocks, so that a mechanism for incorporating industry differences exists. Structuralists have shown that differing market institutions can also be built into these models (Taylor; De Janvry and Sadoulet). However, FDI is an investment activity, so dynamic versions of these models based on some growth theory are needed. Determining the allocation of investment funds across sectors has been difficult for these models—often dynamic CGE models assume investment allocations follow historical patterns, since this performs better empirically than does the Heckscher-Ohlin assumption that capital moves to equalize rates of return across sectors. While CGE models may be specified to make capital movements across sectors sluggish, the empirical basis for describing these relationships is weak.

Incorporating FDI into such a model requires addressing at least the following three issues. FDI as a foreign capital flow can affect the trade balance relationship assumed in CGE models. FDI may bring additional capital, allow countries to run a trade deficit for a period, and may bring about a structural change in the exchange rate determination mechanism assumed in these models (if any such mechanism is assumed at all). FDI may alter the allocation of capital across sectors. For example, with a greater level of FDI, allocation may be more efficient, since foreign firms may embody different advantages than do domestic firms, and so may exploit profit opportunities due to different sectoral rates of return left untouched by domestic firms. Domestic firms may invest in what they know, yielding the result that sectoral allocation of capital follows historical patterns, but FDI may change this. FDI may also bring better management, economies of scale and new technology to a country. Efficiency effects from this may lead to outward shifts in production possibility frontiers. Each of these issues suggests potential structural changes in the specification of a CGE model, and one must be concerned with how many sectors can be examined for such potential structural changes.

Treating middlemen and the role of the marketing and distribution system is more problematic. While price linkages in these models must account for the margins collected by these agents, alternative entry modes are not incorporated. Wholesale and retail trade account for 16 percent of economic activity (GDP) in the 1992 U.S. input-output table (Council of Economic Advisors). In many agricultural CGE models this activity is just part of services. Thus, a grocery store in such models is a service, neither buying nor selling agricultural products. In other specifications, whether distribution is treated as an input to manufacturing or an output purchasing the product of manufacturing and agricultural sectors, it is nevertheless treated as a fixed margin activity, with value added possibly depending on capital and labor allocations in a sector where capacity is an elusive concept.

Issues on how internationalization modes are chosen depend crucially on how each sector of the economy relates to wholesale and retail trade. Market structures can vary, even within a narrow subsector. The food processing industry sells its products to groceries, restaurants or specialty stores (e.g. liquor stores), and the importance of each avenue for sales can vary by product. Within a sector, individual firms may pursue different strategies, as our cases on wine and beverage trade will illustrate later.

The most difficult problem with CGE analysis of these issues, however, concerns aggregation and data availability. To keep model size and implementation demands manageable, and given data availability constraints, rather highly aggregated models are generally specified. While that is appropriate for many issues, firm and industry specific advantages are at the heart of internationalization mode choices. Trade trends in a world with intra-industry and intra-firm trade, decisions between FDI and trade, and factors determining sectoral competitiveness are likely to depend on information not specified in these models. Effort is better spent understanding in detail the sector of concern.

One difficulty with assumptions invoked to create practical models is firm symmetry. Many of the results in trade theory and the business strategy literature, as well as our case study results, point to firm asymmetries as important components of business strategy and competitiveness outcomes. Disaggregating CGE models to capture these firm-level specificities is simply not possible.

Aggregation leads to theoretical difficulties as well. It is one reason why typical CGE models adopt Armington assumptions, yet those assumptions generate terms of trade effects and thus market power (Brown). While market power is likely to be important for narrowly defined sectors, and product differentiation is important for processed food trade, the level of aggregation in a CGE model is likely to get the magnitude of these effects wrong.

Incorporating phenomena related to firm behavior and addressing the issues of business strategy are far easier in a theoretical general equilibrium model than in an empirical CGE model. In any approach to investigating internationalization mode choice and its affect on trade, data will be the limiting factor. In modeling firm behavior, however, we need to recognize that the information available to a firm when making such decisions is far better than that available to modelers.

Internationalization Mode and Competitiveness Assessment: A Microeconomic Approach

The problems of adapting general equilibrium models to empirical investigations and the need to find a microeconomic equivalent are not new to policy practitioners in economic development. Their approach is to conduct a cost-benefit analysis, with shadow prices possibly taken from economy-wide models where the general equilibrium issues have been addressed (although that method of shadow pricing has worked better in theory than in practice). That approach is adapted here to the investigation of internationalization mode choice by firms.

Exhibit 8.1 presents the elements of a cost-benefit analysis framework for choosing where to produce (at home or abroad) and how to market processed food products. Decision options in this framework correspond to the alternative internationalization modes characterized along the lines

EXHIBIT 8.1 Cost-Benefit Framework for International Mode Choice Evaluation

Objective: Profit maximization

Profit = Revenue – Cost = P(Q)*Q – C(Q)

where P(Q) is inverse residual demand *(oligopoly, market power)*, and

C(Q) is cost, composed of production and support activity costs—*marketing and distribution costs are a significant component*

Decision Options

Production (Q) – Quantity and Product Characteristics (*Differentiation*)

Multiproduct decisions and complementarities

Sequential product innovations (Vernon)

Internationalization Mode (Table 8.1 categorizes options – Root):

Location of production – Home or Abroad (Export or FDI)

Control over supporting activities – Contract or Invest

Marketing, Distribution,

Service, R&D, etc.

Demand and Revenue Implications

Economic conditions affect demand over time, opportunities (e.g. exchange rate)

Revenue and markups determined by residual demand (new trade theory)

Residual demand varies by internationalization mode choice

Cost Implications

Transactions Cost Theory—

Variable costs of physical production – marginal cost

Fixed (*sunk) costs* due to investment (Sutton)

production facilities and marketing infrastructure

Firm specific assets and advantages

Transactions costs (Coase, Williamson)

ex-ante for contracting and support activities

information

marketing and distribution

service, R&D, etc.

ex-post from opportunistic behavior due to partner self-interest

bounded rationality (contingencies not exhaustive)

Dynamics due to *learning and scale economies*

Constraints (and shadow prices)

Regulations—domestic product standards, trade barriers, capital controls

Industry structure—initial conditions matter

Resources and prices by country *(HOS trade theory)*

of these two key decisions in Table 8.1. Following standard practice, profit maximization by a firm is chosen as the objective. Residual demand functions facing a firm, costs associated with alternative decisions, and constraints and consequences from the economic environment condition the outcomes from decisions. Exhibit 8.1 also presents (in italics) where the various issues in new trade theory, industrial organization, business strategy, and competitiveness assessment are incorporated into this framework.

The profit maximization objective of this framework is the difference between revenue and cost. Residual demand functions must capture market power in determining the demand faced by a firm in an oligopolistic industry (believed to be important for processed food markets [Marion]). They must also incorporate the consequences of product differentiation, and Hill and Kim have shown that residual demand functions may vary by internationalization mode. One reason to export directly rather than indirectly may be to advertise and so differentiate a product, or to face the demand curve in the target market in order to exploit any market power. Economic conditions, such as the exchange rate, will also affect not only the residual demand function faced, but the marketing strategy, as identified in the pricing to market literature (Pick and Park, Knetter).

For trade up to the retail level in processed foods, marketing and distribution costs can be a significant component of total cost. The transaction cost literature (Coase, Williamson), internalization (Ethier, 1986, 1994; Hortsman and Markusen; Dunning, 1981, 1988), and the relevance of sunk costs are all pieces of the puzzle facing firms going abroad. The role of information related to transaction and opportunity costs from contracting as an alternative to trade or FDI are other important themes in this literature that must be taken into account when specifying costs of alternative modes in this framework. The Spanish wine case will show that these costs are substantial and that "sunk transaction costs" may be important. A dynamic strategy is followed in which intermediaries must become familiar with a specific wine before greater volumes are stocked. Several firms from both Spain and Australia appear to have set up marketing subsidiaries that shrink in importance over time, once their initial mission has been accomplished.

Trade policy, nontariff trade barriers, food safety regulations, and other economic policies set the economic environment within which these decisions are made. Industry structure and firm-level specific advantages may also cause calculations to differ by firm. These factors are viewed as constraints, giving rise to shadow prices of resources. Resource endowments and factor prices, the driving force behind the HOS model, are thus only a subset of the determinants of trade patterns. The magnitude of transaction costs for food products make them at least as important as tariffs, wages, or interest rates.

Spanish-Australian Competition in the U.S. Wine Market

To illustrate the utility of this cost-benefit framework on a conceptual level, we use it to investigate competition between Spain and Australia in exporting wine to the United States. (Firm-level data sources for the following cases are documented in Appendix A.) Spain, a traditional wine exporter, has been losing market share to Australia (and to Chile to a lesser extent) in the U.S. market, prompting concerns that it is losing competitiveness. Comparison of correlations in market share over time shows Australia to be Spain's principal competitor, who has been winning this lost market share and presumably gaining in competitiveness (Solana and Abbott, 1996). Thus, a new market entrant seems able to dissipate a natural resource advantage of Spanish wine producers. Further investigation suggests that Australia's advantage lies as much in its marketing strategy as in its production cost. Some Spanish firms have been as successful in this market as have been Australian firms, in spite of this national trend, by following marketing strategies similar to those of the Australians.

Table 8.4 is intended to demonstrate the overwhelming importance of marketing, distribution, and the magnitudes of wholesale and retail markups (a fact cited earlier) for this product. It also illustrates why direct exports dominate indirect exports and why little additional gain seems to result from IFT. While the average Spanish producer receives fifty cents per liter for his wine (as when exports are indirect and producers sell to a Spanish marketing agent), direct exporters who sell to a U.S. importing agent realize $3.98 per liter, reflecting quality differentials due to product differentiation, transportation, and transaction costs, plus any rents due to market power. IFT in this industry involves sales directly to wholesalers by marketing subsidiaries, yielding on average $5.37 per liter and a much smaller markup than over producer cost. Thus, there is a substantial advantage to be gained from direct exports, and the key to success is getting the firm's wine carried by U.S. wholesalers.

Given these margins, it is not surprising that Table 8.5 shows the dominant entry mode into the U.S. wine market for Australia and Spain is direct exporting, with some IFT and very little indirect exporting. Table 8.6 shows the firm-level data on which these results are based; it also shows information on entry mode and marketing strategy by firm. Hillebrand is an international marketing agent, not a Spanish firm, that deals in several European as well as Australian wines. In this table we see

TABLE 8.4 Markups on Spanish Wine Exports to the United States

Point in Marketing Chain	Price/Cost ($ per liter)	Entry Mode
Spanish Wine Producer Price	***0.50***	Indirect
Exporter Margin (and quality differential)	2.83	
Exporter Price FOB Spain (per liter)	***3.33***	
Transport and insurance to U.S.	0.23	
Input Price (CIF, U.S.)	3.56	
Port costs	0.06	
Import + Federal Tax	0.36	
Importers Cost	***3.98***	Direct
Importer Markup (35%)	1.39	
Wholesale Cost	***5.37***	IFT
Wholesale Markup (40%)	2.15	
Retailer Cost	***7.52***	
Retail Markup (50%)	3.76	
Retail Sale Price	***11.29***	
"Lost" Markups		
Retail Price – Spanish Producer Price	10.79	
as % of Retail Price	96%	Indirect
Retail Price – Importer Price	7.31	
as % of Retail Price	65%	Direct
Retail Price – Wholesale Price	5.91	
as % of Retail Price	52%	IFT

Sources: Instituto Español de Comercio Exterior (ICEX), Spanish Wines (New York Office), and Elizari (1993).

the very successful Spanish firms that have been following strategies similar to those of Australian firms.

Several observations from these tables are relevant. First, IFT has been declining over time, especially for Australian firms. It is interesting to note that IFT here is a strategy for a new entrant rather than a strategy for mature market participants. Marketing subsidiaries invest in advertising and promotion (a sunk transaction cost) until a wine becomes known by the wholesale trade, when this activity diminishes. The role of these subsidiaries is marketing support, not acting as an importing agent, as firms mature. Individual firms, however, may follow mixed entry modes, at the same time engaging in some IFT via the marketing subsidiary and along with direct exports to importing agents.

Success of firms is more strongly related to relationships with consignees than with entry mode (defined as the path of entry). Figure 8.2 shows

TABLE 8.5 Entry Mode into the U.S. Wine Industry (% of Total Sales)

Entry Mode	1989	1990	1991	1992	1993
			Spanish Firms		
Direct Exports	98.39	93.7	94.1	91.4	93.6
Indirect Exports	0.45	4.1	5.4	8.0	4.9
IFT	1.16	2.2	0.5	0.6	1.5
			Australian Firms		
Direct Exports	53.63	62.1	62.1	79.6	80.7
Indirect Exports	0.00	0.9	2.4	4.3	5.6
IFT	46.37	37.0	35.6	16.2	13.7

Sources: PIERS Database, *Journal of Commerce*, various years.

the path followed by the more successful firms (Path A indicates increasing sales to a few consignees before expanding the distribution network), as well as alternative paths followed by less successful firms. Path A involves gaining a foothold in a market and expanding from that base. Consolidation into a few agents (Path B) appears not to be a successful strategy for this product. Statistical tests on firm performance (sales growth) show that path of entry, not mode of entry or country of origin, determines success. Performance of the second and third largest Spanish firms show that consolidation of consignees can be a very unsuccessful strategy.

U.S. Beer and Soft Drink Manufacturers Going Overseas

To illustrate the important differences that product characteristics can make, even within a narrow subsector of the food industry, we looked at internationalization strategies of some U.S. beer and soft drink manufacturers going overseas. For these firms, location of production is much less important and is not perceived as an essential differentiating characteristic of a product (as it appears to be for wine). Foreign markets are important, however. Profit margins overseas are twice the U.S. levels, and foreign sales are one-third of total sales for the U.S. beverage industry (Compact Disclosure). Internationalization mode choices are quite different, though. FDI or licensing is more predominant for beer and soft drinks than for wine. Differences exist between beer and soft drinks, as well.

The PIERS data for 1993 show that the leading exporter of soft drinks is the military, supplying overseas bases, and accounting for 7.6 percent of exports, followed by Pepsi with 6.4 percent of exports and Coke with 6 percent of exports. There are many indirect exporters of soft drinks with

TABLE 8.6 Firm Level Data on Spanish and Australian Wine Exports to the United States

Firm	Sales (Tons)	Sales Growth (% per year)	Market Share*	Consignees in the U.S.	Entry Mode	Path of Entry[a]
Period	*1993*	*1989–93*	*1993*	*1993*	*1989–93*	*1989–93*
SPANISH FIRMS						
Freixenet	12163	12	34.1	89	Direct	A
Team Ib.It.	2079	-76	5.8	65	Direct	B
J Gibert	1886	-12	5.3	33	Direct	B
Hillebrand	1368	910	3.8	44	Indirect	A
Harvey	1246	-34	3.5	10	Direct	B
S.Vinicola	1148	285	3.2	12	Direct	A
R.Barbier	1117	1521	3.1	31	Direct	A
Vinival	1054	1353	3	2	Direct	C
Intl.G.V	940	609	2.6	6	Direct	C
Age	928	-33	2.6	4	Direct	B
Multi T.I	710	84	2	9	Direct	B
Osborne	692	1481	1.9	5	Direct	C
Segura V.	655	-71	1.8	15	Direct	B
Garvey	606	-31	1.7	20	Direct	A
M.Torres	522	-37	1.5	16	Direct	B
U.Vitivini.	496	1281	1.4	11	Direct	A
Domecq	198	20	0.6	13	IFT	A
AUSTRALIAN FIRMS						
Penfolds	4411	1100	15.6	49	Direct	A
Mildara	3251	357	11.5	30	Direct	A
Lindemans	2308	6	8.1	6	DIFT	B
Rosemount	2121	218	7.5	4	IFT	C
OWG	2113	-30	7.5	24	Direct	B
BRL	1392	147	4.9	29	Direct	A
Hillebrand	1303	2147	4.6	8	Indirect	A
Orlando	1243	34	4.4	32	Direct	A
Fine WA	882	257	3.1	11	Direct	A
Negociants	817	327	2.9	10	DIFT	A
SAI	777	1349	2.7	4	Direct	C
TNT	591	432	2.1	1	Direct	C
Schenkers	566	100	2	7	DIFT	C
Hartrodt	555	2334	2	5	DIFT	C
Tyrell	542	850	1.9	20	Direct	A
Mitchelton	448	2105	1.6	6	IFT	C
AW	150	425	0.5	4	Direct	C

[a]See text and Figure 8.2.

Key for Entry Mode Direct = Direct Exports
Indirect = Indirect Exports
IFT = Intrafirm Trade
DIFT = Decreasing Intrafirm Trade
*Market share is percent of a country's exports supplied by that firm

Source: PIERS Database, 1989–93, *Journal of Commerce.*

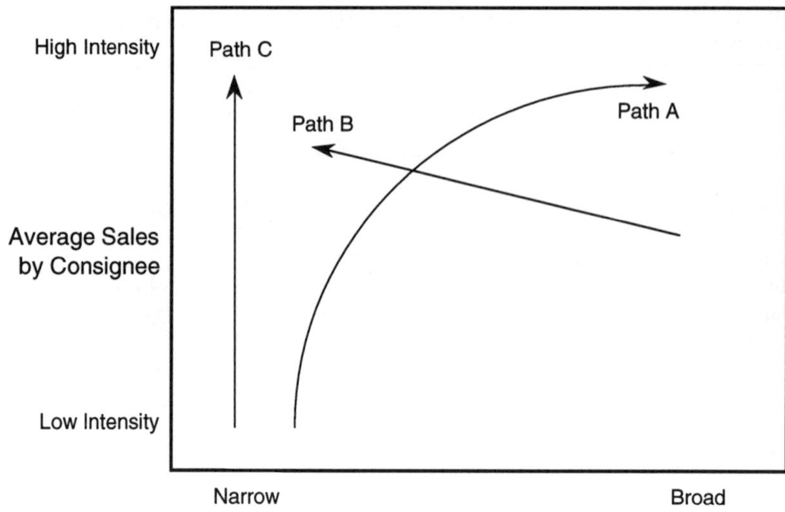

FIGURE 8.2 Path of Entry into the U.S. Wine Market.

small market shares. Foreign sales are 69 percent of total sales for Coke and 35 percent for Pepsi, largely through foreign affiliates. Strategies of these two leading firms are also quite different as Coke specializes more in soft drinks, while Pepsi is diversified into the food industry, marketing products through ownership of fast food chains.

Destination data also suggest that FDI replaces exports when markets become sufficiently large. In 1992 Argentina was the largest destination for Coke exports at 60 percent, but fell to 2 percent in 1993 after additional production capacity in Argentina was constructed. The leading export destinations for both Coke and Pepsi are small markets such as the Virgin Islands and the Cayman Islands.

For beer, exports are more concentrated and are direct. Anheuser Busch handles 31 percent of total U.S. beer exports, Miller exports 28 percent, and Pabst is next at 6.5 percent. Anheuser Busch only exports or licenses, with Puerto Rico, Japan, and the U.K. accounting for 70 percent of their exports. Intra-industry trade is important in this sector, with much foreign beer imported into the United States, but with much more FDI (production of "foreign" beer in the United States) than is the case for wine.

One aspect of competitive advantage and marketing strategies by U.S. firms as compared to European firms is illustrated by these cases. Location of production is an important aspect of European marketing strategies, both in foreign and domestic markets. Brand names however, often confer advantages to U.S. firms independent of production location.

Conclusions

Information on internationalization mode choices for the food industry and for specific beverage industries has highlighted the importance of sector specific marketing strategies in determining the most cost effective internationalization mode. Data on mode choices of food and kindred product processors was shown to be different from those of manufacturers. While direct exports dominate trade mode choices, FDI was more often preferred by food processors, and this tendency was even more pronounced for beverages. Marketing strategy was found more important than country of origin in determining firm level performance in the case of wine exports to the U.S. by Spain and Australia.

A more general observation is that the means by which firms penetrate the distribution network in a target market is critical to firm-level success and hence competitiveness of a product in a market. Marketing costs and alternative strategies appear in the cases considered here to be quantitatively more important than trade policies (with the exception of food safety regulations) in determining trade patterns and choices among alternative internationalization modes.

Some empirical results contradict certain theoretical expectations from the trade and business strategy literature. Diminishing rather than increasing IFT by Australian wine exporters is the result of sunk transaction costs to build reputation among distributors, for example, which becomes less important over time. Firms do not appear to move toward more IFT or FDI as they mature in that sector. These results depend upon industry and firm specifics, including intangible assets, which can be critical to the nature and magnitude of transactions costs. The data show that internationalization mode choices can differ by narrow subsector, by firm, and even by market for a single firm. Furthermore, competitiveness assessments that appear to be true for a country may well not apply to individual firms in that country.

In assessing market behavior where industry specific characteristics are so important, empirical work is likely to rely much more on cost-benefit analysis and case studies than on CGE modeling. Lessons from business strategy, competitiveness, and industrial organization literatures need to be incorporated in both theoretical and empirical research. It is much easier to accommodate these issues in a generic theoretical model than to specify sufficient detail in their empirical counterpart, the CGE model. Appropriate theory may vary by industry at a finely detailed level, and by firm in that industry; firm asymmetry, market power and aggregation, and the varying role of marketing and distribution strategies at the firm level are difficult to capture in aggregate models. Cost-benefit or simulation methods need to focus effort on understanding market structure, firm specific advantages, and transaction costs associated with alternative mode choices at the firm level. The limiting factor for both approaches appears to be data, especially on cost, for international transactions.

Policy implications from this analysis are limited, as is what should be the role of government. These issues are reminiscent of results from the new trade theory: export subsidies may emerge as optimal policy interventions under certain market institutions, but we seldom have enough detailed information to know which sectors might merit targeting of subsidies, or if market structure will lead to expected results. Simple misunderstandings of market structure assumptions can reverse subsidy impacts. Targeting may require identifying not only appropriate sectors, but also worthy firms in that sector. Price is also only one of several variables under a firm's control, since product characteristics, marketing strategy, and industry dynamics matter. Distribution markups are substantial, so subsidies could easily get lost in noncompetitive sectors. If a government is to intervene, and do it well, better use of available theory and more sophisticated empirical investigations along the lines described above are needed to project consequences. Provision of market information, or other public goods (technology or infrastructure, for example) are however, a more appropriate role for government.

References

Abbott, P. C. and M. E. Bredahl. 1994. "Competitiveness: Definitions, Useful Concepts and Issues." *Competitiveness in International Food Markets,* M. Bredahl, P. Abbott, and M. Reed, editors, Westview Press. Boulder, CO.

Balasubramanyam, V. N. and D. Greenaway. 1993. "Regional Integration Agreements and Foreign Direct Investment." *Regional Integration and the Global Trading System,* N. K. Anderson and R. Black Hurst, editors. St. Martin's Press, New York.

Benvignati, A. M. 1990. "Industry Determinants and 'Differences' in U.S. Intrafirm and Arms'-length Exports." *Review of Economics and Statistics* 72:481–488.

Bolling, H. C. 1992. "The European Community's Presence in U.S. Agribusiness." *Foreign Agricultural Economic Report No.245.* ERS, USDA, Washington, DC.

Brown, D. K. 1992. "The Impact of the North American Free Trade Area: Applied General Equilibrium Models." *North American Free Trade: Assessing the Impacts,* N. Lustig, B. Bosworth, and R. Lawrence, editors, Brookings Institution, Washington, DC.

Buckley, P. J. 1985. "Testing Theories of the Multinational Enterprise: A Review of the Evidence." *The Economic Theory of the Multinational Enterprise,* P. J. Buckley and M. Casson, editors. St. Martin's Press, New York, NY.

Bureau of Economic Analysis (BEA). 1995a. *U.S. Direct Investment Abroad,* 1993 and previous years. U.S. Department of Commerce, Washington, DC.

———. 1995b. *Foreign Direct Investment in the United States,* 1993 and previous years. U.S. Department of Commerce, Washington, DC .

Casson, M. 1987. "Multinational Firms." *The Economics of the Firm,* R. Clarke and T. McGuinness, editors. Basil Blackwell, Oxford.

———. 1982. "Transaction Costs and the Theory of the Multinational Enterprise." *New Theories of Multinational Enterprise,* A.M. Rugman, editor. St. Martin's Press, New York, NY.

Caves, R. E. 1971. "International Corporations: The Industrial Economics of Foreign Direct Investment." *Economica* 38:1-27.

———. 1982. " Global Strategy and Multinationals—Entry Mode Choice." *Multinational Enterprise and Economic Analysis.* Cambridge University Press, Cambridge.

Coase, R. 1937. "The Nature of the Firm." *Economica* 4:386–405.

Connor, J. M. 1977. *The Market Power of Multinationals.* Praeger Publishers, New York, NY.

______. 1983. "Determinants of Foreign Direct Investment by Food and Tobacco Manufacturers." *American Journal of Agricultural Economics* 65:395–404.

Connor, J. M. and K. Wang. 1993. *Determinants of Intra-Firm International Trade.* Staff Paper SP 93-11. Department of Agricultural Economics, Purdue University, West Lafayette, IN.

Connor, J. M., R. T. Rogers, B. W. Marion, and W. F. Mueller. 1985. *The Food Manufacturing Industries: Structures, Strategies, Performance, and Policies.* Lexington, Lexington, MA.

Council of Economic Advisors. 1995. *Economic Report of the President.* U.S. Government Printing Office, Washington, DC.

De Janvry, A. and E. Sadoulet. 1987. "Agricultural Price Policy in General Equilibrium Models: Results and Comparisons." *American Journal of Agricultural Economics* 69: 230–246.

Dunning, J. H. 1981. "Explaining the International Direct Investment Position of Countries: Towards a Dynamic or Developmental Approach." *Weltwirtschaftliches Archiv* 117:30–64.

———. 1988. "The Eclectic Paradigm of International Production: A Restatement and Some Possible Extensions." *Journal of International Business Studies* 19:1–31.

Elizari, C. 1993. *Mercado del Vino de la Agrupacion de Exportadores de Rioja Alavesa.* Situacion Mimeo. ICEX. Madrid.

Ethier, W. J. 1986. "The Multinational Firm." *Quarterly Journal of Economics* 102:805-833.

———. 1994. "Conceptual Foundations from Trade, Multinational Firms, and Foreign Direct Investment Theory." *Competitiveness in International Food Markets,* M.E. Bredahl, P.C. Abbott, and M.R. Reed, eds. Westview Press, Boulder, CO.

Ethier, W. J. and H. Horn. 1990. "Managerial Control of International Firms and Patterns of Direct Investment." *Journal of International Economics* 28:5–45.

Gestrin, M. and A. M. Rugman. 1994. "The Strategic Response of MNEs to NAFTA." *Foreign Investment and NAFTA*, A.M. Rugman, editor. University of South Carolina Press, Columbia, SC.

Graham, E. and P. Krugman. 1989. *Foreign Direct Investment in the United States.* Institute for International Economics, Washington, DC.

Handy, C. R. and D. R. Henderson. 1994. "Assessing the Role of Foreign Direct Investment in the Food Manufacturing Industry." *Competitiveness in International Food Markets,* M. E. Bredahl, P. C. Abbott, and M. R. Reed, editors. Westview Press, Boulder, CO.

———. 1991. "Implications of a Single EC Market for the U.S. Food Manufacturing Sector." *EC 1992 Perspectives on World Food and Agriculture Trade.* D. R. Kelch, editor. Staff Report No. AGES 9133. USDA, ERS, Washington, DC.

Handy, C. R. and J. M. McDonald. 1989. "Multinational Structures and Strategies of U.S. Food Firms." *American Journal of Agricultural Economics* 71:1247–1254.

Helleiner, G. K. 1979. "Transnational Corporations and Trade Structure: The Role of Intra-Firm Trade." H. Giersch, editor. *Intra-Industry Trade.* J. C. B. Muhr, P. Siebeck, Tübingen.

Helleiner, G. K. and R. Lavergne. 1979. "Intra-Firm Trade and Industrial Exports to the United States." *Oxford Bulletin of Economics and Statistics* 41:297–311.

Helpman, E. 1985. "Multinational Corporations and Trade Structure." *Review of Economic Studies* 52:443–458.

Helpman, E. and P. R. Krugman. 1989. *Trade Policy and Market Structure.* MIT Press, Cambridge, MA.

Henderson, D. R. and I. M. Sheldon. 1992. "International Licensing of Branded Food Products." *Agribusiness: An International Journal* 8:399–412.

Henneberry, S. and J. Russell. 1989. "Transfer Pricing in Multinational Firms: A Review of the Literature." *Agribusiness* 5:121–137.

Hertel, Thomas W. (ed). 1997. *Global Trade Analysis: Modeling and Applications.* Cambridge University Press, Cambridge.

Hill, C. W. and W. Chan Kim. 1988. "Searching for a Dynamic Theory of the Multinational Enterprise: A Transaction Cost Model." *Strategic Management Journal* 9:93-104.

Hirschberg, J. G., I. M. Sheldon, and J. R. Dayton. 1994. "An Analysis of Bilateral Intra-Industry Trade in the Food Processing Sector." *Applied Economics* 26:159–167.

Horstman, I. and J. Markusen. 1987. "Licensing Versus Direct Investment: A Model of Internalization by the Multinational Enterprise." *Canadian Journal of Economics* 20:464–481.

———. 1996. "Exploring New Markets: Direct Investment, Contractual Relations and the Multinational Enterprise." *International Economic Review* 37:1–19.

Hymer, S. H. 1960. *The International Corporations of National Firms: A Study of Direct Foreign Investment.* MIT Press, Cambridge, MA.

Jones, G. R. and C. W. Hill. 1988. "Transaction Cost Analysis of Strategy-Structure Choice." *Strategic Management Journal* 9:159–172.

Knetter, M. M. 1989. "Price Discrimination by U.S. and German Exporters." *American Economic Review* 79:198–210.

Kravis, I. B. and R. E. Lipsey. 1992. "Sources of Competitiveness of the United States and of Its Multinational Firms." *Review of Economics and Statistics* 74:193–201.

Krugman, P. 1989. "Industrial Organization and International Trade." *Handbook of Industrial Organization*, R. Schmalensee and R. D. Willig, editors. North-Holland, Amsterdam.

Lall, S. 1978. "The Pattern of Intra-Firm Exports by U.S. Multinationals." *Oxford Bulletin of Economics and Statistics* 40:209–222.

Lancaster, K. 1980. "Intra-Industry Trade under Perfect Monopolistic Competition." *Journal of International Economics* 10:151–176.

Leontief, W. 1968. "Domestic Production and Foreign Trade: The American Capital Position Reexamined." *Readings in International Economics*, R. E. Caves and H. G. Johnson, editors. Irwin, Homewood, IL.

Marion, B. W. 1986. *The Organization and Performance of the U.S. Food System*. Lexington Books, Lexington, MA.

Markusen, J. R. 1984. "Multi-Plant Economies and the Gains from Trade." *Journal of International Economics* 16:205–226.

McCorriston, S. and I. M. Sheldon. 1991. "Intra-Industry Trade and Specialization in Processed Agricultural Products: The Case of the U.S. and the E.C." *Review of Agricultural Economics* 13:173–184.

Patterson, P. M. and P. C.Abbott. 1991. *An Evaluation of the PIERS Data for Use in Economic Analysis of U.S. Agricultural and Food Product Trade*. Occasional Paper Series OP-28. Organization and Performance of World Food Systems. North Central Regional Project.

Pick, D. H. and T. A. Park. 1991. "The Competitive Structure of U.S. Agricultural Exports." *American Journal of Agricultural Economics* 73:133–141.

Porcano, T. M. 1993. "Factors Affecting the Foreign Direct Investment Decisions of Firms from and into Major Industrialized Countries." *Multinational Business Review* 1:26–36.

Porter, M. E. 1990. *The Competitive Advantage of Nations*. Free Press, New York, NY.

Ravara, F. A. 1994. *Food Multinational Enterprises Investment Strategies: An Option Theory Perspective*. Ph.D. Dissertation, Department of Agricultural Economics, Purdue University, W. Lafayette, IN.

Reca, A. and P. Abbott. 1995. "Foreign Direct Investment and Regional Integration: MERCOSUR and Argentine Processed Food Trade," Purdue Agricultural Economics Department Staff Paper 95-3, presented at the NCR 182 Conference on Foreign Direct Investment and Processed Food Trade, Washington, DC.

Reed, M. R. and M. A. Marchant. 1992. "The Global Competitiveness of the U.S. Food Processing Industry." *Northeastern Journal of Agricultural and Resource Economics* 21:60–70.

Reed, M. R. and Y. Ning. 1995. "Foreign Investment Strategies of U.S. Multinational Firms." *Industrial Organization and Trade in the Food Industries*, I. M. Sheldon and P. C. Abbott, editors. Westview Press, Boulder, CO.

Root, F. R. 1987. *Entry Strategies for International Markets*. Lexington Books, Lexington, MA.

Rugman, A. M. 1980. "Internalization as a General Theory of Foreign Direct Investment: A Re-Appraisal of the Literature." *Weltwirtschaftliches Archiv* 116:365–379.

Solana, J. and P. Abbott. 1996. "International Entry Modes and Spanish Competitiveness in the U.S. Wine Industry." Presented at OENOMETRIE VI, Zaragoza, Spain.

Srinivasan, T. N. and J. N. Bhagwati. 1978. "Shadow Prices for Project Selection in the Presence of Distortions: Effective Rates of Protection and Domestic Resource Costs." *Journal of Political Economy* 86:97–116.

Siddharthan, N. S. and N. Kumar. 1990. "The Determinants of Inter-Industry Variations in the Proportion of Intra-Firm Trade: The Behavior of U.S. Multinationals." *Weltwirtschaftliches Archiv* 126:581–591.

Spanish Wines 1995. *Guia para la Exportacion de Bebidas Alcoholicas a los Estados Unidos.* Mimeo. New York.

Spulber, D. F. 1992. "Economic Analysis and Management Strategy: A Survey." *Journal of Economics and Management Strategy*, 1:535–573.

———. 1994. " Economic Analysis and Management Strategy: A Survey Continues." *Journal of Economics and Management Strategy*, 3:355–406.

Sugden, R. 1983. "The Degree of Monopoly, International Trade, and Transnational Corporations." *International Journal of Industrial Organization* 1:165–187.

Sutton, J. 1991. *Sunk Costs and Market Structure.* MIT Press, Cambridge, MA.

Taylor, L. 1983. *Structuralist Macroeconomics.* Basic Books, New York.

United Nations. 1993. *International Trade Statistics Yearbook—1993* and previous years, Statistical Office, Department of Economic and Social Affairs, New York, NY.

———. 1990. "Statistical Papers, Commodity Trade Statistics, According to Standard International Trade Classification, Series D." Statistical Office, Department of Economic and Social Affairs, New York, NY.

———. 1988. *Transnational Corporations in World Development: Trends and Prospects.* United Nations Center on Transnational Corporations, New York, NY.

Vernon, R. 1966. "International Investment and International Trade in the Product Cycle." *Quarterly Journal of Economics* 91:190–207.

Williamson, O. E. 1975. *Market and Hierarchies: Analysis and Antitrust Implications.* Collier Macmillan Publishers, New York, NY.

———. 1989. "Transactions Cost Economics." *Handbook of Industrial Organization*, R. Schmalensee and R. D. Willig, editors. North-Holland, Amsterdam.

Yannopoulus, G. N. 1990. "Foreign Direct Investment and European Integration: The Evidence from the Formative Years of the European Community." *Journal of the Common Market Studies* 28:235–259.

Appendix A. Data Sources Used in this Research.

Journal of Commerce. *PIERS (Port of Import/Export Reporting Service).*

Reports data on U.S. imports and exports shipped by ocean freight derived from U.S. Customs reports. There are 10 product classifications: the one used here was "foodstuffs." The database consists of raw data recorded by *Journal of Commerce* agents from customs declarations, therefore additional handling is necessary for its use in research. Time series data on sales by country and by firm, number of consignees, and product market shares may be constructed. This data base, together with additional information on computer-based trade directories, was very useful in classifying firms by entry mode and marketing strategy and associating that with performance. Price data are not disclosed in this data base. For a more thorough explanation of the use of the PIERS data base for economic analysis see Patterson and Abbott (1991).

Bureau of Economic Analysis, U.S. Department of Commerce. *U.S. Direct Investment Abroad*

Reports activities of U.S. parents and their foreign affiliates by country and by industry. From this database we obtained figures for intra-firm trade, sales by foreign affiliates of U.S. parents, and royalties and license fees of U.S. parents. The food and kindred products sector is disaggregated to grain mill and bakery products and beverages. Activities are also reported based on whether the U.S. parent holds a majority position or not. These data are based on annual surveys according to a distribution of firms from a benchmark year.

Bureau of Economic Analysis, U.S. Department of Commerce. *Foreign Direct Investment in the United States*

Reports activities of U.S. affiliates of foreign companies, intra-firm trade, sales of U.S. affiliates of foreign companies, and royalties and license fees to foreign parent companies by country and by industry. Food and kindred products are disaggregated to beverages and other.

International Trade Statistics Yearbook. *UN-Data.*

This data base reports for each country export (FOB) and import (CIF) data in weight and value for commodities classified by SITC (Standard International Trade Classification) codes. For some commodities up to five digits of disaggregation are available. These data are useful to study trends in food industry and agricultural trade flows as well as to calculate unit values.

Compact Disclosure-Worldscope Global®

by Worldscope/Disclosure Partners (W/D) 1000 Lafayette Blvd., Bridgeport, CT 06604.

Reports financial data for twelve thousand companies worldwide. Disaggregation is at the firm level. Some useful items are: net income margin (at home and abroad), foreign assets share of total assets, foreign sales share of total sales, product and geographic segment data.

Instituto Español de Comercio Exterior (ICEX). Data base: OFERES.

Spanish government agency concerned with exports. Reports firm-level trade statistics with distribution of foreign sales by SIC and by country. Years 1989–94.

9

Vertical Markets in International Trade

Ronald W. Jones

Introduction

All markets in which production takes place are vertical. That is, inputs are transformed into outputs. Of central concern in this chapter is a situation in which an input and an output are both traded on international markets. In models in which markets are perfectly competitive, the size of firms becomes indeterminate, but the relationship between prices of traded inputs and outputs is important in analyzing a nation's real income. Commercial policy may be employed by a country in order to gain advantage over other countries by obtaining better terms of trade in one or both markets. In markets that are imperfectly competitive a firm may be able on its own to affect prices. In particular, a firm may be vertically integrated, and it may supply foreign markets with both inputs and outputs. Indeed, it may be in competition with rivals abroad on the output side, while at the same time supplying them (at a profit) with the inputs that these rivals require. In the case of imperfect competition, new trade theory has suggested that the exercise of commercial policy may appear rather different from its form in a competitive world.

The theory of international trade has often prided itself with its use of general equilibrium analysis. However, most of classical trade theory involves only two traded commodities, with each being exported by a separate country to the other. Since this implies only one traded market, the pride of technique turns into a pretty empty boast. In the case of vertically related markets studied in this paper, however, the interrelationship between markets becomes crucial and the analysis a bit more difficult than in the standard case. Although imperfect market behavior has features that are different from those found in competitive markets, there are important similarities that stem from the relations between vertically connected markets, and these are laid out in a core model in the second section of this chapter. In this setting, the prices of items exported by one country tend to go up and down together. By contrast, the third section discusses the variation in which a country's two terms of trade may move in opposite directions. The fourth section pursues the analysis of the core model in a situation in which trade agreements may prevent a country from interfering in some markets, but not in others, so that a distortionary wedge can be introduced in only one of the two markets. The fifth section turns to the kind of imperfectly competitive behavior analyzed in detail in two papers by Spencer and Jones (1991, 1992) in which a vertically integrated firm is engaged in duopolistic competition with a foreign firm, but has an asymmetrically strong position in producing an input required by its rival. The role of government commercial policy in this imperfectly competitive setting is discussed in the sixth section, and contrasted with policy in the competitive case. The seventh section turns to some other modelling strategies concerning vertical markets that have been put forth in the literature, and the eighth section provides concluding remarks.

The Core Model

In discussing the issue of vertical relationships in trade it is useful to refer to a simple core model. Assume that an intermediate good or factor, z_1, is used (along with labor) to produce a final commodity, x_1. Both x_1 and z_1 are traded, with X_1 denoting exports from the home country (with negative values, i.e. imports of good 1, M_1, sometimes considered) and Z_1 exports of z_1. To avoid complications assume in this core setting that z_1 is not produced—it is available each period in a given flow amount. This fits the concept of a given and non-reproducible capital stock in the earlier literature on foreign investment [e.g. Kemp (1966) or Jones (1967)], and in the fourth section more attention is paid to asymmetries between countries in supply conditions for intermediates. To round out the picture assume there is some other commodity, x_2, produced with labor and its own specific resource or capital. This commodity is freely traded (in a competitive market—even in later sections) and serves as numeraire. Pure competition prevails, but governmental commercial policy may insert tax or subsidy distortions—wedges between domestic prices of x_1 and z_1, denoted by p_1 and r_1, and world prices, p_1^* and r_1^*. Thus the production structure of the core model is of the specific-factors variety, with trade at final and intermediate good levels.

The budget constraint can be expressed either in terms of domestic prices (in which case tax or subsidy amounts get listed explicitly) or, more simply, in terms of world prices, as in (1), with the consumption bundle shown by (D_1, D_2).

$$p_1^* D_1 + D_2 = p_1^* x_1 + x_2 + r_1^* Z_1 \tag{1}$$

Of special interest are changes to equilibrium values caused by commercial policy and the consequent alteration in real national welfare, *dy*, defined as the domestic price-weighted sum of consumption changes

$$dy \equiv p_1 dD_1 + dD_2 \tag{2}$$

Any changes *along* the transformation schedule linking outputs x_1 and x_2 involve only a second-order small change in the value of aggregate production at initial domestic prices, but an increase in exports of the intermediate good causes the home transformation schedule to shrink inwards. In a competitive setting such a *shift* is related to the domestic price of z_1, r_1. Thus,

$$p_1 dx_1 + dx_2 = -r_1 dZ_1 \tag{3}$$

With these relationships at hand, the budget constraint (1) can be differentiated to reveal the sources of any change in aggregate real income,

$$dy = \{X_1 dp_1^* + Z_1 dr_1^*\} + \{(p_1^* - p_1)dX_1 + (r_1^* - r_1)dZ_1\} \tag{4}$$

Equation (4) is fundamental in the analysis of trade in vertically related markets. Two items are traded (in addition to the numeraire good 2), and for each there is a terms-of-trade effect (shown in the first bracket) and a volume-of-trade effect (shown in the second bracket). The terms-of-trade effect states that an improvement in the world price of any item exported increases real income by an amount that is proportional both to such a price rise and to the volume of exports. The volume-of-trade effect suggests that if there exists a positive gap between world and domestic prices for any exported item (tax- or subsidy-inspired in this competitive case), an increase in such exports raises national income by an amount proportional both to the extent of the gap and the increase in exports. In popular parlance, "it pays to buy cheap and sell dear;" if, say, p_1^* exceeds p_1, a unit of X_1 can be bought at home for p_1 and sold abroad for the greater amount, p_1^*. Of course, in our competitive model this spread is captured by the government in the form of an export tax.

To proceed with the analysis it is important to recognize the technological and market links between the pair of world prices (p_1^*, r_1^*) and trade volumes (X_1, Z_1). In general, all input prices are related to commodity prices and the resource base (including the volume of intermediate goods available for production). The foreign technology thus determines the nature of the dependence of r_1^* on the price of x_1 abroad, p_1^*, and the only element in the foreign input base that is being changed, namely Z_1. Thus,

$$r_1^* = r_1^*(p_1^*, Z_1) \tag{5}$$

Differentiating,

$$dr_1^* = \frac{r_1^*}{p_1^*}\gamma_1^* dp_1^* - \frac{r_1^*}{Z_1}\delta_1^* dZ_1 \tag{6}$$

Two elasticities have been introduced. The expression γ_1^*, the relative change in the price of specific intermediates, r_1^*, compared to a given relative increase in the price of final goods abroad, p_1^*, exceeds unity in this specific-factors model.[1] The term δ_1^* is positive (if the home country exports the intermediate) and indicates the extent to which the return to Z_1 is driven down abroad as more of this input is added to a given foreign resource base.[2]

A second relationship involves market-clearing for commodities. In particular home exports, X_1, must be balanced by foreign imports, M_1^*, and these, in turn, depend upon foreign price, p_1^* (as shown by movements along a foreign offer curve for imports) and changes in Z_1 (which cause the foreign offer curve to shift):

$$X_1 = M_1^*(p_1^*, Z_1) \tag{7}$$

Thus,

$$\hat{X}_1 = -\varepsilon_1^* \hat{p}_1^* + \frac{1}{X_1}\frac{\partial M_1^*}{\partial Z_1} dZ_1 \tag{8}$$

ε_1^* is the elasticity of foreign demand for imports along its offer curve (defined so as to be positive). The breakdown of $\partial M_1^*/\partial Z_1$ involves both changes in foreign demand for imports at constant prices, $\partial D_1^*/\partial Z_1$, and changes in foreign production, $\partial x_1^*/\partial Z_1$. The former involves just an income effect (since p_1^* is held fixed). Thus, $\partial D_1^*/\partial Z_1$ equals (m_1^*/p_1^*) times $\partial y^*/\partial Z_1$, where m_1^* is the foreign marginal propensity to consume the first commodity. Assuming the foreign country is passive in the sense of not imposing trade taxes or subsidies, $\partial y^*/\partial Z_1$ reflects only a terms-of-trade effect, $-Z_1(\partial r_1^*/\partial Z_1)$, or $r_1^*\delta_1^*$. The output effect, $\partial x_1^*/\partial Z_1$, reveals that at constant prices an increase in Z_1 increases output of the first commodity, x_1^*. But by the reciprocity theorem due to Samuelson (1953), this term is related to γ_1^* since it states that

$$\frac{\partial x_1^*}{\partial Z_1} = \frac{\partial r_1^*}{\partial p_1^*}$$

Thus $\partial x_1^*/\partial Z_1 = (r_1^*/p_1^*)$ times γ_1^*. Putting these together,

$$\frac{\partial M_1^*}{\partial Z_1} = \frac{m_1^*}{p_1^*} r_1^* \delta_1^* - \frac{r_1^*}{p_1^*} \gamma_1^* \tag{9}$$

In words, an increase in flows of the intermediate good abroad at constant p_1^* serves to change foreign demand for imports since it causes r_1^* to fall and thus to improve foreign real incomes, but it also increases foreign supply. In principle the foreign offer curve can shift in either direction, but I assume the supply shift dominates so that an increase of Z_1 shifts the offer curve inwards (see endnote 2).

Assembling these various components into the general expression (4) for welfare changes at home yields:

$$dy = \frac{\partial y}{\partial p_1^*} dp_1^* + \frac{\partial y}{\partial Z_1} dZ_1 \tag{10}$$

$$\text{where } \frac{\partial y}{\partial p_1^*} = X_1 \left\{ \left(1 + \mu^* \gamma_1^*\right) - \frac{\left(p_1^* - p_1\right)}{p_1^*} \varepsilon_1^* \right\},$$

$$\frac{\partial y}{\partial Z_1} = \left[1 - \left(\frac{p_1}{p_1^*} m_1^* + m_2^* \right) \delta_1^* - \frac{\left(p_1^* - p_1\right)}{p_1^*} \gamma_1^* \right] r_1^* - r_1$$

where μ^* is the ratio of the two trade flows, $r_1^* Z_1 / p_1^* X_1$.

Consider the separate roles of the commodity terms of trade, p_1^*, and the extent of resource trade, Z_1, starting from a position of initial free trade in both markets. An increase in p_1^* drives up r_1^* as well. Thus if the home country exports both the intermediate good and the final good, an export tax can be expected to improve the terms of trade in *both* markets. As (10) reveals, however, once a gap is opened up between p_1^* and p_1, there is a drag on the improvement in real income as greater values of p_1^* reduce foreign demand along the foreign offer curve—the volume-of-trade effect. The exercise of setting $\partial y / \partial p_1^*$ in (10) equal to zero would reveal the formula for the optimal export tax. Let this ad valorem tax rate be denoted by τ, such that

$$p_1^* = (1 + \tau) p_1. \tag{11}$$

Thus, the optimal export tax formula is:[3]

$$\tau_{opt} = \frac{[1 + \mu^* \gamma^*]}{\varepsilon^* - [1 + \mu^* \gamma^*]}. \tag{12}$$

Turn now to the optimal tax rate on intermediate exports, Z_1. Assume t is the ad valorem rate applied to the foreign price, r_1^*, so that

$$r_1 = (1 - t) r_1^* \tag{13}$$

From (10) this implies that

$$t_{opt} = \left(\frac{p_1}{p_1^*} m_1^* + m_2^* \right) \delta_1^* + \frac{\left(p_1^* - p_1\right)}{p_1^*} \gamma_1^* \tag{14}$$

Thus at the initial free trade point $t_{opt} = \delta_1^*$, which is positive, a result that parallels that for an export tax on the final good. That is, for an active home country exporting both a final good and an intermediate good used in its production, starting to restrict exports of either good from a position of free trade serves to raise real income.

How does the optimal tax distortion in each market depend on the distortion existing in the other market? Figure 9.1 summarizes the results. It suggests that the greater the export tax on final commodities, the more incentive there exists to insert a tax wedge between the price of the intermediate abroad and its price at home. Rewrite (14) as (14′) to incorporate explicitly the tax rates:

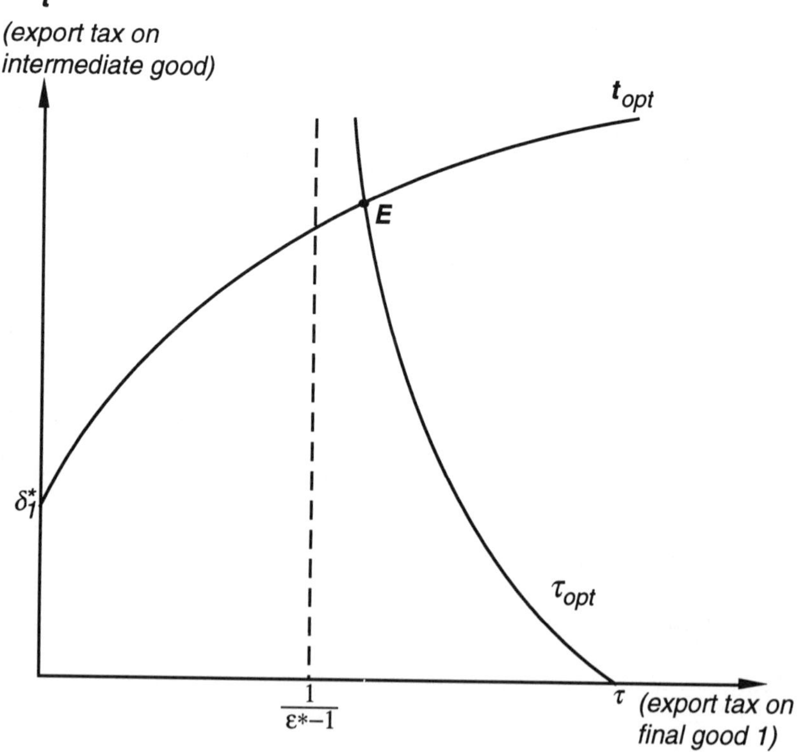

FIGURE 9.1 Relationship between optimal export taxes on intermediate and final goods.

$$t_{opt} = \left[\frac{1}{1+\tau} m_1^* + m_2^*\right]\delta_1^* + \frac{\tau}{1+\tau}\gamma_1^* \tag{14'}$$

The higher is τ the lower is the first expression in (14'), but the higher is the second. Comparing these effects, assuming parameters m_1^*, δ_1^*, γ_1^* remain constant, leads to

$$\frac{dt_{opt}}{d\tau} = \frac{\gamma_1^* - m_1^*\delta_1^*}{(1+\dot{\tau})^2} \tag{15}$$

I have assumed this term is positive since γ_1^* exceeds unity, and δ_1^* is assumed to be less than unity. That is, a restriction on intermediate exports not only serves to raise r_1^*, but by reducing production of the final good abroad (more than demand is reduced by assumption) it also leads to a positive volume-of-trade effect. This latter gets larger the greater the gap between the foreign price, p_1^*, and the home price, p_1.

By contrast, an inverse relationship exists between the optimal tax rate on final goods exports and the tax rate on the intermediate good. In equation (12) recall that μ^* indicates the ratio of revenue earned from sales of the intermediate, $r_1^* Z_1$, to that stemming from sales of the final good, $p_1^* X_1$. Assume, now, that the primary effect of an increase in the export tax on intermediates is to reduce their exports, Z_1, relative to final exports, X_1, thus reducing μ^*. From (12) this has the effect of reducing the optimal tax rate on final goods. Note that the optimal level of τ exceeds the level it would have if there were no trade in intermediates $[1/(\varepsilon^* - 1)]$, since the fact that both terms of trade move together makes raising p_1^* with a tariff more valuable the greater the value of trade in intermediates. This explains the negative relationships shown in Figure 9.1. Full optimization has the tax distortion shown by point E.[4]

Variations on a Trading Theme: Opposed Terms of Trade

Two basic features of the core model resulted in the home country's terms of trade for final goods and for intermediates moving in the same direction. An increase in the price of the final good would, at given export levels for intermediates, result in a magnified increase in the price of those sector-specific intermediates.[5] It was assumed, as well, that the home country exported both commodities. But the trading pattern might be different: The home country might import the final commodity that uses the country's exported intermediate. In such a case, a price rise for imports, a deterioration in final goods terms of trade, is associated with an increase in the price of its intermediate export, an improvement in intermediate goods terms of trade.

Such a scenario may reflect the trading pattern associated with the tail end of the Vernon (1966) product cycle. Initially a country has developed a resource that is specifically used in its export commodity. Eventually it establishes production facilities abroad by sending its intermediate to a branch plant. Alternatively, it may export the intermediate in arms-length transactions to a rival final goods producer abroad. In either case, home production of the final good may fall short of home demand, and the home country may end up importing the commodity that uses its exported intermediate.

Another interpretation fits the scene found in many less-developed countries: Exports are concentrated in a raw material whose production requires little value added at home. The country desires to expand its own production of the secondary industry whose output uses the exported raw material, but it is still at a stage where it imports the final good using this raw material.

In either of these cases it is clear from equation (10)'s expression for $\partial y/\partial p_1^*$ that the sign of $(1 + \mu^*\gamma_1^*)$ is crucial in determining optimal commercial policy, where μ^* is now the negative number $(-r_1^* Z_1/p_1^* M_1)$. The value of $(1 + \mu^*\gamma_1^*)$ could still be positive if imports of the final good strongly dominate exports of the raw material. In such a case optimal policy calls for taxing imports of final good 1, despite the fact that this will drive down r_1^*, the terms of trade on material exports. Of more interest is the possibility that $(1 + \mu^*\gamma_1^*)$ is negative, a result guaranteed if the value of raw material exports is at least as great as that of final imports of good 1 (since $\gamma_1^* > 1$). Optimal policy then calls for a subsidy on imports of the final good in order to raise the foreign price of intermediates. As the expression for t_{opt} in (14) reveals, in this case of a subsidy on imports of the first commodity, p_1^* once again exceeds p_1, and the case for restricting exports of the raw material gets strengthened.

Trade Controls Only on Intermediates

The preceding sections have discussed the case in which the home country can control prices or trade volumes both for final goods and for intermediates (or materials). However, international agreements may tie a country's hands in final goods trade. Markets for raw materials or intermediates are a different matter. Often a country maintains controls over exports of such inputs. Consider such a case. The home country can control Z_1, but there is a free trade agreement for final goods so that p_1 remains equal to foreign p_1^*. What then is the effect of a restriction on Z_1 (which forces r_1^* above r_1) on the common price of final good 1? If the home country exports at both ends of the vertical chain, are its terms of trade in these markets positively correlated?

There is an argument for such a positive correlation in a competitive general equilibrium setting, a presumption that becomes more powerful if markets are imperfectly competitive (See the following section). Referring to equation (10), dp_1^* and dZ_1 are connected by the condition that the world market for final good 1 clears. Thus:

$$\frac{dy}{dZ_1} = \frac{\partial y_1}{\partial p_1^*}\frac{dp_1^*}{dZ_1} + \frac{\partial y}{\partial Z_1} \tag{10'}$$

Suppose the home country exports both the final good and the intermediate. If such exports are based on the home country devoting a larger share of its national income to production of good 1 than does the foreign (importing) country, there is a presumption that an increase of Z_1 will increase world output of final good 1 and thus probably eventuate in a fall in p_1^* (as well as in r_1^*).[6]

The reasoning behind this presumption is laid out in Jones (1987, 1989) and makes use of the Samuelson (1953) reciprocity theorem, whereby in each country $\partial x_1/\partial z_1$ equals $\partial r_1/\partial p_1$. With free trade in goods, p_1 and p_1^* are equal, and in the initial absence of taxation on materials trade so are r_1 and r_1^*. Therefore world output of good 1 rises with an increase in materials export if γ_1^* exceeds γ_1. A commonly shared increase in the price of final good 1 will presumptively raise the home wage rate by relatively more than the foreign wage rate if the x_1-sector is relatively a larger share of incomes at home than abroad. If so, there is a presumption that the relative increase in return to intermediates at home, although exceeding $\hat{p}_1$ (or $\hat{p}_1^*$) will not be as great as it is abroad. That is, the presumption is that γ_1^* exceeds γ_1, suggesting that an increase in Z_1 raises total world output of good 1 and lowers p_1^* as well as r_1^*. In equation (10′), dp_1^*/dZ_1 is negative, leading to an even greater negative value for dy/dZ_1 than for $\partial y/\partial Z_1$. The case is strong for restriction of raw materials exports.[7]

Firm Behavior in Imperfect Markets

In 1986 the United States levied a 35 percent duty on Canadian exports of cedar shakes and shingles (final goods), in an attempt to force greater Canadian exports of cedar bolts and logs (raw materials). In a separate action in the 1980s, Japanese producers of DRAM semiconductors were hit by an American antidumping action. This encouraged a significant increase in the price of these chips to American computer firms, which were locked into duopolistic competition with Japanese firms such as Toshiba and NEC. Both these cases provided examples in which a country's exports bore a vertical relationship to each other (Canada in cedar products and Japan in computers and parts) and were faced with commercial policy instigated in the importing country. In a pair of papers, Barbara Spencer and I analyzed optimal policies for firms and governments in both exporting and importing countries when final goods were produced in a duopolistic market, but the production of intermediates bore strong asymmetries in the two countries.[8] Here I sketch out the basic features of this analysis and relate it to the core model discussed earlier.

Let a vertically integrated firm in the home country export both the final and intermediate good to the foreign country. Production technology is now more simple than in the core model. Only the intermediate good is required to produce the final good and the marginal cost of producing the intermediate good at home is constant. Further to simplify, all final output, x_1, is shipped abroad as exports; there is no local demand for this good. The foreign country also has a firm producing the final good, with both firms engaged in Cournot fashion in deciding output. It is in producing the intermediate good that a strong asymmetry appears; abroad there is a competitive fringe of price-taking producers, with price, r_1^*, determined by the home firm, whose dominance allows it to set a value for r_1^* exceeding marginal (and average) cost, c_1. Decisions are made in stages, with the foreign firm's output decision for final goods taken as of precommitment by the home firm of an intermediate price, r_1^*. This price, in turn, is based on a given set of taxes or subsidies set by governments in both countries.

The key question for the vertically integrated home firm is what price to charge for the intermediate product, in full awareness that, once it commits to this price, Cournot competition in the final goods market determines the final good's price and each country's output share. The home firm must consider the option of charging such a prohibitive price for the intermediate that it forecloses sales in this market. The foreign firm may have its own supplies of the intermediate, but if not, such a vertical foreclosure decision squeezes the foreign firm out of the final goods market. Two key elements bear upon the foreclosure decision. First of all, the foreign government may levy a tariff on its imports of the final good from the home country, thus lowering the profit margin in this market relative to profits to be earned by supplying the intermediate.[9] This response can be illustrated in Figure 9.1, where τ, the export tax on final goods, now represents the profit margin in this market. As this is lowered by the imposition of the foreign tariff, the optimal "tax" on materials exports also falls. This "tax" now represents the excess of price charged to foreigners for materials, r_1^*, over the local cost, c_1. Reducing the profit margin on final goods reduces as well the incentive of the vertically integrated home firm to charge a high price for materials exports in order to gain advantage over its rival in the final goods market. It was this concern with spillovers in the final market (which in the imperfectly competitive case is referred to as the "strategic effect") that causes the optimal tax rate schedule in Figure 9.1 to rise from its vertical intercept at δ_1^*.

The other feature of the model that bears upon the vertical foreclosure issue is the nature of supply conditions for materials in the foreign country. Reconsider expression (4) for real income changes in a competitive market. An analogous expression holds for profit changes for a vertically integrated firm with home prices, p_1 and r_1, replaced by the home firm's (constant) marginal costs, c_1. The more elastic foreign supply of materials is, the more home exports, Z_1, will be stimulated by a reduction in price charged, r_1^*. Thus, sufficiently sensitive foreign supply will encourage home supply of materials exports.

In the competitive model the positive relationship between the terms of trade in final and intermediate goods was provided by technology—as of a given resource base a rise in the price of the final good caused the price of the specific intermediate to rise by a magnified relative amount. In the imperfectly competitive setting with Cournot duopoly in the final goods market, there once again emerges this relationship between the two export prices, but for a different reason. Prices are not anchored to costs since profits can be earned, and the margin of profits varies depending on government taxes and the price charged for intermediates.

Suppose the vertically integrated home firm raises the price, r_1^*, it charges the foreign firm for materials. This shifts the foreign firm's reaction curve in Figure 9.2 inwards, resulting in a new Cournot equilibrium (from A to B) with reduced foreign output, increased home output, and a reduction in total world supply, which serves to increase final price, p_1^*.[10] Consider the extent of the rise in p_1^* if the effect of a rise in home output is temporarily ignored: The foreign firm's marginal cost schedule has shifted upwards by the increase in r_1^*, and this serves to raise p_1^* along the demand curve facing the foreign firm (as of given home output). But if the marginal revenue curve is steeper than the demand curve (as I will assume), p_1^* does not rise by as much as marginal revenue (or r_1^*). As well, since p_1^* exceeds r_1^* (as a profit margin is assumed to exist), the relative increase in final goods price, $\hat{p}_1^*$, falls short of $\hat{r}_1^*$, as in the competitive model (for different reasons). Now take into account the fact that home output actually rises somewhat along the home reaction curve (from A to B), and the increase in p_1^* is even smaller.

I described earlier the presumptive positive relationship between r_1^* and p_1^* in the "second-best" scenario in which the home country is bound by free trade in final goods but could restrict intermediate exports, Z_1, and thus raise r_1^*. The presumption rested on the argument that world output of final commodity 1 would fall in competitive markets with such a restriction on intermediate exports. In the present Cournot setting this presumption is greatly strengthened—the move from *A* to *B* in Figure 9.2 ensured a price rise for the final commodity.

The equilibrium position for the active home firm setting r_1^* results in

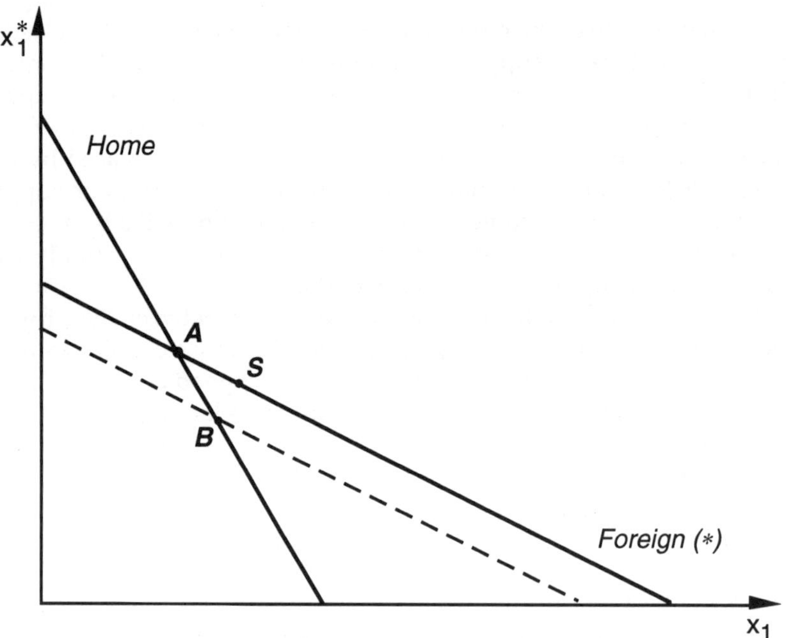

FIGURE 9.2 Cournot reaction functions of vertically integrated home and foreign competitors.

profit margins in each of the two markets that may not be equal. Generally speaking, the higher foreign supply elasticity is the more attractive a lowering of r_1^* to capture more material sales abroad is, even though this entails a lower profit margin in this market than in the final goods market (a drop in r_1^* causes p_1^* to fall, but by less).

Government Policy in Imperfect Markets

The analysis of the core model suggested a strong role for an activist country engaged in trade in vertically related markets. Given that firms were assumed to be price-taking competitors, the role of commercial policy was to exercise control over markets so as to achieve better terms of trade, subject to the volume-of-trade constraint on the exercise of monopolistic power. With imperfect competition, firms are no longer passive price takers, and it is natural to ask what role is left for government interference.

If all exports were of a single type and controlled by a single monopolistic firm, would the unencumbered exercise of profit maximization by such a firm yield the nation's welfare-maximizing outcome? Probably not, and this for two basic reasons: (1) The firm's objective function (profit maximization) generally does not take account of domestic consumer interests, and (2) The firm may not be able to discriminate between local and foreign consumers and thus duplicate optimal commercial policy. Even if it could discriminate, it might not do so in the same way. For example, a discriminating monopolist may face more elastic demand for its product abroad and thus charge foreign consumers a lower price than at home. This is akin to an export subsidy rather than a national income optimum export tax.

The assumption typically made in the imperfect competition literature that no domestic consumption of the exported good takes place obviates much of these difficulties. If the firm could credibly act as a Stackelberg leader in our Cournot setting, there would then be no need for government interference, and in Figure 9.2 a position such as *S* could be attained. But this may not be possible, and our discussion in the preceeding section suggests that the strong asymmetric supply condition for materials or intermediates could allow a home vertically integrated firm to commit to a price, r_1^*, for intermediate exports, but then it has to compete in a Cournot duopoly market for the final good. The home firm does have some control over price and can shift the foreign reaction curve by changing r_1^*. But it takes home government commitment in the form of tax or subsidy policy to replicate the optimal Stackelberg outcome and effectively shift the home reaction curve.

The key to optimal government policy is the comparison between profit margins in the final and intermediate markets. As demonstrated in Spencer and Jones (1991), the government will subsidize the firm's exports of final goods if the profit margin there exceeds that in materials trade, but otherwise a tax on final exports is appropriate. In the celebrated article by Brander and Spencer (1985), optimal policy called for an export subsidy (on final goods). This result, which did much to promote the analysis of strategic trade policy, seemed diametrically opposed to classical trade theory, which called for taxes on trade in order that a country improve its terms of trade. In my view these results are similar in that in each case the role of commercial policy is to see that trade is optimally *restricted*. Under perfectly competitive conditions firms have no incentive to restrict exports so that all trade restriction must be done by government taxation. By contrast, in Cournot duopoly the home firm is aware of its ability to raise price, but if it operates under the belief that foreign output is unchanged, it will "overshoot" and restrict output too much. Hence the role of government is to subsidize trade so as to encourage a bit more exports. In the case of vertically connected trade, the role of government is to encourage a switch away from final trade toward exports of the intermediate *if* the profit margin there is higher. This is obviously not the case if there were no intermediate trade, and the positive profit margin for final goods uniformly leads to subsidies on exports in that market.[11]

The preceeding section discussed the role of government policy in the foreign country that is importing both final and intermediate goods. Because of the strategic connection between markets, the vertically integrated firm has charged a higher price for intermediate exports even than would a monopolist firm in that area. By diminishing the importance of the final goods market, the foreign tariff induces the vertically integrated firm to lower r_1^*, whereas a pure monopolist dealing only with intermediates would be tempted to raise export price since foreign demand for such intermediates is stimulated by the tariff's support of the local final goods sector. Much the same argument was presented for competitive markets in Jones and Spencer (1989) and, as the previous section discussed, can be illustrated in Figure 9.1 by movements along the t_{opt} schedule.[12]

Other Facets of Vertical Markets

The international trade literature has been concerned with some other facets of markets with vertical structures. Here I briefly sketch some of the directions in which this literature has proceeded.

International Predation

Suppose that each of two countries has a firm in the same (downstream) market (perhaps with exports to a third country), but that in one of the countries the firm is vertically integrated with a branch producing a raw material or intermediate. These firms are locked into duopolistic competition, much as in the discussion earlier. Bernhofen (1996a) analyses the advantages that the vertically integrated firm has over its foreign rival if predation occurs, involving losses in the downstream market. If profits are made in the materials market, these funds can be used to subsidize temporary losses by the firm at the downstream end and thus give the vertically integrated firm an advantage in its duopolistically competitive struggle. This opens up a temporal dimension to the arguments presented in the previous section.

Bargaining

Karp and Sioli (1995) discuss trade between two countries, in each of which there is an upstream and a downstream firm, and, instead of price-setting at the upstream (materials) end, there is bargaining. This is like moving from noncooperative to cooperative equilibria. Some of the novelties include a sequence in which bargaining takes place first between upstream and downstream firms in the same country and then between firms in the the two countries. Complications also appear since resale of intermediates may or may not be possible.

Quality Differences

The final good produced in the two countries may not be of the same quality. Chang and Kim (1989) have a setting in which a DC (developed country) is in competition with an LDC (less developed country), selling a high-quality export good to third markets, whereas the LDC sells a lower-quality good. The LDC is dependent upon imports of an important intermediate from the DC, which gives the DC power to affect market outcomes. Indeed, they assume that the DC can act like a Stackelberg leader [as also in Chang and Chen (1994)], as opposed to the earlier discussion in Spencer and Jones (1991), where the vertically integrated firm can set conditions in the intermediate good market but must compete in Cournot fashion in the final goods market. This difference supports the Chang and Kim conclusion that the optimal policy for the DC is one of non-intervention—there is no distortion that the government needs to offset. The LDC government, on the other hand, may find it in its interest to tax imports of the required intermediate. In Chang and Kim (1991) the scenario is enriched by allowing the LDC to produce a substitute intermediate good. Then if the LDC uses the intermediate from the DC, it produces a medium-quality good, inferior to the good produced by the DC but of higher quality than the good produced with the home-grown intermediate. Skeath (1993) emphasizes quality differences on the input side, which in turn lead to quality differences on the output side. A model with quality differences is more amenable to the analysis of Bertrand competition, and, with such competition for final goods, a tariff on inputs will drive the downstream output firm out of business. Skeath points out the relevance of the analysis to the over 60 percent tariff applied in the United States in 1991 on display screens for laptop computers supplied by Japan.

Services and Trade

The volume of international trade in intermediates, producer goods, raw materials, and other middle products is rising even relative to the total volume of trade. This reflects the increased *fragmentation* of the production process into separate vertical components. As modelled in Jones and Kierzkowski (1990), one element that makes this possible is the kind of increasing returns suggested long ago by Adam Smith—increased specialization and division of labor. In their model, the production process is made up of separate *production blocks*, connected and coordinated by *service links*. As scale of productive activity expands, so does the division into production blocks, and it is primarily the costs of service links—information, communication, and transportation—that have been decreasing at the international level, aiding and abetting the process whereby vertical production structures get fragmented and spread around to various countries, each of which may have a comparative advantage in a separate part of the production process. These activities may be coordinated at arms length, or production may take place under the rubric of a multinational enterprise. In the literature on the latter [see especially Helpman (1984) and Helpman and Krugman (1985)] the rationale for multinationals involves the distinction between production and headquarters services, and the setting is one in which factor endowment proportions between countries may be sufficiently different that, in order to maintain factor-price equalization, headquarter services (presumably capital intensive) are located in the capital-abundant country and, some of the production activity (using only labor) is located in the labor-abundant country. This scenario is close to the earlier Kemp (1966) and Jones (1967) models in which a country uses some of its capital abroad as foreign investment and the sector-specific version of that model is the basis for the core model. Thus there is vertical trade in which a country produces and exports a commodity using inputs (services), which are also "exported" (i.e. used) abroad (even if they do not travel).

Concluding Remarks

International trade in vertically related products is an important feature in world markets. For any country that trades in a final product and, as well, in an input that is used to produce that product, the relationship between the two terms of trade is crucial in determining national commercial policy or, if such trade is conducted by a vertically integrated firm, is important in deciding that firm's pricing or output strategy. The core model outlined in the second section revealed how technology as well as trade flows helps determine links among input and output prices. In the specific-factors framework adopted there, the price of the final product and the price of the traded specific input are positively related, so that if a country exports at both ends of the vertical spectrum it has an interest in restricting trade in both items to achieve better terms of trade. The interplay between markets is more subtle, and the analysis underlying Figure 9.1 reveals how a higher gap between the world price of an exported final good and the (lower) price or cost domestically of that item encourages even more restrictions on exports of an intermediate or raw material used to produce the final good.

In a purely competitive framework agents take prices as given, so that any effort to achieve better terms of trade for a country becomes the responsibility of government. In less competitive settings, much of this effort can be undertaken by private firms, but commercial policy is still required for a national optimum if the firm's objective function does not take into account interests of domestic consumers, or if, as in the case of Cournot equilibria, the firm cannot credibly shift its own reaction locus. Therefore once again there is a possible use for commercial policy. Nonetheless, the basic rationale for interference—to take account of possible terms-of-trade gains subject to volume-of-trade constraints—is applicable to firms as well as countries, and this breakdown proves useful in the analysis of optimal distortions in a context in which both final goods and intermediate products are traded on world markets.

Notes

1. Details of the relationships among input and output prices in a specific-factors model can be found in Caves, Frankel, and Jones (1996), supplement to chapter 6. If p_1^* rises, the return to the mobile factor, w_1^*, rises but by a dampened amount: $\hat{w}^* = \beta_1^* \hat{p}_1^*$ with β_1^* a positive fraction. (A hat "^" over a variable denotes a relative change). Thus the competitive profit equations of change require that $\hat{r}_1^*$ equals $\left(1-\beta_1^*\theta_{L1}^*\right)/1-\theta_{L1}^*$ times $\hat{p}_1^*$ where θ_{L1}^* is labor's distributive share abroad in the first sector. The coefficient of $\hat{p}_1^*$ is γ_1^*.

2. In what follows I assume δ_1^* is less than unity. It equals the fraction of the foreign resource base represented by the flow from the home country (Z_1/z_1^*) times the elasticity $\left\{-\left(\partial r_1^*/\partial z_1^*\right)\cdot\left(z_1^*/r_1^*\right)\right\}$.

3. It is important to note that optimal trade restriction must be sufficient to yield an equilibrium point along the foreign offer curve such that ε^* is high enough to ensure a positive denominator in (12).

4. Strictly speaking the curves in Figure 9.1 should be relabeled as $\{\partial y/\partial p_1^* = 0\}$ for τ_{opt} and $\{\partial y/\partial Z_1 = 0\}$ for t_{opt}. Curves corresponding to $\{dy/dp_1^* = 0\}$ and $\{dy/dZ_1 = 0\}$ would also intersect at *E* but capture more indirect effects as well. Some of these are discussed in a later section (Trade Controls Only on Intermediates).

5. In Kemp (1996) and Jones (1967) investment of non-specific capital abroad took the place of the core model's export of a sector-specific intermediate good. In that Heckscher-Ohlin model it was possible that the final commodity exported by the country engaged in foreign investment was produced by labor-intensive techniques in the host country. In such a case the investor's two terms of trade move in opposite directions.

6. The increase in Z_1 changes r_1^* and thus reallocates real incomes between countries. The assumption made here is that the resulting change in world demand for commodity 1 (if any) is outweighed by supply changes. For details see Jones (1987).

7. With reference to Footnote 4 and Figure 9.1, this is an argument for a curve showing $\{dy/dZ_1 = 0\}$ to lie above the t_{opt} curve shown in Figure 9.1 for t smaller than the optimum shown at E. Starting from a point on the t_{opt} curve, a slight

restriction of Z_1 exports would not affect real income if p_1^* is held constant. However, if p_1^* rises following a restriction in Z_1, real incomes would rise as well, calling for a higher optimal value of *t* than shown by the curve in Figure 9.1. A similar kind of argument can be used to show that below E, a curve showing $\{dy/dp_1^* = 0\}$ would have optimal t greater than shown in Figure 9.1.

8. See Spencer and Jones (1991, 1992) as well as an analysis in a competitive setting in Jones and Spencer (1989).

9. Indeed one of the motives behind the 1986 U.S. tariff on cedar shakes and shingles from Canada was to encourage more Canadian sales of raw cedar bolts and logs.

10. The reaction loci in Figure 9.2 need not be linear. What is assumed, however, is that outputs are strategic substitutes—an increase in the output of one firm lowers marginal revenue in the other. The home reaction curve is steeper than a 45 degree line, so that world output at B is lower than at A.

11. A similar kind of argument, pointing out the possibility of a desired export tax (instead of subsidy) on final goods if there are also profits earned by intermediate exporters, is made in Bernhofen (1996b).

12. Lin (1994) explores the possibility that restrictions on raw material exports get tightened rather than loosened if the foreign country imposes a tariff on exports of the final good.

References

Bernhofen, Daniel M. (1996a). "Vertical Integration and International Predation," *Review of International Economics*, vol. 4, pp. 90–98.

———. (1996b). "Strategic Export Policy in a Model of Vertical Equilibrium," unpublished manuscript.

Brander, James and Barbara Spencer (1985). "Export Subsidies and Market Share Rivalry," *Journal of International Economics*, vol. 18, pp. 83–100.

Caves, Richard E., Jeffrey A. Frankel and Ronald W. Jones (1996). *World Trade and Payments*, 7th edition, Harper Collins, New York.

Chang, Winston and Fang-yeuh Chen (1994). "Vertically Related Markets: Export Rivalry Between DC and LDC Firms," *Review of International Economics*, vol. 2 (June), pp. 131–142.

Chang, Winston and Jae-Cheol Kim (1989). "Competition in Quality-Differentiated Products and Optimal Trade Policy," *Keio Economic Studies*, pp. 1–17.

———. (1991). "Strategic Tariff Policy in a Model of Trade in Intermediate and Final Products," in Takayama, Ohyama, and Ohta (eds.), *Trade, Policy, and International Adjustments.* Academic Press, New York pp. 36–59.

Helpman, Elhanan (1984). "A Simple Theory of International Trade with Multinational Corporations," *Journal of Political Economy*, vol. 92, pp. 451–71.

Helpman, Elhanan and Paul R. Krugman (1985). *Market Structure and Foreign Trade* (M.I.T. Press, Cambridge, MA).

Jones, Ronald W. (1967). "International Capital Movements and the Theory of Tariffs and Trade," *Quarterly Journal of Economics*, vol. 81, pp. 1–38.

———. (1987). "Tax Wedges and Mobile Capital," *Scandinavian Journal of Economics*, vol. 89, no. 3, pp. 335–46.

———. (1989). "Co-Movements in Relative Commodity Prices and International Capital Flows: A Simple Model," *Economic Inquiry*, vol. 27, (January), pp. 131–141.

Jones, Ronald W. and Barbara Spencer (1989). "Raw Materials, Processing Activities and Protectionism," *Canadian Journal of Economics*, vol. 22, pp. 469–86.

Jones, Ronald W. and Henryk Kierzkowski (1990). "The Role of Services in Production and International Trade: A Theoretical Framework," in Jones and Krueger (eds): *The Political Economy of International Trade* (Basil Blackwell).

Karp, Larry and Lucy Sioli (1995). "Vertically Related Markets and Trade Policy in a Bargaining Framework," CEPR Discussion Paper #1175.

Kemp, Murray C. (1966). "The Gain from International Trade and Investment: A Neo-Heckscher-Ohlin Approach," *American Economic Review*, vol. 56 (September), pp. 788–809.

Lin, Chyi-Ing (1994). "Processing and Exporting Raw Materials: The Theory of Optimal Policy," unpublished (University of Missouri).

Samuelson, Paul A. (1953). "Prices of Factors and Goods in General Equilibrium," *Review of Economic Studies*, vol. 21, pp. 1–20.

Skeath, Susan E. (1993). "Quality Differentiation and Trade in Vertically Related Markets: Protecting a Low Quality Input Producer," Wellesley College Working Paper 93–01.

Spencer, Barbara and Ronald W. Jones (1991). "Vertical Foreclosure and International Trade Policy," *Review of Economic Studies*, pp. 153–70.

———. (1992). "Trade and Protection in Vertically Related Markets," *Journal of International Economics*, vol. 32, pp. 31–55.

Vernon, Ray (1966). "International Investment and International Trade in the Product Cycle," *Quarterly Journal of Economics*, vol. 80, pp. 190–207.

10

International Vertical Markets in Processed Foods

Frances Antonovitz, Brian Buhr, and Donald J. Liu

Since Tom Urban popularized the phrase "industrialization of agriculture" nearly five years ago, numerous studies of this phenomenon have been conducted (e.g., Boehlje; Drabenstott; and Hurt). Generally, the industrialization of agriculture refers to the trend toward larger production units (to capture economies of scale) and the increasing occurrence of vertical integration and coordination among the adjacent stages of the food and fiber system. Barkema; Drabenstott; and Kinsey as well as others have suggested that it is today's discriminating consumers who are the driving force behind this industrialization because of their demands for refined product specifications that have overwhelmed the traditional market system.

A trend concurrent with industrialization is the globalization of commercial agriculture and its products. Advances in transportation, storage, and electronic information systems have improved the ability to coordinate activities across greater distances and have drawn world markets closer together. The icons of globalization are the multinational agribusiness corporations. Rather than being involved solely in the export of home-country commodities, for example, these firms have ownership of production-related activities in foreign countries.

This chapter focuses on the nexus of agricultural globalization and industrialization, with the specific goal of providing insights to the following question: What are the incentives for agricultural firms to vertically integrate across national boundaries?[1] To begin the discussion, it is necessary to define international vertical integration (IVI). Following the literature in industrial organization (e.g., Perry, 1989), we define vertical integration as the consolidation of two successive productive processes in which the output of the upstream stage is used as an intermediate input in the downstream stage. The consolidation is such that contractual and open market exchanges between the upstream and downstream subsidiaries are eliminated and replaced by internal exchanges within the consolidated firm. Thus, our working definition of international vertical integration will be the case where a firm vertically integrates into a neighboring productive stage located in a different country, with the implicit requirement that the downstream subsidiary must import one of its intermediate inputs from the upstream affiliate for the purpose of producing the output.

Evidence of IVI

Given this definition, do we observe international vertical integration in agriculture? In other words, is this chapter an exercise in providing a theory for potential anomalies or an attempt to identify reasons for the observed behavior of firms? To begin this search for observed agricultural international vertical integration, we begin with the previous descriptive literature on international foreign direct investment (FDI) in food processing. Most recently, Henderson, Sheldon, and Pick (Ch. 2, this volume) offered descriptions of trade patterns in processed foods. These patterns include: (1) intra-industry trade, (2) foreign direct investment or contractual arrangements, and (3) international vertical ties. While the authors noted numerous examples of international horizontal integration, they were unable to discern from their data any specific instances of international vertical integration.

Two earlier papers (Connor; Pagoulatos) examined the nature and extent of foreign investment in retail firms. Connor breaks the theories explaining foreign direct investment into three categories, (1) ownership-specific, (2) industry-specific, and (3) location-specific, and discusses them as related to the firm, the industry, and the national economy, respectively. Pagoulatos points out that most theoretical explanations for foreign direct investment are related to market imperfections. A general summary of these two papers reveals that there is significant foreign direct investment in food manufacturing, that FDI is generally executed by merger or acquisition, that FDI tends to be by firms in developed countries into similarly developed countries, and that FDI tends to be by firms that are large and diversified. However, both authors focus on horizontal forms of foreign direct investment rather than vertical direct investment.

So, do agricultural firms vertically integrate across national boundaries? Two observed cases indicate that there are incentives for agricultural firms to do so. Nippon Meat Packers (Japan's largest meatpacking company) owns Texas Farm (a swine production operation) with the intention of producing hogs for slaughter in the United States and shipping the pork to Japan. The pork product will be branded and marketed as a premium quality product (Staleup). The key reasons cited for Nippon locating in Texas include environmental factors such as climate and ability to manage animal waste. However, these reasons are not sufficient for explaining why a Japanese meat-packing firm would want to raise hogs in the United States rather than purchasing them from U.S. hog farmers. There must be something more than the environmental concerns, and the answer likely lies closer to the consumer. We will come back to this issue in a later section.

There is also the case of U.S. swine production firms owning sow farrowing facilities in Canada and transporting the weaned pigs to facilities in the U.S. Midwest for finishing out for market. The reason for this is again due to environmental conditions, but in this case the reduced level of swine pathogens in rural areas of Canada (due to the lower population density of hogs). The firms have found it more cost effective to ship the hogs to the Midwest rather than keep them in Canada which has slightly higher grain costs and smaller/less efficient packing plants.

Theoretical Considerations in IVI

To this point, it has been established that there do exist instances of international vertical integration in agriculture. The issue here is what the incentives are for doing so. The approach taken is to review the theoretical literature in the areas of "new" trade and "new" industrial organization and to draw inferences on international vertical integration. The relevant industrial organization literature deals directly with the various incentives of vertical integration at the firm level, without specific references to national differences in factor endowments and other trade-related issues. On the other hand, the relevant trade literature is mainly concerned with the economy-wide production patterns (and hence trade patterns) of individual countries when the trade involves both intermediate inputs and final outputs. While useful in understanding such vertically-related issues as multinational enterprises and industry complexes, the trade literature in general does not dwell on the decision aspect of individual firms. Given that the focus here is on firms' incentives for vertical integration, the trade literature discussion will be relatively brief compared to the industrial organization literature.

The New Trade Literature

A long tradition in the exposition of international economic theory is to start with two autarky economies (say, Home and Foreign), which then are allowed to trade with each other. From pursuing the answer to the effect of the unification, one gains positive and normative insights into a wide range of issues in international trade. This is in contrast to the integrated economy approach taken by the authors of the new trade literature focusing on imperfect competition and increasing returns (e.g., Helpman and Krugman). The integrated economy approach goes in the reverse direction, starting from a unified economy, then breaking it up into Home and Foreign and asking "what must a divided economy do to neutralize the effects of that division?" Among other things, if the factors of production are not too unevenly divided between the nations, it is then possible through specialization and trade to achieve exactly the same global output and consumption as before. As such, trade has the effect of reproducing the integrated economy, and one could describe such a restoration as the purpose of international trade.

Industry Complexes

Consider now the intermediate good models surveyed in Krugman's review of new trade theory. Imagine an economy in which two of its many sectors (say, N) are denoted by X and Y. Industry X is monopolistically competitive, producing differentiated goods subject to scale economies, while each of the other industries (including Y) is of homogeneous and constant returns. The varieties of X do not enter into final consumption; rather they are used as intermediate inputs in the production of Y. If all the goods are costless to trade, the integrated economy solution dictates that each variety of X is produced only in one country so as to take advantage of the scale economies in the production of that variety. Accordingly, the trade pattern of X is of intra-industry as Home and Foreign produce different varieties of X, while the trade patterns of other products (including Y) are of inter-industry reflecting the traditional forces of comparative advantage in the sense of Heckscher-Ohlin-Samuelson (e.g., see Krugman).

On the other hand, if X is not tradeable (or subject to nontrivial transportation costs), the integrated economy solution requires an "industry complex"—consisting of X and Y—be established and concentrated either in Home or in Foreign. The other N-2 industries can then be allocated between the two nations, based on the principle of comparative advantage, to fully employ their resources. In this case, there will be no trade in X, and the trade patterns of other products (including Y) will be of inter-industry. Notice that, while the solution in this case dictates the establishment of an industry complex in one of the two countries, the model says nothing about vertical integration per se, because the formation of the complex does not require firms in X and in Y to be vertically integrated. However, the solution does imply that if vertical integration between X and Y is to occur, it must be of domestic type.

Multinational Enterprises

Again, imagine an economy in which two of its many sectors are denoted by X and Y, where X is an intermediate input in the production of Y. However, it is now assumed that both X and Y are differentiated products, with X_i being the intermediate input for Y_i (where i denotes variety). For concreteness, let us think of activities in X as "headquarters" and activities in Y as "factory production." Now, assume that it is difficult to sell headquarters services to producers of Y via arms-length transactions, and hence each headquarters and its corresponding production unit are under common ownership (i.e., X_i and Y_i are vertically integrated). To focus on the comparative advantage forces (without the complication of scale economies), assume that the production of all the N sectors are of constant returns.

The model can be used to explain the phenomenon of multinational enterprises. With additional assumptions, Krugman shows that one can pin down the extent of the control of a foreign factory (Y_i in Foreign) by a domestic headquarters (X_i in Home). Since the technology is of constant returns, these foreign direct investments, like trade in goods, are dictated by comparative advantage forces.[2] On the other hand, suppose multinational enterprises are prohibited by the national government for some reason, then each Y_i factory and its headquarters X_i must be in the same country. As such, the economy can be thought of as consisting N-1 industries with the vertically integrated XY being counted as one. The integrated economy solution then dictates that the N-1 industries should be allocated between the two nations based on comparative advantage principle. Thus, there will be some headquarters/factory pairs located in Home and others in Foreign, leading to intra-industry trade in Y but no foreign direct investments.

While the above multinational enterprise model admits international vertical integration (or domestic integration if multinational enterprises are prohibited), it does not explain why vertical integration has occurred in the first place. That is to say, the integration between X_i and Y_i is not the outcome of the model; rather it is imposed by assumption. In the last chapter of Helpman and Krugman, the production technology of headquarters services is, instead, assumed to be of increasing returns to scale. The authors then justified their assumption by invoking the industrial organization arguments on firm-level incentives for vertical integration. The need for understanding firm-level motivations leads us to the survey of the industrial organization literature presented later.

Technological Economies Arguments for Vertical Integration

One reason given for the occurrence of vertical integration by industrial organization theorists is that there may be technological economies associated with the integration because it takes less of the other intermediate inputs to produce the same output in the downstream process (Perry, 1989). In processed meats, a clear example is the relationship between meat processors (defined as fabricating final cuts such as pork chops or processed meats such as Johnsonville Brats) and grocery store butcher shops. For all practical purposes the technologies involved in the cutting and packaging are identical. Therefore, meat-cutting personnel and equipment would seem to be redundant inputs for one or the other stage. The primary practical reason for the lack of integration is that individual grocery stores may attempt to satisfy their particular customers' demands for specific cut specifications. Inventory control and product distribution may also be limiting factors in further integration. However, as meat products become more homogeneous (due to producer and processor technologies) and inventory control and information systems technologies improve, it is likely that greater levels of integration will occur, most likely with processors developing case-ready products and the retailer removing their redundant butcher shops.

Very intriguing cases arise when considering the international dimensions of technological economies. It is readily apparent that technical efficiencies arise when livestock and crop production can occur in the same place (linking production to idiosyncratic country factor endowments) because it is then possible to use the manure to improve crop yields and at the same time reduce inputs associated with pollution abatement. This crop-livestock complementarity explains why it may be more efficient for Japanese and Taiwanese packers (e.g., the Nippon meat packing case) and processors to integrate backwardly into the livestock production stage in the United States, rather than importing feed grains from the United States and raising the animals there.

Neoclassical Theories of Vertical Integration

In addition to technological economies, there are other motivations for which firms integrate. In the neoclassical theory of vertical integration the focus has been on market imperfections, including imperfect competition and imperfect information.

Imperfect Competition

Focusing on the case of imperfect competition, we will examine three different motivations for vertical integration: internalization of market distortions arising from imperfect competition, price discrimination, and entry blocking.

Internalization of Efficiency Losses. Consider a vertical situation in that the upstream firm is a monopoly which provides one of the intermediate inputs used by the downstream competitive firms. Due to monopoly pricing, there exists a distortion in the usage of intermediate inputs by the downstream industry as firms shift away from the monopoly input in favor of other intermediate inputs that are competitively supplied. The size of this distortion depends on the elasticity of substitution among the inputs of downstream production. The monopolist would have the incentive to capture the efficiency loss from the distortion by integrating forward into the downstream stage (i.e. purchasing as many of the downstream firms as possible), thus expanding the usage of its own intermediate good. This suggests that one possible incentive for vertical integration is to internalize efficiency losses arising from imperfectly competitive pricing (e.g., McKenzie; and Vernon and Graham).[3]

Just as monopoly pricing may cause inefficiencies, there are clear distortions created at the international level by trade policies such as nontariff barriers. Similar in concept to avoiding monopoly distortions by vertically integrating, it may be possible to capture or avoid some of the nontariff trade barrier distortions with international vertical integration. An example for incentives to integrate occurs within the context of the European Community's ban on beef imports from countries who use certain anabolic hormones in production. After processing, it is not possible to tell which beef products are from treated animals without expensive tests. Therefore, all the beef from countries that have approved use of the banned hormones is effectively excluded from the E.C. whether it is treated or not. The only way to assure no use is for a firm in the E.C. to be directly involved in raising the cattle itself and certify them as hormone-free. The U.S. firm IBP (a major beef packer) is actively pursuing integrated marketing in the E.C. to ensure hormone-free beef, and personal contacts suggest they are stepping up efforts in response to the recent bovine spongiform encephalophthy (BSE, or mad cow disease) incidents in Great Britain.

Price Discrimination Motivations. As pointed out in the literature (e.g., Stigler; Perry, 1978a), another incentive for vertical integration under imperfect competition is to separate downstream markets for the purposes of price discrimination. For example, consider the case where an upstream monopoly is able to classify its downstream competitive industries into two groups: one with an elastic intermediate input demand for the monopoly product and the other with an inelastic derived demand. The Robinson-Patman Act prohibits the monopoly from engaging in explicit price discrimination, that is, charging a different price to each downstream group. Yet, through forwardly integrating into the stages with elastic derived demand, the monopoly can expand input usage for its product in those stages, meanwhile raising the open market price to the inelastic group by charging the monopoly price.[4]

Perry (1978b) gives an interesting backward-integration story to illustrate the incentive for price discrimination by a downstream monopsony. To integrate back into the competitive upstream industry, the monopsony needs to acquire the assets of the competitive firms at the price that equals the rents that the assets generate. Instead of acquiring all of the upstream firms outright, the monopsony can extract some of the initial rents by buying one at a time. More specifically, the partially integrated monopsony then expands the production of its subsidiaries, hence buying even less from the remaining independent firms. In turn, this has the effect of lowering the rents of the assets of the remaining independent suppliers, which makes it possible for the monopsonist to acquire those firms at a lower price as it chooses to further integrate.

A good domestic market example of the above price discrimination theory is given by the meat packing and processing industries. After the slaughter process, the carcass may move on to several alternative stages that require different amounts of further processing (e.g. further cutting for consumption in the fresh market vs. additional processing such as canned hams, luncheon meats, etc.). If the demand elasticities are different for the fresh and the more extensively processed meat products, then the theory can be used to suggest which of the two processing stages the packer is likely to choose for integration. For example, Kesavan and Buhr estimate that the retail demand for fresh cuts of pork (hams, pork chops, sirloin roasts) is less elastic than the demand for pork sausage. Based on the criteria of price discrimination, if a packer chooses to integrate into one of these two processing stages, it would pick the sausage. This may be evidenced by the fact that further processed sausages and canned hams in a typical grocery store meat counter are branded by the packer or processor, while most of the fresh cuts (pork chops, loins, etc.) are typically store label. One can make similar arguments at the international level. For example, if Country A's demand for pork sausage is less elastic than Country B's, then the U.S. packing firm would choose to integrate into the sausage-processing stage in Country B, ceteris paribus.

Entry Blocking Motivations. Bain proposes a third incentive for vertical integration under imperfect competition. He argues that vertical integration has the effect of creating entry barriers by forcing potential entrants to contemplate entry at two stages of production rather than just one. Salop and Scheffman discuss a situation where a dominant firm may engage in backward integration into the input production stage so as to raise the costs of its downstream competitors in the final good market. More specifically, by sufficiently integrating into the upstream stage and consequently leaving the upstream open market thin, the final-good competitors (existing or potential) are forced into a situation where they find themselves not being able to expand without driving up the input price significantly.

We can also discuss the issue of entry barriers in the context of resolving them. Vertical integration can be used to overcome barriers to entry into international markets. For example, Japanese meat wholesale companies have had a difficult time acquiring particular pork products for their markets due to different cultural preferences and the fact that a commodity mentality of U.S. meatpackers prevents them from meeting the Japanese demands. To overcome this factor, three Japanese firms (Mitsubishi, Central Soya, and Ferruzzi) have purchased and operate IPC (a pork packing plant) in Indiana with the explicit objective of procuring hogs and processing them in a manner consistent with their meat sales in Japan. Hence, backward vertical integration in this case has eliminated an institutional or cultural barrier of entry for Japanese firms procuring pork products from the U.S. market.

Imperfect Information

Now, turn to the case of imperfect information. We will discuss several incentives for vertical integration under this category including: supply assurance, diversification, and information acquisition.

Supply Assurance Motivations. First, consider the notion of "supply assurance." As pointed out by Perry (1989), this concept entails the possibility of a rationing disequilibrium in the sense that the firm may not be able to procure the desired quantity of input at the prevailing open market price. The salient feature of this concept can be explained by Carlton's model in which the upstream manufacturers endogenously choose to ration the supply of the necessary intermediate input to downstream retailers. To ensure adequate supplies of the input, the retailers have an incentive to integrate back into the manufacturing stage, but only to the extent that it guarantees the satisfaction of the portion of consumer demand that will arise with high probability. The retailers then resort to the open market to buy additional quantity of input called for by any greater consumer demand that arises with low probability.

An example of this phenomenon is the so-called captive supply of cattle. Captive supply refers to packers using contract cattle, packer-owned cattle, or cattle procured via some type of business arrangement (such as forward contracting) as a strategic attempt to offset expected shortages during the year due to the seasonality in the supply of cattle.[5] Clearly, captive supply may work to the benefit of packers by insuring a given supply of cattle. However, to the detriment of cattle producers, markets may become thin and prices received for fed cattle may be lower and/or market information is reduced due to fewer reported price transactions established in the open market (Barkley and Schroeder; Ward et al.).

We can also discuss the analogous concept of demand assurance as it relates to international vertical integration. Interesting examples occur in the markets for red meat as well as the market for broilers. Animal anatomy dictates that specific animal parts or cuts are produced in relatively fixed proportions even though consumers may prefer one part or cut over another. In this country for example, consumers have an aversion toward many of the offals or by-products of meat animals such as livers, brains, kidneys, hearts, blood, and tongues. However, the tastes and preferences of consumers in the former Soviet Union and some Asian countries are quite different; many of these offals and by-products are as highly valued as the red meat itself (e.g., see Hayes et al.; and Wong and Khan). As to the broiler example, U.S. consumers have a strong preference for breast meat, while this is not observed in many other countries. Clearly, it is optimal for the U.S. livestock and broiler industries to expand their international markets into countries with stronger demand for the parts or cuts not demanded in the U.S. market. Foreign captive demands for these parts or cuts can be established by vertical integration into their retail distribution systems.[6] For example, Perdue and Cargill (U.S. broiler firms) have made extensive inroads toward integration in Russia and other former Soviet countries. Recently (March 1996), Russia tried to restrict chicken imports from the United States because, it argued, U.S. imports did not meet its sanitary requirements. However, most market analysts agreed that this was an attempt to protect their chicken producers and processors from the intense competition from U.S. integrated firms.

Diversification Motivations. Can vertical integration be used as a tool to deal with uncertainty arising from demand and supply shocks? To provide a partial answer, consider the model by Perry (1982). Consumers purchase the final good from retailers who in turn purchase the good from an intermediate market supplied by manufacturers who in turn obtain from the factor markets the inputs needed for the production of the good. There is also a foreign demand for the good at the intermediate market level. Through market linkages, retail profits can be affected by shocks in consumer demand, foreign demand, and factor supply. Now, suppose Retailer X and Manufacturer Y are to be consolidated. The integrated firm will still be affected by economic elements affecting consumer demand and factor supply. Moreover, even though it may no longer be involved in the intermediate input market, the integrated firm is not immune to shocks in foreign demand, as those shocks will eventually affect factor and final output prices. This suggests that vertical integration will not inherently insulate firms from economic shocks within the system.

Although vertical integration cannot insulate firms from price fluctuations, it may provide the benefit of diversification. For example, when the shocks are mainly fluctuations in foreign demand in the intermediate market (increasing demand for the manufacturing stage, but reducing supply and raising price for the retail stage), the returns from retail and manufacturing stages are negatively correlated,[7] which would present a diversification incentive for vertical integration. On the other hand, if the shocks are mainly fluctuations in domestic demand (raising the demand in the same direction in both stages), the returns from retail and manufacturing operations are positively correlated, and hence the diversification incentive would favor disintegration.

Information Acquisition Motivations. Given that firms operate under uncertainty, is it possible that the reason they engage in vertical integration is because they want to acquire information relevant to the resolution of the uncertainty? Consider Arrow's model in which there is a group of competitive manufacturers supplying intermediate inputs to a group of competitive retailers. The intermediate input price is stochastic because of production shocks associated with the manufacturing stage. While the production shocks are observable by the upstream firms prior to the marketing of the intermediate good, this information is not revealed to the retailers until aggregated into the equilibrium price. As such, the retailers have to make business decisions without knowing the intermediate input price. Obviously, if a retailer is to integrate back into the manufacturing stage, he will be able to observe the production shock of his subsidiary. Assuming production shocks are generally positively correlated across the manufacturers, Arrow argues that backward integration facilitates decision making as it enables the retailer to obtain a better forecast of the intermediate input price.[8]

Additional insights on the information acquisition motivation for vertical integration can be found in Riordan and Sappington. There are three vertical stages: research and development (R&D) determining output quality, manufacturing, and retailing. The developer has private information about the cost of R&D, while the manufacturer (whose identity is to be determined) has private information about the cost of producing the final good. The retailer sells the product at a known price. Now, both the retailer and developer can do the manufacturing and are equally proficient in doing it. The retailer's problem is to decide whether to manufacture the product himself or let the developer do it. It turns out that, when the R&D cost shock and the production cost shock are positively correlated, the developer has an added incentive to overstate the cost of R&D if he is also manufacturing. Thus, it is beneficial for the retailer in this case to vertically integrate into the manufacturing stage. On the other hand, when the cost shocks are negatively correlated, the developer's incentive to overstate the cost of R&D is restrained if he is also manufacturing. Hence it may be best for the retailer to let the developer do the manufacturing.[9]

Finally, we would like to discuss an issue related to information acquisition incentives to vertically integrate when there is inaccuracy in the transmission process. For example, the production/processing/marketing system wants to produce meat with characteristics that are highly valued by consumers. However, knowledge and understanding of consumers' preferences for individual characteristics must be accurately transmitted through many disintegrated stages in the system to the genetics and production management stages where most of the final product characteristics are determined. Hence, there may be some incentive to shorten this information chain through vertical integration so as to improve the accuracy and speed of information transmission. This also raises the issue of nonidentifiable product attributes that consumers may deem important. Organically produced meat and produce, rbST (recombinant bovine somatotropin)-free milk, and animal welfare-friendly production methods are all developments directly related to meeting specific consumer preferences. Many disintegrated sectors make it difficult and expensive to track these attributes, which are only identifiable by the labels placed on them once they leave their point of production origin. To ensure differentiation, they must remain outside the marketing channel of other products whose producers could incorrectly make the same claim. In addition, many of these products command market premiums providing incentives for intermediaries to misrepresent the products. These cases may in fact require consumer cooperative ownership or integration of the production process to vouch for the attendance of the desired attributes.

Transaction Cost Economics Viewpoint of Vertical Integration

Having discussed the neoclassical theories of vertical integration, consideration now turns to the transaction cost economics literature that focuses on vertical bilateral monopoly exchanges (Coase; Williamson). A bilateral monopoly between a buyer and a seller of successive stages occurs because of ownership of exchange-specific assets, a concept Williamson referred to as "asset specificity." According to this theory, vertical integration is merely one method of carrying out the bilateral monopoly exchange, and there are other ways such as contracting. As the environment becomes more complex, however, the probability of a contract failing to specify the terms of performance for particular states of nature increases. In such states, due to asset specificity, a firm may find itself held hostage by the other firm's threat to relinquish the relationship unless certain concessions are granted. A solution to this opportunistic behavior is vertical integration. Obviously, the stronger the asset specificity, the more opportunistic the other party can be and, hence, the more preferable is the vertical integration solution. For a given degree of asset specificity, the relative costs of governance between vertical integration and contractual arrangement then dictate the choice of the governance structure.

It is important to emphasize that transaction costs in livestock industries have many applications such as grading, quality of inputs, and food safety. For example, consider PSE syndrome in hogs.[10] PSE could be eradicated from the U.S. swine herd as it has been in Denmark. However, at least in this country, the costs of doing so would outweigh the benefits at the present time because only a small proportion of hogs have this genetic defect. Since the Japanese have a strong preference for PSE-free pork, they must carefully inspect each carcass imported from the United States to ensure that it does not have PSE. Apparently, there are significant transaction costs to the Japanese associated with this type of nonintegrated bilateral arrangement. Alternatively, the Japanese could vertically integrate into the U.S. hog production sector, produce PSE-free pork themselves, and ship it back to Japan. The earlier case of Nippon Meat Packers' vertical integration with Texas Farm may be viewed as an attempt to minimize transaction costs of measuring and testing PSE pork.

Summary and Implications for Future Research

The industrialization of agriculture is characterized by more specific product attributes to suit consumers' preferences, and by the increased coordination necessary to assure delivery of those attributes that may not be transparent to the final consumer or a downstream user of intermediate inputs. Meanwhile, increased trade in commodities and processed foods reflects the globalization of agriculture. To present a rationale for the overlap of these observed trends, this chapter presents an overview of the vertical integration theories appearing in trade and industrial organization literatures and examines the relevancy of these theories to the study of industrialization and globalization using the meat sector as a readily available case study. Whereas the industrial organization literature deals directly with the various incentives of vertical integration at the firm level, the trade literature is mainly concerned with the economy-wide production and trade patterns of individual countries when intermediate inputs are involved in the trade. The nexus of these two literatures is scant, and there is a need to synthesize the two sets in a way that allows for studying international vertical integration issues on a solid firm-level foundation. Without paying close attention to the firm-level idiosyncracies it will be difficult if not impossible to explain why international vertical integration occurs.

Finally, several broader research issues evolve from the chapter. As discussed earlier, vertical integration and coordination can allow an economy to recapture inefficiencies in the system while at the same time creating additional distortions. The question is whether there is an overall gain or loss to the society. In addition, we must put all of these debates in a global context when international vertical integration arises. Clearly, issues of global welfare and distribution must be examined as well as impacts on national food security, trade patterns, and future direction of multinational trade negotiations.

Acknowledgments

Senior authorship is shared. The authors wish to thank Daniel Otto and James Kliebenstein for helpful suggestions. This study evolves under the umbrella of the research program of the Retail Food Industry Center at the University of Minnesota.

Notes

1. There are other "governance structures" that can cross international borders. Somewhere in between the extremes of vertical integration and open market exchange lie the various degrees of vertical coordination arising from contractual arrangements between firms at the successive stages. See Antonovitz et al. for a brief review of the theory behind vertical coordinations.

2. The issues of multinational enterprises can also be addressed within a framework of segmented world economy, in which goods are costly to transport while services are not (Krugman). Then, rather than be dictated by comparative advantage forces, firms go multinational in order to improve their access to markets (i.e. to avoid transportation costs or other barriers to trade).

3. Subsequently researchers have raised the question of whether vertical integration by the monopolistic manufacturer into the retail stage will in turn create a monopoly distortion in that stage, thus increasing consumer prices to such an extent that it actually reduces overall welfare compared to the preintegration situation (see the review in Perry, 1989).

4. Notice that the above scheme will not work if the monopoly's forward integration is with respect to the inelastic group. The optimal pricing strategy for the monopoly in this case would appear, on the surface, to be to reduce the usage of its product by the inelastic subsidiaries while lowering the open market price for the elastic independent firms. But this cannot be optimal because the resulting higher retail prices in the inelastic stages would certainly be undercut by new entrants who can obtain the input at the lower open market price.

5. In this example the supply is "rationed" by Mother Nature. That is, supply at any given point in time is fixed due to biological lags in animal production.

6. One can think of situations in which the foreign distribution systems might choose to "ration" their net import demand for the U.S. products.

7. The negative correlation result requires that the elasticity of the retail demand for the final good exceeds the elasticity of substitution among intermediate inputs used in production of the final good.

8. While being simple, as pointed out in Perry (1989), Arrow's model suffers a degeneracy problem of a sort. That is, since the manufacturers are competitive, they cannot benefit from withholding their private information on production shocks, and hence the retailers could easily purchase the information from them. As such, vertical integration is not needed in the model. See Crocker for a model illustrating the acquisition of private information while avoiding Arrow's degeneracy.

9. Consider the following application and a slight variation of Riordan and Sappington's model in the area of export promotion. There are three vertical stages: Excel (a U.S. packing firm) exporting beef to Japan, advertising and promotion

activities at the Japanese retail level, and the Japanese retail stage. The Japanese retailers have private information about the cost of retailing, while the promoter (whose identity is to be determined) has private information about the cost of promotion. Either Excel or the Japanese retailers can perform the promotion activities. Perhaps the theory can be used to predict where the vertical integration may occur. If the retail cost shock and promotion cost shock are positively correlated, the Japanese retailers have an added incentive to overstate the cost of retailing if they are also doing the promotion. Thus, it is beneficial for Excel in this case to vertically integrate into the export promotion stage. On the other hand, when the cost shocks are negatively correlated, the retailers' incentive to overstate the cost of retailing is restrained if they are also doing the promotion. Hence, it may be best for Excel to let the Japanese retailers do the promotion.

10. PSE is a genetically transmitted condition in which the muscle tissue of the hog will react to stress before slaughter, diminishing its palatability. Many foreign consumers have a much stronger aversion to these characteristics (pale, soft, exudative, i.e. PSE) than the average U.S. consumer.

References

Antonovitz, F., B. Buhr, and D. J. Liu. "Vertical Integration Incentives in Meat Product Markets." Dept. of Applied Econ., Staff Paper P9613, University of Minnesota, August 1996.

Arrow, K. J. "Vertical Integration and Communication." *Bell J. Econ.* 6(1975):17383.

Barkema, A. "New Roles and Alliances in the U.S. Food System." In *Food and Agricultural Markets: The Quiet Revolution*. L.P. Schertz and L. M. Daft, eds., Washington, D.C.: National Planning Association Report No. 270, 1994.

Barkley, A. P., and T. C. Schroeder. "The Role of Captive Supplies in Beef Packing: Long-Run Impacts of Captive Supplies." In Reports to Packer & Stockyards Programs, Grain Inspection, Packers and Stockyards Administration, USDA, 1995.

Bain, J. S. *Barriers to New Competition*. Cambridge, Mass.: Harvard University Press, 1956.

Boehlje, M. "Industrialization of Agriculture: What are the Implications?" *Choices*, Fourth Quarter 1996:30–33.

Carlton, D. W. "Vertical Integration in Competitive Markets under Uncertainty." *J. Industrial Econ.* 27(1979):189–209.

Coase, R. "The Nature of the Firm." *Economica* 4(1937):386–405.

Connor, J. M. "Determinants of Foreign Direct Investment by Food and Tobacco Manufacturers." *Amer. J. Agr. Econ.* 65(1983): 395–404.

Crocker, K. J. "Vertical Integration and the Strategic Use of Private Information." *Bell J. Econ.* 14(1983):236–48.

Drabenstott, M. "Industrialization: Steady Current or Tidal Wave." *Choices*, Fourth Quarter 1994:4–8.

Hayes, D., B. Chernyakov, and S. Sotnikov. *Meat Marketing in the Former USSR: A Guide for U.S. Meat Exporting Companies.* Midwest Agribusiness Trade Research and Information Center, Iowa State University, 1993, pp. 12–14.

Helpman, E., and P. R. Krugman. *Market Structure and Foreign Trade: Increasing Returns, Imperfect Competitions, and the International Economy.* Cambridge, MA: MIT Press, 1985.

Hurt, C. "Industrialization of the Pork Industry." *Choices,* Fourth Quarter 1994:9–13.

Kesavan, T., and B. Buhr. "Price Determination and Dynamic Adjustments: An Inverse Demand System Approach to Meat Products in the United States." *Empirical Econ.* 20(1995):681–98.

Kinsey, J. "Changes in Food Consumption: From Mass Market to Niche Markets." In *Food and Agricultural Markets: The Quiet Revolution.* L. P. Schertz, and L. M. Daft, eds., Washington, D.C.: National Planning Association Report No. 270, 1994.

Krugman, P. "Increasing Returns, Imperfect Competition and the Positive Theory of International Trade." In *Handbook of International Economics,* Vol. III, eds. G.M. Grossman and K. Rogoff, Amsterdam: North-Holland, 1995, pp. 1244–77.

McKenzie, L. W. "Ideal Output and the Interdependence of Firms." *Econ. J.* 61(1951):785–803.

Pagoulatos, E. "Foreign Direct Investment in U.S. Food and Tobacco Manufacturing and Domestic Economic Performance." *Amer. J. Agr. Econ.* 65(1983):405–412.

Perry, M. K. "Vertical Integration: Determinants and Effects." In *Handbook of Industrial Organization,* Vol. 1, eds. R. Schmalensee and R. Willig, Amsterdam: North-Holland, 1989, pp. 183–255.

Perry, M. K. "Vertical Integration by Competitive Firms: Uncertainty and Diversification." *Southern Econ. J.* 49(1982):201–08.

———. "Price Discrimination and Forward Integration." *Bell J. Econ.* 9(1978a):209–17.

———. "Vertical Integration: The Monopsony Case." *Amer. Econ. Rev.* 68(1978b):561–70.

Rhodes, V. J. "The Industrialization of Hog Production." *Rev. of Agr. Econ.* 17(1995):107–118.

Riordan, M. H., and D. E. M. Sappington. "Information, Incentives and Organizational Mode." *Quart. J. Econ.* 102(1987):243–63.

Salop, S. C. and D. T. Scheffman. "Raising Rivals' Costs." *Amer. Econ. Rev.* 73(1983):267–71.

Staleup, L. "Panhandle Pork: A Boom in Texas and Oklahoma Hog Production may Redraw the Industry's Borders." *Hogs Today* (1996): 54–56.

Stigler, G. J. "The Division of Labor is Limited by the Extent of the Market." *J. Polit. Econ.* 59(1951):185–93.

Vernon, J. and D. Graham. "Profitability of Monopolization by Vertical Integration." *J. Polit. Econ.* 79(1971):924–25.

Urban, T. "Agricultural Industrialization: It's Inevitable." *Choices,* Fourth Quarter (1991):4–6.

Williamson, O. E. *Markets and Hierarchies: Analysis and Antitrust Implications.* New York:Free Press, 1975.

Ward, C. E., S. R. Koontz, and T. C. Schroeder. "Short-Run Captive Supply Relationships with Fed Cattle Transaction Prices." In "Reports to Packer & Stockyards Programs," Grain Inspection, Packers and Stockyards Administration, USDA, 1995.

Wong, J., and L. Khan. "Meat Marketing in Taiwan." In *Meat Marketing in Taiwan: A Guide for U.S. Meat Exporting Companies,* D. Hayes, ed., Midwest Agribusiness Trade Research and Information Center, Iowa State University, 1989, pp. 94–98.

11

Theory and Practice in Perspective

Ian M. Sheldon and Dennis R. Henderson

This chapter draws together themes from the preceding chapters that contribute in a systematic way to the search for a framework that can be used to analyze observed patterns of international commerce in the processed food sector. Documented in the earlier chapters, international transactions in this sector portray features that are not explained by the neoclassical theory of international (inter-industry) trade, as generally represented by the Heckscher-Ohlin-Samuelson (HOS) model. Even so, the processed food sector is not unique in this respect. Foreign direct investment, transnational product licensing and franchising, intra-industry trade, and international vertical market linkages have also been observed in many other sectors throughout the industrial world.

Due to the frequency with which international transactions other than inter-industry trade are observed, a number of theories have been developed to explain such phenomena. These theories provide much of the analytical foundation for the preceding chapters. The intent of this chapter is to examine how well this body of thought provides a coherent means for understanding what is observed in the food sector, and how useful it is as a guide to analysis of public policy. The chapter is organized into two parts: First, unique contributions of chapters 2 through 10 to an understanding of patterns of international commerce in processed foods are reiterated; second, the individual contributions are drawn together in order to assess the extent to which a general framework emerges.

Specific Themes

Jones and Blandford (Ch. 3, this volume) make the case for a wide range of policy issues to be considered in order for the benefits of liberalized international commerce in the food sector to be realized fully. They demonstrate that reform of agricultural policy is just one strand of the policy fabric, albeit one that has only recently been brought into the international policy arena. Using the milk sector as an example, they show how policy-induced distortions in individual markets for agricultural commodities (e.g. price supports, production or marketing quotas, and monopoly export boards) can affect the structure and performance of the downstream processing industries (e.g. the location of processing plants, size of industrial output, and operating efficiency). A policy learning curve is also demonstrated. In light of the downstream effects, many countries have introduced modifications in commodity policy that are aimed at reducing these distortions. In the absence of any multinational body for coordinating farm policy, their illustration of how multilateral trade policy has been used as an engine to drive change in national farm policies is of particular significance.

In much the same vein, Jones and Blandford show that multilateral trade liberalization has stimulated efforts for international agreement on policies that directly affect global commerce in processed foods. Specifically, the Uruguay Round Agreement of the GATT on sanitary and phytosanitary (SPS) rules forces participating countries toward a greater concurrence with global standards on such things as food safety regulations. Likewise, the agreement on trade-related investment measures (TRIM) moves countries toward a more common policy for regulating foreign direct investment. Also, though not addressed by Jones and Blandford, as a result of the Uruguay Round Agreement on trade-related intellectual property (TRIP), countries are moving toward a more consistent policy for defining and protecting intellectual property (e.g. brands, geographical indications, and proprietary information on processing technology and recipes).

Jones and Blandford also discuss competition (or industrial structure) policy, as another important part of the policy agenda aimed at liberalizing international commerce. In contrast to issues of food safety, foreign investment, and intellectual property, however, multilateral trade agreements have not yet pushed countries toward globally oriented competition policies. While still more policy-related issues are identified in other chapters, a compelling question remains: How much of the policy agenda can be promulgated within the context of trade policy? Is it asking too much of multilateral trade negotiations to bring about rationalization of national policies that affect all traits of international commerce when such commerce includes much that is not captured by the neoclassical models of international trade? The theoretical and empirical contributions of other chapters suggest a more eclectic framework for assessing the expected impacts of policy change on the global food sector.

Karp (chapter 4) examines strategic trade policy in light of observed conditions in the processed food sector (e.g. imperfect competition and government intervention). Following a careful investigation of both static and dynamic representations of strategic trade theory, it becomes apparent that little in the way of general policy prescriptions can be drawn from it. In a static framework, the optimal instrument of government intervention is sensitive to the type of competition among firms. Adding dynamics to the model multiplies the number of factors to which the outcomes of strategic trade policy are sensitive (e.g. the number of variables that can be affected by policy, and the ability of government to commit to future policies).

The conclusion that universal policy cannot be formulated on the basis of static strategic trade theory is not particularly new. However, because strategic trade theory has not previously been fully depicted in a dynamic context, Karp's analysis is all the more compelling in reinforcing the notion that general policy prescriptions are unlikely products of the theory. In short, the idiosyncracies of firm behavior, and the policy environment in the global processed food sector, suggest that strategic trade policy has a very limited normative role. Further, the neoclassical presumption that free trade maximizes economic welfare is not dispelled, and is likely reinforced, by the theory. If strategic trade theory has any real content, it is in highlighting the importance of incorporating imperfectly competitive behavior into positive analysis of the effects of trade policy. For example, Karp cites the "collusion-inducing effects" of import quotas compared to tariffs when there is oligopolistic interaction between domestic and foreign firms—a result that is in conflict with the predicted equivalence of tariffs and quotas under perfect competition.

Carter and Yilmaz (chapter 5) show that neither the presence of intra-industry trade (IIT) nor foreign direct investment (FDI) in processed foods can be explained by neoclassical trade theory, a situation that is similar to other sectors of manufactures. Over the past two decades, a body of literature has evolved in an effort to incorporate these different forms of international commerce. Helpman and Krugman's (1985) model, which draws extensively on this literature, is probably the most developed. Their model incorporates monopolistic competition into a general equilibrium trade model from which hypotheses concerning IIT and FDI can be drawn and tested. Specifically, the Helpman-Krugman model makes predictions concerning the relationship between factor endowments, country size, and the level of IIT, and between factor endowments and FDI. In this sense, the Helpman-Krugman framework is an attempt to generalize the HOS model to allow for IIT and FDI.

Empirical studies of IIT based on Helpman-Krugman and other models have been conducted in numerous industrial sectors, including processed foods. A number of the variables important in these models are, however, notoriously difficult to quantify using generally available data (e.g. the degree of product differentiation and scale economies), and, collectively, the studies do not provide a conclusive test of the theory. Further, Carter and Yilmaz report that some results of empirical studies in the food sector point to factors other than those embodied in the Helpman-Krugman type model as drivers of IIT.

Empirical studies of FDI in the food sector are also examined by Carter and Yilmaz. While these studies lack a common theoretical foundation, they are loosely consistent with Dunning's OLI paradigm, wherein three conditions are necessary and together sufficient for a firm to invest in a foreign affiliate. These are ownership advantages such as intellectual property, location advantages such as transport costs and trade restrictions, and internalization advantages, stemming from conditions such as the existence of high transaction costs that encourage firms to integrate. As with the empirical studies of IIT, quantification problems abound, often making it difficult to test important theoretical ideas. Although the various studies suggest a similar set of factors that motivate FDI, inconsistencies exist in the empirical work and direct ties of the findings to theory are rather sparse.

Overall, Carter and Yilmaz argue that, while neoclassical trade theory comes up short as a framework for explaining two empirically important traits of global commerce in processed foods, the commonly embraced theories of IIT and FDI provide incomplete guides for rationalizing such empirical observations. Neither body of theory displaces neoclassical thought as a general theory, but both add to the mosaic of concepts that help explain, under carefully crafted conditions, why global commerce may not follow the predictions of the neoclassical model.

Markusen (chapter 6) integrates multinational enterprises into the theory of international trade, resulting in a general equilibrium model that generates foreign direct investment endogenously. Drawing on a wide range of literature addressing multinational firms, Markusen grounds the model on sixteen "stylized facts" that characterize firms and countries involved in FDI. These turn on the importance of intellectual property and other firm-specific assets, and on national economic maturation. Such characteristics (e.g. high levels of product differentiation, importance of brand names, and the dominant role of OECD countries in international trade) are central to processed foods and thus reinforce the relevance of this type of model to understanding global commerce in the sector.

Two features are crucial to the Markusen model: first, firm-specific, knowledge-based assets such as product recipe and trademarks that lead to economies of multiple plant operation, and second, plant scale economies. The model demonstrates that FDI is the rational mode of international commerce when, inter alia, firm-specific assets are relatively high and plant scale economies are relatively low. Further, the model predicts that, given the above condition, FDI will tend to be the dominant form of commerce between countries that have high income levels, similar-sized economies, and similar relative factor endowments. This combination of conditions is the predominantly-observed situation in the global processed food sector.

Conversely, the model predicts that trade in goods will prevail in the absence of high firm-specific assets, combined with low levels of transport costs (including the cost of trade barriers such as tariffs) relative to barriers to direct investment. Casual observation suggests that these latter conditions are descriptive of the unprocessed agricultural commodity sector. Thus, Markusen's integrated FDI/trade model serves up predictions of patterns of global commerce that seem to be consistent with observed patterns in both processed foods and in unprocessed commodities.

Rugman (chapter 7) documents the dominant role of Western European, North American, and Japanese multinational enterprises in the global processed food market. Then, drawing largely from transaction cost theory, it is demonstrated why the existence of firm-specific assets in the processed food sector leads firms to internalize foreign operations through FDI. Rugman's work is less general than is the Markusen model in that it accommodates only FDI and not trade in goods, but it is more elegant in identifying specific characteristics of the processed food industries that rationalize the presence of FDI.

Forms of multinational internalization include various contractual relationships (e.g. licensing, franchising, and joint ventures), in addition to direct (physical) ownership of affiliated foreign operations. Such contractual arrangements may be expected when the risk of dissipation of a firm's intellectual property by the foreign partner is relatively low, that is, where easily enforceable contracts can be established, or where strong personal relationships can be maintained. Regardless of form, however, of key importance is the ownership of the skill of managing a procurement, processing, and distribution system which is unique in some degree from that of competing product lines. That is, a firm-specific advantage motivates a firm to internalize, or directly control, the operations of foreign affiliates.

Specific to the processed food sector, Rugman demonstrates that brand names and their associated product formulation, quality control, and distribution regimes constitute a significant firm-specific asset for most multinational enterprises. These have most frequently been internalized internationally through FDI, franchises, and licenses. Some evidence of the international business network or alliance approach, styled after the Japanese keiretsu, is presented, predominantly among food firms either headquartered or doing substantial business in Japan.

Abbott and Solana-Rosillo (Chapter 8) provide empirical insight into foreign market entry decisions by firms. Drawing on a case study of Spanish and Australian firms entering the U.S. wine market, they demonstrate that firms may exhibit a mix of strategies for entering a market, including FDI, direct exporting, and indirect exporting. They also show that the type of aggregate market data used in computable general equilibrium models, which are currently popular in trade policy analysis, miss much of the reality of firm decision-making (e.g. asymmetry of firm behavior and use of multiple strategies) and thus may predict incorrectly the impact of policy change.

As an alternative methodology, a firm-level cost-benefit approach is presented that allows comparison of different mixes of foreign market entry strategies within a profit maximization framework. Using this framework, Abbott and Solana-Rosillo demonstrate the rationality of the use of mixed entry strategies for a given firm, based on circumstances that may be unique to the firm and/or the foreign market. They also show evidence of strategic change in light of experience, which in the case of wine, was displayed as a diminishing commitment to foreign direct investment (sunk costs) and an increase in direct exporting as a firm's experience in the foreign market matured.

It is argued that assessing the impact of policy intervention using such firm-level models yields superior predictions of resulting changes in firm behavior than can be achieved with computable general equilibrium models. That said, however, predicting sector-wide impacts would appear to require aggregation of results from a sufficiently large number of firm-level models to assure representation of all significant firm/market combinations in the sector. This would be a daunting task.

Jones (chapter 9) demonstrates the importance of taking into account international vertical market linkages when considering optimal policy choices. This may be of particular significance in the food sector where both intermediate goods (e.g. unprocessed or semiprocessed commodities) and final goods (e.g. branded foods) are part of the pattern of global commerce. Jones begins by setting up a core model that extends the specific-factors approach to the case where both a final good and an intermediate good used to produce that final good are traded. Given a country that exports both goods and markets that are perfectly competitive, commercial policy in the form of an export tax on either the final or the intermediate good is shown to improve the country's terms of trade. This also raises national income, albeit subject to a volume-of-trade constraint on the ability of the country to exercise monopolistic power in the world market. Essentially, in the core model, Jones extends the conventional optimal export tariff argument to the case of vertical markets.

Drawing on work with Spencer, Jones then applies the analysis of policy and vertical markets to the case of imperfect competition (Spencer and Jones, 1991, 1992). The market structure is one where in the home country there is a vertically integrated firm that controls the exports of both the intermediate good and the final good. This firm then competes in the foreign country with a firm that produces the final good and also has the option of either importing the intermediate good or producing it at higher cost. Selecting policy that ensures optimal economic gains is ever the more subtle when international markets are characterized by these types of vertical linkage. Given that this type of situation may not be unusual in food and agriculture, Jones's analysis is particularly compelling.

Jones focuses first on the case of optimal policy for the government in the home country. In the absence of trade in the intermediate good, and assuming Cournot interaction between the two firms producing the final good, the optimal policy is one of subsidizing exports of the final good. This is essentially the Brander and Spencer (1985) result that Karp (chapter 4) outlines. In the case of trade in both the intermediate and final goods, if profit margins are higher for trade in the former, the optimal policy is a tax on exports of final goods (and perhaps a subsidy for direct investment in a foreign processing affiliate). The point of government policy in this case is to encourage a shift toward trade in the intermediate good. As is typical in the literature on trade and imperfect competition, the opposite result holds if firms play a Bertrand game in the final goods market.

In the case of the foreign country, if the home country supplier of the intermediate good has the opportunity to engage in vertical foreclosure, and assuming Cournot competition in the final good market, Jones shows that it is optimal for the foreign government to tax imports of the final good. This has the effect of reducing the profit margin on the final good for the home firm relative to the profits it can earn from exporting the intermediate good, hence reducing its incentive to vertically foreclose in the intermediate good. This result follows from the fact that the tariff on the home final good, by shifting market share to the foreign competitor, generates an increase in demand for the imported intermediate good.

Numerous other examples of the complexity of optimal policy design in the presence of international vertical linkages can be gleaned from this work. For example, Jones draws on Chang and Kim (1989, 1991) to focus on the case of a developed country firm that sells a high-quality final good in a third market in competition with a developing country firm selling either a low-quality good that uses a domestically produced low-quality intermediate good or a medium-quality final good that requires import of a high-quality intermediate good from the developed country. Assuming the developed country firm acts as a Stackelberg leader in the final good market, its government need not provide an export subsidy for the final good because the developed country firm is already capturing maximum rents. It may be optimal, however, for the less developed country to tax either imports of the high-quality intermediate good or exports of the medium-quality final good. This type of analysis may be of special relevance when considering the processed food sector, particularly if the firm in the developing country is a multinational firm making decisions concerning from where to source its raw materials.

Antonovitz, Buhr, and Liu (chapter 10) address the incentives for vertical integration in the global food sector. This is framed within the context of the often-discussed trend toward industrialization in U.S. agriculture and with it increased consolidation of control over the production of both intermediate and final goods in the food sector.[1] Two examples are provided of cases where food firms have vertically integrated across national boundaries: a Japanese meat packing firm integrating upstream into a swine production operation (farm) in Texas, and U.S. swine production firms (farms) integrating upstream into sow farrowing facilities in Canada.

As the authors point out, the theory of vertical integration is well developed. Drawing on this body of thought, it is shown that, in the presence of imperfect competition, vertical integration can result in a reduction of economic inefficiency due to monopolistic price distortion in an intermediate good. It can be profit enhancing if it facilitates price discrimination between own use and market sales of the intermediate, and it may be used to retard entry of nonintegrated competitors. Further, it can be used to overcome information asymmetries and to offset high (market) transactions costs. These incentives would appear to be applicable to cross-border, as well as within-border, situations. Thus, the presence of international vertical integration can be explained with economic rationality. Less obvious at this point is how the presence of international vertical integration affects the analysis of global commerce and related policy interventions, although Markusen and Jones have provided some direction.

The Works in Context

Neoclassical trade theory, as typified by the HOS paradigm, is an elegant and powerful structure that, prior to the late 1970s, dominated theoretical and empirical work in international trade. Its weakness, and a common theme that can be drawn from all of the preceding chapters, is the notion that application of the neoclassical model to global commerce in sectors such as processed foods may miss much of what actually occurs. Other models and theories provide some insight as to why this is so.

Yet, even though it captures observed characteristics of international markets such as product differentiation and economies of scale, and yields insights into analyzing policy in the presence of imperfect competition, this newer body of literature does not yet provide a general framework. To quote Krugman, "the central problem of international trade is how to go beyond the proliferation of models to some kind of new synthesis. Probably trade theory will never be as unified as it was a decade ago" (1989, p. 1214). Implicit in this is a warning that while policy analysis based on the neoclassical model may miss certain outcomes, the new body of theory does not provide a new general benchmark for trade policy. It is in this context that the preceding chapters should be considered.

Several of the chapters in this volume can be viewed as logical extensions of the new trade literature. However, with the exception of the work by Markusen, we appear to be little closer to a new general theory. The set of theories reviewed by Carter and Yilmaz that address intra-industry trade, for example, are quite elegant and rich in conceptual understanding and seem to offer rationale for an aspect of global commerce that is actually observed in the processed food sector. However, because there are several different theories that draw on a variety of market structures, representations of demand, and production technologies, each serves mainly to clarify only a piece of the mosaic that makes up the pattern of global commerce.

Most of these models require detailed and unique data for empirical application, data that typically are either not collected at all, or, if collected, do not match well the phenomena of interest, for example, product differentiation and scale economies. As a result, much of the cross-industry empirical work in this field suffers from many of the methodological problems that characterized the empirical analysis grounded on the structure-conduct-performance paradigm of the industrial organization literature. In addition, tests of the predictions of the Helpman-Krugman model, while focusing on the country-level characteristics of intra-industry trade such as factor endowments and country size, have not explicitly tested whether the underlying assumptions concerning market structure and product differentiation are reasonable. Nevertheless, it should be recognized that it may be asking too much of *any* theory to generate a singular explanation of what is clearly a complex phenomenon.

Due to the assumptions about perfect competition, constant returns to scale, and factor mobility, it is perhaps not surprising that neoclassical trade theory has very little to say about foreign direct investment and multinational firms. With the exception of a few papers such as Helpman (1984) and Markusen (1984), which incorporate multinational firms into a framework characterized by imperfect competition, economies of scale, and product differentiation, there has not been a general theory of trade to date that embodies foreign direct investment.

As Markusen notes in chapter 6, an extensive, informal microeconomic literature on multinationals has evolved, drawing on a variety of concepts from industrial organization, transaction cost theory, and business economics. Rugman's chapter in this book stands as an example of one aspect of this approach. Much of the empirical analysis to date on multinational firms in the food processing sector also draws on this eclectic body of literature, and some of these ideas have been incorporated into the works by Helpman and Markusen. As Markusen points out, it is only recently that explicit attempts have been made to integrate general equilibrium trade theory with the microeconomic theory of multinational firms.

There are three features in Markusen's work suggesting that many of the observed traits of international commerce in processed food can be endogenized in a relatively simple framework. First, sensible predictions can be made in a general equilibrium model about what conditions will lead to foreign direct investment, intra-industry trade, and inter-industry trade. Second, the issue of which type of international arrangement firms will choose is addressed. Third, although Markusen focuses only on horizontal arrangements for multinational firms, he submits that the general equilibrium analysis equally applies to the case of vertically integrated multinational firms; further, it would probably not require much effort to extend the analysis to the choice of international vertical market arrangement. In addition, recent work in location theory, for example Venables (1993, 1995), may be useful in understanding decisions regarding the international location of production of intermediate and final goods in the food processing sector.

In the case of trade policy, the chapters by Karp and Jones lend validation to what has been widely observed about trade policy under conditions of imperfect competition, to wit:

> "The resulting literature is full of special cases, models, and results that do not generalize in any simple fashion. The strategic trade policy literature is not a useful guide to government policy at this time. Yet, taken together, this collection of special cases may help us better understand how our global economy's trade is increasingly dominated by large, multinational firms." (Markusen, et al. 1995, p. 293)

Karp (Chapter 4), by applying strategic trade policy analysis in a dynamic framework, serves a warning that strategic trade policy outcomes, as in the static case, will not only be sensitive to the nature of competition between firms but also to factors such as the ability of governments to commit to future policies. Jones (Chapter 9) adds to this by pointing out the extra complexity of implementing strategic trade policy when there are vertical market linkages. Not only may policymakers pick the wrong instrument because they are unable to observe the game firms are playing, they may also pick the wrong stage of a vertical market at which to apply that instrument. Nevertheless, the theory does highlight the importance of capturing imperfect competition in trade models when evaluating either the impact of a particular policy or the effects of trade liberalization.

In conclusion, the complexity of international commerce in the processed food sector is reflected in the lack of a simple, general framework for analyzing factors such as foreign direct investment, intra-industry trade, and vertical market linkages. Encouragingly, recent work of Markusen and others is moving in this direction. Perhaps the bigger challenge is how to implement this new body of theory empirically. Progress has been made in the agricultural economics literature in estimating market power in international markets, incorporating imperfect competition into computable general equilibrium models, measuring and explaining intra-industry trade and foreign direct investment, and evaluating the effects of imperfect competition on trade policy. As pointed out earlier, however, this research is usually hampered by data problems; empirical research on multinational firms in the context of models such as those outlined by Markusen is virtually nonexistent, as is work on international vertical market linkages. Nevertheless, both more extensive and intensive empirical work in the processed food sector may aid the search for a tractable general theoretical framework. As Krugman notes, "it would be desirable to see empirical work begin to narrow the range of things that we regard as plausible outcomes." (1989, p. 1214).

Notes

1. This type of consolidation is often loosely referred to as vertical coordination. It encompasses vertical integration and a variety of vertical contracts other than spot market exchange.

References

Brander, J. A. and B. J. Spencer (1985). "Export Subsidies and International Market Share Rivalry," *Journal of International Economics*, 18: 83–100.

Chang, W. and J. C. Kim (1989). "Competition in Quality Differentiated Products and Optimal Trade Policy," *Keio Economic Studies*, 26: 1–17.

———. (1991). "Strategic Tariff Policy in a Model of Trade in Intermediate and Final Products," in A. Takayama, M. Ohyama, and H. Ohta (eds.), *Trade, Policy, and International Adjustments*, New York: Academic Press.

Helpman, E. (1984). "A Simple Theory of Trade with Multinational Corporations," *Journal of Political Economy*, 92: 451–471.

Helpman, E. and P. R. Krugman (1985). *Market Structure and Foreign Trade*, Cambridge: MIT Press.

Krugman, P. R. (1989). "Industrial Organization and International Trade," in R. Schmalensee and R. Willig (eds.), *Handbook of Industrial Organization*, Amsterdam: North-Holland.

Markusen, J. R. (1984). "Multinationals, Multi-Plant Economies, and the Gains from Trade," *Journal of International Economics*, 16: 205–226.

Markusen, J. R., J. R. Melvin, W. H. Kaempfer, and K. E. Maskus (1995). *International Trade: Theory and Evidence*, New York: McGraw-Hill.

Spencer, B. J. and R. W. Jones (1991). "Vertical Foreclosure and International Trade Policy," *Review of Economic Studies*, 58: 153–170.

———. (1992). "Trade and Protection in Vertically Related Markets," *Journal of International Economics*, 32: 31–55.

Venables, A. J. (1993). "Equilibrium Location of Vertically Linked Industries," Centre for Economic Policy Research, Discussion Paper, No. 802.

———. (1995). "Economic Integration and the Location of Firms," *American Economic Review—Papers and Proceedings*, 85: 296–300.

PART TWO

Related Studies

12

Wine Quality and Price: A Hedonic Approach

Günter Schamel, Silke Gabbert, and Harald von Witzke

Introduction

Premium wine is a good with highly differentiated quality characteristics. An overall measure for wine quality is difficult to derive. Many sensoric quality attributes are highly subjective including color and intensity, aroma and sweetness, as well as acidity, mouth-feel, and body. Additional outer quality attributes that may advance or hinder the sale of a particular wine involve factors such as label and bottle design or the reputation of wine-growing regions and wine producers. It has frequently been observed that the retail price for a bottle of premium wine may vary widely despite similar sensoric quality characteristics. For instance, French wines typically sell at a higher price than comparable American wines. Therefore, it is reasonable to postulate that a consumer's decision to buy a particular wine is often based on outer quality attributes. In particular, the reputation of a region as a reliable producer of high-quality wine may play a key role as it seems plausible that a consumer is prepared to pay a higher price for a reputable wine from a well known origin. Although a few empirical studies exist that analyze a number of quality attributes and characteristics for wine (Golan and Shalit 1993; Oczkowski 1994; Nerlove 1995), no special attention has been paid to wine-growing regions worldwide and their reputation as a key characteristic in determining the price of a premium wine.

This chapter presents an empirical analysis examining sensoric wine quality as well as outer quality attributes (e.g. regional origin). A hedonic pricing model of the premium wine market in the United States is developed, estimating implicit prices for several key quality attributes. The main objective is to analyze the impact on price of sensoric quality, variety, regional origin (e.g. the reputation of selected wine-growing areas), and vintage. *The Wine Spectator*, a U.S. trade magazine that publishes average retail prices for premium wines along with relatively consistent sensoric quality ratings (so-called scores), as well as information on regional origin, varieties, and other distinguishing quality characteristics, was the source of data. In an effort to evaluate important premium wines, a large number of white wines (chardonnay) and red wines (cabernet sauvignon) were selected from a variety of wine-growing regions around the world. They are American wines from Napa and Sonoma Valley as well as from Washington State, French wines from Bordeaux and Burgundy, Australian wines and Chilean wines.

In the following section, a brief literature review surveys the current research on hedonic pricing models, particularly with regard to wine and other agricultural commodities. Next, we discuss the theoretical foundation of our analysis, followed by the empirical model and its results. The main conclusions of our analysis and their implications for producers and consumers are discussed in the last section.

Brief Literature Review

Hedonic price analysis is based on the hypothesis that every good can be treated as a bundle of attributes that define its quality and differentiate closely related products. Producers and consumers can evaluate any bundle of product attributes (e.g. features of a car, indicators of air or water quality). The observed market price is the sum of implicit prices paid for each quality attribute. In a classic paper, Rosen (1974) presents a model of product differentiation based on the hypothesis that any good is valued for its utility-generating attributes, which in turn define implicit prices. Assuming a competitive market, he develops a theoretical model that allows him to construct implicit markets for characteristics embodied in differentiated products. Rosen recognizes an identification problem for supply and demand functions derived from hedonic price functions, because implicit prices are equilibrium prices jointly determined by supply and demand conditions. Consequently, implicit prices do not only reflect consumer preferences, but also factors that determine production. Solving the identification problem would require that the supply and demand conditions that determine the market price of a product be separated from each other. Arguea and Hsiao (1993) examine some econometric issues when estimating hedonic price functions. They argue that Rosen's identification problem is essentially a data issue that can be avoided by pooling cross-section and time-series data characteristics on a particular side of the market.

Uri et al. (1994) developed a hedonic pricing model for wheat to investigate the effects of quality attributes on wheat prices. Specifically, they addressed the question of whether the quality characteristics for wheat assigned by the U.S. Federal Grain Inspection Service (FGIS) have an impact on price. Intriguingly, they claim that identification is not an issue to be concerned with because their empirical estimation does not analyze a particular side of the market, but rather focuses on an overall market evaluation of the quality attributes.

Currently, three empirical studies exist that apply the hedonic pricing technique to wine. Nerlove (1995) estimated a hedonic price function for the Swedish wine market, which is small relative to the overall world market. Moreover, there is no domestic production, and the prices are controlled by the government. This allowed him to presume that prices are exogenous as opposed to assuming that supply is exogenous, thus avoiding Rosen's identification problem. He estimated a reduced-form hedonic price function by regressing quantities sold on various quality attributes and prices. Thus, Nerlove assumed that Swedish wine consumers express their valuation of a particular quality attribute by varying the derived hedonic demand for it. Oczkowski (1994) estimated a log-linear hedonic price function for Australian premium table wine. His regression analysis relates retail prices to six attribute groups represented by dummy variables and various interaction terms. Although he stressed the applicability of Rosen's pure competition equilibrium framework, he fails to address the identification problem throughout the paper. Golan and Shalit (1993) developed another empirical model, identifying and evaluating quality characteristics for Israeli wine grapes relative to Californian wines. In contrast to Nerlove's analysis, they analyzed hedonic grape pricing, that is, the supply side of the wine market in Israel. Their premise is that high quality wines are produced only when growers are given a strong enough price incentive to supply better grapes. In a two stage model, they first developed a quality index by evaluating the (relative) contributions of various physical grape attributes to wine quality. Second, they constructed a quality-price function relating the price of California wine to the quality index developed in the first stage. It is interesting to note that similar to Nerlove, they circumvent Rosen's identification problem by assuming that the price is exogenously given.

In contrast to these studies, the identification problem is avoided here by arguing that the supply of premium wines is largely determined by exogenous factors for at least three reasons. First, vineyards suitable for growing premium wines can be laid out only in selected locations satisfying their unique growing demands (e.g. climate, soil). Their acreage is fixed, at least in the short and medium run. Despite the fact that yields from premium vineyards may vary over time (e.g. due to weather), generally they cannot be increased by much without loss of quality. Second, compared with average- and low-quality grapes, processing and storage of premium wine require more attention. For example, the wines are often stored in oak barrels and the ripening process has to be carefully controlled. Moreover, mechanical harvest of grapes may not be possible. Thus, although technical progress also affects premium wines, it may have limited effects on production capacities. Third, production and processing of premium wines depend to a large extent on industry-specific human capital, that is, on the experience and know-how of the wine grower and vintner. Consequently, it seems unlikely that the supply of premium wines can be increased significantly by new players, at least not in the short run. Given these facts, the supply of premium wines is determined by variables that are primarily exogenous. Therefore, a standard regression of price on quantity would allow one to estimate the price elasticity of demand (Schultz, 1938).

The Model

Lancaster (1966) presented a theory of consumer behavior that argues that utility is enhanced not by the consumption of an economic good, but by the characteristics of that good. Therefore, the market price of the good is the sum of the prices consumers are willing to pay for each characteristic that improves their utility. The demand functions derived from maximizing this utility function provide the foundation for hedonic price analysis.

Wine, like other economic goods, is composed of n attributes or characteristics, $\mathbf{Z}=z_1, \ldots, z_n$ (e.g. variety, quality score, region of origin, vintage). Associated with the bundle of attributes that define the type of wine is a unit price $P(\mathbf{Z})$. A hedonic price function describes the price of a wine i (Pw_i) as a function of its characteristics:

$$Pw_i = Pw(z_{i1}, \ldots, z_{ij}, \ldots, z_{in}) \tag{1}$$

Following Rosen (1974), the utility maximization problem for a representative individual is

$$\text{Max } U = U(X, \mathbf{Z}) \qquad \text{s.t.} \quad M - Pw_i - X = 0 \tag{2}$$

where X is a composite (numeraire) commodity and M is income. An implicit assumption of equation (2) is that each individual purchases only one unit of wine i during the relevant time period. Thus, the model presumes that the quantity consumed is given and that consumers express their valuation of a particular quality attribute by varying their willingness to pay for it. The first-order condition for the choice of characteristic z_j is given by

$$\frac{\partial U/\partial z_j}{\partial U/\partial X} = \frac{\partial Pw}{\partial z_j}. \quad (3)$$

Condition (3) simply states that the consumer's marginal willingness to pay for attribute z_j is equal to the marginal cost of purchasing more of z_j. $\partial Pw/\partial z_j$ is the marginal implicit price for characteristic z_j and corresponds to the regression coefficients when estimating equation (1).

The utility function U can be rewritten as

$$U = U(M - Pw_i, z_{i1}, \ldots, z_{ij}, \ldots, z_{in}). \quad (4)$$

Inverting condition (4), solving for Pw_i, and holding all but characteristic z_j constant, yields a bid curve B_j:

$$B_j = B_j(z_j, \mathbf{Z}^*, U^*) \quad (5)$$

Equation (5) describes the maximum amount a representative individual would pay to obtain a unit of a particular wine as a function of z_j, holding other things constant. Note that U^* is the optimal utility level associated with the utility maximization problem (2), and $\mathbf{Z}^*$ is the vector of optimally chosen quantities for all other characteristics. A well-behaved bid curve ought to exhibit a diminishing willingness to pay for z_j or a diminishing marginal rate of substitution between z_j and X. Because of differences in preferences and/or incomes, consumers can have different bid curves $B_j^1(z_j)$ and $B_j^2(z_j)$ as shown in Figure 12.1 for individuals 1 and 2.

On the supply side of the market, firms' costs of production depend on the levels of the characteristics of the product (wine) that they produce. Firms are heterogeneous with respect to cost functions. Inverting a firm's cost function yields an offer curve for characteristic z_j:

$$C_j = C_j(z_j, \mathbf{Z}^*, \pi^*) \quad (6)$$

Equation (6) describes the minimum price a firm would accept to sell a unit of wine as a function of z_j, holding other things constant. Note that π^* is the profit level associated with the firm's profit maximization problem (i.e. $\pi^* = 0$ assuming perfect competition). Offer curves $C_j^1(z_j)$ and $C_j^2(z_j)$ for two individual wine producers are also shown in Figure 12.1. In an equilibrium, all bid and offer curves for quality attributes and for each market participant must be tangent to the hedonic price function $Pw(z_j)$, which is an equilibrium locus for all individual bid and offer curves.

However, we do not formally model the supply side of the wine market, because our interest is in the values of quality characteristics to buyers of wine. Instead, we assume that the wine market is competitive and in equilibrium. That is, all individuals have made their utility-maximizing choices given the prices of alternative wines and their characteristics, all firms have made their profit-maximizing decisions, the produc-

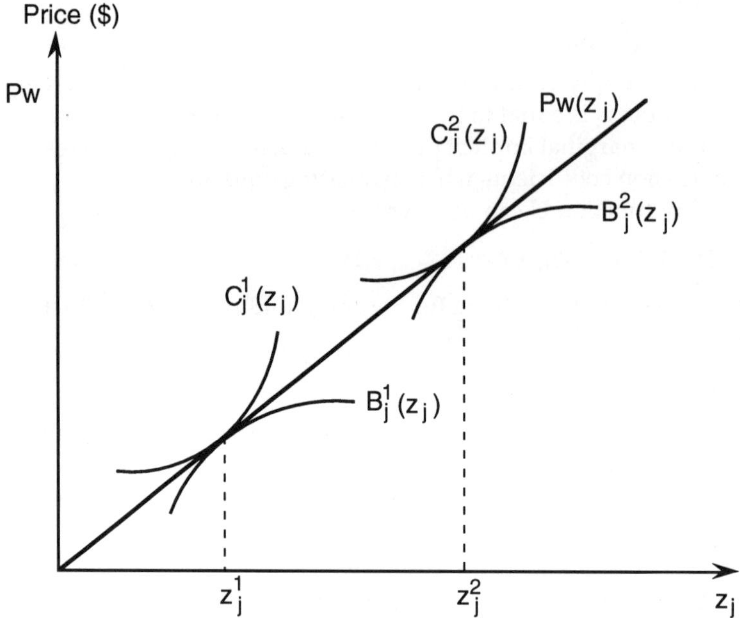

FIGURE 12.1 Bid curves of consumers and offer curves of producers in a hedonic market.

tion costs of alternative wines and their characteristics, and resulting prices that clear the market. According to Freeman (1992), this assumption implies that implicit prices for the ith wine can be specified without modeling the supply side of the market.

Empirical Estimation and Results

Hedonic pricing is a well-known tool for economists to relate the price of a product to its various attributes or characteristics. Premium wine is a highly differentiated product and any measurable variable (quantitative or qualitative) that affects the utility of consumers (or the costs to producers) is a potential candidate to be included in the hedonic price function. Therefore, the choice of appropriate variables must be guided by our two main objectives, given the availability of suitable and consistent data.

First, we are interested in the overall value of wine quality to consumers. Therefore, we do not consider technical wine quality attributes such as sugar level or acidity as done by Nerlove (1995) and Golan and Shalit (1993). Rather, we use the wine ratings that are published in the monthly

U.S. magazine *The Wine Spectator* in order to quantify wine quality, an intrinsically subjective product attribute. Their ratings are obtained by a certified tasting panel, and all the wines are blind tasted. The tasters are only told the general type of wine (e.g. variety) and the vintage. The tasting panel uses a one hundred-point scale, and their ratings reflect how highly a particular wine is regarded relative to other wines. The wines are sampled one at a time. Sometimes close-scoring wines of a similar type are sampled again before assigning a final score (Shanken 1994). Moreover, we employ a qualitative variable to distinguish a typical red wine (cabernet sauvignon) and a typical white wine (chardonnay) in order to evaluate the differences between two widely recognized premium wine types.

Second, we focus on whether and how the reputation of a particular wine-growing area affects the price of premium wine. In order to achieve this goal, we employ regional origin as a conceptual dummy variable categorizing wines from North America (Napa and Sonoma Valley, Washington State), France (Bordeaux and Burgundy), Australia, and Chile. Napa Valley was selected as a reference category to avoid the dummy variable trap.

The variable "vintage" denotes the year in which a wine was harvested and vinified and is included to determine whether time-contingent price differences exist. The price data signify a current retail price of a particular wine as a weighted average of prices obtained primarily from catalogs, retail advertisements, and wine auctions. A brief description of data and variables used in our analysis is provided in Table 12.1.

Initially, standard tests (e.g. Park, Goldfeld-Quandt) were applied for both the linear and log-linear forms. The linear model revealed a signifi-

TABLE 12.1 Description of the Data

Variable	*Description*
Price	weighted retail price (dependent variable)
Score	sensoric wine quality score (maximum score = 100 points)
Red/White	red wine = 1 (cabernet sauvignon), white wine = 0 (chardonnay)
Napa	dummy for Napa Valley wines
Sonoma	dummy for Sonoma Valley wines
Washington	dummy for wines from Washington State (red wines only)
Chile	dummy for Chilean wines
Australia	dummy for Australian wines
Bordeaux	dummy for wines from Bordeaux, France
Burgundy	dummy for wines from Burgundy, France
Vintage	year of harvest and vinification (1986–91)

Source: Shanken, 1994.

cant degree of heteroskedasticity. Thus, the log-linear form was chosen to estimate the hedonic price function; the results are presented in Table 12.2. The "full sample" column reports implicit prices for all variables listed in Table 12.1, including a shifter for red wines.[1] The other columns show results for subsamples of red and white wines, respectively. Given the nature of the data set, only the logarithms of the dependent variable "Price" and of the independent variable "Score " can be taken. Thus, the "Score" coefficient measures the price elasticity of premium wine with respect to sensoric wine quality. A dummy variable coefficient is interpreted as a percentage price impact relative to Napa Valley wines.

In discussing individual results, first consider the coefficients except regional origin. The coefficient for wine quality (Score) is significant for all three samples, suggesting that wine quality is an important criterion to consumers across wine varieties. The elasticity is larger for red wines, indicating a higher-quality premium for them compared to white wines. The shifter for red wines (Red/White) in the full sample is also significant, indicating that a remarkable 12.4 percent price difference is paid for premium red wines compared to white wines from Napa Valley. The vintage coefficients are not significant in all three samples, which suggests that time-contingent price differences do not exist.[2]

Now consider the coefficients for regional origin. They denote percentage premiums for reputation that are paid for wines from a particular growing area relative to wines from Napa Valley. For the full sample, the

TABLE 12.2 Hedonic Pricing Model Estimates[a]

Variable	*Full Sample* n=305 R^2=0.6661	*Red Wines* n=162 R^2=0.7196	*White Wines* n=142 R^2=0.6198
Constant	-16.7 (-8.58)[b]	-19.4 (-7.23)[b]	-13.7 (-4.89)[b]
Score	4.38 (9.97)[b]	5.05 (8.42)[b]	3.07 (5.82)[b]
Red/White	0.124 (2.36)[b]	---	---
Sonoma	-0.041 (-0.48)	-0.135 (-1.13)	0.050 (0.412)
Washington	-0.389 (-3.59)[b]	-0.465 (-3.89)[b]	---
Chile	-0.772 (-8.03)[b]	-0.898 (-7.00)[b]	-0.569 (-3.52)[b]
Australia	-0.521 (-5.97)[b]	-0.499 (-4.10)[b]	-0.536 (-4.42)[b]
Bordeaux	0.145 (1.65)	0.053 (0.43)	0.342 (2.81)[b]
Burgundy	0.602 (6.91)[b]	0.656 (5.30)[b]	0.563 (4.68)[b]
Vintage	0.028 (1.10)	0.0079 (0.209)	-0.0031 (-0.076)

[a]t-statistics are in parentheses.

[b]significanct at the 5% level.

dummies categorizing regional origin are significant for all wine-growing areas except Sonoma Valley and Bordeaux, indicating that the reputation of wines from Napa and Sonoma Valley and from Bordeaux can be regarded as similar. The coefficients denoting the reputation of Washington State, Australia, and Chile are all negative and highly significant. It suggests that, in general, wines from these origins are less preferred than wines from Napa and Sonoma Valley as well as from Bordeaux. However, a large positive coefficient for Burgundy wines demonstrates that they enjoy a very high reputation resulting in a 60 percent price difference relative to comparable wines from Napa Valley.

For red wines, a similar result holds. Significant price differences due to regional origin can be reported for all regions except Sonoma Valley and Bordeaux, and it seems that premium red wines from these areas reach a comparable reputation in the eyes of consumers. For premium white wines, regional origin seems to be even more important because an insignificant price difference can be reported only for Sonoma Valley. In general, the coefficients on regional origin are highly significant and seem to indicate that the wine-growing area strongly matters to consumers of premium wines in the United States. However, when their attention is on buying a particular variety, it looks as if regional origin matters even more for white wines than for red wines. Finally, note that all significant parameters reported in Table 12.2 exhibit the signs that were expected a priori.

Marketing and Policy Implications

Our empirical results contain some important marketing and policy implications. Sensoric wine quality is an important utility-generating attribute for consumers. However, increasing the quality of wine would benefit producers of red wines more than producers of white wines, with elasticities of 5.05 and 3.07, respectively. Variety is another important quality attribute to consumers. On average, producers can get a 12.4 percent higher price for a red wine than for a white wine of the same quality and origin. Even though only a six-year time horizon was analyzed, no time trend is observable, indicating that relative prices have not changed significantly over time.

Interesting conclusions can be drawn from categorizing regional origins across premium wine varieties. Relative to Napa Valley, red as well as white wines from Sonoma Valley have reached an equal reputation in the eyes of consumers. In general, it appears that French wines (especially from the Burgundy area) enjoy a high reputation in the United States. However, while the reputation of red wines from Bordeaux and red wines from Napa and Sonoma Valley is comparable, this is not the case for white wines from Bordeaux. This indicates that premium Napa and Sonoma Valley white wines lag somewhat behind in their reputation relative to red wines from both valleys. It was to be expected that wines from Washington State are regarded less favorably than comparable Californian wines of equal sensoric quality. However, it is surprising that consumers are willing to pay even less for premium Australian wines compared to Washington State wines given the great success of Australian wines at international wine competitions and auctions. The reputation of Chilean wines represents the low end in our analysis with a 90 percent discount relative to Napa Valley wines. However, it is interesting to note that Chilean white wines are valued similarly to Australian white wines but significantly higher than Chilean red wines.

The estimated hedonic price function may also have important policy implications. Because regional reputation is a public good, it may be desirable for governments or regional marketing boards to engage in activities to enhance the reputation of a particular wine-growing area or of a variety from a particular region. For example, Australian wine producers may want to foster the reputation of their wines in North America, given that they lag significantly behind other regions despite very favorable international ratings for their wines.

In conclusion, we emphasize that sensoric wine quality is a highly significant factor influencing a consumer's willingness to pay for premium wine. In addition to wine quality, the reputation of the wine-growing area is a crucial determinant influencing the price of premium wine. However, significant regional differences exist across wine varieties. Also, since region of production imparts quality to a wine, a wine with a specific regional identity cannot be produced in an importing country. Therefore, unlike trade in many other food and beverage products where production can be moved to the country where the consumers live, the wine must be traded in order to maintain its regional characteristic.

Notes

1. Note that Napa Valley wines are missing in Table 12.2 because the category was chosen to avoid the dummy variable trap. Thus, the estimated parameters have to be interpreted relative to wines from that area.

2. Of course, time-contingent price differences may exist for older premium wines (e.g. port wines).

References

Arguea, N. and Hsiao, C. (1993). "Econometric Issues of Estimating Hedonic Price Functions." *Journal of Econometrics*. Vol. 56, pp. 243–67.

Freeman, M. (1992). *The Measurement of Environmental and Resource Values: Theory and Methods*. Resources for the Future: Washington. D.C., chapters 4 & 11.

Golan, A. and Shalit, H. (1993). "Wine Quality Differentials in Hedonic Grape Pricing." *Journal of Agricultural Economics*. Vol. 44, pp. 311–21.

Lancaster, K. J. (1966). "The New Approach to Consumer Theory." *Journal of Political Economy*. Vol. 74, pp. 132–57.

Nerlove, M. (1995). "Hedonic Price Functions and the Measurement of Preferences: The Case of Swedish Wine Consumers." *European Economic Review*. Vol. 39, pp. 1697–716.

Oczkowski, E. (1994) "A Hedonic Price Function for Australian Premium Table Wine." *Australian Journal of Agricultural Economics*. Vol. 38, pp. 93–110.

Rosen, S. (1974). "Hedonic Prices and Implicit Markets: Product Differentiation in Pure Competition." *Journal of Political Economy*. Vol. 82, pp. 34–55.

Shanken, M. (1994). *Wine Spectator' Ultimate Guide to Buying Wine, 4th ed.* Wine Spectator Press:New York.

Schultz, H. (1938). *The Theory and Measurement of Demand*. The University of Chicago Press: Chicago.

Uri, N. D., Hyberg, B., Mercier, S., and Lyford, C. (1994). "The market valuation of the FGIS grain quality characteristics." *Applied Economics*. Vol. 26, pp. 701–12.

13

Export Subsidy Switching Under the Uruguay Round Commitments: The Case of Wheat and Wheat Flour

Stephen Haley and Philip L. Paarlberg

Introduction

Under the terms of the Uruguay Round (UR) of the General Agreement on Tariffs and Trade (GATT), wheat and wheat flour form one commodity grouping. Analyses of the effect of UR commitments follow this grouping by treating wheat and flour as a composite good. This treatment ignores the differences in marketing arrangements and structures between the bulk commodity wheat and its value-added transform, flour. There is no consideration of the wheat processing sector, neither its effect on achieving commitment levels nor on the effect of the UR on the sector.

The purpose of this chapter is to analyze the effect of adjustment to the commitment levels on the wheat and flour sectors in the United States. The analysis emphasizes trade-offs reaching commitment levels between wheat and flour in the United States and the European Union (EU). An analytical framework developed at the U.S. Department of Agriculture's Economic Research Service (ERS) is used for the analysis. The framework is a price-based modeling system that simulates the balancing of world trade in wheat, flour, and other grains. It predicts medium-term adjustments resulting from transitioning from an initial state of equilibrium to one that results from a set of policy changes. In this instance, the policy changes consist in complying with the terms of the UR for wheat and flour by the United States and the EU.

A contribution of the approach is that it allows the wheat milling sector to be affected by wheat market developments and simultaneously to influence the wheat market. Two factors are emphasized: (1) the substitutability of nonwheat inputs for wheat in the milling process, and (2) how the availability of wheat from Canada affects predicted outcomes of meeting UR commitments in the United States.

World Flour and Wheat Trade

World flour trade is small compared to wheat trade. Over the 1985–86 to 1993–94 period, flour exports have averaged 7.2 million metric tons (mmt), or about 7.4 percent of combined wheat/flour exports. Over this period, the world's largest importer has been Egypt, taking in about 18 percent of all imports. Other large importers include Libya, Syria, Yemen, and, as a group, sub-Saharan African countries.

The EU and the United States are the largest flour exporters—world export shares averaging 58 percent (about 4.2 mmt/year) and 19 percent (about 1.4 mmt/year), respectively. Both the EU and the United States have subsidized flour exports. The EU unit flour export restitutions subsidy is generally kept in line with that for wheat—about 1.4 times as much, reflecting a flour/wheat milling ratio of about 0.73. Important importers of EU flour are sub-Saharan countries: Egypt, Syria, Libya, and Yemen.

The United States has subsidized flour exports through its Export Enhancement Program (EEP). Unlike the EU, it does not try to coordinate unit values between flour and wheat. While subsidized U.S. flour volume has been only 2.8 percent of subsidized wheat volume, the value of flour subsidy expenditures has been 7.4 percent of wheat subsidy spending. The average EEP bonus for flour has been $94.34 per metric ton, contrasting with $34.15 per metric ton for wheat. The largest flour EEP markets have been Egypt and Yemen.

UR Wheat and Flour Commitments

Terms of the UR call for the United States and the European Union to reduce wheat/flour export subsidy expenditure by 36 percent and the volume of subsidized exports by 21 percent, relative to base period levels averaged from 1986 through 1990. By 2001 subsidized wheat/flour exports from the EU will be constrained at 13.436 mmt, and expenditure constrained to 1,141.1 million ECU. Likewise, maximum EEP exports from the United States will be set at 14.522 mmt, and spending will be limited to $363.8 million.

Theoretical Expectations

Nondurum food wheat is a material input into flour production. Demand for flour forms the primary basis for the demand for wheat. Figure 13.1 shows the main effects of a wheat export subsidy on domestic, foreign, and world markets for wheat and flour. The top panel represents wheat markets: domestic, world, and rest-of-world (ROW). D_W and S_W, and D'_W and S'_W, represent wheat demand and supply schedules in the domestic and ROW markets, respectively. Differences between supply and demand are expressed as excess supply in the domestic market (ES_W in the middle panel), and excess demand in ROW (ED_W in the middle panel). Equilibrium in the world market consists of excess supply being balanced with excess demand through world wheat price clearing at P_W. The lower panel shows corresponding markets, supply and demand schedules, and the world price for flour.

The diagram shows domestic policymakers extending an export subsidy to the ROW wheat importer. The effective excess demand facing exporters becomes ED'_W. World equilibrium trade increases from X_W to

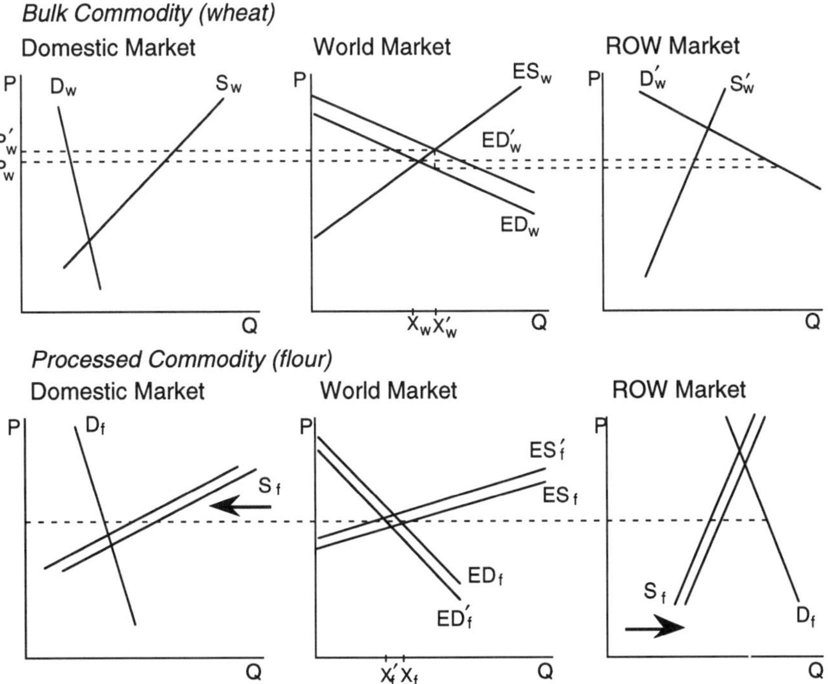

FIGURE 13.1 Export Subsidy in the Bulk Commodity.

X'_W. To generate additional supplies to the world market implied by this increase, the exporter's price increases to P'_W. The price offered to ROW to increase demand to clear the world market is shown in the diagram as the dashed line from the middle to the right panel. It lies below P'_W by the amount of the unit value of the export subsidy.

These wheat price changes affect the supply of flour in the domestic and ROW markets. A higher-priced input in the domestic flour market (bottom left panel) causes the supply schedule to shift upward. At each level of production, higher input prices require a higher compensating product price to balance revenues with higher costs. Excess flour supplies to the world market are lower: ES_f shifts leftward to ES'_f. In the ROW (bottom right panel), a lower wheat price allows the unit price of flour to be lower in order to match revenue from sales with reduced costs: S_f shifts downward, and excess demand in the middle panel shifts from ED_f to ED'_f.

If there were no subsidies in flour markets, simultaneous excess supply and demand curve shifts imply that there will be reduced trade in flour, X_f to X'_f. Increased trade in the input in effect displaces the trade in the output. The effect on the price of flour is ambiguous because of the simultaneous, exogenous reductions in excess supply and demand.

Figure 13.2 shows the effects of an export subsidy on flour. World excess demand shifts up by the amount of the unit subsidy: ED_f to ED'_f (bottom middle panel). Flour exports expand X_f to X'_f, and the domestic flour price increases to P'_f. The ROW flour price is equal to P'_f less the unit subsidy amount, leaving it lower than initial price P_f in order to absorb the added flour supply. In wheat markets, domestic demand shifts upward reflecting the pressures of an expanding flour supply. In the ROW wheat market, the opposite occurs because of lower flour prices. Excess wheat supply and demand curves shift leftward in the world market panel, predicting a drop in wheat trade from X_W to X'_W and leaving the effect on price indeterminant.

This graphical analysis shows the effect of a single policy change made by only one of the exporters. Given that flour reductions must always be accompanied by some reduction in wheat to meet UR commitments (flour subsidies and trade are still small relative to wheat), additional complexity must be introduced in designing a modeling system that can keep track of the many simultaneously occurring events.

Analytical Framework and Scenario Description

The analytical framework is an extension of a world trade modeling system developed for wheat differentiated by class and source-country (Haley, 1995). Extensions for the current analysis are constituted by: (1) an inclusion of flour milling, consumption, and world trade; and (2) an inclusion of a demand and production system for feedgrains.[1]

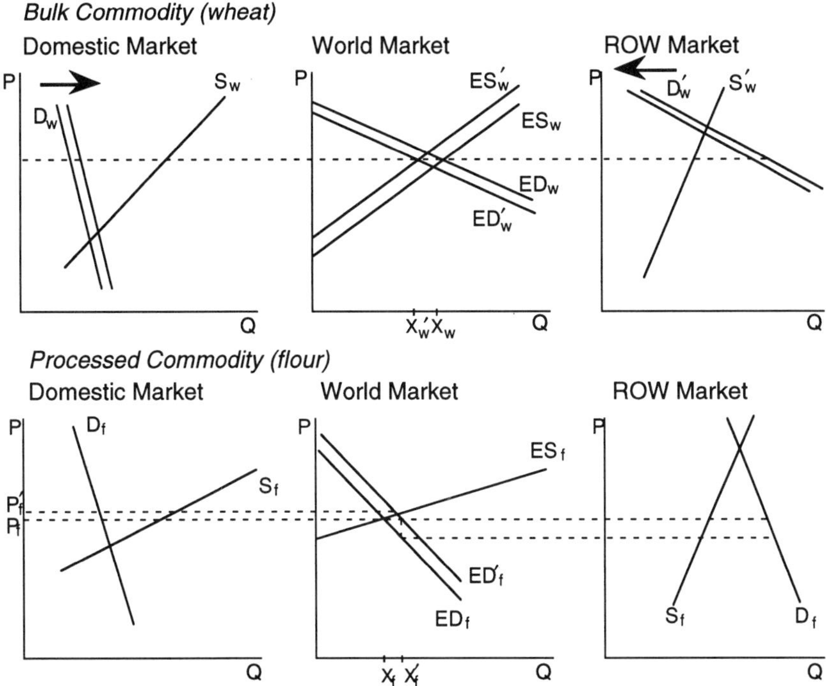

FIGURE 13.2 Export Subsidy in the Processed Product.

The system is a static, partial equilibrium, nonspatial modeling framework of equations representing supply, demand, and their difference: net trade. Both supply and demand are functions of own- and cross-prices. Domestic incentive prices depend on the level of consumer and producer support and on world prices denominated in local currency. Price transmission elasticities regulate the extent to which domestic prices change when world prices change. World markets clear when net trade of a commodity across all regions sums to zero. Haley's framework relies on a constant elasticity of substitution (CES) specification traceable to Armington (1969) to account for substitution possibilities between wheat classes and sources.

Because the framework is comparatively static, analysis consists in comparing one precommitment equilibrium with one that assumes that the commitments have been achieved. The analysis does not consider the details of arriving at the new equilibrium. The model takes the July 1992–June 1993 crop year as its base. Production, consumption, trade, export price, transport, and non-U.S. export data are from the World Grain

Statistics (International Grains Council, 1994). U.S. EEP data for wheat and flour are from the U.S. Department of Agriculture (USDA).

Calculated subsidy levels are reduced to levels specified in the UR for 2001, the sixth and final year of the adjustment period for the United States and the EU. Because not all U.S. wheat exports are subsidized (i.e., the EEP bonuses are targeted to specific importers), the United States satisfies its commitments by reducing EEP expenditure, with the volume commitment as necessary but analytically secondary. For the EU, the volume commitment is as analytically important as the expenditure commitment because most, if not all, EU wheat and flour exports are shipped with subsidy. In the description that follows, the necessary EU volume reductions are emphasized.

Table 13.1 describes four scenario possibilities, labeled I-A, I-B, II-A, and II-B. The EU attains its commitments through: (I) no reduction of its flour subsidies—that is, all the adjustment is in wheat; and (II) total elimination of subsidies for flour and therefore less of a reduction in wheat to meet its commitment level. For each case, the United States is modeled with the same alternatives: (A) no reduction in the flour EEP, therefore all adjustment in wheat; and (B) total elimination of the flour EEP, less of a reduction in wheat.

TABLE 13.1 Description of Modeling Scenarios

EU Volume Commitment Under the UR: 13.436 million metric tons (mmt)				
I.	*No Flour Reduction*			
	Flour Exports	= 4.882	Wheat Exports	= 15.812
	Reduction	= 0	Reduction	= 7.258
	Balance	= 4.882	Balance	= 8.554
II.	*Full Flour Reduction*			
	Flour Exports	= 4.882	Wheat Exports	= 15.812
	Reduction	= 4.882	Reduction	= 2.376
	Balance	= 0	Balance	= 13.436
U.S. Expenditure Commitment Under the UR: $363.8 million				
A.	*No Flour Reduction*			
	Flour Exports	= $69.8	Wheat Exports	= $687.4
	Reduction	= 0	Reduction	= $393.4
	Balance	= $69.8	Balance	= $294.0
B.	*Full Flour Reduction*			
	Flour Exports	= $69.8	Wheat Exports	= $687.4
	Reduction	= $69.8	Reduction	= $323.6
	Balance	= 0	Balance	= $363.8

Sensitivity of Results to Technology Specification

Many parameter values are important to the framework and therefore to this analytical exercise. Especially important are those affecting demand for wheat. One of the primary parameters, indirectly accounted for in the actual specification of the framework, is the elasticity of substitution between wheat and the nonwheat composite input. The value of this elasticity reflects the degree to which wheat and nonwheat inputs can substitute for each other in flour milling. The elasticity value, along with wheat's distributive or cost share in flour milling and the own-price demand elasticity for flour, determine the value of the own-price demand elasticity for wheat. Table 13.2 shows computational details (Wohlgenant and Haidacher, 1989).

The consensus among ERS analysts who reviewed both model structure and elasticity values was that, for the United States, an own-price demand elasticity for flour should be about -0.07 (Huang, 1985). The corresponding elasticity value for food wheat should be about -0.25 (Sullivan and others, 1992). If these values were accepted and with wheat's cost share equal to 0.8186, then it would imply a value of 1.05 for the underlying elasticity of substitution between wheat and the nonwheat

TABLE 13.2 Key Sensitivity Parameters: Technology

Elasticity of Substitution between wheat and non-wheat inputs into flour production governs the extent to which changes in the demand for flour translate into changes in demand for wheat as a material input in flour milling:

ε_{wheat} = $-(1-Share_{wheat})*\sigma + Share_{wheat}*\varepsilon_{flour}$

η_{flour} = $(1-Share_{wheat})/Share_{wheat})*\sigma$, where:

ε_{wheat} = Own-price wheat demand elasticity

ε_{flour} = Own-price flour demand elasticity

η_{flour} = Own-price flour supply elasticity

$Share_{wheat}$ = Cost share of wheat in flour production

σ = Elasticity of substitution between wheat and non-wheat composite input in flour milling

Implications for Demand and Supply Elasticities

Exporter	*Substitution Elasticity*	*Own-Price Demand Elasticity: Food Wheat*	*Own-Price Demand Elasticity: Flour*	*Own-Price Supply Elasticity: Flour*
United States	1.05	-0.25	-0.07	0.23
	0	-0.25	-0.30	0
EU	1.05	-0.29	-0.12	0.23
	0	-0.29	-0.35	0

composite input. These values in turn imply an own-price flour supply elasticity of 0.23.

ERS analysts were confident in estimating own-price demand elasticities for the EU and other regions but were not able to speculate confidently regarding flour elasticities. For this reason, the U.S. value for the elasticity of substitution was used for all regions comprising the framework in order to generate own-price flour demand and supply elasticity values. Recognizing limitations in this approach, the value of zero was used as an alternative. A value of zero is more compatible with other modeling approaches (typically general equilibrium) that use fixed input-output ratios in specifying intermediate demand.

Implications of a zero elasticity of substitution are shown for the U.S. and EU wheat and flour specifications in Table 13.2. The own-price wheat demand elasticity is assumed fixed, and the flour elasticities are allowed to change according to the presumed value of the elasticity of substitution. For the United States the flour demand is -0.30 (wheat demand of -0.25 divided by the cost share 0.8186), and for the EU it is -0.35.

Sensitivity of Results to U.S. Wheat Import Demand

U.S. imports of Canadian wheat constituted over 6 percent of U.S. food wheat consumption in 1992–1993. There is no consensus regarding the effect of EEP reductions from meeting UR commitments on the level of imports. If EEP has contributed to lower wheat prices in Canada and thereby added to the attractiveness of shipping to the United States to take advantage of higher U.S. prices attributable to the EEP, then EEP reductions would lessen this incentive. If, on the other hand, the Canadian Wheat Board (CWB) (through which all Western Prairie Canadian food wheat is marketed) is assumed to have matched EEP subsidies to remain competitive in certain shared markets, then an EEP reduction would allow the CWB to lessen its subsidies.

Unlike the United States, Canadian wheat exports do not receive subsidies from government sources; rather, subsidies (if considered as such) are indirectly producer-financed through CWB pool accounts. The idea is that if the CWB reduces producer-financed "subsidies" as EEP bonuses are lowered, the savings get reflected in larger pool accounts (or higher initial CWB producer payments) that cause the average producer return from wheat to be higher. The higher return would imply more production of Canadian wheat. Higher production and fewer sales to the EEP markets (now no longer as heavily subsidized) would imply expanded sales domestically and to other offshore markets, including (possibly) the United States.

In order to take these effects into account, each scenario is viewed from three perspectives (or cases) regarding imports from Canada. For case i, no special assumption is made regarding CWB behavior. The CWB is assumed to adjust passively according to the framework's overall structure and already specified parameter values. One would expected an increase in Canada's export price to all importers, including the United States. U.S. consumption of Canadian wheat would fall.

For case ii, Canadian imports are held fixed at the initial baseline level. This case allows an examination of the case where all U.S.-derived wheat demand changes require adjustments from U.S. wheat sources alone.

For case iii, the CWB is assumed to have priced its wheat to be competitive in certain EEP markets shared with the United States. Specifically, it is assumed that Canadian wheat commands a $10 per metric ton premium over U.S.-sourced wheat due to a perceived higher-quality Canadian product. The markets include Venezuela, Brazil, the former Soviet Union, China, Algeria, and EEP markets in the Near and Far East Asian regions. EEP reductions in those countries are matched by the CWB in order to retain the $10 premium. Savings are passed back to the Canadian producer and are assumed to directly increase the producer incentive price. Wheat production increases and exports to the United States are permitted to reach equilibrium levels implied by the framework's structure and parameter value settings.

Results and Conclusions

Results from each of the scenarios (I-A, I-B, II-A, and II-B) are shown, respectively, in Tables 13.3a, b, c, and d. Each table shows two layerings of results. The first divides results between the high ($\sigma = 1.05$) and low ($\sigma = 0$) elasticities of substitution for wheat and the nonwheat input into flour milling. Within each of these groupings, results are divided according to cases i (passive CWB), ii (constant U.S. wheat imports), and iii (CWB "price-to-market").

Price and Quantity Effects: Scenario I-A

In this scenario (Table 13.3a), the EU reduces export restitutions for wheat but not for flour; and the United States reduces the EEP for wheat but not for flour. Most notably, the United States expands flour exports. For $\sigma = 1.05$, a higher flour price induces an increased supply of U.S. flour and increases the domestic demand for wheat. A higher flour price helps to limit magnitude of fall in the U.S. wheat price so as to maintain sufficient wheat supply to meet domestic needs. For $\sigma = 0$, export flour growth stems from reduced domestic demand for flour rather than increased supply as in the previous case. Because flour supply is perfectly inelastic with respect to its own price, changes in flour prices do not cause

TABLE 13.3a U.S. Wheat and Flour Price and Quantity Effects: Scenario I-A

Elasticity Value	*Case**	*U.S. Wheat Producer Price*	*Supply of U.S. Wheat*	*Demand for U.S. Wheat*	*Demand for Imported Wheat*	*Exports of U.S. Wheat*	*Supply of U.S. Flour*	*Demand for U.S. Flour*	*Exports of U.S. Flour*
		(Dollar/MT)	(1000 MT)						
Base	N/A	119.00	58182	23404	1386	34778	22192	20762	1430
					Change from Base				
1.05	i	-.90	-379	662	-549	-1041	160	-162	322
	ii	-1.71	-578	28	0	-606	109	-161	271
	iii	-2.77	-843	-2	190	-842	247	-161	409
0	i	-2.16	-677	234	-562	-911	-271	-656	385
	ii	-2.93	-868	-389	0	-478	-321	-655	334
	iii	-3.91	-1114	-366	148	-748	-180	-655	475

* Case i = Passive CWB
Case ii = Constant U.S. wheat imports
Case iii = CWB "price-to-market"

increased production. Flour supplies are reduced but the reductions are limited by wheat price reductions.

Domestic demand for U.S.-produced wheat depends on CWB policies. For case i (that is, passive CWB response), U.S. wheat prices are falling due to decreased export demand as EEP bonuses are removed; at the same time, Canadian wheat prices are increasing as demand for Canadian wheat in offshore markets increases due to reduced U.S. and EU excess supplies. Domestic demand for U.S. wheat increases, while U.S. demand for Canadian wheat decreases.

In case iii, in contrast, the CWB follows the United States out of EEP markets and increases pooled returns to producers. Wheat supply expands, and consequently so does Canadian excess supply. Wheat shipments increase to the non-EEP markets, including the United States, and the unsubsidized world price drops between $5.59 and $6.09 per metric ton. This level of reduction exceeds the drop in the U.S. domestic wheat price, thereby increasing the demand for Canadian wheat vis-à-vis U.S. wheat for both $\sigma = 1.05$ and $\sigma = 0$. The decrease in the U.S. wheat price (case i to case iii) is about $1.75 per metric ton greater if an aggressive CWB price-to-market strategy is assumed.

Price and Quantity Effects: Scenario I-B

In this scenario (Table 13.3b), the EU reduces export restitutions for wheat but not for flour, and the United States reduces EEP for both wheat and flour. Unlike scenario I-A, the United States reduces flour exports. For $\sigma = 1.05$, the primary adjustment is in flour supply. Although there is less domestic demand for wheat, the reductions in U.S. wheat prices are not too much more than those in I-A. There is less reduction in demand for U.S. wheat in export markets because of fewer wheat EEP bonus reductions.

For $\sigma = 0$, U.S. flour demand and supply are reduced to validate the flour export reduction. A reduction in domestic flour demand requires an even greater reduction in flour supply. Derived demand for wheat falls more, with the fall being reflected in larger wheat price reductions.

Increasing Canadian imports going from case i to iii causes a fall in U.S. wheat prices by about $1.50 per metric ton. This decline is about $0.25 less per ton than in I-A because the wheat EEP reduction and the consequent CWB reaction to it are less.

Price and Quantity Effects: Scenarios II-A and II-B

The EU eliminates export restitutions for flour (Tables 13.3c and 13.3d); the EU also reduces wheat export restitutions for wheat, but not as much as in scenarios I-A and I-B. Because EU wheat restitution reductions are not as great, EU wheat exports do not drop as much, thereby reducing

TABLE 13.3b U.S. Wheat and Flour Price and Quantity Effects: Scenario I-B

Elasticity Value	*Case**	*U.S. Wheat Producer Price*	*Supply of U.S. Wheat*	*Demand for U.S. Wheat*	*Demand for Imported Wheat*	*Exports of U.S. Wheat*	*Supply of U.S. Flour*	*Demand for U.S. Flour*	*Exports of U.S. Flour*
		(Dollar/MT)	(1000 MT)						
Base	N/A	119.00	58182	23404	1386	34778	22192	20762	1430
					Change from Base				
1.05	i	-1.27	-453	-318	-548	-135	-537	-135	-403
	ii	-1.99	-632	-915	0	283	-562	-134	-428
	iii	-2.84	-844	-884	-7	41	-530	-135	-395
0	i	-2.45	-730	-732	-564	2	-1070	-559	-511
	ii	-3.14	-903	-1323	0	420	-1092	-557	-535
	iii	-3.92	-1098	-1247	-51	149	-1071	-560	-511

* Case i = Passive CWB
Case ii = Constant U.S. wheat imports
Case iii = CWB "price-to-market"

TABLE 13.3c U.S. Wheat and Flour Price and Quantity Effects: Scenario II-A

Elasticity Value	*Case**	*U.S. Wheat Producer Price*	*Supply of U.S. Wheat*	*Demand for U.S. Wheat*	*Demand for Imported Wheat*	*Exports of U.S. Wheat*	*Supply of U.S. Flour*	*Demand for U.S. Flour*	*Exports of U.S. Flour*
		(Dollar/MT)	(1000 MT)						
Base	N/A	119.00	58182	23404	1386	34778	22192	20762	1430
					Change from Base				
1.05	i	-5.22	-1362	811	-514	-2173	372	-160	531
	ii	-5.97	-1550	224	0	-1775	330	-160	489
	iii	-7.01	-1817	158	240	-1975	479	-161	640
0	i	-5.93	-1536	409	-529	-1945	-99	-660	561
	ii	-6.65	-1718	-172	0	-1546	-142	-659	518
	iii	-7.61	-1965	-188	198	-1777	8	-663	671

* Case i = Passive CWB
Case ii = Constant U.S. wheat imports
Case iii = CWB "price-to-market"

TABLE 13.3d U.S. Wheat and Flour Price and Quantity Effects: Scenario II-B

Elasticity Value	*Case**	*U.S. Wheat Producer Price*	*Supply of U.S. Wheat*	*Demand for U.S. Wheat*	*Demand for Imported Wheat*	*Exports of U.S. Wheat*	*Supply of U.S. Flour*	*Demand for U.S. Flour*	*Exports of U.S. Flour*
		(Dollar/MT)	(1000 MT)						
Base	N/A	119.00	58182	23404	1386	34778	22192	20762	1430
					Change from Base				
1.05	i	-5.63	-1447	-226	-516	-1221	-369	-133	-236
	ii	-6.30	-1617	-781	0	-835	-386	-133	-253
	iii	-7.12	-1826	-777	27	-1049	-348	-134	-213
0	i	-6.27	-1604	-597	-532	-1008	-931	-563	-369
	ii	-6.91	-1769	-1148	0	-620	-948	-562	-386
	iii	-7.67	-1961	-1103	-15	-858	-923	-568	-355

* Case i = Passive CWB
Case ii = Constant U.S. wheat imports
Case iii = CWB "price-to-market"

opportunities for U.S. wheat to expand into EU export markets. U.S. wheat prices therefore drop between $3.70 and $4.40 per metric ton more than corresponding cases in "I" scenarios.

U.S. flour suppliers take advantage of lower wheat input prices by either expanding flour production more than in "I" scenarios ("A" and $\sigma = 1.05$) or by reducing flour supplies by less ("A", $\sigma = 0$, and "B", $\sigma = 1.05, 0$).

For "A" scenarios, U.S. flour exports expand. As above, the expansion results from a supply expansion for $\sigma = 1.05$, and the expansion results from a demand contraction for $\sigma = 0$. For "B" scenarios, U.S. flour exports decrease. Not unexpectedly, for $\sigma = 1.05$ supply factors are more important, and for $\sigma = 0$ demand factors are more important.

For "A" scenarios, increased Canadian imports imply about a $1.70 per metric ton further wheat price reduction. For "B" scenarios, increased Canadian imports imply about a $1.45 per metric ton further wheat price reduction. As before, the wheat EEP reduction for the "B" scenarios is less than for the "A", so the CWB reaction to it is less.

Analysis of U.S. Producers' Receipts

In order to focus on export subsidy switching trade-offs available to U.S. policymakers, producer receipts for U.S. wheat and flour producers from each set of scenarios are examined. Wheat receipts are calculated as the producer price times the amount produced. Flour receipts are calculated as the producer price times the amount produced less the cost of purchasing wheat as an input. Table 13.4 shows U.S. wheat and flour producer receipts averaged over cases i-iii and over $\sigma = 1.05$ and 0.

Averaged across versions of all scenarios, flour producers gain $510 million and wheat producers lose $403 million. In no version do flour producers lose revenue or wheat producers gain revenue. Results (summarized immediately below) indicate that making all adjustments in wheat EEP bonuses (and consequently none in flour EEP bonuses) should be a preferred policy option, even for wheat producers.

Regardless of EU choice, a U.S. policymaker who wishes to maximize the combined returns of U.S. wheat and flour sectors chooses option "A"; that is, the option that does not reduce flour EEP but rather makes all reductions in wheat EEP bonuses. For EU choice "I," the combined gain is about $109 million ($272.5 million gain from "A" less $163.2 million gain from "B"). For EU choice "II," the combined gain is about $117 million ($44.7 million gain from "A" less the $72.6 million loss from "B").

Regardless of EU choice, U.S. wheat producers weakly prefer option "A" to "B," although differences in producer receipts are hardly significant. For EU choice "I," the gain is only about $16 million ($225.9 million loss from "A" less the $241.7 million loss from "B"). For EU choice "II," the

TABLE 13.4 Summary of Averaged Revenue Changes for U.S. Producers ($million)[a]

Scenario	Producer	I	II
A	Wheat	-225.9 (82.3)	-558.9 (66.6)
	Flour	498.4 (29.6)	603.6 (34.8)
	Sum	272.5	44.7
B	Wheat	-241.7 (72.1)	-578.2 (56.3)
	Flour	404.9 (27.1)	505.6 (33.2)
	Sum	163.2	-72.6

[a]Results averaged over cases i-iii and over $\sigma = 1.05$ and $\sigma = 0$; Wheat producer receipts = (wheat production)*(producer price of wheat); flour producer receipts = (flour production)*(producer price of flour) – (wheat consumption by flour producers)*(consumer price of wheat). Standard Deviation in parenthesis below average.

gain is only about $19 million ($558.9 million loss from "A" less the $578.2 million loss from "B").

Regardless of EU choice, U.S. flour producers prefer option "A" to "B." For EU choice "I," the gain is about $94 million ($498.4 million gain from "A" less the $404.9 million gain from "B"). For EU choice "II," the gain is about $98 million ($603.6 million gain from "A" less the $505.6 million gain from "B"). Not unexpectedly, lower wheat input prices associated with the "B" option do not offset the directly negative effect of eliminating EEP flour bonuses.

When the EU chooses option "I," the U.S. wheat producer gains about $330 million more compared to option "II," implying that the U.S. wheat producer prefers that EU cuts be made entirely in wheat. The flour producer, on the other hand, loses about $100 million more, so that the U.S. flour producer prefers the EU mix of flour and wheat subsidy reductions. However, the combined U.S. wheat and flour sectors gain more as the EU emphasizes the reduction of wheat restitutions against flour restitutions.

Conclusion

The terms of the Uruguay Round of the GATT have constrained U.S. policymakers by placing restrictions on agricultural commodities that receive direct export subsidies and also on the magnitude of the subsidies.

Although policy options are much constrained, the terms of the UR still provide some latitude for policymakers to select within narrow product groupings the commodities to be subsidized and the allocations of permissible amounts to individual commodities.

This chapter has examined meeting UR commitments in the wheat and flour category. This analysis has tried to incorporate those factors whose uncertain nature might influence predicted outcomes the most. Chief among them have been: export subsidy shifting between flour and wheat for EU and U.S. policymakers, the nature of demand for wheat by flour millers, and export policies of the Canadian Wheat Board. The analysis has been carried out in a setting that assumes that wheat is differentiated by class and production sourcing.

This analysis indicates that returns to U.S. producers from meeting UR commitments are uneven. U.S. wheat producers lose income, and flour producers gain income. On average, flour producer gains exceed wheat producer losses. Flour producers gain because they face lower input costs as wheat prices decline.

It is more difficult to predict the magnitude of wheat producer outcomes than flour producer outcomes. U.S. wheat producer receipts are lower as: (1) EU policymakers cut back on wheat export restitutions as opposed to flour restitutions; (2) the more input substitutability there is between wheat and nonwheat inputs in the milling industry; and (3) the extent to which Canadian wheat imports do not grow as a result of the United States adjusting to UR commitments.

Both flour and wheat producers tend to gain more (or lose less) income as wheat EEP subsidies are cut and flour EEP bonuses remain intact. Results seem robust for flour producers, less so for wheat producers. If flour bonuses are eliminated, the reduction in domestic wheat demand is about even with or offsets slightly the effect of less reduced wheat export demand. Wheat producers seem more vulnerable to external influences, especially EU policymakers' choices and potentially those of the CWB as well.

Notes

This research is supported through USDA cooperative agreement No. 43-3AEL-4-80078, entitled "Export Subsidies and High Valued Products Trade in Agriculture." The authors acknowledge the assistance in modeling development of the following individuals: James Rude, Agriculture Canada; Kim Hjort, Suchada Langley, Patrick O'Brien, and Agapi Somwaru, Economic Research Service. The authors acknowledge the manuscript review and the helpful comments of the following individuals: Carlos Arnade, Nicole Ballenger, Suchada Langley, Stephanie Mercier, Daniel Pick, and Jim Stout, Economic Research Service.

1. Details are described in an appendix to the longer version of this chapter (Haley and Paarlberg, 1996).

References

Armington, P. C. (1969) "A Theory of Demand for Products Distinguished by Place of Production," *International Monetary Fund Staff Papers*. Vol. 16, pp. 159–78.

Haley, Stephen L. (1995) *Product Differentiation in Wheat Trade Modeling*. Technical Bulletin No. 1838, Econ. Res. Serv., U.S. Dept. Agriculture.

Haley, S. L. and P. L. Paarlberg. "Export Subsidy Switching under the Uruguay Round Commitments: The Case of Wheat and Wheat Flour," Staff Paper 96-17, Dept. of Agricultural Economics, Purdue University, August 1996, 44 pp.

Huang, Kuo S. (1985) *U.S. Demand for Food: A Complete System of Price and Income Effects*. Technical Bulletin No. 1714, Econ. Res. Serv., U.S. Dept. Agriculture.

International Grains Council. (1994) *World Grain Statistics 1993*. London.

Sullivan, John, Vernon Roningen, Susan Leetmaa, and Denice Gray. (1992) *A 1989 Global Database for the Static World Policy Simulation (SWOPSIM) Modeling Framework*. Staff Report No. AGES 9215, U.S. Dept., Econ. Res. Serv., U. S. Dept. of Agriculture.

U.S. Department of Agriculture, Economic Research Service, Commercial Agriculture Division. Data on Export Enhancement Program and PL-480 Program.

Wohlgenant, Michael K., and Richard C. Haidacher. (1989) *Retail to Farm Linkage for a Complete Demand System of Food Commodities*. Technical Bulletin No. 1775, Econ. Res. Serv., U.S. Dept. of Agriculture.

14

Sources of Growth and Competitiveness of U.S. Food Processing

Munisamy Gopinath, Terry Roe, and Mathew Shane

Introduction

Processed food is a growing share of foreign trade.[1] High-value exports, including processed foods, accounted for 56 percent of total U.S. agricultural exports in 1993, compared with an average of less that 35 percent prior to 1980. The sector's real Gross Domestic Product (GDP) grew by an average 1.04 percent per year over the period 1959–91. This performance reflects efficiency gains at both the primary agriculture and food processing levels. Annual growth in agricultural output averaged a robust 2.16 percent over the period 1959–91, but its output prices declined at an average rate of 1.19 percent per year. Therefore, its real GDP growth was only 0.97 percent. The major source of agricultural output growth was the relatively high rate of growth of total factor productivity (TFP), at 2.31 percent (Gopinath and Roe, 1995). The rising importance of the food processing sector in foreign trade is, in part, due to a transfer of the efficiency gains in primary agriculture through increased availability of primary inputs at declining real prices. The growth of TFP in food processing is transferred, in part, back to the primary sector by increasing its demand and thus mitigating the price decline that might otherwise occur. These linkages facilitate growth in both sectors by increasing their capacity to compete for economy-wide resources.

The nature and magnitude of these linkages are an important public policy issue since many of the sources of growth in TFP originate outside the sector, such as public investments in research and development (R&D). Moreover, growth in TFP may yield larger benefits to other sectors than to the sector within which growth originates. Understanding the extent to which other sectors benefit is important in determining the social profitability of the various sources of economic growth that are external to a sector. The means of internalizing the technological externalities, the nature of which is discussed in the "new" growth theory (Lucas, 1993; Romer, 1990; and Stokey, 1988), include public investments in R&D, public infrastructure, patent protection, and learning by doing.

This chapter assesses the sources of growth in the U.S. food processing sector's real GDP and contrasts them with the results obtained for primary agriculture. Sources of growth in GDP are attributed to changes in relative output prices and input levels, and to growth in TFP. The first two effects are referred to as level effects, the latter as a rate effect. Level effects link the sector to prices in other sectors of the economy and to the competition among sectors for economy-wide resources. The contribution from TFP to growth is particularly important since this dynamic (rate) effect determines the long run rate of growth for food processing and its capacity to compete for economy-wide resources (i.e., its competitiveness). In addition, it raises questions as to how these efficiency gains are shared with the rest of the economy.

Results indicate that annual growth in the food processing sector's GDP was negatively affected by a decline in its index of real output prices, but growth in material and other inputs has tended to more than offset the price decline. The material input category includes primary agricultural output as the single largest input subcategory, accounting for 26 percent of total input costs (U.S. Input Output Tables, ERS, U.S. Department of Agriculture). The contribution from TFP to the sector's GDP growth is low relative to primary agriculture, suggesting fewer technological externalities because the returns to inventing a new product such as a cake mix or a cereal are captured by the increased level of resources devoted to this activity by the respective food processing firms.

For primary agriculture, public R&D expenditures do not appear among the resources allocated within the sector. Firm-specific investments are not a technological externality per se, while the public R&D addresses an externality whose effect on growth is captured by our estimates of TFP. Since the output of primary agriculture appears in the material input category of the food processing sector, TFP effects in primary agriculture translate into level effects in food processing. Thus, policies that tend to distort markets by, for example, raising the price of primary agricultural outputs, will adversely affect the competitiveness of the food processing sector. Policies that induce productivity growth by lowering production costs in either sector will tend to increase the competitiveness of both sectors.

The conceptual and empirical framework is outlined in the next section (for a definition of competitiveness see the appendix), following which are results, conclusions, and policy suggestions. The data are described in Appendix I of Gopinath, Roe and Shane (1996).

The Model

Consider the case of an economy with three outputs (vectors) y_j , j = primary agriculture (A), food processing (F), and nonagriculture (N), and four categories of inputs (v_A, v_F, v_N, v_E), where the input vector v_j, j = A, F, N, is specific to sector j, and v_E is a vector of economy-wide factors, such as labor and material inputs. Following Woodland (1982), define the economy-wide GDP function as the maximum value of output, given the level of inputs and prices.

$$G(p_A, p_F, p_N, \bar{v}_A, \bar{v}_F, \bar{v}_N, \bar{v}_E; \gamma) \equiv \max_x \left\{ \sum\nolimits_{j=A,F,N} p_j Y_j \left(v_j, v_E^j \gamma_j \right) \right\}$$

$$X = \left\{ \left(v_A, v_F, v_N, v_E^A, v_E^F, v_E^N \right) : v_A \leq \bar{v}_A, v_F \leq \bar{v}_F, v_N \leq \bar{v}_N, v_E^A + v_E^F + v_E^N \leq \bar{v}_E \right\} \quad (1)$$

and Y_j (v_j ,v_E^j;γ_j) for j=A,N,S is a constant returns to scale or vintage production function (Diewert, 1980). The Lagrangian multipliers of this maximization problem (λ_A, λ_F, λ_N, λ_E) are the shadow prices for the three sector-specific inputs and one economy-wide factor. The feasible set X is bounded by the endowments of the private sector. The variable γ_j in Y_j is an externality in the sense that it is not a choice variable of the individual firm. It broadly represents the level of efficiency or in other words, technology. The sources of efficiency gains or technological progress include learning-by-doing, public investments in infrastructure, and research and development.

Given the solutions $\left(v_E^{j*}, \bar{v}_A, \bar{v}_F, v_N \right)$ to the problem in equation 1, redefine it as:

$$\max_x \sum\nolimits_{j=A,F,N} p_j Y_j \left(v_j, v_E^j; \gamma_j \right)$$

$$X = \left\{ \left(v_A, v_F, v_N, v_E^A, v_E^F, v_E^N \right) : v_A \leq \bar{v}_A, v_F \leq \bar{v}_F, v_N \leq \bar{v}_N, v_E^j \leq v_E^{j*} \text{ for all } j \right\} \quad (2)$$

The solution to the problem in equation 2 is given by:

$$G(p_A, p_F, p_N, \bar{v}_A, \bar{v}_F, \bar{v}_N, \bar{v}_E; \gamma) \equiv \sum\nolimits_{j=A,F,N} g_j \left(p_j, v_E^{j*}, \bar{v}_j, \gamma_j \right) \quad (3)$$

The function g_j is the GDP function for the jth sector, and, under certain regularity conditions, completely characterizes the underlying technology set (following Diewert, 1974). This product function is homogeneous of degree one in each of p_j and (v_E^{j*}, v_j*), and has the same envelope properties as the economy-wide GDP function. The function g_j and its specific (translog) functional form are the basis for the non-parametric analysis (see Kohli, 1993, for the terminology) of contributions to growth in sectoral GDP.

The food processing sector is given by g_F (hereafter, for notational convenience, g) with four outputs, one sector-specific input, and three economy-wide inputs. For given real prices[2] and the levels of the sector-specific and economy-wide inputs used in this sector, define the period t theoretical productivity index in the food processing sector (Diewert and Morrison, 1986) as

$$R^t\left(p, v_E^F, \bar{v}_F\right) \equiv \frac{g\left(p, v_E^F, \bar{v}_F; \gamma_F^t\right)}{g\left(p, v_E^F, \bar{v}_F; \gamma_F^{t-1}\right)} \tag{4}$$

The index R^t represents the percentage increase in food processing GDP (valued at reference prices) that can be produced by the period t technology relative to the period t-1 technology. Two special cases of R^t are:

$$R_L^t \equiv \frac{g\left(p^{t-1}, v_E^{F,t-1}, \bar{v}_F^{t-1}; \gamma^t\right)}{g\left(p^{t-1}, v_E^{F,t-1}, \bar{v}_F^{t-1}; \gamma^{t-1}\right)} \text{ and } R_P^t \equiv \frac{g\left(p^t, v_E^{F,t}, \bar{v}_F^t; \gamma^t\right)}{g\left(p^t, v_E^{F,t}, \bar{v}_F^t; \gamma^{t-1}\right)} \tag{5}$$

The index R_L^t is a Laspeyres-type index (period t-1 base), while R_P^t is a Paasche-type productivity index (period t base). Since the indices in equation 5 are not observable, a geometric mean of the two can be obtained using a translog sectoral GDP function. For an explicit specification refer to appendix 3 of Gopinath and Roe (1995). It follows that GDP in food processing equals the sum of the value of individual outputs, or the sum of payments to all factors of production.

$$g\left(p^t, v_E^t, v_F^t; \gamma^t\right) \equiv \sum_{l=1}^{3} \lambda_{El}^t v_{El}^t + \lambda_F^t v_F^t \equiv \sum_k p_k^t y_k^t \tag{6}$$

where, v_E is the vector of economy-wide factors and λ_F is sector-specific factor returns. Then,

$$\left(R_L^t R_P^t\right)^{\frac{1}{2}} = \frac{a}{b*c*e}; \text{ where } a = \frac{p^t y^t}{p^{t-1} y^{t-1}}$$

$$\ln b = \frac{1}{2} \sum_{k=1}^{4} \left(\frac{p_k^t y_k^t}{p^t y^t} + \frac{p_k^{t-1} y_k^{t-1}}{p^{t-1} y^{t-1}} \right) \left(\ln \frac{p_k^t}{p_k^{t-1}} \right) \tag{7}$$

$$\ln c = \frac{1}{2} \left(\frac{\lambda_F^t v_F^t}{p^t y^t} + \frac{\lambda_F^{t-1} v_F^{t-1}}{p^{t-1} y^{t-1}} \right) \left(\ln \frac{v_F^t}{v_F^{t-1}} \right) \tag{8}$$

$$\ln e = \frac{1}{2} \sum_{l=1}^{3} \left(\frac{\lambda_{E1}^t v_{E1}^t}{p^t y^t} + \frac{\lambda_{E1}^{t-1} v_{E1}^{t-1}}{p^{t-1} y^{t-1}} \right) \left(\ln \frac{v_{E1}^t}{v_{E1}^{t-1}} \right)$$

Note that the right-hand side of equation 7 can be evaluated using aggregate price and quantity data. In equation 7, a is growth in real value of output (GDP), b is a translog output price index, so (a/b) is an implicit output quantity index, while c and e are primary and economy-wide input quantity indexes. Individual real price and input contributions to growth in real food processing GDP can be obtained by disaggregating the indexes in equation 8 (Diewert and Morrison, 1986). The output (real) price effect for each good k is given by $ln\ b_k$ while, for each input l, input level effect is given by $\ln e_l$ (ln c for sector-specific input).

Results

Estimates of the contributions to the food processing sector's real value of output (GDP) due to changes in real prices (ln b in equation 8), input levels (ln c and ln e in equation 8), and TFP (a/bce in equation 7) are presented in Tables 14.1, 14.4, and 14.5. We draw on the work of Gopinath and Roe (1995, 1996) to compare the level and rate effects on growth in this sector's GDP with that of primary agriculture and the aggregate U.S. economy (Tables 14.2 and 14.3). Tables 14.6–9 present the estimates for the four subsectors of food processing: crops, grains, dairy, and meat.

Aggregate Food Processing

Table 14.1 provides estimates of the average annual rates of growth of the food processing sector's GDP and its decomposition into the effects of TFP, input levels, and changes in real prices (level effects) for the period 1959–91. During this period, the rate of growth in food processing GDP averaged 1.04 percent annually. The major contributor to this rate of growth is the rise in the levels of input (ln e). The rise in input levels

TABLE 14.1 Components of U.S. Food Processing GDP Growth (percent)

Year	*GDP growth*	*Real price effect*	*Input contribution*	*TFP growth*
1959-91	1.04	-0.83	1.46	0.41
Std. Devn.	3.14	3.27	1.78	1.05
1959-63	0.95	-1.79	1.84	1.00
1964-68	1.61	-1.03	2.34	0.34
1969-73	3.52	1.54	1.46	0.52
1974-78	1.84	-0.51	2.64	-0.29
1979-83	-1.46	-2.27	-0.09	0.90
1984-88	0.78	-1.15	1.14	0.79
1989-91	-0.64	-0.94	0.59	-0.29

Source: Gopinath, Roe, and Shane (1996)

caused, all else being constant, the GDP of food processing to rise by an average rate of 1.46 percent per year. TFP accounted for 0.41 percent of the average growth rate (equation 7). Of course, not all else is constant. The real price index of food processing declined at an annual rate of 0.83 percent (equation 8), which partially offset the positive effects from inputs and TFP. Nevertheless, this negative effect stands in contrast to the positive effect of the rise in the price index of the services sector on growth of the U.S. economy (Table 14.2). The rate effect (TFP) on growth in food processing is relatively small. The growth rate of TFP has declined from about 1.0 percent in 1959 to 0.3 percent in 1991, resulting in an average rate of 0.41 percent annually over the period.[3] Relatively low growth rates in TFP should not necessarily be alarming, since it is likely that sources of technological externalities may be small.[4]

In contrast, growth in primary agriculture is largely due to TFP, while aggregate input growth has been stagnant. Moreover, the real price decline in the agricultural sector exceeded that of the food processing sector by a factor of about one and a half. As mentioned earlier, growth in real agricultural GDP averaged 0.97 percent with TFP growth at 2.31 percent and real prices declining at 1.19 percent per year over the period 1959–91 (Table 14.3). The USDA/ERS official estimate of TFP growth in primary agriculture is 2.08 percent (Ball et al., 1995) for the same period. The difference between the two estimates, although small, is largely due to our accounting for the terms of trade effects (real prices) on agricultural real GDP growth. Table 14.2 includes comparable estimates for the aggregate U.S. economy. U.S. real GDP grew at an annual average rate of 2.92 percent for the period 1958–92. While price effects on growth are negative for primary agriculture and food processing, terms of trade effects on growth for the entire economy tend to be positive. These domestic terms of trade effects are largely due to the rise in the price index of the services sector of the U.S. economy relative to the agricultural and manufacturing (including food processing) sectors.

For the economy, the level effects of resources on growth are important. Capital and labor inputs account for 81 percent of the growth (40 and 41 percent, respectively) in the U.S. economy, while the contribution from

TABLE 14.2 Components of U.S. Real GDP Growth (percent)

Year	*GDP growth*	*Agri. price*	*Mft. price*	*Serv. price*	*Labor*	*Capital*	*TFP growth*
1958-92	2.92	-0.03	-0.23	0.35	1.18	1.18	0.47
Percent contribution	100	-1	-8	12	41	40	16

Source: Gopinath and Roe (1996).

TABLE 14.3 Components of U.S. Agricultural GDP Growth (percent)

Year	*GDP growth*	*Real price effect*	*Input contribution*	*TFP growth*
1959–91	0.97	-1.19	-0.15	2.31

Source: Gopinath and Roe (1995).

TFP growth averaged 16 percent (i.e., an economy-wide TFP growth rate of 0.47 percent per year). Thus, the growth rate of TFP in primary agriculture is large in contrast to that of food processing in particular, and to the more aggregated sectors of manufacturing and services in general. This result suggests that agriculture is likely to be more responsive to technological externalities than many other sectors of the U.S. economy.

Consider next a more detailed decomposition of the level effects on growth. Table 14.4 presents a decomposition of the price effects on growth for the four categories: crops, grains, dairy, and meat. All four subsectors experienced a decline in their respective real prices. The effect on growth in food processing GDP from price declines is largest for the processed products associated with the meat sector (0.36 percent) followed by the prices of crops (0.21 percent), grains (0.14 percent), and dairy (0.13 percent), although year-to-year variations are fairly large as suggested by standard deviations. The largest variability appears in the processed crops and meat sectors. These results suggest that the declines in these real prices amount to gains to consumers as the output of these sectors flow to consumers at lower real prices.

As noted, the largest contributor to growth in food processing output is the level effects from inputs. Table 14.5 provides estimates of the contribution from individual inputs: labor, capital, energy, and materials (includes agricultural output). Two-thirds of the level effects originate from growth in the material inputs, including the output of primary agriculture. Growth in capital accounts for the remainder. The contribution of labor is negative (-0.06 percent), suggesting that this resource is departing the sector. The contribution from energy is small (0.02 percent).

These results need to be interpreted in light of the declining prices of the

TABLE 14.4 Real Price Effects on U.S. Food Processing GDP Growth (percent)

Year	*Crops price*	*Grains price*	*Dairy price*	*Meat price*	*Aggregate price*
1959–91	-0.21	-0.14	-0.13	-0.36	-0.83
Std. Devn.	1.60	0.89	0.34	1.86	3.27

Source: Gopinath, Roe, and Shane (1996).

TABLE 14.5 Input Contributions to U.S. Food Processing GDP Growth (percent)

Year	*Labor*	*Capital*	*Energy*	*Materials*	*Aggregate input*
1959–91	-0.06	0.49	0.02	1.01	1.46
Std. Devn.	0.14	0.17	0.03	1.64	1.78

Source: Gopinath, Roe, and Shane (1996).

food processing sector's outputs, its relatively low TFP, and, while relatively high, a nevertheless stagnant growth in primary agriculture's TFP. In this context, these results suggest that the food processing sector is employing a declining share of the economy's resources and thus, the sector's domestic competitiveness is declining in the sense that its relative ability to bid resources away from the rest of the economy appears to be falling. If, for example, agriculture and/or food processing had a higher rate of growth in their respective TFP, then food processing should have been able to maintain its growth in labor, material, and capital inputs unless, in a large country context, the resulting increase in food supply would have resulted in an even faster decline in output prices. As we discuss in the next section, not all of the food processing subsectors are losing resources. Closer inspection suggests that the sector is in the process of specialization and division of labor wherein some subsectors decline, effectively transferring resources to other subsectors that are growing.

The social welfare implications of this evolution depend on whether policy, at home or abroad, distorts markets and whether markets reward factors of production for their full contribution to productivity. The new growth literature suggests that the nonrival and partially nonexcludable nature of knowledge embodied in technology cause markets to fail in this regard.

On average, the decline in the real prices of primary agricultural products has benefited the processing sector in the form of cheaper inputs. To illustrate, recall that the share of primary agricultural output in food processing output is 26 percent. A price decline of 1.19 percent in the primary sector translates into a 0.31 percent (0.26*1.19) decline in the procurement costs to the food processing sector. If the food processing sector's price has declined at the rate of 0.31 percent, then all the gains from the decline in the price of primary agricultural output are passed on to consumers. However, the decline in the real prices of the food processing sector averaged 0.83 percent. This suggests that the additional price decline in the food processing sector (0.83 – 0.31 = 0.52 percent) has come from efficiency gains within the sector. Since the TFP growth within the food processing sector has been only 0.41 percent per year, the ultimate gains from efficiency growth in the primary and food processing sectors are to consumers (through retail and wholesale trade, hotels and restaurants).

The efficiency gains in primary agriculture in the United States as well as its major competitors lead to supply shifts that cause a global decline in the prices of agricultural output, given a relatively lower growth rate in demand. It is in this way that the rate effects of primary agriculture translate into level effects for the food processing sector. Investments in public agricultural R&D and public infrastructure have been found to be robustly associated with TFP growth in agriculture (Gopinath and Roe, 1995). While these investments have served to sustain a growth rate in real agricultural GDP of about 0.97 percent, they have contributed to the competitiveness of the food processing sector through lower primary agricultural product prices.[5]

Subsector Results

While all the four of the subsectors (processed crops, grains, dairy, and meat) experienced positive real rates of growth in their respective GDP, the processed crops and grains subsectors have benefited from larger input level effects on growth than have processed dairy and meat. It can be said that the processed grains and crops subsectors have, on average, been relatively more competitive than processed dairy and meat. Clearly, the reasons for this competitiveness are not solely due to efficiency growth within these processed subsectors per se, but also due to the efficiency gains experienced in the production of crops and grains (see Gopinath and Roe, 1995, for further discussion of a disaggregated primary agriculture).

Processed Crops Sector. The growth accounting results for the processed crop products, which account for 45 percent of food processing sector GDP, are presented in Table 14.6. Among the four sectors considered, the processed crops sector experienced the largest growth in its GDP, at 1.69 percent, on average, over the period 1959–91. The level effects from all inputs account for almost nine-tenths of the growth in the real value of output in this sector (1.56 percent). Of the input level effects, the largest are from material inputs, followed by capital. The level effect from energy is positive and that from labor is negative; both, however, are

TABLE 14.6 Components of U.S. Processed Crops Sector GDP Growth (percent)

Year	*GDP growth*	*Real price effect*	*Input contribution*	*TFP growth*
1959–91	1.69	-0.43	1.56	0.56
Std. Devn.	3.74	3.59	2.30	1.59

Source: Gopinath, Roe, and Shane (1996).

relatively small. While price effects contributed negatively to growth in its value added (-0.43 percent), they are nevertheless smaller than are the price effects in the other sectors. The growth effect of TFP averaged 0.56 percent per year, which exceeds the average of the other subsectors but shows a declining trend. Overall, this subsector appears the most competitive, on average, in its competition for resources relative to the other subsectors.

Processed-Grains Sector. This subsector's share of food processing GDP averaged 18 percent. On average, over the period 1959–91, the annual rate of growth in this subsector's GDP is 0.81 percent (Table 14.7). The effects of declining real prices are 0.80 percent, which is similar to the price effects on the aggregate food processing sector. As above, the level effects from inputs contributed the most to growth in this subsector's GDP. Material inputs and capital contributed almost equally (0.71 and 0.62 percent, respectively) to this subsector's GDP growth. The contribution from energy is again small and positive, while that of labor is relatively large and negative (-0.14 percent). TFP growth accounted for about 50 percent of its GDP growth. On average, the effects of this subsector's TFP, in conjunction with the efficiency gains in primary agriculture, appear to have caused unit processing costs to fall sufficiently to offset the real decline in output price. This offsetting effect induced the sector to increase its derived demand for material inputs. In a large country context, this increase in demand likely mitigated the decline in the real price of grain at the farm level. Through the decline in the real price of processed grain, the efficiency gains of both the primary and the processing subsector were passed to wholesale and retail markets. In spite of the adverse terms of trade effects, this subsector appears relatively competitive in attracting resources.

Processed-Dairy Sector. The processed dairy sector experienced the lowest rate of growth in its GDP, compared with the other subsectors. It accounts for 13 percent of food processing sector's GDP. This is largely due to negative real prices effects which, if all else were constant, would have caused this subsector's value added to fall at an average rate of 1.00 percent per year (Table 14.8). This negative effect almost offsets the positive effects on growth in GDP attributable to inputs and TFP. As with

TABLE 14.7 Components of U.S. Processed Grains Sector GDP Growth (percent)

Year	*GDP growth*	*Real price effect*	*Input contribution*	*TFP growth*
1959–91	0.81	-0.80	1.21	0.40
Std. Devn.	4.35	5.18	1.47	1.97

Source: Gopinath, Roe, and Shane (1996).

TABLE 14.8 Components of U.S. Processed Dairy Sector GDP Growth (percent)

Year	*GDP growth*	*Real price effect*	*Input contribution*	*TFP growth*
1959–91	0.16	-1.00	0.95	0.22
Std. Devn.	2.78	2.64	2.63	2.33

Source: Gopinath, Roe, and Shane (1996).

the processed grains sector, growth in material inputs and capital contributed the most to growth in GDP. While energy inputs had relatively small effects on GDP, labor input's contribution to growth in the dairy sector GDP is large and negative (-0.23 percent). This result implies that labor has departed the subsector as it became more capital intensive. The contribution of TFP is the smallest of all subsectors, although the standard deviation is large in all cases.

Processed Meat Sector. The processed meat sector has grown at an annual average rate of 0.65 percent over the period 1959–91. Of the four sectors, the processed-meat sector experienced the largest negative effect on growth in its value added from a decline in real prices. All else constant, the decline in real prices would have decreased the growth in value added by 1.42 percent per year (Table 14.9). The level effects from inputs on the growth of its GDP is also the largest of the subsectors. With a relatively lower contribution from TFP growth (0.28 percent), the level effects of inputs are largely offset by the decline in real prices. In addition, the real prices of the processed meat sector exhibits high variability (standard deviation of 7.56 percent).

Conclusions

The major factor contributing to growth in food processing GDP (1.04 percent annually) during 1959–91 is the level effects from inputs. Material inputs including primary agricultural products, account for almost all growth in food processing GDP. However, the contribution from other inputs to growth in the sector's real GDP are offset by the 0.83 percent decline in real price for the sector's output. Total factor productivity

TABLE 14.9 Components of U.S. Processed Meat Sector GDP Growth (percent)

Year	*GDP growth*	*Real price effect*	*Input contribution*	*TFP growth*
1959–91	0.65	-1.42	1.81	0.28
Std. Devn.	5.32	7.56	3.59	2.14

Source: Gopinath, Roe, and Shane (1996).

growth in food processing is relatively low at 0.41 percent. This compares with a TFP growth rate of 0.47 percent for the economy and 2.31 percent per year for primary agriculture.

Decomposing growth in the food processing sector, in an economy-wide context, provides insights into the nature and magnitude of its linkages to the primary agricultural sector. The domestic terms of trade effects among the various sectors in an economy suggest that the food processing sector benefited from the decline of 1.19 percent in the real output prices of primary agriculture. This decline is mostly an outcome of efficiency gains (TFP effects), in the United States and its major competitors in the presence of a relatively lower growth rate in food demand. Due to the decline in primary output prices, the processed food sector was able to increase its employment of material inputs even though it experienced a price decline for processed food. It is in this way that rate effects in primary agriculture are transferred into level effects in food processing. Since the output of agriculture accounts for about 26 percent of the material inputs in food processing, the decline of 0.83 percent in the price of processed food implies that more than the entire price decline experienced by primary agriculture has been, on average over the period, passed on to wholesale and retail markets. In other words, efficiency gains from both the primary agriculture and processed food sectors translate into lower real prices for consumers.

Thus, policies that tend to distort markets by, for example, raising the price of primary agricultural outputs will adversely affect the competitiveness of the food processing sector. Policies and programs that tend to induce productivity growth in either sector, such as public agricultural R&D that lowers production costs, will tend to increase the competitiveness of both sectors. The rate effects (TFP) in primary agriculture are the major source of growth in its GDP. TFP growth is found to be robustly associated with public investments in sector-specific R&D and infrastructure (e.g., Gopinath and Roe, 1995). These investments, while maintaining the viability of the farm sector, contribute significantly to the competitiveness of the food processing sector as well, with ultimate gains to consumers in the form of lower real food prices. Other sectors of the economy receive indirect benefits from the savings in food expenditures that can be allocated to purchases of nonfood goods and services.

Notes

1. Processed food sectors, as used in this chapter, include forty-nine four-digit industries under food and kindred products (SIC code 20), and four four-digit industries under tobacco products (SIC code 21), respectively.

2. We derive the real prices by deflating the sectoral price indices by a GDP deflator, in principle, discounting them for average price increases in the economy.

3. Empirically TFP includes unanticipated changes in exogenous variables such as weather and other shocks to the economy. So we employed the Hodrick-Prescott filter to smooth the series and obtained a declining trend in TFP growth (see Gopinath, Roe, and Shane 1996).

4. Note that efficiency gains due to investments of the firms that are captured by the industry are not included in TFP.

5. To the extent that the fall in primary agriculture's output prices is in response to efficiency gains, technological change has been almost immiserizing.

References

Ball, V. E., J. C. Bureau, R. Nehring, and A. Somwaru (1997). *Agricultural Productivity Revisited.* U.S.D.A., Economic Research Service (forthcoming).

Bartelsman, E., and W. Gray (1994). Manufacturing Productivity Database, 1959–91, Electronic form, National Bureau of Economic Research, New York.

Diewert, W. E. (1974). "Applications of Duality Theory," *Frontiers of Quantitative Economics, Volume II.* M. D. Intriligator and D. A. Kendrick (eds.), North-Holland, Amsterdam.

———. (1976). "Exact and Superlative Index Numbers," *Journal of Econometrics,* 4:115–145.

———. (1980). "Aggregation Problems in the Measurement of Capital," *The Measurement of Capital, Studies in Income and Wealth, Volume 45.* D. Usher (ed.), National Bureau of Economic Research, New York.

Diewert, W. E., and C. J. Morrison (1986). "Adjusting Output and Productivity Indexes for Changes in Terms of Trade," *The Economic Journal,* 96:659–679.

Gopinath, M., and T. L. Roe (1995). *Sources of Sectoral Growth in an Economy-Wide Context: The Case of U.S. Agriculture.* Bulletin 95-7, Economic Development Center, University of Minnesota, Minneapolis-St.Paul.

———. (1996). "Sources of Growth in U.S. GDP and Economywide Linkages to the Agricultural Sector," *Journal of Agricultural and Resource Economics,* 21 (2):325–340.

Gopinath, M., T. L. Roe and M. D. Shane (1996). *Growth and Competitiveness of Food Processing: Linkages from Primary Agriculture.* Staff Paper No.9608, U.S.D.A., Economic Research Service.

Kohli, U. R. (1993). "GNP Growth Accounting in the Open Economy: Parametric and Non-parametric Estimates for Swizerland," *Swedish Journal of Economics and Statistics,* 129:601–615.

Lucas, R. E. (1993). "Making a Miracle," *Econometrica,* 61(2):251–272.

Romer, P. M. (1990). "Endogenous Technological Change," *Journal of Political Economy,* 98 (5): S71–S102.

Stokey, N. L. (1988). "Learning by Doing and the Introduction of New Good," *Journal of Political Economy,* 96:701–717.

U.S. Department of Commerce, Bureau of Economic Analysis (1996). National Income and Product Accounts of the United States, 1929–1995. Database.

Woodland, A. D. (1982). *International Trade and Resource Allocation.* North-Holland, Amsterdam.

Appendix

Definition of Competitiveness

The following provides an analytical definition of the concept "competitiveness." It focuses on relative rates of growth rather than absolute growth. As we use it, competitiveness is a relative concept with two dimensions: domestic and international. If within an economy, say the United States, the rate of growth in agriculture's real GDP exceeds that of the economy, that is,

$$d(\ln GDP_A)/dt > d(\ln GDP)/dt \tag{A2.1}$$

then agriculture (A) is increasing its competitiveness relative to the other sectors of the economy. In other words, agricultural GDP is growing relative to the rest of the economy. The derivative in equation (A2.1) is total rather than partial, and suggests that the sources of this change can be decomposed into level effects of prices and factors, and the rate effects of TFP.

Now, consider a comparison of agricultural sectors of two countries, say that of the United States and country X:

$$\frac{d(\ln GDP_{A,US})/dt}{d(\ln GDP_{US})/dt} > \frac{d(\ln GDP_{A,X})/dt}{d(\ln GDP_{X})/dt} \tag{A2.2}$$

In this case, U.S. agriculture is growing relative to country X and is said to be gaining bilateral competitiveness. Note that this is again a function of the underlying sources of growth in agricultural GDP.

For the United States to be globally competitive, it has to be the case that:

$$\frac{d(\ln GDP_{A,US})/dt}{d(\ln GDP_{US})/dt} > \frac{d(\ln GDP_{A,W})/dt}{d(\ln GDP_{W})/dt} \tag{A2.3}$$

where, GDPA,W =Σx GDPA,X is world agricultural GDP. In a competitive economy, this result implies that, in the aggregate and on average over a period, U.S. farmers are competing more successfully for world consumers of food, including U.S. consumers, than are the rest of the world's farmers.

15

Looking in All the Right Places: Where Are the Economies of Scale?

Nicholas G. Kalaitzandonakes, Hong Hu, and Maury E. Bredahl

Introduction

Most research on agricultural food trade has been directed to agricultural commodities. As Bredahl et al. noted, however, such attention may have been misplaced as the value of trade in processed foods far exceeds that of agricultural commodities. In recent years, increasing attention has been given to the trade of processed foods and some of its characteristics including intra-industry trade (Christodoulou, and McCorriston and Sheldon) and the importance of foreign direct investment as a means of accessing foreign markets (Handy and Henderson).

Economies of scale have been explicitly tied to intra-industry trade (IIT) but have played a far less important role in explaining observed trade flows or foreign direct investment (FDI) in food production and distribution (Hartman et al.). Drawing on the firm strategy and industrial organization literature (Caves, Dunning), observed FDI patterns in food markets have been related to differential transaction costs related to market access (Goldsmith and Sporleder) or to the appropriability of rents embodied in intangible assets, such as intellectual property, image, and brand name (Bjornson, Connor, Henderson et al.).

In this chapter we argue that analysis of economies of scale may provide significant insights not only about IIT but also about the patterns of trade and access to international markets through multinational activity. Our argument is in line with findings that firms strategically position themselves to take advantage of economies of scale, and in the process they influence industry structure and the flows of consumption and capital goods (Chandler). In order to extract useful insights regarding trade and FDI, however, the sources of economies of scale must be clarified and explicitly taken into account. Along these lines we develop a two-country two-sector model with different economies of scale and illustrate their role in FDI and trade. We subsequently contrast the predictions of our model with U.S. pork production, trade, and incidence of FDI.

Economies of Scale and Relevance to Trade

In the trade literature, economies of scale (ES) are typically not precisely defined, though in most studies they indicate increasing returns from a proportional increase in all inputs or associated reductions in unit costs. The concept of ES has a long history going back to Adam Smith's famous pin factory example. Adam Smith identified division of labor and specialization as the sources of increased returns in larger factories.

Alfred Marshall provided a distinction between internal and external ES. In particular, ES are external to a firm when a firm's unit costs decrease as the industry's (rather than the firm's) operations expand. Division of labor and specialization are once again seen as sources of such economies (Chipman). Presumably, a larger industry allows for the creation of a larger labor pool with more skilled workers and concomitant increases in productivity. Increased industry size at a given location can also generate external ES (Krugman, 1991). Geographic concentration of firms and industries, presumably, tends to create economies not only from increased labor specialization and creation of supporting industries but also from spillovers of technology and information. In any case, with external ES all firms in the industry, large and small, benefit.

More recently, ES, both internal and external, along with imperfect competition and product differentiation, have been employed to amend the standard trade theory (Ethier, Krugman 1980, Helpman and Krugman). The traditional factor-endowment trade theory is basically consistent with the stylized facts of inter-industry trade, but it is at odds with the growing phenomena of IIT as well as intra-firm trade by multinational corporations. Allowing for ES rectifies some of these shortcomings. For example, one argument is that, when two countries are similar, each may specialize in producing parts of a final product in order to take advantage of the external ES from labor division and specialization. Despite the absence of comparative advantage, there will be (intra-industry) trade in differentiated intermediate goods (Ethier).

On the Concept of Economies of Scale

Along with considerations of product differentiation and imperfect market structures, ES have clearly enriched international trade theory. Important conceptual issues with respect to the role of ES on market structure and trade, however, remain.

In general, theorists have continued to use a rather narrow concept of ES that is unduly restrictive. The concept of ES typically used involves increases in the size or capacity of production units under constant factor proportions. By implication, unchanged technology and a constant product mix are also assumed. In essence, ES are presumed to be created from an expanded duplicate of the smaller scale unit. Defining ES in such a way has contributed to the fuzziness of the concept since no insights about the sources of the expected benefits are provided (Gold). This is particularly true since it has been demonstrated that firms modify their input and output configurations and change technology in order to capture ES (Chandler).[1] In Chandler's words, firms capture ES by "improving and rearranging inputs; by using improved machinery; by reorienting processes of production within the plant; by placing the several intermediary processes employed in making a final product within a single works" (p. 22).

Loss of sight of the sources and benefits of ES has been worsened by another formalistic preoccupation regarding the concept within standard neoclassical trade models. Given that increasing ES are, in principle, inconsistent with perfectly competitive markets leading to national monopolies, interest of trade economists concentrated primarily on the concept of external ES which provides no inherent advantage for any particular firm and are consistent with observed market structures (Chipman). A variety of sources for external ES have been considered including division of labor, creation of complementary industries, technological spillovers, and improved infrastructure (Krugman, 1991), the size of national markets (Shariff), or even the size of international markets (Ethier). When internal ES have been considered, the preoccupation of trade economists has been with the existence of an optimal tax structure (Olson and Zeckhauser) or the justification of IIT. The sources of internal ES have been left largely unexplored and unspecified in trade models.

Specifying the sources of ES can provide useful insights regarding trade flows. Recent studies focusing on firm location decisions (Horstman and Markusen, Brainard) have begun to specify where internal ES reside and have obtained useful results regarding the impact of ES on trade and FDI. Within such a framework, the decision between trade and overseas expansion is determined by tradeoffs between proximity to markets and economies from concentration.

Sources and Dimensions of Economies of Scale

Students of industrial structure and business historians have described a much richer concept of (internal) ES than the one formalized within the neoclassical theory of the firm (e.g. Chandler, Pratten). ES are multifaceted, involving not only efficiencies in production but also in marketing, distribution, and the financial operations of a firm. These efficiencies may also involve multiple dimensions. For example, ES in production may involve increased rate of production, standardization, augmented capacity, and others. In distribution, ES may involve size of consignment, geographical concentration of customers, or some other dimension. Along these lines, ES may be defined as reductions in average costs attributable to different positions along varying dimensions of scale (Pratten).

There is a multitude of sources from where ES is derived as well. These include:

(a) *Indivisibilities* in inputs: When inputs are lumpy in nature or nonrival in consumption, they are, at least in part, independent of scale and their costs can be spread over a larger level of output, resulting in lower unit costs. Such inputs include capital, research and development (R&D) and advertising.

(b) *Specialization* in inputs: When the scale of the plant or the firm increases, opportunities for specialization for both the labor force and the capital equipment become available, resulting in increased efficiencies.

(c) *Lower input costs:* Input costs may be lowered due to volume discounts, lower transaction costs, reduced inventories, and other similar cost efficiencies resulting from large scale of operations.

(d) *Advanced techniques and organizations:* Expanded scale of operations may make possible more efficient methods of production and distribution (e.g. automation) and allow improved organization of resources, resulting in efficiency gains.

(e) *Learning:* Efficiencies may result from increased scale due to rapid learning. Such economies are more readily available in production and distribution processes involving high degrees of tacit knowledge.

Diseconomies of scale (DS) are also possible. Increased unit costs may result from increased scale of operations. Contributing sources to such DS are:

(a) *Management and labor inefficiencies:* Beyond a certain scale, the cost of management may increase more than proportionately or its effectiveness may decrease. Similarly, in large operations, labor effort may decrease and supervision costs may increase. DS of this nature are thus the result of increased coordination, motivation, and monitoring costs.

(b) *Marketing and distribution:* As the scale of output increases, marketing and distributing goods in increasingly diverse and geographically dispersed markets may be necessary. Such operations tend to involve larger transportation costs. Furthermore, coordination costs (e.g. costs of gathering information and accessing potential customers) per unit of output may also increase, leading to DS.

It is interesting to note here that sources of cost efficiencies or inefficiencies described are quite different in nature. Some relate to production operations, some to transactions, and some to organizational and technological innovation. What is important is not what function of the firm these efficiencies or inefficiencies are associated with, but rather that they vary in a predictable way with scale so that the firm can strategically decide how to expand in order to capture ES.

Equally interesting to note is that an increase in the scale of operations may result in both ES and DS that derive from different sources. For example, scale expansion at the plant level to capture ES in production may result in DS from marketing and distributing goods in increasingly distant and dissimilar markets. From a firm's point of view it is the *net* effect of various ES and DS that determines its strategic positioning rather than any particular source of ES in isolation. Thus, focusing attention on any one singular type of ES may be misleading.

Close scrutiny of the sources of scale-related cost efficiencies and inefficiencies also reveals that some of the ES and DS are *location-specific,* while others are not anchored to any particular geographic location. For example, ES deriving from indivisibilities in physical capital assets and automation reside in particular plants, and hence they are location-specific.[2] Alternatively, ES deriving from indivisibilities in R&D, and cost efficiencies through volume discounts in input sourcing and in learning may be available to multiplant firms independent of plant size and location. Such ES are more related to the overall scale of firm operations and may be shared by plants in multiple locations.

The implication is that when ES are location-specific, trade must be used to access markets from the particular location where the economies reside. Depending on the level of the optimal scale at the specific location relative to the total market size, the geographic segmentation of the market, and other relevant structural characteristics, trading large quantities of output from a particular location may result in DS deriving from increased coordination, monitoring, and transportation costs.

When ES are independent of location, the firm may access multiple markets through multiple production and distribution plants while still capturing ES that are tied to its overall scale of operations. In the context of international trade, this decision may imply accessing foreign markets through horizontal or vertical FDI. Locating multiple production plants close to markets may decrease DS from marketing and distribution but may increase DS from increased management costs that result from attempting to supervise and coordinate functions across multiple locations and operations. Once again, it is the net effect of all relevant ES and DS that is important.

Based on the foregoing observations, it is clear that the optimal level and degree of localization of ES could vary significantly along a value-adding chain that involves numerous diverse operations. Accordingly, the strategic behavior of firms in production, distribution, and trade of capital and consumer goods could vary from one stage of the value-adding chain to another. Hence, differentiating ES on the basis of optimal level, degree of localization, and operations on which they reside could enhance our understanding of their role in trade and FDI.

A Theoretical Trade Model with Differential Economies of Scale

Following the arguments developed in the previous section, we develop a two-country two-sector model while allowing for multiple production stages and differential ES. In particular, we assume two similar countries: a and b, and two sectors: manufacturing and agriculture. Following Bredahl and Abbot's categorization of agriculture, we assume that there are three subsectors involving primary production (P), production of intermediate or semiprocessed goods (I), and production of a final or consumer-ready good (F). For simplicity, we assume the two countries have identical factor endowments, and thus trade or FDI are not caused by endowment differences.

Manufacturing production and primary agricultural production are characterized by constant return to scale and perfectly competitive markets. The intermediate and final agriculture markets are characterized by monopolistic competition. The undifferentiated primary products are used as input in the intermediate sector and the differentiated intermediate products are used as inputs in the final sector. Markets are assumed to be segmented so the producers can practice price discrimination.

There are n_a and n_b firms in each country's intermediate sector with identical technology, each producing one variety of intermediate products. All intermediate product varieties contribute symmetrically to the production of the final product. These producers choose to either set up one plant in the home country and export to the other country, or set up two plants, one in each country. There is a fixed cost A_1 associated with the overall operations of the firm and a fixed cost A_2 associated with each plant the firm operates. Hence, there are internal economies of scale at both the firm and plant level. In addition to fixed costs, there are constant marginal costs b in intermediate good production measured in the primary good units. If the price of the primary good is s, and the quantity of an intermediate firm's production is x, the cost function of the firm is $C(x)=A_1+k_IA_2+sbx$, where $k_I=1$ or 2 is the number of plants that the firm chooses to set.

There are m_a and m_b firms in each country's final agricultural subsector with identical technology, each producing one variety of differentiated final product. Let the amounts of intermediate inputs that the ith firm in country a uses be u^a_{ia} and u^a_{ib}. Also, let the production function of the ith firm in country a be $y_{ia} = (n_a+n_b)^{\alpha}[(\Sigma u^a_{ia}{}^{\beta} + \Sigma u^a_{ib}{}^{\beta}/(n_a+n_b)]^{1/\beta}$. The production function displays external economies of scale with respect to the number of varieties of intermediate inputs (n) when $\alpha>1$.

Similar to the intermediate sector, the final producers can choose either to set up one plant in the home country where the firm's headquarters are located and export to the other country or to set up two plants, one in each country. There is a fixed cost A_3 associated with the overall firm operations and fixed costs A_4 that are specific to each plant that is set up. Hence, there are internal economies of scale in both firm and plant level. Under these conditions, the cost function of the ith firm in the final sector is given by $C(y_{ia})=A_3+k_FA_4+VC(y_{ia})$, where $k_F=1$ or 2 is the number of plants that the firm chooses to set up while $VC(y_{ia})$ is the variable cost of producing y_{ia}.

Within the above setup, differential firm- and plant-specific ES are specified for the two downstream stages of the agricultural value-adding chain. Fixed unit costs t_P, t_I, t_F, (with $t_P,t_F,t_I>1$) associated with all relevant costs of trading from one country to the other, including transportation and transaction costs, are also specified.

Following Hortsman and Markusen, and Brainard, a firm's choice between FDI and trade is determined by benefit-cost comparisons. There are tradeoffs between benefits from locating close to markets and cost efficiencies from locating in a single location and exploiting plant-specific ES. Let

y^l_{ik} be the quantity of final product produced by the ith firm in country k and consumed in country l;

y_{ik} be the total quantity of final products produced by the ith firm in country k, $y_{ik} = y^a_{ik} + y^b_{ik}$;

p^l_{ik} be the supply price of final product produced by the ith firm in country k and sold in country l;

u^{lr}_{ik} be the quantity of intermediate product produced by the ith firm in country k and used in a plant of country l that is located in country r; and

q^{lr}_{ik} be the supply price of intermediate product produced by the ith firm in country k and used in a plant of country l that is located in country r.

The equilibrium structure is determined in a two-stage procedure. In the first stage, all the firms in final and intermediate agricultural subsectors choose to set up 0, 1, or 2 plants simultaneously. In the second stage, all producers choose prices so that they maximize profits. The game is solved backwards for the maximum profit for each firm. By considering four cases in all, we can specify the payoffs of intermediate and final subsector firms under various trade/FDI scenarios. Such payoffs will tend to determine the firms' optimal choices.

Case 1. No FDI in Final Sector (One Plant/Firm); No FDI in Intermediate Sector (One Plant/Firm)

Consumer Behavior. Following Brainard and Ethier we assume that consumers have homothetic preferences over manufactured and agricultural goods. Thus, consumer choice involves two decisions: First, the allocation of income between manufactured and agricultural goods, and second the allocation of the agricultural budget among different varieties. Consumers of country a then allocate income between manufacturing good M and aggregate agricultural final good Y by maximizing a Cobb Douglas utility function subject to an income constraint as:

$$\max Y^{\delta}M^{1-\delta}$$

$$\text{s.t. } P_M M + \Sigma p^a_{ia} y^a_{ia} + \Sigma p^a_{ib} t_F y^a_{ib} = I^a$$

where $Y=\Sigma y^a_{ia} + \Sigma y^a_{ib}$

Solving the first order conditions yields expenditure shares for each of the aggregate goods that are independent of income:

$$P_M M/I^a = (1-\delta)$$

$$(\Sigma p^a_{ia} y^a_{ia} + \Sigma p^a_{ib} t_F y^a_{ib})/I^a = \delta$$

Consumers then allocate the fixed portion of income δI^a among the differentiated agricultural varieties through a second (sub) utility maximization. Here we assume consumers have identical preference over different varieties of final goods characterized by a constant elasticity of substitution utility function that has been used by Krugman (1980). This second-stage optimization is specified as

$$\max \Sigma {y^a_{ia}}^{\theta} + \Sigma {y^a_{ib}}^{\theta}$$

$$\text{s.t. } \Sigma p^a_{ia} y^a_{ia} + \Sigma p^a_{ib} t_F y^a_{ib} = \delta I^a$$

where $\theta=(\sigma-1)/\sigma$, $\sigma>1$, is the elasticity of substitution among varieties. Solving the first order conditions yields

$$(y^a_{ia}/y^a_{ja}) = (p^a_{ia}/p^a_{ja})^{1/(\theta-1)}$$

$$(y^a_{ia}/y^a_{jb}) = (p^a_{ia}/p^a_{jb} t_F)^{1/(\theta-1)} \quad (1)$$

and

$$p^a_{ia} = [y^a_{ia}{}^{\theta-1}/(\Sigma y^a_{ia}{}^{\theta} + \Sigma y^a_{ib}{}^{\theta})]\delta I^a$$

$$p^a_{ib} = [y^a_{ib}{}^{\theta-1}/(\Sigma y^a_{ia}{}^{\theta} + \Sigma y^a_{ib}{}^{\theta})]\delta I^a \quad (2)$$

From (1) and (2) the elasticity of demand is equal to

$$\varepsilon = -(p^a_{ia}/y^a_{ia})/(dp^a_{ia}/dy^a_{ia}) = -(p^a_{ib}/y^a_{ib})/(dp^a_{ib}/dy^a_{ib}) \approx 1/(1-\theta) = \sigma (3)$$

Thus, consumers treat home and foreign goods indifferently as the demand elasticities for final agricultural goods from countries a and b are the same. Similar analysis for country b yields symmetrical results.

Final Producer Behavior. The profit maximization of the ith final producer in country a may be viewed as a two-step procedure. First the producer minimizes costs by choosing the optimal level of intermediate input, and second they maximize profits by choosing the optimal level of output.

The cost minimization process is then given by

$$\min A_3 + A_4 + \Sigma u^{aa}_{ia} q^{aa}_{ia} + \Sigma u^{aa}_{ib} q^{aa}_{ib} t_I$$

$$\text{st. } y_{ia} = (n_a+n_b)^{\alpha}[(\Sigma u^{aa}_{ia}{}^{\beta} + \Sigma u^{aa}_{ib}{}^{\beta})/(n_a+n_b)]^{1/\beta}$$

Solving the first order conditions yields

$$(u^{aa}_{ia}/u^{aa}_{ja}) = (q^{aa}_{ia}/q^{aa}_{ja})^{1/(\beta-1)}$$

$$(u^{aa}_{ia}/u^{aa}_{jb}) = (q^{aa}_{ia}/q^{aa}_{jb} t_I)^{1/(\beta-1)} \quad (4)$$

with the elasticity of demand being equal to

$$\varepsilon = -(q^{aa}_{ia}/u^{aa}_{ia})/(dq^{aa}_{ia}/du^{aa}_{ia}) = -(q^{aa}_{ib}/u^{aa}_{ib})/(dq^{aa}_{ib}/du^{aa}_{ib}) = -1/(\beta-1)$$

In the second stage, profit maximization of the ith final producer in country a is then given by

$$\max p^a_{ia} y^a_{ia} + p^b_{ia} y^b_{ia} - [A_3 + A_4 + VC(y_{ia})]$$

Solving the first-order conditions yields the standard marginal cost equal to marginal revenue condition

$$p^a_{ia} = p^b_{ia} = VC'(y_{ia})/[1-(1/\varepsilon)] = VC'(y_{ia})/\theta \quad (5)$$

From (5) it is apparent that the final producer will choose the same price in both the home and foreign markets. No price discrimination is exercised since demand elasticities in both markets are the same. To solve for the equilibrium prices and quantities, we need the structure of the variable cost in the production of the final good. The marginal cost $VC'(y_{ia})$

depends on the quantities and prices of intermediate inputs that the ith firm in the final sector chooses. Hence, the optimization problem of the intermediate producer must be considered first.

Intermediate Producer Behavior. The ith intermediate producer in country a maximizes profit given the derived demand implied by (4):

$$\max m_a q^{aa}{}_{ia} u^{aa}{}_{ia} + m_b q^{bb}{}_{ia} u^{bb}{}_{ia} - [A_1 + A_2 + bsm_a u^{aa}{}_{ia} + bsm_b u^{bb}{}_{ia}]$$

Solving the problem yields

$$q^{aa}{}_{ia} = bs/[1-(1/\varepsilon)] = bs/\beta \equiv q$$

$$q^{bb}{}_{ia} = bs/[1-(1/\varepsilon)] = bs/\beta = q$$

Similarly, $q^{aa}{}_{ib} = q^{bb}{}_{ib} = bs/\beta = q$. Combining these results with those in equation (4), we obtain

$$u^{aa}{}_{ia} = u^{aa}{}_{ja}$$

$$u^{bb}{}_{ib} = u^{bb}{}_{jb}$$

$$uaa_{ib} = t_I{}^{1/(\beta-1)} u^{aa}{}_{ia}$$

$$ubb_{ia} = t_I{}^{1/(\beta-1)} u^{bb}{}_{ib}$$

With the supply function of the intermediate producer at hand, the final producer's variable cost function can now be specified. Subsequently, the equilibrium conditions can be solved to yield the price and quantity schedules, and the profits of the final and intermediate producers can be derived. We bypass all the derivations and present only the final results that are of interest to this chapter, which are the payoffs of the intermediate and final producers. In particular, we estimate the profit of each final producer in country a to be

$$\pi_{F1} = p^a{}_{ia} y^a{}_{ia} + p^b{}_{ia} y^b{}_{ia} - [A_3 + A_4 + VC(y_{ia})]$$

$$= (1-\theta)\delta(I^a + I^b N^{\theta(\beta-1)/\beta(\theta-1)} M t_F{}^{1/(\theta-1)})/(m_a + m_b N^{(\beta-1)\theta/\beta(\theta-1)} t_F{}^{\theta/(\theta-1)})] - (A_3 + A_4)$$

with

$$N \equiv (n_a + n_b t_I{}^{\beta/(\beta-1)})/(n_b + n_a t_I{}^{\beta/(\beta-1)}) \text{ and}$$

$$M \equiv (m_a + m_b N^{-(\beta-1)\theta/\beta(\theta-1)} t_F{}^{\theta/(\theta-1)})/(m_b + m_a N^{(\beta-1)\theta/\beta(\theta-1)} t_F{}^{\theta/(\theta-1)})$$

Similarly, we estimate the profit of each intermediate producer in country a to be

$$\pi_{I1} = q_{ia} m_a u^{aa}{}_{ia} + q_{ia} m_b u^{bb}{}_{ia} - (A_1 + A_2 + bsm_a u^{aa}{}_{ia} + bsm_b u^{bb}{}_{ia})$$

$$= \theta\delta(1-\beta)(m_a + m_b t_I{}^{1/(\beta-1)} N^{1/\beta})[I^a/(m_a + m_b N^{-(\beta-1)\theta/\beta(\theta-1)} t_F{}^{\theta/(\theta-1)})$$

$$+ I^b N^{(\beta-1)\beta}/(m_b + m_a N^{(\beta-1)\theta/\beta(\theta-1)} t_F{}^{\theta/(\theta-1)})]/(n_a + n_b t_I{}^{\beta/(\beta-1)}) - (A_1 + A_2)$$

Following procedures similar to those described in case 1, we derive the profits of the final and intermediate producer for the three additional cases, each under a different configuration of market presence among final and intermediate firms.

Case 2. No FDI in Final Sector (One Plant/Firm); FDI in Intermediate Sector (Two Plants/Firm)

In this case, the profit of each final and intermediate producer in country a are

$$\pi_{F2} = q_{ia}m_a u^{aa}_{ia} + q_{ia}m_b u^{bb}_{ia} - (A_1 + A_2 + bsm_a u^{aa}_{ia} + bsm_b u^{bb}_{ia})$$

$$= (1-\theta)\delta(I^a + I^b M' t_F^{1/(\theta-1)})/(m_a + m_b t_F^{\theta/(\theta-1)})] - (A_3 + A_4)$$

$$\pi_{I2} = q_{ia}m_a u^{aa}_{ia} + q_{ia}m_b u^{bb}_{ia} - (A_1 + 2A_2 + bsm_a u^{aa}_{ia} + bsm_b u^{bb}_{ia})$$

$$= \theta\delta(1-\beta)(m_a + m_b)[I^a/(m_a + m_b t_F^{\theta/(\theta-1)}) + I^b/(m_b + m_a t_F^{\theta/(\theta-1)})]/(n_a + n_b) - (A_1 + A_2)$$

$$= \theta\delta(1-\beta)(m_a + m_b)(I^a + I^b M')]/[(n_a + n_b)(m_a + m_b t_F^{\theta/(\theta-1)})] - (A_1 + 2A_2)$$

where $M' = (m_a + m_b t_F^{\theta/(\theta-1)})/(m_b + m_a t_F^{\theta/(\theta-1)})$.

Case 3. FDI in Final Sector (Two Plants/Firm); No FDI in Intermediate Sector (One Plant/Firm)

The profit of each final producer in country a is given by

$$\pi_{F3} = p^a_{ia}y^a_{ia} + p^b_{ia}y^b_{ia} - [A_3 + 2A_4 + VC(y_{ia})]$$

$$= (1-\theta)\delta(I^a + I^b)/(m_a + m_b) - (A_3 + 2A_4)$$

The profit of each intermediate producer in country a is equal to

$$\pi_{I3} = qm_a(u^{aa}_{ia} + u^{ab}_{ia}) + qm_b(u^{bb}_{ia} + u^{ba}_{ia}) - [A_1 + A_2 + bsm_a(u^{aa}_{ia} + u^{ab}_{ia}) + bsm_b(u^{bb}_{ia} + u^{ba}_{ia})]$$

$$= \theta\delta(1-\beta)(I^a + I^b)(1 + t_I^{1/(\beta-1)})/(1 + t_I^{\beta/(\beta-1)})(n_a + n_b) - (A_1 + A_2)$$

Case 4. FDI in Final Sector (Two Plants/Firm); FDI in Intermediate Sector (Two Plants/Firm)

The only difference between cases 3 and 4 is that there are two plants for each intermediate sector, and there is no need of transportation and transaction costs for accessing distant markets in either sector:

$$\pi_{F4} = (1-\theta)\delta(I^a + I^b)/(m_a + m_b) - (A_3 + 2A_4)$$

$$\pi_{I4} = \theta\delta(1-\beta)(I^a + I^b)/(n_a + n_b) - (A_1 + 2A_2)$$

Nash Equilibrium

In principle, every final and intermediate producer has three choices: to set up 0, 1, or 2 plants. The payoff matrix for both intermediate and final producers can now be specified under each one of the aforementioned choices as

		Intermediate Producers		
		0	1	2
Final	0	(0, 0)	(0, 0)	(0, 0)
Producers	1	(0, 0)	(π_{F1}, π_{I1})	(π_{F2}, π_{I2})
	2	(0, 0)	(π_{F3}, π_{I3})	(π_{F4}, π_{I4})

where the entries of the matrix were specified in each of the four cases recounted above. Given this payoff matrix we can now begin to analyze the choices of firms under differential ES, efficiencies due to market proximity and varying degrees of product differentiation.

Final Producer's Choice

When there is only one plant per intermediate producer, a final producer will choose FDI if the following conditions hold:

$$B = \pi_{F3} - \pi_{F1} > 0 \text{ and } \pi_{F3} > 0$$

$$B = (1-\theta)\delta(I^a + I^b)/(m_a+m_b) - (A_3 + 2A_4)$$

$$-(1-\theta)\delta(I^a + I^b N^{\theta(\beta-1)/\beta(\theta-1)} M t_F^{1/(\theta-1)})/(m_a+m_b N^{(\beta-1)\theta/\beta(\theta-1)} t_F^{\theta/(\theta-1)})] + (A_3+A_4)$$

$$= -A_4 + (1-\theta)\delta I^a[1/(m_a+m_b) - 1/(m_a+m_b N^{(\beta-1)\theta/\beta(\theta-1)} t_F^{\theta/(\theta-1)})]$$

$$+(1-\theta)\delta I^b[1/(m_a+m_b) - N^{\theta(\beta-1)/\beta(\theta-1)} t_F^{1/(\theta-1)}/(m_b+m_a N^{-(\beta-1)\theta/\beta(\theta-1)} t_F^{\theta/(\theta-1)})]$$

Hence, $dB/dA_4 = -1 < 0$. This result indicates that the higher the fixed cost necessary to set up the second plant is, the lower the benefit of choosing FDI over trading from a single location will be. Hence, as the level of plant-specific ES increases, firms will tend to choose trade over FDI.

Given monopolistic competition, profits in the relevant industries will be driven to zero. This zero profit condition will imply that all firms in both the intermediate and the final sector will behave symmetrically (Brainard). Under the assumption of complete symmetry of the two countries (i.e., $I^a=I^b=I$, $m_a=m_b=m$, $n_a=n_b=n$), B is simplified and

$$dB/d(t_F) = \delta I[t_F^{(2-\theta)/(\theta-1)}(1+t_F^{\theta/(\theta-1)}) - \theta t_F^{1/(\theta-1)}(1+t_F^{1/(\theta-1)})]/m(1+t_F^{\theta/(\theta-1)})^2 > 0$$

as long as $\theta < 1/t_F$ (i.e., $1 < \sigma < t_F/(t_F-1)$).

This result suggests that gains from FDI increase as transportation and transaction costs as well as other DS associated with trading from a distant location increase. This decision is only valid when the elasticity of substitution among varieties is not very large, that is, when consumers are less likely to substitute a firm's product for another due to a marginal price increase. Given that the elasticity of substitution decreases as the degree of differentiation increases, producers of highly differentiated products are more likely to benefit from FDI.

The conditions that determine a final producer's choice of FDI when there are two plants per intermediate producer are qualitatively similar to the results above.

The Intermediate Producer's Choice

When there are two plants per final producer, an intermediate producer will choose to trade if the following condition is true:

$B = \pi_{I3} - \pi_{I4} > 0$ and $\pi_{I3} > 0$

$B = \theta\delta(1\text{-}\beta)(I^a + I^b)(1+t_I^{1/(\beta-1)})/(n_a+n_b)(1+t_I^{\beta/(\beta-1)}) - (A_1+A_2) - \theta\delta(1\text{-}\beta)(I^a + I^b)/(n_a+n_b) + (A_1+2A_2)$

$= A_2 + \theta\delta(1\text{-}\beta)(I^a + I^b)[(1+t_I^{1/(\beta-1)})/(1+t_I^{\beta/(\beta-1)})\text{-}1]/(n_a+n_b).$

Hence, $dB/dA_2 = 1 > 0$. This result indicates that, as in the case of final producers, gains of trade over FDI increase as the fixed cost of the second plant become larger. As plant-specific ES in the intermediate sector become large, intermediate producers will tend to choose trade over FDI:

$dB/d(t_I) = -\theta\delta(I^a+I^b)t^{(2-\beta)/(\beta-1)}[1+t_I^{\beta/(\beta-1)} - t_I\beta(1+t_I^{1/(\beta-1)})]/(n_a+n_b)(1+t_I^{\beta/(\beta-1)})^2 < 0$ as long as $b<1/t_I$

Similar to the case of final producers, gains of intermediate producers by trade over FDI decrease as the trading costs increase. This decision is only valid when β is not very large or in other words only when intermediate products are relatively differentiated (a small β is associated with increasing product differentiation). If intermediate products are not sufficiently differentiated, intermediate producers will be better off to set up a single plant in the home country and trade.

The conditions that determine an intermediate producer's choice of exports when there is one plant per intermediate producer are qualitatively similar to the results above.

Confronting the Real World

Our model suggests that along a value-adding chain, the level of ES and their degree of localization along with the degree of product differentiation will tend to impact how firms expand to capture scale efficiencies and how they trade or engage in FDI at each stage of the chain. We now confront these predictions with trade and FDI patterns in the fresh and processed pork sector. We segment the pork value-adding chain in three stages: (a) primary swine production, (b) slaughter and processing (e.g. fresh and chilled pork), and (c) manufacturing of differentiated and branded products (e.g. sausage, ham, luncheon meats, canned meats). We focus on the structure of the U.S. pork industry, but similar structures are observed among other leading pork producing countries (e.g., Denmark and the Netherlands).

ES in the primary sector seem to be exhausted at very low levels of production. As illustrated in Table 15.1, there is a large number of pork farms with very limited size that produces the bulk of the industry's output. Despite the appearance of some very large producers in recent years (e.g. Murphy Family Farms, Carrol's Foods, Premium Standard Farms), plant-level ES seem to be exhausted at rather small output levels. Large farms tend to operate multiple plants (houses) of limited size, which are replicated as long as capital resources and management can be secured (Kalaitzandonakes and Pierce). Hence, plant-level ES are exhausted at rather small levels of primary production. ES at the firm level deriving from improved inventory management, sourcing of inputs and volume discounts, improved access to credit, and faster learning may still be significant (Pierce and Kalaitzandonakes).

At the slaughter/processing stage of the value-adding chain, there is significant concentration both at the firm and plant level. As indicated in Table 15.2, in 1995 less than twenty firms processed 98 percent of pork produced in the U.S. using only forty-two slaughter plants. Industry experts maintain that the industry standard is a plant with single processing line with a capacity of 6,000 to 8,000 head per day per shift, operating with two shifts. An important constraint is that the carcasses must be chilled overnight before processing, so the refrigerated capacity must equal the daily kill. The two largest firms, IBP and Smithfield, operate twelve plants on two shifts and process from 13,000 to 17,000 head per day for a total annual capacity of over 18 million head. Hence, with an average size slaughter house of over 2.5 million head/year, these figures suggest that plant-specific ES are exhausted at very large output levels.

Judging the existence of ES and their degree of localization for the processing of consumption-ready products is more difficult. As indicated in Table 15.3, in 1992 approximately fifty plants produced, on average,

TABLE 15.1 U.S. Pork Primary Production Sector

Total Number of Farms	*Average Farm Size All Farms*	*Number of Farms with >2000 head*	*Output Share of Farms >2000 head*
207,980	264 head	4,630	37.0%

Source: Nass, 1995.

TABLE 15.2 U.S. Pork Slaughter Sector

Number of Firms	*Number of Plants*	*Average Size (head)*	*Share of Total Output*
19	42	2,500,000	98.0%

Source: National Pork Producers Council, 1996.

50% of manufactured pork, suggesting that the U.S. pork manufacturing sector is less concentrated than the packing sector. Eliciting the optimal scale and degree of localization of ES in the manufacturing sector is complicated by the fact that plant capacity data may not be directly comparable across firms and plants given that often significant differences exist in the preparation modes of branded and highly differentiated products. However, plant-specific ES appear to still be available since fewer than fifty plants produced a very large portion of the industry's total output.

Given the results of the theoretical model, these figures would suggest that trade of primary pork products will likely be small. Firms with (single or multiple) small plants may be located anywhere, and proximity to the market will tend to minimize the transaction costs of trading (mainly transportation in this case). At the slaughter/processing stage, however, where plant-specific ES are large, trade is likely. Since the output of the sector is not highly differentiated, DS associated with trading in diverse markets will likely be small. Hence, trading large amounts of output from a single location where a large plant is located will tend to be profitable for firms.

DS from trading large amounts of output from a single location may be more significant in the case of highly differentiated and branded pork products. Most pork processors produce and distribute a large variety of products under several brand names directed to diverse and multiple markets. Assessing the demand and accessing consumers in multiple markets from a distance is likely to increase transaction costs. Hence, tradeoffs between plant-specific ES and DS associated with trade and

TABLE 15.3 U.S. Pork Processing Sector

	Number of Large Plants	*Output Share of Large Plants*	*Four-Firm Concentration Ratio*
Processed Pork	49	59%	31%
Sausage	46	41%	38%

Source: McDonald, et al., 1996.

distribution are likely to determine the proportion of trade from a single location and FDI in manufactured pork.

Pork Trade

Actual trade patterns seem to confront well the predictions of the model. U.S. pork exports are dominated by fresh and frozen pork, and they have increased significantly in recent years (Figure 15.1). The value of exports of fresh and frozen pork is several times greater than those of live swine or of processed pork products. Global pork trade is also dominated by trade in fresh and frozen pork, and trade in that product, reflecting liberalization in key markets, has grown dramatically in recent years (Figure 15.2.) Trade in fresh and frozen pork has increase from less than $1 billion the 1960s to over $15 billion in recent years. Processed pork trade has grown slowly and has reached $2 billion in recent years. Trade in live swine has been very similar to that of processed pork.

Pork trade has been influenced by a host of nontariff barriers as well as by the trade-distorting effects of domestic agricultural policies. Trade among the member states of the European Union would have been less influenced by such factors and would, then, reflect economies of scale and other economic factors affecting trade. Figure 15.3 shows the pork trade among the member states of the European Union. As was the case with global pork trade, trade within the European Union is dominated by trade in fresh and frozen pork.

Exports Versus Foreign Direct Investment

The choice betweem exports and FDI as a means for accessing foreign markets among a selected set of U.S. pork processors and manufacturers also seems to be consistent with the predictions of the theoretical model. We have segmented a set of selected firms with presence in the slaughter and manufacturing sectors for which data on exports and sales from foreign affiliates are available in three groups. The first group, composed by IBP and Farmland, includes firms that market mainly fresh and frozen meat. The second group, composed by Thorn Apple Valley, Hormel, ConAgra, and Wilson's Foods, includes firms that market some fresh and chilled meat but also produce manufactured pork products such as ham, bacon and cured meats. The third group, composed by Sara Lee, Smithfield, and Doskocil, involves firms that produce and distribute highly differentiated branded pork products.

As illustrated in Table 15.4, there is a clear pattern in the choice of FDI and exports for accessing foreign markets across the three groups. Firms operating primarily in the processing sector and selling undifferentiated fresh meat products (group 1) use exports as the exclusive vehicle to

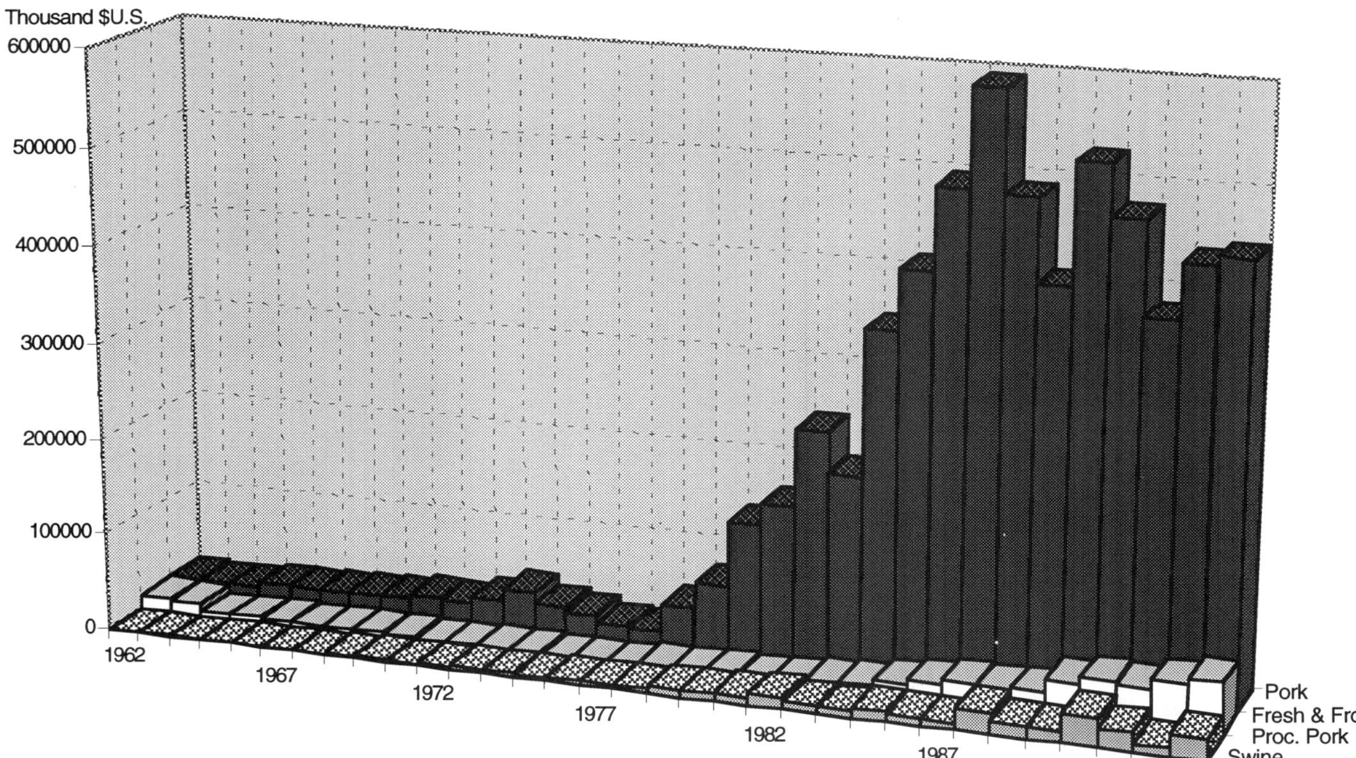

FIGURE 15.1 U.S. Trade in Swine, Pork, and Processed Pork Products. *Source:* USDA/ERS unpublished data.

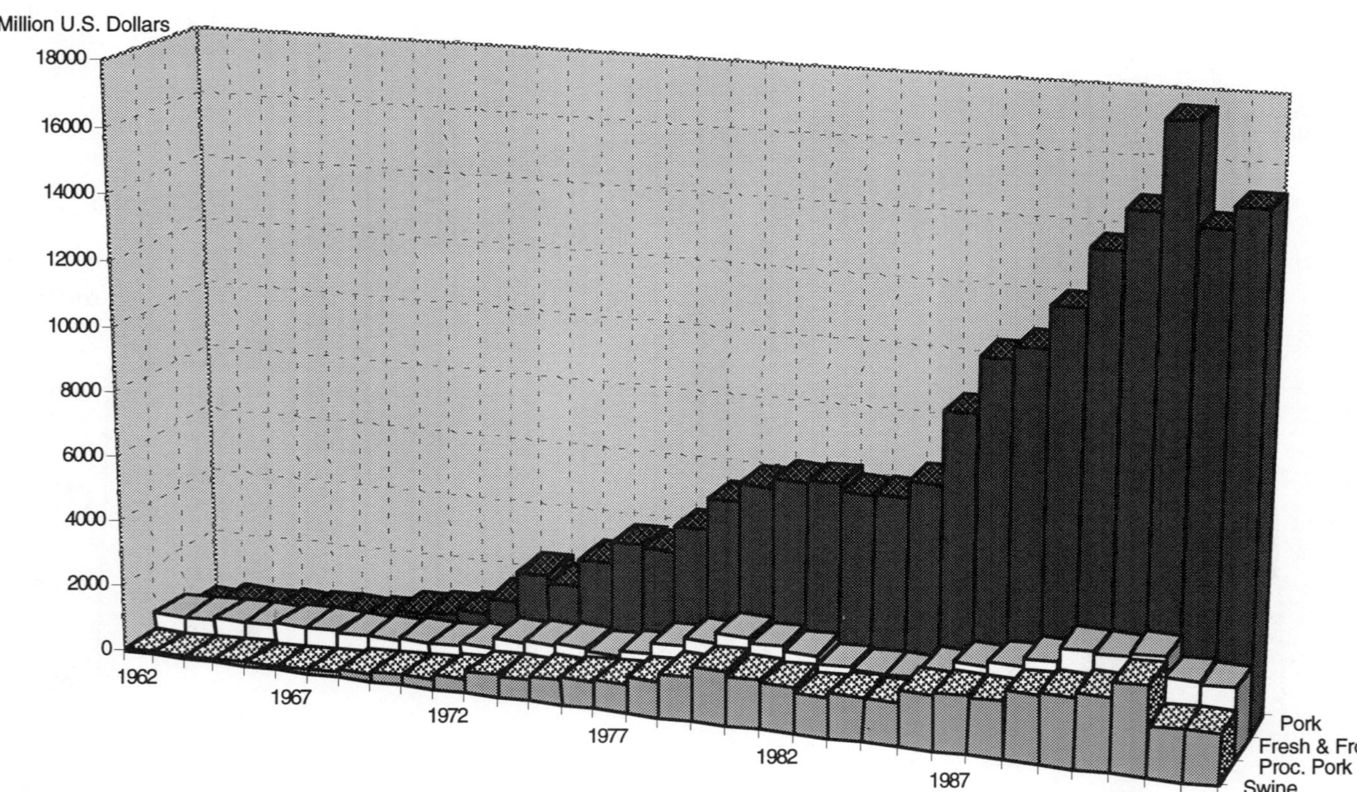

FIGURE 15.2 Global Trade in Swine, Pork, and Processed Pork Products. *Source:* USDA/ERS unpublished data.

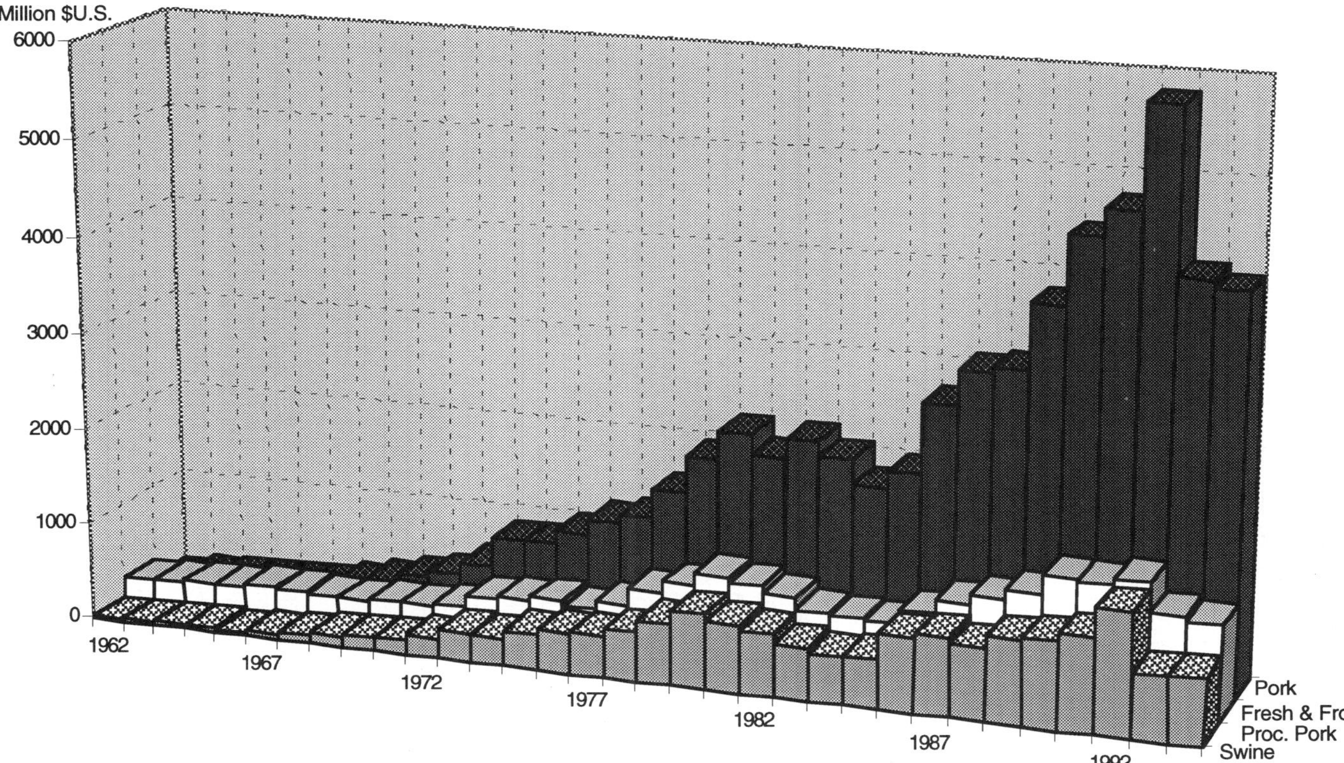

FIGURE 15.3 Trade in Swine, Fresh and Frozen Pork, and Processed Pork Products, European Union. *Source:* USDA/ERS unpublished data.

TABLE 15.4 Exports and Sales of Foreign Affiliates of Selected Pork Processors Measured as a Percent of Food Sales

	Group 1		*Group 2*		*Group 3*	
	Exports	FDI	Exports	FDI	Exports	FDI
1988	4.75	—	2.20	2.35	0.51	9.31
1990	4.78	—	1.82	1.13	0.39	9.49
1991	9.40	—	2.10	4.62	1.11	10.43
1992	12.72	—	3.16	3.26	0.92	13.90
1993	11.90	—	4.22	2.33	2.43	10.33
Average	8.71	—	2.70	2.74	1.07	10.69

Source: USDA/ERS, unpublished data.

international markets. As the product mix becomes more balanced between undifferentiated fresh meats and somewhat differentiated processed products (group 2), both FDI and exports are used. For firms in group 3 that produce almost exclusively highly differentiated and branded products, FDI is ten times more important than exports.

These FDI/export patterns are consistent with those predicted by the theoretical model. To be sure, these results are only suggestive since no statistical tests of formal hypotheses are carried out. Furthermore, given that the samples are very thin, the choice of firm can meaningfully impact the conclusions. Nevertheless, the observed trade and FDI patterns reviewed here seem to lend support to the argument that disaggregating the value chain and examining the sources and optimal levels of ES may provide significant insights regarding the strategic choices of firms in accessing foreign markets.

Notes

1. The above concept of ES is not only conceptually but also empirically limiting. Empirical measures of ES are rarely consistent with the theoretical concept of ES since fixed input and output configurations are not generally observed in reality as scale of operation of firms and industries continuously changes (Gold).

2. Location-specific ES need not be related only to production activities. For example, location-specific ES may derive from indivisibilities in consignment or market segmentation and hence may relate to distribution. Similarly, location-specific ES need not be internal to the firm. ES that derive from labor specialization and technological spillovers for geographically clustered industries are external to individual firms but still location-specific.

References

Abbott, P. and M. E. Bredahl. 1994. "Competitiveness: Definitions, Useful Concepts and Issues." In *Competitiveness in International Food Markets*, M. E. Bredahl, P. Abbott and M. Reed, eds. Boulder, CO: Westview Press.

Bjornson, B. 1995. "Investment by US Food Manufacturers: Growth, Rents, and Multinationality." Working Paper, University of Missouri, Columbia.

Brainard, S.L. 1993. "A Simple Theory of Multinational Corporations and Trade with a Trade-off Between Proximity and Concentration." National Bureau of Economic Research, Working Paper No. 4269.

Bredahl, M. E., P. Abbott and M. R. Reed. 1994. *Competitiveness in International Food Markets*. Boulder, CO: Westview Press.

Caves, R. 1982. *Multinational Enterprise and Economic Analysis*, Cambridge: Cambridge University Press.

Chandler, A.D. 1990. *Scale and Scope: The Dynamics of Industrial Capitalism*. Cambridge, MA and London: Harvard University Press.

Chipman, J. 1970. "External Economies of Scale and Competitive Equilibrium." *Quarterly Journal of Economics*, 134:347–385.

Christodoulou, M. 1992. "Intra-Industry Trade in Agrofood Sectors: The Case of the EEC Meat Market." *Applied Economics*, 24:875–884.

Connor, J. M. 1983. "Foreign Investment in the U.S. Food Marketing System." *American Journal of Agricultural Economics*, 65:395–404.

Dunning, J. H. 1981. *International Production and the Multinational Enterprise*. London: Allen and Unwin.

Ethier, W. 1979. "Internationally Decreasing Cost and World Trade." *Journal of International Economics*, 9:1–24.

Gold, B. 1981. "Changing Perspectives on Size, Scale, and Returns: An Interpretive Survey." *Journal of Economic Literature*, 19:5–33.

Goldsmith, P. D. and T. L. Sporleder. 1996. "Analyzing Boundary Decisions of Firms: Foreign Direct Investment by Food Manufacturers." Working Paper, McGill University.

Handy, C. R. and D. R. Henderson. 1994. "Assessing the Role of Foreign Direct Investment in the Food Manufacturing Industry." In *Competitiveness in International Food Markets*, M. Bredahl, P. Abbott, and M. Reed, eds. Boulder, CO: Westview Press.

Hartman, D. A., D. R. Henderson, and I. M. Sheldon. 1993. "A Cross-Section Analysis of Intra-Industry Trade in the U.S. Processed Food and Beverage Sectors." *Agricultural and Resource Economics Review*, 23:189–198.

Helpman, E. and P. R. Krugman. 1985. *Market Structure and Foreign Trade*. Cambridge, MA: MIT Press.

Henderson, D. R., P. R. Voros, and J. G. Hirschlberg. 1996. "Industrial Determinants of International Trade and Foreign Investment by Food and Beverage Manufacturing Firms." In *Industrial Organization and Trade in the Food Industries*, I. Sheldon and P. Abbott, eds. Boulder, CO: Westview Press.

Horstman, I. and J. Markusen 1992. "Endogenous Market Structures in International Trade" *Journal of International Economics*, 32:109–29.

Kalaitzandonakes, N. and V. Pierce. 1996, "Industrialization in the U.S. Hog Industry: An Empirical Analysis of Causal Factors." Working Paper, University of Missouri, Columbia, MO.

Krugman, P. 1991. *Geography and Trade.* Louvain, Belgium. Leuven University Press and Cambridge, MA: MIT Press.

———. 1980. "Scale Economies, Product Differentiation and the Pattern of Trade." *American Economic Review*, 70:950–959.

Marshall, A. 1920. *Principles of Economics.* London: Macmillan. Eighth edition.

———. 1923. *Industry and Trade.* London: Macmillan. Fourth edition.

McCorriston, S. and I. M. Sheldon. 1991. "Intra-Industry Trade and Specialization in Processed Agricultural Products: The Case of the U.S. and the EC." *Review of Agricultural Economics*, 13:173–184.

McDonald, J., M. Ollinger, K. Nelson, and C. Handy. 1996. "Structural Change in Meat Industries: Implications for Food Safety Regulation." Presented paper, ASSA meetings, San Francisco.

Olson, M. and R. Zeckhauser. 1970. "The Efficient Production of External Economies." *American Economic Review*, 60:512–17.

Pierce, V. and N. Kalaitzandonakes. 1995. " Quasi-Vertical Contracts in the U.S. Hog Industry: A Source of Efficiency and Productivity?" Working Paper, University of Missouri, Columbia, MO.

Pratten, C. F. 1971. *Economies of Scale in Manufacturing Industry.* Cambridge: Cambridge University Press.

Shariff, I. 1971. "The Concept of External Economies of Scale in Economic Development." *Indian Journal of Economics*, 19:7–18.

Smith, A. 1971. *An Inquiry Into the Wealth of Nations.* London: Strahan and Cadell. Sixth edition.

16

Farm Output and Employment Links From Processed Food Exports: A Comparison of Brazil, Mexico, and the United States

Mary E. Burfisher, Sherman Robinson, and Karen Thierfelder

Introduction

Global trade in processed agricultural products has grown rapidly, and now exceeds the value of world trade in bulk agricultural commodities (United Nations, 1990). This trend has stimulated much interest in the characteristics of processed food trade, and discussion about whether and how countries should increase their role in this dynamic segment of the global agricultural market. One motivation to expand processed food exports is to stimulate farm output and employment. An increase in processed food exports raises the level of domestic economic activity directly, through an expansion of food processing, and indirectly, through increases in input demand, largely from farm sectors.[1]

Estimating the effects of expanded processed food exports on farm output and employment requires an economy-wide perspective. Input-output analysis is a standard approach to quantify the economy-wide implications of a shock in one sector through its backward and forward linkages. A standard input-output model uses national input-output accounts to quantify the backward linkages among sectors through input provision, and the forward linkages to output utilization.[2] While the input-output model captures the general equilibrium linkages that operate through changes in intermediate demand, it has important limitations.

For example, one must assume linearity in production, no input substitution, a perfectly elastic supply of inputs, and exogenous trade flows.

A computable general equilibrium (CGE) model provides a richer perspective than an input-output model. It includes the intermediate input relationships and changes in consumer income accounted for in an extended open input-output model as well as the household and government accounts included in a SAM-based model. However, a CGE model extends the input-output framework by allowing for endogenous prices, price responsive nonlinear supply and demand behavior, resource constraints, and explicitly modeled trade relationships. The model also incorporates other policy and factor market distortions that may influence the effects of an increase in processed agricultural exports.

Trade and production characteristics of a CGE model yield results that may differ from input-output analysis. Since there is two-way trade at the sectoral level, higher demand for raw inputs can raise domestic farm prices and induce increased imports of raw products. "Leakages" can therefore occur in the linkage from food processing to farm sectors, as demand for inputs falls on both domestic and imported products. On the export side, assuming imperfect transformation between production for domestic and export markets can magnify the effects of export growth on food output, since production increases for both foreign and home markets. When raw agricultural sectors expand, competition for a fixed, fully employed supply of capital and labor by sectors with different factor intensities causes factor prices to change. In turn, changes in wages affect the linkage from food processing to employment in raw agricultural sectors, as farm producers' employment decisions respond to changes in labor costs. The CGE model also captures the real exchange rate and demand effects that follow export growth. These features are important in determining the size of trade leakages and enable us to show that it matters how export growth is achieved.

In this chapter we use a CGE model to provide an empirical perspective on linkages from processed agricultural export growth to farm output and employment in Brazil, Mexico, and the United States. These countries are particularly relevant case studies because of the prospects for the western hemisphere free trade agreement to stimulate trade in processed foods.

The remainder of the chapter is organized as follows. In the second section, we describe the raw and processed agricultural sectors in the economies and trade of Brazil, Mexico, and the United States. In the third section, we describe the model. In the fourth section, we present the simulations and results. Our conclusions are in the final section.

Raw and Processed Agriculture in Brazil, Mexico, and the United States

Raw farm and processed agriculture are important components of total trade for the three countries (see Table 16.1).[3] Trade dependency in production, measured as the share of production that is exported, varies among crops in the three countries (see Table 16.2). Brazil has the highest trade dependency in processed products, with 10.9 percent of food exported, compared to 3.2 percent for Mexico and the United States. In contrast, Mexico and the United States have higher trade dependencies for the production of raw products than Brazil. For example, the United States exports 36.8 percent of the corn it produces, and Mexico exports 40.3 percent of its fruits and vegetables.

Export shares are important because they affect the responsiveness of a sector to world price shocks and real exchange rate movements. In the processed food sector, large trade shares mean that export growth leads to proportionately larger linkages to farm output and employment. In the case of the United States and Mexico, there are large trade shares in farm sectors that do not provide inputs to processed foods. When these highly traded farm sectors adapt to world price shocks, there can be important indirect effects on farm linkages following an expansion of food exports.

In all three countries, the trade shares in consumption are higher in raw agricultural sectors than they are in processed agriculture. Only a small share of processed food consumption is imported in each country. When import shares are small, changes in world prices and real exchange rates result in small income effects on demand. This suggests that there will be minimal income effects from real exchange rate appreciation on the demand for both imported and domestic varieties of processed food. Again, indirect effects of trade shares are important. In Mexico, for example, the large share of imports in consumption of corn will be shown to have

TABLE 16.1 Characteristics of Agricultural Trade of Brazil, Mexico, and the United States, 1992 (percent)

	Brazil		*Mexico*		*United States*	
	Exports	Imports	Exports	Imports	Exports	Imports
Agricultural share of total trade	27.7	9.6	10.5	11.3	7.2	4.7
Processed food share of total trade	13.8	2.6	3.6	5.2	2.9	2.2
Processed food share of agric. trade	49.8	26.7	34.3	45.7	39.9	46.9

Source: Robinson, Lewis, and Hinojosa, 1994.

TABLE 16.2 Share of Trade in Agricultural Production and Consumption, 1992

	Brazil	*Mexico*	*United States*
Export share in production			
Processed	10.9	3.2	3.2
Raw	5.3	9.8	7.9
Corn	0.0	0.0	36.8
Grains/oilseeds	19.3	1.2	24.2
Horticulture	1.4	40.3	7.5
Other agriculture	3.2	7.8	1.0
Import share in consumption			
Processed	2.1	3.9	3.7
Raw	2.3	8.2	6.1
Corn	0.0	15.8	0.0
Grains/oilseeds	5.4	24.5	3.8
Horticulture	2.2	9.1	12.2
Other agriculture	0.0	0.0	5.9

Source: Robinson, Lewis, and Hinojosa, 1994.

Note: Other agriculture includes livestock, tropical products, and miscellaneous other farm sectors.

important indirect effects on farm employment linkages from increased processed food exports.

The characteristics of agriculture are very different in the three countries. Notably, backward linkages from food processing to intermediate inputs are strong in Mexico and the United States, but relatively weak in Brazil (see Table 16.3). Farm production is much more labor intensive, relative to processed agriculture, in Mexico and Brazil as compared to the United States.

The Input-Output and CGE Models

The standard input-output model is a multisector accounting framework in which final demand, including trade, is assumed exogenous. Sectors are linked through their demands for intermediate inputs. Intermediate and labor input coefficients are fixed. There are benefits to using an input-output model to assess economy-wide changes following a policy shock, and this class of model is widely used to analyze linkage effects. Since the model accounts for direct and indirect effects, it captures some general equilibrium properties of the economy. However, the input-output model makes strong assumptions, namely fixed factor input coefficients, exogenous adjustment to import shares, and constant prices.

TABLE 16.3 Backward Linkages and Total Labor Intensity of Farm and Processed Food Sectors[a]

	Brazil		*Mexico*		*United States*	
	Backward linkage	Labor intensity[b]	Backward linkage	Labor intensity	Backward linkage	Labor intensity
Corn	1.00	1.77	0.81	3.70	0.96	0.80
Grains/oilseeds	1.00	1.77	0.85	1.50	0.84	0.91
Horticulture	0.96	2.04	0.77	1.80	0.85	1.45
Other agric.	0.98	1.50	0.97	1.30	1.19	1.31
Processed food	0.95	0.67	1.30	0.68	1.29	1.05

[a]The indicators are normalized to one. A value greater than one indicates that the sector's demand for intermediate or labor inputs is greater than the economy wide average.

[b]Labor intensity includes both direct and indirect (through inputs) labor demand.

A CGE model includes the fixed coefficient, intermediate linkages that are the core of input-output analysis. However, prices are endogenous and affect decisions in a CGE model. Output and employment effects of an exogenous shock satisfy market equilibrium conditions based on the nonlinear responses of producers and consumers to changing price signals. Furthermore, final demand, trade, and factor coefficients are endogenous in a CGE model.

We use a multicountry CGE model, WHFTA-CGE, to analyze the effects of an increase in food processing exports.[5] It consists of ten linked "country" models: the United States, Mexico, Argentina, Brazil, Chile, Peru, Bolivia, Ecuador, Colombia, and Venezuela. The model includes a simple representation of the rest of the world, with export-demand and import-supply curves for tradeable goods. Each country has a separate CGE model that determines: sectoral supply, demand, exports, imports, and market clearing prices; factor supply, demand, and market-clearing wages; and the real exchange rate. The countries are linked by trade flows, and the model solves for world prices that equate export supply and import demand for all traded goods. Domestically produced and traded goods are specified as imperfect substitutes, which provides for a realistic continuum of "tradability" and two-way sectoral trade.

The WHFTA-CGE model focuses on real trade flows, relative prices, and the real exchange rate. The aggregate price level in each country is taken as exogenous, and the model does not include money or other assets. The model includes the basic macro aggregates for each country, including the government deficit, the balance of trade, and the savings-investment balance. The balance of trade for each country is fixed exogenously. Government revenue is determined endogenously, while government expenditure is fixed exogenously. The government deficit is endogenous. Aggregate investment in each country is assumed to be a fixed share of GDP (gross domestic product), and aggregate savings is assumed to adjust to equate savings and investment.

In the CGE model, unlike the input-output model, there are resource constraints as the supply of each input is assumed to be fixed and fully employed in each country. This implies that certain sectors must contract as others expand. Producers also respond to economy-wide changes in factor returns. Factor shares in production are important for the sectoral reallocation of labor and capital following a shock.

The production and trade relationships are distinctly different in the CGE model compared to the input-output model. In the CGE model there is joint production, where the allocation of output between domestic and export markets is described by a constant elasticity of transformation (CET) function. Export supply is a function of relative prices, the transformation elasticity, and the export share of output. The export share and elasticity of export transformation are two key parameters in the CGE model. Since the producer price is a weighted aggregation of the export and domestic sales prices, a large export share raises the pass-through of increased world prices to the domestic market. A high elasticity of transformation reduces the domestic production effects of export growth. When domestic sales shift easily into the export market, there is less expansion and, therefore, weaker linkage effects.

Similar to the allocation of domestic production between domestic and exports, consumers allocate their total expenditure on each composite commodity between imported and domestic varieties of that good. Demand for domestic and imported varieties is modeled using an Almost Ideal Demand System (AIDS) specification, in which import expenditure shares are a function of total expenditure on the composite commodity and relative prices. A shock that affects the price of imports will affect the quantity of imports relative to domestic goods consumed. The imperfect substitution between imports and domestic goods pertains to all components of final demand, including intermediate good purchases. When imports satisfy an increase in demand for inputs, there is a weaker link to the intermediate good sector than one would expect using input-output analysis.

With the CGE model, we can analyze the linkages from an increase in processed food exports to farm employment and output effects. The linkages take into account (1) resource constraints; (2) the leakage of processors' demand for raw farm inputs onto imported inputs; and (3) general equilibrium effects, including changes in terms of trade and exchange rates.

Scenarios and Results

Scenarios

We use the CGE model to simulate three scenarios. In the first two scenarios, we focus on Brazil as an illustrative example. In the first scenario, we assume an increase in world demand for Brazil's processed food exports. This demand shock could occur as other countries reduce their trade barriers, or because of income growth in Brazil's trade partners. We implement the scenario in both the CGE and the input-output models and compare linkages to farm output and employment in detail. In the second scenario, we introduce an export subsidy to processed foods in Brazil with no change in world demand conditions. The subsidy could arise if the country is pursuing an aggressive trade policy to expand global market share in processed foods trade. We then compare linkages under the two export expansion scenarios. In the last section, we compare linkages in the three countries from food export growth due to a demand shock, and we analyze the sensitivity of results to trade elasticities.

Brazil: Linkages in the CGE and Input-Output Models

Linkages from food processing to farm sectors depend, first, on the size of the output change in food induced by the export shock. In the input-output model, food processing output increases 2.9 percent due to the increase in export sales, plus the implied increase in intermediate demand for food inputs based on input-output relationships (see Table 16.4). In the CGE model, output in the food sector increases by 2.95 percent, slightly more than in the standard input-output model. The slightly higher level of food output in the CGE model has three key components. First, there is an expansion of composite output (domestic and exports) as producers respond to the higher producer price caused by an outward shift in foreign demand. The output response increases with the trade share because producers respond to a price that is a composite of the export and the domestic sales price. Because Brazil exports 10.9 percent of its food production, there is a strong production response. Second, we assume some jointness in production for exports and domestic markets. The ease with which goods can be shifted out of domestic sales and into the export market is described by a transformation elasticity. Higher transformability between the home and the export markets reduces the need to expand food output to meet export growth. Since exports and domestic goods are imperfect substitutes, we find that a 25 percent increase in exports is

TABLE 16.4 Brazil: Effects of a 25% Increase in Processed Agricultural Exports due to an Increase in Export Demand (% change from base)

	Own Sector	*Input Sectors*			
	Processed agriculture	Corn	Grains and oilseeds	Horticulture	Other agriculture
Input-output model:					
Output and employment	2.89	0.51	1.16	0.30	0.16
CGE model:					
Output	2.95	0.39	0.93	0.13	-0.87
Exports	25.00	0.00	-1.53	-4.76	-2.19
Imports	4.72	0.00	9.77	3.05	2.02
Domestic sales of domestic output	0.26	0.39	1.15	0.20	-0.11
Employment	4.52	0.32	1.05	-0.03	-0.34

Note: In the input-output model, labor input ratios are fixed so that employment and output effects are identical. In the CGE model, output is linearly aggregated over domestic and export sales so it is comparable to the input-output specification.

accompanied by an increase in production and a small increase in domestic sales.

Finally, general equilibrium effects influence food output in the CGE model. As world demand for Brazil's food processing exports increases, there are terms of trade gains as Brazil's export price increases. This increase in income is spent on all commodities, including processed foods. As a result, the domestic food price increases despite the increase in domestic supply due to joint production.

Real exchange rate changes accompany the export shock. An increase in exports must be met by an increase in imports, given the constant foreign balance constraint. The export shock, a 25 percent increase in food export demand, causes the real exchange rate to appreciate 1.2 percent. This causes the composite (imported and domestic) consumer price of goods to decrease slightly, reflecting the small (2.1 percent) import share of consumption. The income effect causes an increase in consumption of the composite good and contributes to an increase in demand and further expansion in food processing. However, the consumption of the composite good now contains a larger share of imports because the appreciation induces consumers to substitute imported goods for the domestic variety. In the case of Brazil, food imports increased 4.7 percent as a result of food export growth.

In Brazil's farm sectors, output effects in all sectors are lower than predicted by the input-output model. Trade effects dampen the linkages to farm sectors. There is an import leakage because higher domestic prices due to rising demand, and lower import prices due to exchange rate appreciation, cause food processors to substitute toward imported inputs. Exchange rate appreciation also causes exports to fall in those sectors that have not experienced an increase in world demand. For example, Brazil's imports of grains/oilseeds, the main raw agricultural sector for food processing, increase almost 9.8 percent, and exports decline 1.5 percent. Resource constraints also limit Brazil's farm output response. Since the supply of resources is fixed in the CGE model, expansion of some sectors forces others to contract. In Brazil, the expansion of output in corn, horticulture, and grains/oilseeds causes the sector "other agriculture" to contract. In the standard input-output model, the labor force implicitly increases to meet demands for additional labor, with no repercussions on wages. Since the input-output model includes fixed labor-input coefficients, labor demand changes proportionately to changes in output. In grains/oilseeds, the primary input to food processing in Brazil, output and employment increase 1.2 percent according to input-output analysis.

In the CGE model, resource constraints, wage changes, and factor substitution influence the linkage from food export growth to farm employment.[6] Given the aggregate resource constraints, an increase in demand for raw agriculture means that rural wages increase, inducing some substitution towards capital. The magnitude of the change in rural wages depends on the factor intensity in both the expanding sectors and the sectors that must contract to release resources. In the CGE model, employment grows by 1.1 percent in Brazil's grains/oilseeds sector, the main raw agricultural input sector for food processing, compared to 1.2 percent in the input-output model. However, grains/oilseeds output increases by a smaller amount in the CGE model. When differences in the level of output are accounted for, a larger employment linkage emerges from the CGE model. Employment increases by more than output in the grains/oilseeds sector. One reason for increased labor use is that resource competition forces output of "other agriculture," a large employer, to contract, and rural labor is released. Higher employment in grains/oilseeds raises a potential policy issue for Brazil. While growth in food exports can stimulate higher employment and wages in the raw input sector for food processing, its repercussions on competing farm sectors must be considered. For example, the sectoral reallocation of rural labor may have adverse welfare effects if employment grows in farm sectors characterized by low labor productivity.

Brazil: Linkages From Export Subsidy vs. Demand Growth

Linkages to farm output and employment are often used as arguments to support the promotion of processed agricultural exports. In this scenario, we analyze two sources of export growth in processed food and compare their linkages to farm output and employment. We compare an exogenous increase in global demand that increases Brazil's food exports by 25 percent to an export subsidy that causes an equal increase in food processing exports. Although a new export subsidy is not currently permissible under the GATT agreement, we pose this scenario to explore the different effects of demand and supply shocks on backward linkages.

Output of processed food is lower when food exports are subsidized, compared to export demand growth, but output and employment in grains/oilseeds, the primary agricultural input sector, are higher (Table 16.5). World price effects, exchange rate changes, and trade behavior drive the stronger linkages of the export subsidy scenario. Consequently, standard input-output models do not capture the differences between the two scenarios.

In the export subsidy scenario, the world price of Brazil's food exports falls, and there is a terms of trade loss. The decline in income causes a decline in consumer demand. There is no income stimulus to domestic demand for food processing as there is when demand expands. Likewise, the income decline causes a decline in demand for imports.

Since the policy shock induces an increase in exports, the exchange rate

TABLE 16.5 Brazil: Effects of a 25% Increase in Processed Agricultural Exports

	Export Subsidy	*World Demand Growth*
Output (% change from base)		
Corn	0.38	0.39
Grains/oilseeds	1.02	0.93
Horticulture	0.10	0.13
Other agriculture	-0.11	-0.09
Food	2.90	2.95
Employment (% change from base)		
Corn	0.30	0.32
Grains/oilseeds	1.18	1.05
Horticulture	-0.07	-0.03
Other agriculture	-0.37	-0.34
Food	4.48	4.52
Welfare change (Million 1992 cruzeiros)[a]	-0.14	0.12
Export revenue gain as a percent of export subsidy	2.00	na
Exchange rate (% change from base)[b]	-1.03	-1.24

[a]Welfare is measured as equivalent variation: a positive number indicates a welfare gain.
[b]A decline in the exchange rate indicates an appreciation.
na = not applicable.

must appreciate to maintain the foreign balance constraint, as in the scenario in which export demand increased. However, less appreciation is needed given the income loss as the terms of trade decline. In the farm sectors, the smaller exchange rate appreciation under a subsidy scheme results in less trade leakage, with a smaller shift toward imported inputs and a smaller decline in farm exports. The employment effect in the grains/oilseeds sector is also stronger when exports increase under a subsidy scheme. Employment in grains/oilseeds increases by 1.2 percent, compared to 1.1 percent under a world demand shock.

Although linkages to farm output and employment are stronger under an export subsidy scheme compared to a demand shock, the gains for raw agricultural sectors are achieved through economy-wide welfare and fiscal costs. Welfare declines under a subsidy scheme, compared to an increase under demand growth, because of the decline in the price of exports relative to imports. This terms of trade loss represents a reduction in income. The increase in total export revenue is only 2 percent of the cost of the subsidy. Fiscal costs of the export subsidy exceed export revenue gains because there is a decline in the world price of the subsidized food exports. Furthermore, the real exchange rate appreciation dampens demand for all Brazilian exports. Through this exchange rate effect, the export subsidy to food processing is essentially a "beggar thy neighboring sector" policy.

Comparing Linkages in Brazil, Mexico, and the United States

In the third scenario, we compare the effects of a 25 percent increase in global demand for the processed food exports of Brazil, Mexico, and the United States. We increase each country's export demand separately. The three countries differ in their trade shares, labor intensity in production, and intermediate demand linkages from food processing.

In Figures 16.1–16.3, we show the sensitivity of changes in the output and employment in food processing to variations in the elasticity of transformation between the export and domestic varieties in the three countries. The diagrams illustrate the role of trade shares. Large trade shares transmit a stronger world price signal to domestic producers. Brazil exports the highest share of its production of food processing, 10.9 percent, compared to 3.2 percent in both the United States and Mexico. For a given transformation elasticity, Brazil has the largest output expansion when export demand increases.

Higher export transformability means that there is less output expansion for a given level of exports, since it is easier to shift sales out of the domestic market. The sensitivity of processed food output in the three countries to the elasticity parameter indicates that robust analyses of

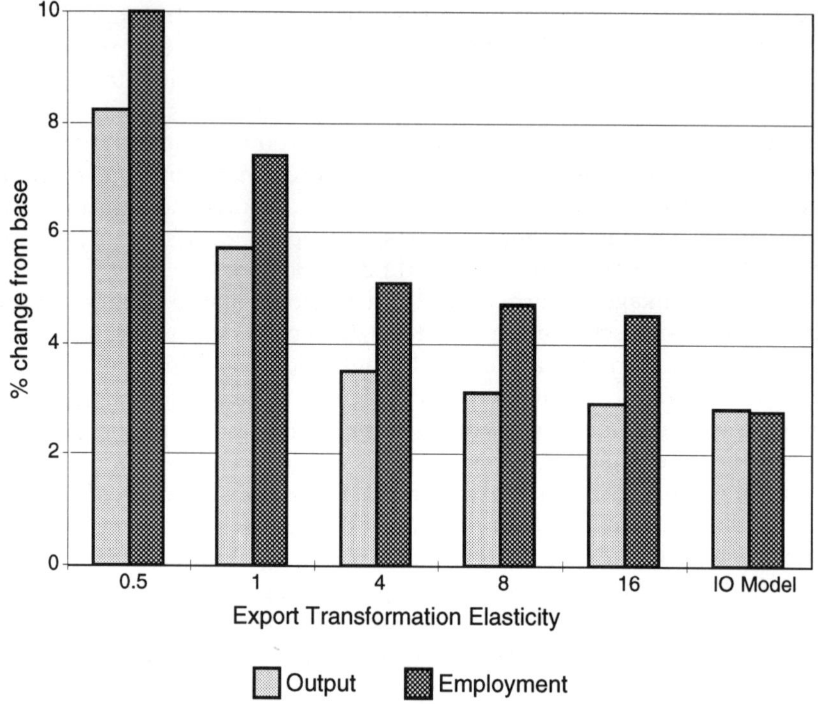

FIGURE 16.1 Brazil—Output and employment in processed food with a 25% increase in export demand.

linkages need to be based on microeconomic studies that can support assumptions about particular values of export transformation.

In all three countries, food processing output in the CGE model always expands more than in the standard input-output model. In the input-output framework, output expands by only the growth in processed food exports. In the CGE model, output expansion is higher because of the joint production effect, which is diminished as the transformation elasticity is increased; the expansion effect, which increases with the size of the trade share; and an income effect caused by real exchange rate appreciation.

In all three countries, employment per unit of output increases in food production due to the general equilibrium effects of expanding processed food exports, which causes output in other labor-intensive manufacturing sectors to contract. This change in labor demand is the most dramatic in Brazil, where food output increases the most as exports expand.

The output response in food processing triggers an increase in demand for inputs from farm sectors. In Figures 16.4–16.6 we consider the effects of a 25 percent expansion in processed food exports on output and employ-

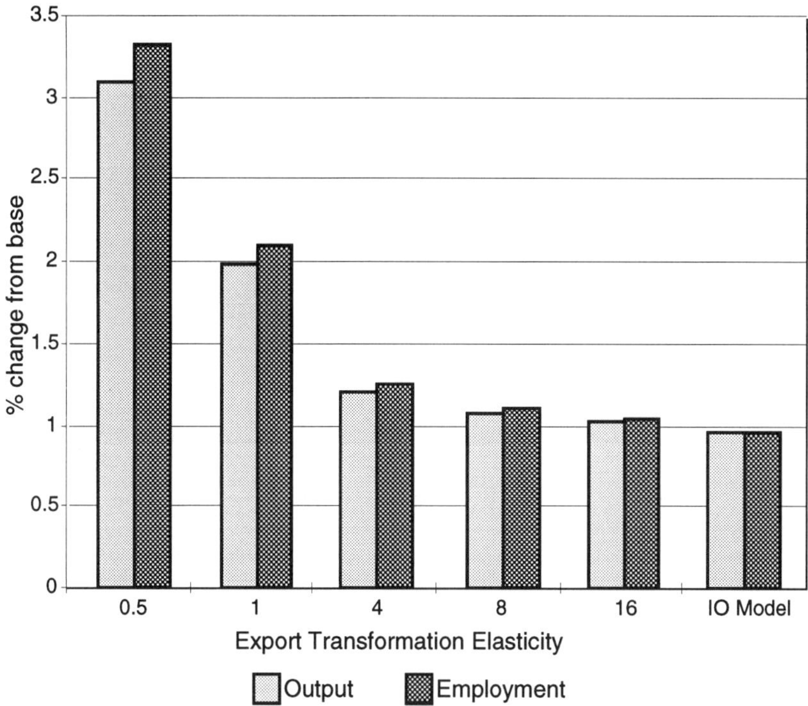

FIGURE 16.2 Mexico—Output and employment in processed food with a 25% increase in export demand.

ment in the main input sector to food processing—grains/oilseeds for Brazil and "other agriculture" for Mexico and the United States. The output response for raw agricultural input sectors is sensitive to import substitution elasticities. The export shock induces an increase in domestic farm prices and a relative price change in favor of imports as the real exchange rate appreciates. As the substitutability of domestic and imported raw agricultural inputs increases, the trade leakage onto imported inputs becomes larger, and the linkage from food export growth to farm output weakens.

The output response in the raw farm sector in Brazil, for a given elasticity of import substitution, is proportionately higher than the output response in Mexico or the United States because exports are a larger share of Brazil's food production. Farm output in Brazil is also more responsive to the elasticity changes, with changes in output ranging from above to below those of the input-output model across the range of elasticities. In Mexico and the United States, linkages to the production of raw inputs are always weaker than in the input-output model. Interestingly, the inter-

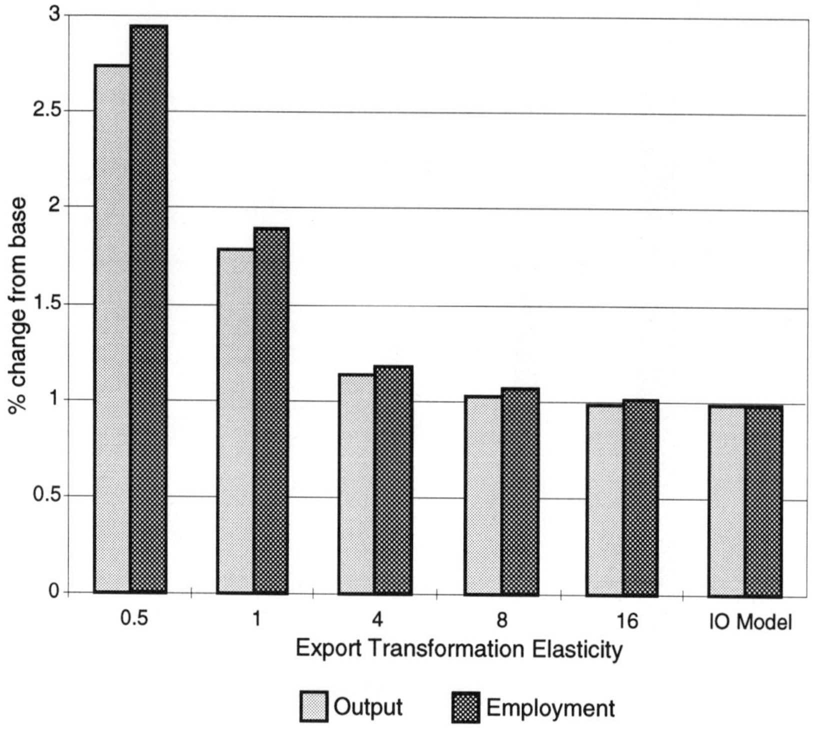

FIGURE 16.3 U.S.—Output and employment in processed food with a 25% increase in export demand.

country differences in parameter sensitivity are not due to differences in import shares, which are quite similar for raw agricultural inputs in the three countries. Once again, the differences can be traced to export trade shares in processed food. The small share of exports in Mexican and U.S. food processing means that export growth leads to only a small appreciation of the real exchange rate in the two countries. The relative price shift in favor of imported inputs is small. Even when import substitution is assumed high, price effects are weak, and the trade leakage to imported inputs is small.

The production structure in the raw agricultural input sectors varies by country. As seen in Figure 16.4, employment per unit of output increases in Brazil's grains/oilseeds sector. In contrast, employment per unit of output in the raw agricultural sector declines in Mexico and the United States (Figures 16.5 and 16.6). The range of employment effects for Mexico's raw agricultural input sector over this sensitivity analysis illustrates the interactions among real exchange rates, trade behavior, factor markets,

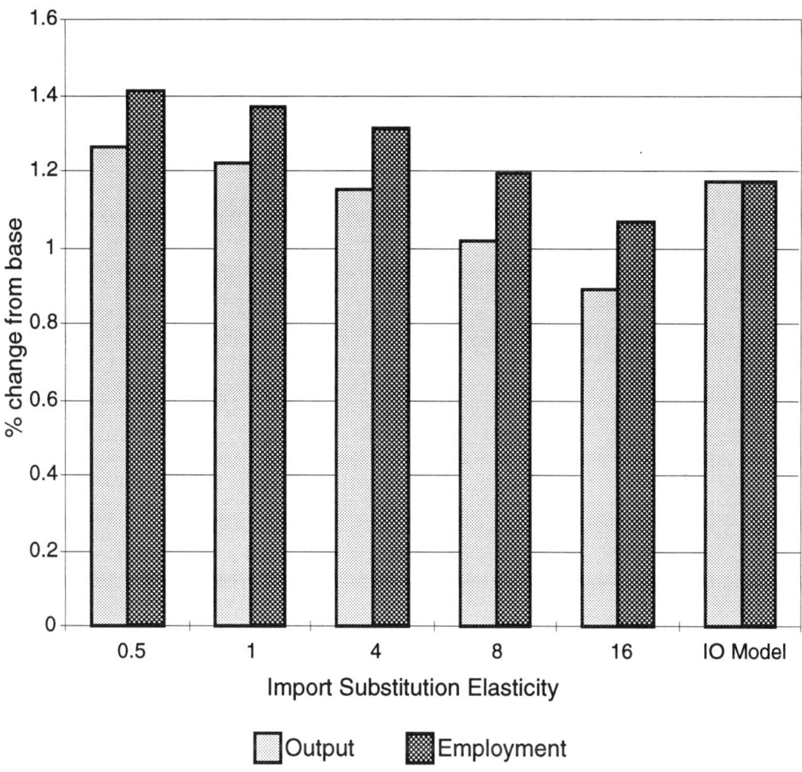

FIGURE 16.4 Brazil—Output and employment in main raw input with a 25% increase in export demand.

and intersectoral linkages in determining employment effects in the CGE model. As seen in Figure 16.5, employment in Mexico's agricultural inputs sector increases by a larger amount as the import substitution elasticity increases. This change in input use in the raw agricultural sector reflects adjustments in other farm sectors. The appreciation of Mexico's real exchange rate due to food export growth causes a shift in consumption toward imported corn. As the assumed substitutability of domestic and imported varieties is increased, corn imports rise and domestic production falls. Corn, a large and relatively labor-intensive sector, releases labor which is employed in the main agricultural input sector. The adjustments in corn strengthen the linkage from Mexican food export growth to employment in its main agricultural input sector over the range of import substitution elasticities.

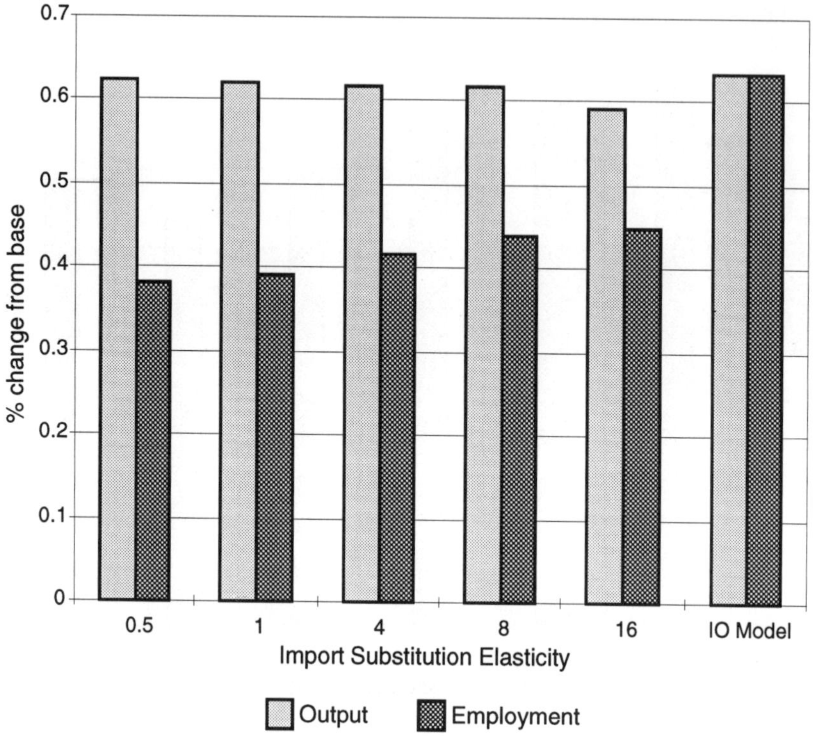

FIGURE 16.5 Mexico—Output and employment in main raw input with a 25% increase in processed food export demand.

Conclusions

We use an eleven-sector, ten-country CGE model of the western hemisphere to analyze and compare the effects of a 25 percent increase in the processed agricultural exports of three countries: Brazil, Mexico, and the United States. We show that linkages to farm output and employment are more complex than in a standard input-output model that only considers technical input-output relationships.

Linkages from the processed food exports to raw agricultural input sectors depend, first, on the size of the output change in food induced by the export shock. The input-output model tends to understate the effects of export growth on processed food output. In the CGE model, we assume that increased production for exports occurs jointly with some increase in production for domestic sales. Even when joint production is minimized, real exchange rate appreciation and the consequent increase in domestic demand that accompany export growth stimulate domestic processed food output.

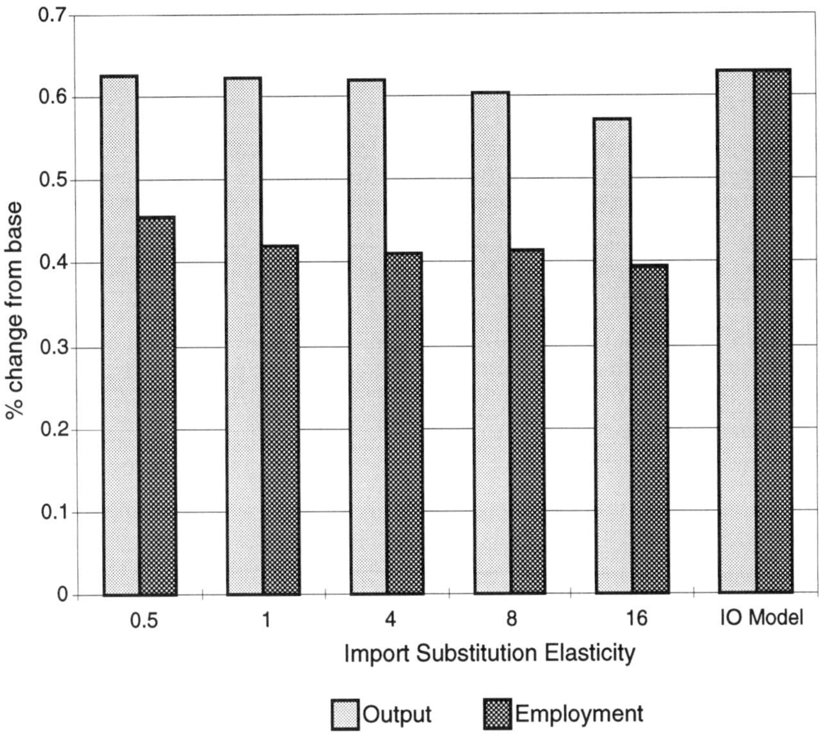

FIGURE 16.6 U.S.—Output and employment in main raw input with a 25% increase in processed food export demand.

The extent of the increase in farm output following an increase in processed food output depends on tradability in the raw agricultural sector. When domestic and imported inputs are easily substituted, the increase in demand for raw agricultural inputs can be met by imports. Once again, real exchange rate effects are important. This time, the appreciation that accompanies the expansion of food processing exports serves to weaken the linkage to farm output because it makes imported raw agricultural inputs more attractive. Real exchange rate appreciation also lowers export demand for the raw input and other farm sectors. We also find that output and employment in both the raw and processed agricultural sectors are quite sensitive to trade elasticities. This suggests that microeconomic studies would help to refine our understanding of the effects of export growth in food processing sectors.

In the input-output model, the assumptions of fixed labor-input coefficients and a perfectly elastic supply of labor mean that employment in raw agricultural input sectors increases by the same percent as does output. In the CGE model, an increase in the domestic supply of raw agricultural inputs to food processing comes at the expense of production in other farm sectors. Structural change and factor competition among sectors with different factor intensities change factor prices, factor demand, and factor use per unit of output. Our comparison of three countries shows that linkages to farm employment depend not just on changes in farm output, but also on changes in factor intensities.

Finally, we find that the method by which processed food exports are increased is quite important. An export subsidy reduces welfare because the world price of processed food exports declines. In contrast, export demand growth, as other countries reduce their trade barriers, generates welfare gains. Furthermore, the cost of the subsidy program exceeds the gains in aggregate export income. It is a "beggar thy neighboring sector" policy because export growth in food processing causes real exchange rate appreciation and a decline in demand for exports in other sectors.

Notes

The authors would like to thank Larry Deaton, Stephanie Mercier, Daniel Pick, Gerald Schluter, David Skully, and Thomas Vollrath for helpful comments. This paper was prepared under USDA Cooperative Agreements No. 43-3 AEK-4-80109 and 43-3AEK-4-80111.

1. For example, Schluter and Edmondson (1989) show that a shift from raw to processed exports increases farm output and employment. The export of $1 million of wheat as flour instead of grain generates an additional $9.1 million in U.S. national business activity, almost half from farm sectors.

2. We describe a standard input-output model in which all components of final demand are exogenous. Extended input-output models include induced, or second-round, effects whereby the increase in production raises household income and private consumption expenditure and magnifies the size of the original shock. A SAM-based (social accounting matrix) model includes linkages to household and government accounts, and all components of final demand can be treated endogenously.

3. Our definitions of raw farm commodities and processed foods follow the standard commodity classification conventions from national input-output accounts. In the United States, for example, the raw farm sectors are Standard Industry Classification (SIC) sectors 1 and 2, and forestry and fishery sectors (SIC 7–9). Processed foods sectors are SIC 20 and tobacco products. We define agriculture as processed plus raw agriculture.

4. The input-output methodology and recent extensions are reviewed in Skolka (1989) and Peterson (1991). See Midmore (1991) for recent applications of input-output analysis to agriculture.

5. See Robinson, Lewis, and Hinojosa (1994) on the WHFTA (Western Hemisphere Free Trade Area)-CGE model, and Lewis, Robinson, and Wang (1995) for a more detailed description of the multicountry CGE model.

6. In the CGE model, we assume that rural labor remains within farm sectors, while other labor types are mobile across the nonfarm sectors. We assume full employment, so that rural labor is reallocated among farm sectors following a policy shock.

References

Burfisher, Mary, Sherman Robinson, and Karen Thierfelder (1994). "NAFTA, Mexican Agricultural Policy Reform and Labor Mobility," in Thomas Grennes and Gary Williams, eds., *NAFTA: Will the Experiment Work?* International Trade Research Consortium: Minneapolis, MN.

Lewis, Jeffrey D., Sherman Robinson, and Zhi Wang (1995). "Beyond the Uruguay Round: The Implications of an Asian Free Trade Area." *China Economic Review*, Vol. 6, No. 1, pp. 35–95.

Midmore, Peter, ed. (1991). *Input-Output Models in the Agricultural Sector*. Hants, England: Avebury Academic Publishing Group.

Peterson, William, ed. (1991). *Advances in Input-Output Analysis*. Oxford: Oxford University Press.

Robinson, Sherman, Jeffrey Lewis, and Raul Hinojosa (1994). "Regional 10-country CGE Model of the Western Hemisphere." Unpublished model and database.

Schluter, Gerald and William Edmondson (1989). "Exporting Processed Instead of Raw Agricultural Products." U.S. Department of Agriculture, Economic Research Service, Staff Report No. 89-58. Washington, D.C.

Skolka, Jiri (1989). "Input-Output Structural Decomposition Analysis for Austria." *Journal of Policy Modeling*. Vol. 11, No. 1, pp. 45–66.

U.S. Department of Agriculture, Economic Research Service (1995). *NAFTA: Year One*. Washington, D.C., April.

United Nations (1990). "Statistical Papers, Commodity Trade Statistics, According to Standard Industrial Trade Classification, Series D. " Statistical Office, Department of Economic and Social Affairs.

17

Foreign Production by U.S. Food Processing Firms: A Transaction Cost Approach

James M. Hagen

Introduction

The basic question this chapter addresses is whether observed business practice in the food processing industry is consistent with the transaction cost theory of foreign production. The answer is yes, and the inquiry also reveals several factors of importance to foreign production in the food industry. The chapter considers the food processing industry as a manufacturer of finished foods, primarily in a state ready for retail sale. It is specifically focused on two groups of products: processed meats (Standard Industrial Classification [SIC] code 2013) and preserved fruits and vegetables (SIC code 203). Foreign production here is focused on horizontal integration (producing and selling approximately the same products in new markets), rather than vertical integration (e.g., sourcing food in one country for sale in another). The chapter builds on, and adds to, earlier work on determinants of foreign production in food processing (e.g. Horst, 1974; Connor, 1983; Handy and Henderson; 1994; Vaughan, Malanoski, West, and Handy, 1994). It differs from previous research by identifying major producers of specific product groups and seeking to explain why they do or do not have foreign production in select foreign markets.

The first section is a very brief discussion of the theory of foreign production, with emphasis on the transaction cost theory; the second is an abbreviated review of determinants of foreign production in the food sector; the third reports on the findings from interviews of industry executives and a statistical analysis of firm and product determinants of foreign production by U.S. processors of SIC 2013 and SIC 203 products. The concluding section summarizes the assets which firms take overseas and proposes how they might better be measured in future studies.

The Transaction Cost Theory of Foreign Production

The transaction cost approach has become fundamental to foreign production literature. *Internalization, eclectic,* and *comparative institutional theories* are among the related theories that incorporate fundamental ideas central to the transaction cost approach. It is a description of those ideas that follows in this section.

Williamson (1975) drew from earlier scholarship (especially Coase, 1937) in noting that, even when there exists a willing buyer and a willing seller for a good or service, sometimes there is no effective market for transacting the good or service. In particular, market transaction costs can be so high as to influence either the would-be buyer and seller to take over functions of the other or essentially merge with the other so that the asset is transferred internally by hierarchical decree from one part of the organization to the other. An application of this to foreign production is when a firm in one country cannot effectively sell (or license) its assets to a user in another, encouraging the home-country firm to establish or acquire a host-country user so that the asset is transferred internally. The types of transaction costs of concern here include the cost of searching for a transaction partner, negotiating the transaction, measuring or monitoring the goods or services received, and enforcing the sales agreement.

Intangible assets (knowledge and reputation derived, in particular) have been widely identified as subject to high transaction costs. If knowledge embodied in a recipe or in process technology is sold, it may be difficult for the buyer to be certain of what it is getting when the price is negotiated, and the precautions on the part of the seller to assure that the buyer does not use the knowledge beyond the terms of the agreement (e.g., by competing with the seller) may be costly. Also, in the case of selling reputation (typically by licensing a product brand name), it may be difficult for both parties to be sure the other is maintaining the integrity of the name. Interestingly, intangible assets also contribute to a firm's growth trajectory in the first place. Johnson (1970) argued, and Horstmann and Markusen (1989) emphasized, that an important property of knowledge-based intangible assets is their public good characteristic in that they may be exploited at additional production facilities at minimal marginal cost.

Knowledge and reputation are two key intangible assets most commonly identified as subject to high transaction costs. Knowledge has generally been measured as the ratio of research and development (R&D)

expense to sales at either the industry or firm level. Grubaugh (1987), Kimura (1989), Kogut and Chang (1991), and Hennart and Park (1994) are among those who found a positive relationship between R&D and foreign production. An intangible asset of perhaps more critical importance, managerial knowledge, has received much less attention. Pugel (1981) rated the managerial knowledge of industries as a ratio of managerial to total employment. In another approach to measurement of knowledge, Swedenborg (1979) measured experience by the number of years from the foundation date of a firm's first manufacturing affiliate. She found a significant and positive relationship between her knowledge proxies and foreign production.

The other intangible asset that has been the target of much investigation is reputation. Specifically, a high ratio of advertising to sales is presumed to indicate that a product is highly differentiated, meaning it embodies reputation. Gatignon and Anderson (1988) are among those who found a positive relationship between this measure and foreign production. A number of studies and, in particular, those studying foreign production by Japanese firms (e.g., Hennart and Park, 1994), found no such relationship, indicating that failure of the market for conveying brand reputation was not a necessary driver of foreign production.

The above research highlights the close connection drawn between intangible assets and foreign production. Intangible assets are also central to the analyses of foreign production specific to the food sector. This sector-specific research is briefly reviewed in the next section.

Foreign Production by U.S. Food Processing Firms

An early, pretransaction cost theory, contribution to the study of foreign production focused on the food processing sector (Horst, 1974). Horst concluded that U.S. firms needed foreign territory for growth, and he identified the knowledge that advertising was a profitable undertaking as a key asset that U.S. firms exploited in their European operations.

Several more recent studies of foreign production in food processing have sought to identify determinants of foreign production. Connor (1981) found that size of firm sales, advertising intensity, and diversification were positive determinants of the extent of foreign food firms' ownership of U.S. operations. He also reported regression results on determinants of the foreign to domestic sales ratios of U.S. food firms (Connor, 1983). Firm sales size, advertising and R&D expenditure intensity were all positive determinants, though he expressed skepticism that the benefits of internalization applied to horizontal investments. In an examination of food sector investment into the United States, Pagoulatos (1983) found that foreign investment comprised a much larger percentage of U.S. sales in certain food groups (e.g. cookies and crackers) than others. Connor, Rogers, Marion, and Mueller (1985) stated that testing for determinants of foreign direct investment (FDI) is particularly challenging, because of the need for firm-, industry-, and location-specific factors that must be incorporated. The present research is an effort to address this need.

Handy and McDonald (1989) observed that 82 percent of sales of foreign affiliates of U.S. food processing firms are in the country of production (higher than the 66 percent figure for all U.S. manufacturers), suggesting that foreign production of processed food is primarily motivated by market seeking, the motivation suggested by Horst some fifteen years earlier, and the motivation found in the present study.

Handy and Henderson (1994) found an association between firm size (whether measured by assets, employees, or shipments) and multinationality in a sample of U.S. and other food firms. They found that U.S. firms with foreign affiliates are more diversified (into nonfood sectors) than U.S. firms without foreign affiliates. However, finding that foreign-oriented multinational firms have fewer brand names and product lines than more domestic-oriented multinationals, they were unable to find support for an association of diversification with foreign production. Henderson, Voros, and Hirschberg (1993) analyzed a sample of food and beverage firms and found foreign production (measured by the percentage of firm shipments originating from foreign affiliates) positively associated with high home market share, large size, high net income as a percent of total sales, and high investment in firm-specific assets.

The U.S. Department of Agriculture's Economic Research Service (ERS) has compiled data on foreign production behavior by U.S. food processing firms, described in Handy and Henderson (1994). Reed and Ning (1996) performed a regression analysis on thirty-four U.S. multinational food processing food firms in the ERS sample and found the number of SIC 4-digit industries (as a measure of diversification) to be a significant and positive determinant of foreign production, which was measured by over 10 percent of the firm's assets residing in foreign countries.

Vaughan, Malanoski, West, and Handy (1994) interviewed senior executives of seventeen multinationals (mostly U.S.) regarding their firms' international operations. The most often stated reason for establishment of foreign affiliates was slow growth at home. Interviewees expressed strong desire to maintain control over the following intangible assets: "reputation and quality of branded products, process technologies, commodity trading, customer service, and skills related to marketing and market development" (p. 11). In a study of Australian and Spanish wine entry into the U.S. market, Abbott and Solana (Ch. 8, this volume) found that "internationalization mode choices can differ by narrow subsector, by firm, and even by market for a single firm."

An Analysis of Foreign Production by Two Food Processing Sectors

The above research has taken a variety of approaches to analyzing foreign production in the food processing sector. Three measures of the extent of foreign production were: foreign to domestic sales ratios of firms (Connor, 1983); whether the firm had any foreign affiliates (Handy and Henderson, 1994); and whether over 10 percent of a firm's assets resided in foreign countries (Reed and Ning, 1996). Regarding the establishment of an affiliate in a foreign region as a defining act of the firm, the present research measures foreign production simply by whether the parent firm has a subsidiary (with 50 percent or more ownership) in specific regions. While all of the studies (except for Abbott and Solana, ch. 8, this volume) aggregated all processed food products for analysis, the present study distinguishes between specific product groups. The above focus on firm size and diversification as intangible assets is continued in the present study.

Like some of the previous studies, the present research focuses on foreign production in many countries by U.S. firms. In order to ask why some U.S. firms making a product practice foreign production and others do not, it identifies specific product groups: processed meats (SIC 2013) and preserved fruits/vegetables (SIC 203) and identifies the major U.S. public firms in those groups. Of seventeen total firms, eight are major SIC 2013 firms and eleven are major firms in SIC 203. Two firms, ConAgra and Philip Morris, are active in both areas. The study then identifies whether each firm is producing the indicated product (of which it is a major producer in the United States) in each of nine global regions. Thus, there are 171 observations (nineteen firm/products times 9 regions). Firms in these product groups, as well as some in related groups, were interviewed, and several characteristics of the seventeen firms were tested as determinants of foreign production by regression analysis. This method has the potential of enabling analysis of firm, product, and location variables simultaneously.

Interviews

Interviews of executives of four large food processing firms revealed several insights concerning the motivation for establishment of foreign operations and the nature of intangible assets.[1] Facility visits and on-site interviews included Kraft (Philip Morris), ConAgra, Hormel, and Pillsbury. This chapter also draws on shorter interviews (primarily at trade shows and conferences) of executives or former executives of Smuckers, Dean Foods, Jerome Foods, Nestlé, Universal Foods, Unilever, Procter and Gamble, and others. Additional telephone interviews were with personnel of most of the seventeen firms.

Consistent with findings in the previous section, nearly every interviewee reported going abroad as part of a strategy of growth, based on concern that domestic markets offered little room for growth. One of the larger firms specifically noted that sourcing was not a major motivation for foreign production because "you can go to some broker and have global sourcing without having to go anywhere." A firm with active licensing arrangements overseas but no foreign production illustrated licensing as "putting your toe in the water," compared to foreign production, which was "taking a bath." The firm explained its interest in foreign production as a result of its need for growth and its difficulty in "growing" a license business.

To identify intangible assets that might be central to the firm's foreign production, a question asked of nearly every interviewee was what assets they were bringing to the table as they entered foreign countries with production operations. The answer was almost invariably capital (especially in the case of acquisitions, which characterise the vast majority of foreign production entries), followed by production and marketing knowledge.

While the capital transfer responses may seem like a case of the capital transfer/portfolio theories of foreign investment (Aliber, 1970), the financial flows were not specifically movements of capital from capital-rich to capital-poor countries. Rather, it appears that the local firms were using their reputation and knowledge to gain access to funds that were otherwise unavailable to the target firms. What the multinational firm was really bringing to the table was reputation, not in the brand sense, but as a successful track record in bringing products to market. In at least one case, two firms in the sample competed for the same European acquisition target, with the larger capitalized firm winning. Certainly one determinant of acquisition (or greenfield investment) is the financial strength of the acquiring company.

Management and process control were other assets mentioned by several firms. Critical assets may depend on the host region. One firm that had no European production plants said that successful entry into Europe would require some kind of market distribution advantage over competitors. Lacking such assets, the firm intended to focus on developing countries where its process control knowledge would be particularly valuable.

One large firm, speaking of its foreign acquisitions, said that a major asset it was contributing was an awareness of the benefits of managerial freedom, that it profitably freed the managers from the constraints placed on them by the previous owners. This may also be region- specific, as the one firm with an affiliate in Poland disagreed, arguing that Eastern European managers were not ready for empowerment. On the other side of the transaction, there appeared to be some consensus on the point that a key asset being *acquired* in an acquisition is management. One suggestion was that it is cheaper to buy management by buying the company than by starting from scratch and trying to recruit entirely new staff. That is, labor markets are costly and can be internalized by acquiring entire companies.

The importance of a firm asset that might be called organizational coordinative skill was suggested by a firm with an affiliate in the former East Bloc. It observed that production and distribution knowledge were both present in the host country, but they were administratively separated. A major asset the firm was bringing to the table, it suggested, was the know-how to coordinate the production and marketing sides.

Reputation of the firm was offered as an asset, with one comment that as the firm "positions itself as a global player to be dealt with," its importance goes up, making it easier to gain the cooperation of other firms. The interviewee said that, while other firms may not at first wish to do business with the newcomer, they realize that at some point they may need some technical or other help from the entering firm or its parent. Corporate size is then an important factor in achieving success in international markets. Local governments, suppliers, and distributors wonder what they will do if the foreign-owned operation fails, and that concern is heightened if the foreign operation is not part of a known entity.

A story that revealed problems with trying to transfer reputation through market channels is the case of a firm that had a canned product that had been introduced to several foreign markets through the U.S. military. The firm long ago entered into licensing agreements for production of the product, but as the firm has shifted its perception of foreign markets from a source of bonus income to sources of growth, it has become disappointed that the licensees are not aggressively developing their markets or product lines. The inability to assure aggressive promotion by the licensee is itself a transaction cost. While many profitable licensing agreements exist (and Chiquita is even advertising the availability of its name for license on its Internet home page), it is unclear if that approach is optimal in a strategic sense or if it is the result of unavailable financial resources to engage directly in foreign production.

One of the issues raised in the previous section concerns the influence of diversification in contributing to foreign production. The interviews did not lead to a clear consensus. A common view was that too much diversification is distracting. When asked for opinions of Sara Lee's rather remarkable diversification (food, apparel, shoe polish), two less-diversified firms suggested that Sara Lee's major asset was its chairman who could take any acquisition and inspire its management to make it profitable. One interviewee suggested that a range of products was helpful in entering a new market because, if the initial product failed, the firm would readily have other products in its stable to switch to. There is pressure on expatriate staff to make a production facility successful even if the product is completely different from that originally planned. The primary role of diversification, then, appears to be an experience-based knowledge asset.

If the U.S. firms' assets that are critical to foreign production are best exploited internally, an explanation is needed for the frequency of copacking, whereby the manufacturing of the product is outsourced. The Green Giant brand of canned and frozen vegetables (owned by Pillsbury, which is in turn owned by the British firm Grand Metropolitan), for example, exited processing altogether in the early 1990s in order to focus on marketing. Green Giant, then, is a brand/marketing asset, rather than a production asset. The approach raises the question of why all foreign production is not done on an outsource (i.e. copack) basis. The firm's answer is consistent with the transaction cost view. Namely, outsourcing is hardly a turn-key operation. In Japan, which is Pillsbury's largest international market, for example, Pillsbury invests considerable resources in identifying, training, and monitoring its copackers in order to assure quality standards. The maintenance of those copack relationships and the avoidance of interference of competitors with the copackers is difficult to assure, making the copacker relationship itself a proprietary asset that the firm closely guards.

In another case, a seasoning firm with international operations explained that copacking was not an attractive option because sales to food service and other processors were an important part of its business. Industry customers may trust the reputable seasoning firm with proprietary information about their sales volumes, but they are reluctant to reveal that information to lesser known entities, such as copackers.

It was apparent from the interviews that U.S. food processing firms were going overseas because that is where the greatest growth opportunities appeared to be. While they were taking the assets of management skills and production and marketing knowledge with them, they were also taking organizational reputation, which allows resources (including capital) to be focused in a production/marketing operation. While production technology can be transferred, it must be readily adapted to the dictates of the market, and those adaptation skills are an intangible asset lacking an adequate market. The idea of selling those skills in a consulting capacity could not serve the growth objectives of the firm. Similarly, licensing agreements allow the firm to grow its brand equity but not its product development asset base. The latter appears to be fundamental to the food companies interviewed. These findings indicate that foreign production in food processing is a result of inadequate markets for transferring the skills of the firm in a manner that affords future growth opportunities. The analysis that follows has results that are consistent with this finding.

Regression Analysis

While this model is novel in that it tests for determinants of all foreign production in select regions for specific products, the independent firm variables (size, diversification, and product) are ones suggested by the literature reviewed in the first two sections of this chapter. Data for the study are from 1993, and sources include a database developed by the USDA Economic Research Service as well as direct inquiry of the firms and a variety of secondary sources including 10-k reports, journalistic accounts, and stock analysts' reports.

The host regions considered for the study include Canada, Mexico, Latin America/Caribbean, Western Europe, Eastern Europe, China, Japan, Australia/New Zealand, and the rest of Asia. They were selected to allow differentiation between near countries (Americas and Europe) and more distant countries (Asia and Pacific), and also between industrialized markets and developing economies. Also, the firms indicated that they often targeted regions rather than countries for first entries.

A logistic regression model (Amemiya, 1981; Maddala, 1983) of the following form is used to test for determinants of the probability of foreign production:

$$P(Y_{ijk} = 1) = 1/(1 + \exp(-a - X_{ijk}b))$$

where $Y_{ijk} = 1$ if firm i manufactured product j in country k in 1993, given that it produced product j in the U.S., and $Y_{ijk} = 0$ otherwise. X_{ijk} = the vector of independent variables for the ijkth observation.

Independent variables include a binary categorical variable for product (either 203 or 2013) and the firm-level variables of size, media spending, and diversification. Two location variables (distance from the United States and regional Gross National Product [GNP] per capita) are included as controls. It was expected that firm size and diversification at the SIC four-digit (but not two-digit) level would be positive determinants of foreign production. Also, that shorter distance and higher GNP per capita were expected to positively affect foreign production. The regression results are discussed below and appear in Table 17.1.

Size and Diversification. Size, whether expressed as the log of total firm sales (LOGTSALE) or the log of total firm food sales (LGTFSAL), is highly correlated with the number of product groups at the SIC four-digit level and less so with the number of industries at the SIC two-digit level (Table 17.2). Using a log scale reflects the expectation that an additional increment of sales is expected to have more impact on a relatively small firm such as Smucker than on a large firm such as Philip Morris.

TABLE 17.1 Parameter Estimates for Logistic Regression Model: Determinants of Foreign Production

Variable Name	*Description*	*Coefficient (Wald statistic)*
LOGTSALE	Log of total firm sales	.4710*** (7.9493)
PRODB	Dummy for product 1 = SIC 203 -1 = SIC 2013	1.0032*** (13.0997)
TWODIGB	Number of SIC 2-digit industry codes	-.0968 (1.2726)
DISTANC2	Dummy for distance 1 = Western Hemisphere & Europe -1 = Asia/Pacific	.7613*** (10.0312)
REGGNPT	GNP per capita of region	.0473* (2.8837)
	Intercept	-6.1907*** (2.8837)

*** $p<0.01$ ** $p<0.05$

model chi-square: 38.264
p value: 0.000
N: 171
McFadden's pseudo R square: .24

The high correlation (of size and four-digit product count) makes it difficult to identify the respective effects of diversification and size. While diversification in itself may appear significant, size may be driving both diversification and foreign production. In any event, size and four-digit product count are both highly significant when run separately. The reported regression model excludes four-digit diversification because of this correlation. The experience and knowledge represented in diversifi-

TABLE 17.2 Correlation Matrix of Independent Variables

	DISTANC2	*LGTFSAL*	*MEDIA2*	*PRODB*	*TWODIGB*	*MEDTWOD*	*LOGTSALE*
DISTANC2	1.000						
LGTFSAL	.000	1.000					
PRODB	.000	.064	***-.344	1.000			
TWODIGB	.000	*** .484	-.120	** .156	1.000		
LOGTSALE	.000	*** .938	*** .442	.018	*** .524	*** .516	1.000
REGGNPT	.003	.000	.000	.000	.000	.000	.000

*** $p<0.01$ ** $p<0.05$

cation are assets that were identified in the interviews as valuable for foreign production. As a firm characteristic, there are several reasons to expect the size phenomenon. One is the financial power to establish diverse operations. The interviews suggest that the clout that accompanies size is also an asset of great value in foreign production.

Consistent with the interviews, diversification at the two-digit level is not significant. This is not necessarily inconsistent with Handy and Henderson (1994) finding that food sales accounted for a lower percentage of total firm sales for firms with foreign affiliates than for firms with no foreign affiliate. It may be that some diversity of experience is beneficial, but that diversification into too many sectors may strain managerial resources.

Product. There is much more foreign production activity in the 203 product group than the 2013 group, and accordingly product (PRODB) is a significant and positive determinant of foreign production in the model (Tables 17.1, 17.3, and 17.4). Only the three largest 2013 firms have foreign 2013 production, and none of those firms is in more than two regions. American Home is the only 203 firm with no foreign 203 production. American Home has by far the smallest ratio of food to total sales, and it is quite international in its core medical industry. No evidence was found

TABLE 17.3 Meat Processing (SIC 2013)* Firms, (Data in million $, effective 1993)

Name	*Sales*	*Food Sales SIC*	*Estimated 2013 Sales*	*Foreign Production Food Sales*	*Regions of Foreign Production***
Philip Morris	60,901	33,777	2,000	11,945	w
ConAgra	23,512	18,727	1,400	1,311	w,n
Sara Lee	15,536	7,562	3,100	2,344	m,w
Tyson	4,707	4,707	518	0	
Hormel	2,854	2,854	1,627	0	
Smithfield	1,143	1,143	560	0	
Thornapple Valley	730	723	401	0	
Doskocil	648	648	648	0	
TOTAL	110,031	70,141	10,254	15,600	

*Slaughter operations were excluded to the extent possible in forming this sample.

**Regions considered are: Canada (c); Mexico (m); Latin America (l); Eastern Europe (e); Western Europe (w); Japan (j); China (p); other Asia (a); Australia/New Zealand (n).

Source: Original data (including unpublished data from the USDA, Economic Research Service).

TABLE 17.4 Preserved Fruits and Vegetables (SIC 203) Firms* (Data in millions $ effective 1993)

Name	*Sales*	*Food Sales*	*Estimated 203 Sales*	*Foreign Production Food Sales*	*Regions of Foreign Production***
Philip Morris	60,901	33,777	*2,570	11,945	c,m,l,e,w
ConAgra	23,512	18,727	3,640	1,311	w
American Home	8,305	936	856	0	
Heinz	7,047	7,047	5,642	3,020	p,l,e,w,a,n,j
CPC	6,738	6,738	4,326	5,660	c,m,l,e,w,a
Campbell	6,586	6,586	4,124	1,931	c,m,w,n
Dean Foods	2,431	2,411	787	5	m
DelMonte	1,555	1,555	1,555	230	m,w
Gerber	1,270	803	803	126	l,e
Curtis-Burns	879	879	674	47	c
Smucker	512	512	522	58	c,w,n
TOTAL	119,736	79,971	25,499	24,333	

*This product group includes such diverse products as mayonnaise and dried soups.
**Regions considered are: Canada (c); Mexico (m); Latin America (l); Eastern Europe (e); Western Europe (w); Japan (j); China (p); other Asia (a); Australia/New Zealand (n).
Source: Original data (including unpublished data from the USDA, Economic Research Service).

that the low level of foreign 2013 production was in any way compensated by a high level of licensing.

Several interviewees suggested that, in general, 2013 has more challenging sanitation concerns from raw material input to final consumption, and that fostering a management system for addressing those challenges would be difficult by either license or foreign production. Also, 2013 is the more fragmented of the two industries (evidenced by preliminary unpublished U.S. census data on 1992 industry concentration ratios), very likely on account of the relatively short shelf life of the product. This fragmented characteristic has provided sufficient acquisition targets for growth without need for venturing abroad.

Location. While there is at least some foreign production of the subject products in each of the regions of the study, location is a positive determinant of foreign production. The lesser extent of investment in Asia and the Pacific may be due to the inconvenience of travel. The diverse cultures in that region unfortunately preclude inclusion of a cultural distance variable. The weak degree of significance of GNP per capita is likely due to investment barriers in Japan (one of the higher-income regions) and to an interest in regions that show that potential for rapid income growth. Some of the entries into China and Eastern Europe occurred since those regions were identified as potential rapid growth areas. Analysis by country would add substantial data collection and methodological challenges but enable a richer explanation of foreign production.

Conclusion

The statistical and interview data both indicate that firms engaged in foreign food production possess assets that may be difficult to exploit abroad through export markets, and thus the findings are consistent with the transaction cost theory of foreign production. Technology and brand names are exploited less in foreign production than product development expertise, process management knowledge, and reputation.

The high correlation between size and diversification (by SIC 20 product count) in the sample prevents a conclusion that diversification (irrespective of firm size) is a significant driver of foreign production. The expectation that product characteristics would be important determinants of foreign production was met, and location factors were also found to be significant determinates of foreign production. Unfortunately, the disaggregation of foreign production of specific products by location and firm is very difficult due to unavailability of data. This study is believed to be the first to take this methodological approach, particularly in the food processing sector, and further studies can be envisioned that might build on this approach by the addition of more firm variables (such as a count of new product introductions by the firm) and by comparison with licensing activity in the same regions and products.

Notes

The author gratefully acknowledges the valued comments of Jean-François Hennart, Michael A. Mazzocco, and Thomas Roehl on an earlier version of this chapter, the cooperation of Charles Handy of the USDA Economic Research Service, the executives of food processing firms who generously shared their insights, and the advice of Bruce Chassy. The author takes sole responsibility for any errors or misinterpretations which may appear in the chapter.

1. For confidentiality as well as reader convenience, interviews are characterized as with "firms," though any given firm interview may have actually consisted of interviews of more than one person from that firm.

References

Aliber, Robert Z. (1970). A theory of direct foreign investment. In C. P. Kindleberger (ed.) *The International Corporation*. Cambridge: MIT Press.

Amemiya,T. (1981). Qualitative response models: A survey. *Journal of Economic Literature*, 19: 1483–1536.

Coase, Ronald H. (1937). The nature of the firm. *Economica*, 3: 386–405.

Connor, John M. (1981). Foreign food firms: their participation in and competitive impact on the U.S. food and tobacco manufacturing sector. In Glenn L. Johnson and Allen H. Maunder, eds., *Rural Change:The Challenge for Agricultural Economists*, pp. 552–569. Farnborough, England: Gower Press, 1981.

———. (1983). Determinants of foreign direct investment by food and tobacco manufacturers. *American Journal of Agricultural Economics*, 65(2). May: 395–404.

Connor, John M., Richard T. Rogers, Bruce W. Marion, and Willard F. Mueller. (1985). *The Food Manufacturing Industries: Structure, Strategies, Performance, and Policies*. Lexington, MA: D.C. Heath and Company.

Gatignon, Hubert and Erin Anderson. (1988). The multinational corporation's degree of control over foreign subsidiaries: an empirical test of a transaction cost explanation. *Journal of Law, Economics, and Organization*, 4 (Fall): 305–336.

Graham, Edward M. (1978). Transatlantic investment by multinational firms: A rivalistic phenomenon. *Journal of Post-Keynesian Economics*, Fall: 82–99.

Grubaugh, Stephen. (1987). Determinants of direct foreign investment. *The Review of Economics and Statistics*, 69 (1): 149–152.

Handy, Charles R. & Dennis R. Henderson. (1994). Assessing the role of foreign direct investment in the food manufacturing industry. Foreign investment in food manufacturing. In Maury C. Bredahl, Philip C. Abbott, and Michael R. Reed, eds., *Competitiveness in International Food Markets*. Boulder, Colo.: Westview Press: 203–230.

Handy, Charles R. and James M. McDonald. (1989). Multinational structures and strategies of U.S. food firms. *American Journal of Agricultural Economics*, 71(5): 1246–1254.

Henderson, Dennis R., Peter R. Voros, & Joseph G. Hirschberg. (1993). Industrial determinants of international trade and foreign investment by food and beverage manufacturing firms. Paper presentation at NC-194 Conference, *Empirical Studies of Industrial Organization and Trade in the Food and Related Industries*. Indianapolis. Ind. April.

Hennart, Jean-François. (1982). *A Theory of Multinational Enterprise*. Ann Arbor: University of Michigan Press.

Hennart, Jean-François & Young-Ryeol Park. (1994). Location, governance, and strategic determinants of Japanese manufacturing investment in the United States. *Strategic Management Journal*, 15: 419–436.

Horst, Thomas. (1974). *At Home Abroad: A study of the Domestic and Foreign Operations of the American Food-Processing Industry*. Cambridge, Mass.: Ballinger.

Horstmann, Ignatius J. & James R. Markusen. (1989). Firm-specific assets and the gains from direct foreign investment. *Economica*, 56: 41–48.

Johnson, H. G. (1970). The efficiency and welfare implications of the international corporation," in C. P. Kindleberger, ed., *The International Corporation*. Cambridge, Mass.: MIT Press.

Kimura, Yui. (1989). Firm-specific strategic advantages and foreign direct investment behavior of firms: The Case of Japanese Semiconductor Firm. *Journal of International Business Studies*, Summer: 296–314.

Knickerbocker, F. T. (1973). *Oligopolistic Reaction and Multinational Enterprise*. Boston: Division of Research , Graduate School of Business Administration, Harvard University.

Kogut, Bruce and Sea-Jing Chang. (1991). The effect of national culture on the choice of entry mode. *Journal of International Business Studies*, 19: 411-432.

Maddala, G. S. (1983). *Limited Dependent and Qualitative Variables in Econometrics*. Cambridge, Mass.: Cambridge University Press.

Monteverde, Kirk & David Teece. (1982). Supplier switching costs and vertical integration in the automobile industry. *Bell Journal of Economic*, 13 (Spring): 206–213.

Pagoulatos, Emilio. (1983). Foreign direct investment in U.S. food and tobacco manufacturing and domestic economic performance. *American Journal of Agricultural Economics*, 65(2). May: 405–412.

Pugel, Thomas A. (1981). The determinants of foreign direct investment: An analysis of U.S. manufacturing industries. *Managerial and Decision Economics*, 2: 220–228.

Reed, Michael R. and Yulin Ning. (1996). Foreign investment strategies of U.S. multinational firms. In Ian M. Sheldon and Philip C. Abbott, eds., *Industrial Organization and Trade in the Food Industries*. Boulder, Colo.: Westview Press.

Rugman, Alan. (1981). *Inside the Multinationals: The Economics of Internal Markets*. London: Croon Helm.

Swedenborg, Birgitta. (1979). *The Multinational Operations of Swedish Firms: An Analysis of Determinants and Effects*. Stockholm: The Industrial Institute for Economic and Social Research.

Vaughan, Odette, Margaret Malanoski, Don West, & Charles Handy. (1994). Firm strategies for accessing foreign markets and the role of government policy. Working Paper 5/94. Agriculture Canada. Agri-food Policy Directorate.

Williamson, Oliver E. (1975). *Markets and Hierarchies: Analysis and Anti-Trust Implications*. New York: Free Press.

Yu, Chwo-Ming J. and K. Ito. (1988). Oligopolistic reaction and foreign direct investment: The case of the U.S. tire and textile industries. *Journal of International Business Studies*, 49: 449–460.

About the Editors and Contributors

Philip C. Abbott, Professor, Department of Agricultural Economics, Purdue University.

Frances Antonovitz, Associate Professor, Department of Economics, Iowa State University.

David Blandford, Economist, Directorate for Food, Agriculture and Fisheries of the Organisation for Economic Cooperation and Development (OECD).

Maury E. Bredahl, Professor, Department of Agricultural Economics, University of Missouri.

Brian Buhr, Associate Professor, Department of Applied Economics, University of Minnesota.

Mary E. Burfisher, Economist, Economic Research Service, U.S. Department of Agriculture.

Colin A. Carter, Professor, Department of Agriculture and Resource Economics, University of California, Davis.

Silke Gabbert, Ph.D. Student, Department of Agricultural Economics and Social Sciences, Humboldt University in Berlin, Germany.

Munisamy Gopinath, Assistant Professor, Department of Agricultural and Resource Economics, Oregon State University.

James M. Hagen, Assistant Professor, Department of Agricultural, Resource, and Managerial Economics, Cornell University.

Stephen Haley, Senior Economist, Economic Research Service, U.S. Department of Agriculture.

Dennis R. Henderson, Professor Emeritus, Department of Agricultural Economics, the Ohio State University.

Hong Hu, Graduate Student, Department of Agricultural Economics, University of Missouri.

Ronald W. Jones, Professor, Department of Economics, University of Rochester.

Wayne Jones, Economist, Directorate for Food, Agriculture and Fisheries of the Organisation for Economic Cooperation and Development (OECD) on secondment from Agriculture and Agri-Food Canada.

Larry S. Karp, Professor, Department of Agricultural and Resource Economics, University of California, Berkeley.

Nicholas G. Kalaitzandonakes, Associate Professor, Department of Agricultural Economics, University of Missouri.

Jean D. Kinsey, Director, The Retail Food Industry Center, and Professor, Department of Applied Economics, University of Minnesota.

Donald J. Liu, Associate Professor, Department of Applied Economics, University of Minnesota.

James R. Markusen, Professor, Department of Economics, University of Colorado.

Philip L. Paarlberg, Associate Professor, Department of Agricultural Economics, Purdue University.

Daniel H. Pick, Economist, Economic Research Service, U.S. Department of Agriculture.

Sherman Robinson, Director of the Trade and Macroeconomics Division, International Food Policy Research Institute.

Terry Roe, Professor, Department of Applied Economics, University of Minnesota.

Alan M. Rugman, Professor, Joseph L. Rotman Centre for Management, University of Toronto.

Günter Schamel, Assistant Professor, Department of Agricultural Economics and Social Sciences, Humboldt University in Berlin, Germany.

Mathew Shane, Senior Economist, Economic Research Service, U.S. Department of Agriculture.

Ian M. Sheldon, Associate Professor, Department of Agricultural Economics, the Ohio State University.

Juan B. Solana-Rosillo, Research Assistant, Department of Agricultural Economics, Purdue University.

Karen Thierfelder, Associate Professor, Department of Economics, U.S. Naval Academy.

Harald von Witzke, Professor and Associate Dean, College of Agricultural and Horticultural Sciences, Humboldt University in Berlin, Germany.

Alper Yilmaz, Ph.D Student, Department of Agriculture and Resource Economics, University of California, Davis.